The Man in the Principal's Office

The Man in the Principal's Office

An Ethnography

Updated Edition

HARRY F. WOLCOTT

ALTAMIRA
PRESS

A Division of
ROWMAN & LITTLEFIELD PUBLISHERS, INC.
Walnut Creek • Lanham • New York • Toronto • Oxford

This work was developed under contract from the U.S. Office of Education, Department of Health, Education and Welfare. However, the opinions expressed herein do not necessarily reflect the position or policy of that Agency, and no official endorsement should be referred.

ALTAMIRA PRESS
A division of Rowman & Littlefield Publishers, Inc.
1630 North Main Street, #367
Walnut Creek, CA 94596
www.altamirapress.com

Rowman & Littlefield Publishers, Inc.
A wholly owned subsidiary of The Rowman & Littlefield Publishing Group, Inc.
4501 Forbes Boulevard, Suite 200
Lanham, MD 20706

PO Box 317
Oxford
OX2 9RU, UK

British Library Cataloguing in Publication Information Available

Library of Congress Cataloging-in-Publication Data

Wolcott, Harry F., 1929–
     The man in the principal's office: an ethnography / Harry F. Wolcott –Updated ed.
         p. cm.
     Includes bibliographical references (p.).
     ISBN 0-7591-0529-4 (pbk.: alk. paper)
     1. Elementary school principals—United States—Case studies. 2. Educational anthropology—United States. I. Title.

     LB2831.92.W64 2003
     372.12'012—dc21   2003050278

Printed in the United States of America

♾™ The paper used in this publication meets the minimum requirements of American National Standard for Information Sciences—Permanence of Paper for Printed Library Materials, ANSI/NISO Z39.48–1992.

Contents

Preface, 2003

The Man in the Principal's Office hardly seemed destined to become a classic when I began work on it almost forty years ago. As a matter of fact, it probably survived only because it wasn't costing anything except part of the salary of a beginning assistant professor. Had it not been conceived in so positive a climate for educational research existing at the time, it might easily have been overlooked.

The study was my first independent postdissertation research. It seemed headed in the right direction, but it was not exactly what I would have envisioned had I been free to study anything I wanted, or even free to study anything that dealt so immediately with schools. I had talked about possibilities for research with George Spindler, professor of education and anthropology at Stanford University. Spindler was my mentor and was to become a lifelong friend. We already had discussed the possibility of doing an ethnography of an entire classroom, both in and out of school, which would obviously entail an elementary class to make the study manageable. But upon completing my doctorate, I had accepted a position as a research associate at the University of Oregon's recently inaugurated Center for the Advanced Study of Educational Administration. My study would have to relate specifically to educational administration. Focusing on an elementary school principal, rather than a classroom, had to suffice. However, I was allowed, even encouraged, to conduct the study from an anthropological perspective—whatever that was.

To me, that meant to study the actual behavior of a small number of principals, even one principal if I could get away with it, and to build my account from there. I have written how I almost got off on the wrong foot in *writing up* the research (2003), but at least for the fieldwork part, I was true to what one might expect an anthropologist to do in such circumstances. And exactly what would that be? Well, ethnography, of course. That is what I promised in my first working title for the project: "An Ethnography of the Principalship," which I later changed to "The Ethnography of a Principalship."

Outside anthropological circles, ethnography was not well understood at the time. I am not sure it is well understood even today, in part because it blends so easily into the broader phenomenon of qualitative research that is becoming increasingly difficult to pin down as it becomes more widely employed. Today the label is used in broader and broader circles by researchers who want to have a look around at what people in some other group are doing, or what people in their own group are doing, and sometimes even at what researchers themselves are doing and feeling. Mid–twentieth century ethnographers were much more focused than that.

If there is blame to be shared for those changing circumstances, I probably must take my share, not for being directly responsible but because I happened along as the transition was taking place. In the 1960s, anthropologists still tended to go off to do fieldwork and then come home to write it up. I had done that with my dissertation study among the Kwakiutl Indians of British Columbia, Canada. At the very moment, I was rewriting that study so that George and Louise Spindler could include it in their new series, Case Studies in Education and Culture, launched in 1967.

The new educational research center at the University of Oregon had intended to employ a "pure" anthropologist among its researchers, but the anthropology department offered little support for such an appointment, especially in a department that has always tilted toward archaeology. So those charged with staffing the center had to be satisfied with a "halfie" like me, someone who had studied cultural anthropology to augment doctoral studies in education. But in that regard, I came to Oregon with flying colors, for I was one of Spindler's earliest wave of graduate students in "anthropology and education." I had successfully completed and written up my fieldwork. I was even twice blessed, for it was not Spindler but professor Solon T. Kimball of Teachers College, Columbia University, who had found the job for me. I came recommended by the only two people in the United States who held joint appointments in anthropology and education at the time.

I had no way of appreciating how closely my own career was paralleling the development of anthropology and education or how fortunate I was that what I was doing was actually helping to shape the field. Because publications like this one have remained in print so long, it may seem that I was shaping the field rather than the other way around. But at least it is true that *The Man in the Principal's Office* was something of a pioneering effort in bringing ethnography "home" and bringing it into contemporary studies of schools and schooling. Between the time I began the fieldwork reported here and finally published the book some seven years later, the Council on Anthropology and Education was born, and there was at least a place at the table for things "ethnographic."

There was still not much interest in education on the part of anthropologists, however, and that meant that a few studies like this one became the models for numerous others that were to follow. *The Man in the Principals' Office* was there, in the right place at the right time. I have spelled this out in an article titled "Mirrors, Models, and Monitors: Educator Adaptations of the Ethnographic Innovation" (1982c).

In that article I discuss how this book was intended to speak to principals and to paint a realistic picture of what the principalship was like, based on an intense study of one person. The book did accomplish that and has often been used in classes in educational administration. But that did not become its primary use, which was instead to show students how ethnography itself was done and to give them a model that they could apply in other educational settings. I believe that the true "market" for this book has always been in classes that teach educators about qualitative research. It offers a way of looking that is descriptive rather than judgmental, beginning with the deceptively simple question "What is going on here?" As well, even in the late 1970s educators were also interested in problems of evaluation, and I had to acknowledge that my study sometimes served as a model for evaluative studies, a forerunner of today's "critical ethnography." Thus the "monitor" aspect of a tripartite title that encompasses the various purposes and audiences the book has served.

About Ed Bell

Both *The Man in the Principal's Office* and "Ed Bell" himself have survived the test of time. Ed retired years ago (*finally* retired, as some of his younger colleagues put it). He still lives with his wife in the house where he lived when this study was made. Today it is visits from grandchildren that are eagerly anticipated. As Ed describes life in retirement, he and his wife "keep pretty busy with church friends and family."

We live on opposite sides of town and move in different circles, and our paths do not usually cross. But I was present at his golden wedding anniversary and was happy to inform the guests that Ed was probably the best-known elementary school principal in the United States, albeit by the pseudonym he was assigned in the study. I also made a point of visiting him in 2001 so that I could present him with a copy of a new edition of the book, one translated in Taiwan by Professor Pai, Yi-fong of the National Hualien Teachers College. That edition proved a rather quick read for us both, since the only words we could make out were our respective names.

Trends I thought I could identify earlier have begun to look more like variations on a theme. Local schools and the state are, as usual, strapped for cash; enrollments are declining in the immediate area as people move farther out in search of affordable housing; and old-timers look favorably on what we now call the "good old days." It is not really that the old days were better but that we know how they turned out. The future poses questions yet to be answered before it can become the next generation's "good old days."

Schools of today seem more businesslike than when I was conducting this research, or when I taught in them (mid-1950s), or when I attended them (mid-1930s and 1940s), with far more concern for measurable results and responsibilities toward custodial care, far less for the "whole child." But such pressure comes from above and is more evident in the upper grades. Six-year-olds are still free spirits that have yet to endure the pressure and competition many of them will feel as they move up in the grades. And there are still plenty of people like Ed who are dedicated to making school a pleasant place to be, a constructive "learning environment," and a pleasant memory to carry away.

In Ed's case, the farther he gets from the realities of the classroom, the fonder his memories grow. His memories of the two years I spent following him from 1966 to 1968, and of how I wrote about it afterward, have taken on a similar glow. He has often mentioned how I contributed to his "professional growth" by causing him to take a closer look at himself. I wasn't really trying to do that—whatever impact the study had on him personally would be for him alone to know—but it has been comforting to know that, as usual, he made it into something positive. That was his way.

What contribution did a study like this have to make? My feeling was that we needed a much closer look at how schools operated, especially on a day-to-day basis. If our assigned mission as a research center was their betterment, how might that be accomplished, and to what ends? A study of what went on, an intimate portrait of even one school, would tell us a lot about the realities of public education. And that, it seemed to me, was the kind of contribution an anthropological orientation could make.

Did the study make that contribution? I was ready to defend it at the time, and after forty years, there is no doubt. It not only documented how things were; it pretty well tells the story of how things remain today. Schools operate under a law of limited possibilities—there is always something they should or could do that they are not doing, and there is always something they could do more or better. But when you box in a large group of learners of any age for a predetermined number of hours each day and week, there is only a certain amount you can expect to accomplish. School "keeps." This is a story of one of its keepers and the context in which he worked.

About the Developing Field of "Anthropology and Education"

Spindler himself sidetracked my getting this account written. Although I had already gathered a mountain of data, I spent the better part of a second year doing fieldwork rather than turning to the writing task. About the time that I was ready to settle down and devote my nonteaching time exclusively to writing the book—and with a funded study, there *had to* be a book—Spindler decided that he would revise his well-received *Education and Culture* published in 1963. He intended to retain some old chapters in the revision, but he wanted new material as well, adding material from his own students' recently completed field studies, mine included.

For me that meant preparing two chapters, one from the earlier Kwakiutl study, one from the new and as yet unwritten principal study. The temptation was too great; I wanted to be included in a Spindler-edited book, especially with a publisher waiting in the wings. I also rationalized that having an article from my study would draw attention to the full account and would buy me more time to complete it.

Ideas for his revision grew, and Spindler decided that the growing collection needed a new title, *Education and Cultural Process: Toward an Anthropology of Education*. And I discovered that edited books take a long time to come to fruition. Although taking time out to write the article for Spindler delayed the writing of this book, my book came out a year ahead of his edited version anyway. (The first edition of *Education and Cultural Process* was published in 1974.)

I was pleased with the way my book eventually turned out. I was also delighted to have Spindler accept it for the Education and Culture series, especially when he was willing to live with a longer book than he had been accepting for others in the series. The book is reprinted here exactly as it first appeared, except for this preface that allows me the opportunity to bring things up-to-date.

I was also watching the field of anthropology and education develop. Once I recognized the book's influence on the field, I wished that I had made it even more "anthropological" than it was. That might have created some tension at the research center, but from an anthropological perspective I was sorry that the account was not more about a man who happened to be a principal than about a principal who happened to be a man. And in those days, the elementary principalship was essentially a man's role, the secondary principalship almost exclusively so. Changes brought about by affirmative action were to come along later.

Given some misgivings about making our studies "more anthropological" in spite of their familiar settings, I urged comrades in anthropology and education to demonstrate a more anthropological orientation in their work, giving more emphasis to cultural context and to everyday life rather than only to life in schools. I was also determined to make my own studies more anthropological in the future. My next study conducted under the auspices of the center was *Teachers Vs. Technocrats: An Educational Innovation in Anthropological Perspective* (1977). It bore clear indications of its anthropological roots.

Following the completion of that study and reassignment to full-time teaching, I turned from writing about processes of schooling and toward writing about the educational process writ large. I began with an essay called "The Anthropology of Learning" (1982a) and an anthropological life history titled "Adequate Schools and Inadequate Education: The Life History of a Sneaky Kid" (1983). The latter study now extends over a period of twenty years and was published as *Sneaky Kid and Its Aftermath: Ethics and Intimacy in Fieldwork* (2002).

A careful examination of the bibliography accompanying the original study should give a good idea of the school-related work done to the time of publication, including virtually everything that had been published in "anthropology and education" to that point. Personally I would have been satisfied to see ethnography retain more evidence of its anthropological (and sociological) roots rather than receive broad acclaim as a sometimes-synonym for qualitative studies in general. But it also has been satisfying to watch qualitative research come more into its own. *The Man in the Principal's Office* probably sits right in the middle. It has inspired countless other studies, some more anthropological than others, but many fine studies among them. And I still wrestle with a question that a colleague asked at the time: "Does it really matter whether the studies are *anthropological* or not, as long as they are good studies?"

For this edition, I have added a select bibliography of my own work with this new preface, citing my more educationally relevant pieces that followed the account reported in these pages. Related to the bibliography, I should mention two people who have exerted a major influence on what I have written. George Spindler has watched over my career for forty years and has created opportunities and offered counsel throughout, always with support and encouragement. Mitch Allen is the unseen hand that put *The Man in the Principal's Office* back in print, along with two other early studies, *A Kwakiutl Village and School* and *Teachers versus Technocrats*. For that alone I would be grateful. But Mitch has exerted a major influence on my writing since about 1988, when he first suggested I put together my thoughts for a little monograph about writing up qualitative research (1990b). Since that time he has published (and personally edited) four of my other books (1994, 1995, 1999, 2002). Together with the support of former doctoral students and colleagues, noting especially John Singleton and Phil Young in the latter regard, I have found my way through the maze of university life and unimagined opportunities inherent in the anthropological study of education.

Harry F. Wolcott
Eugene, Oregon
March 2003

Select Bibliography

1973   *The Man in the Principal's Office: An Ethnography.* New York: Holt, Rinehart & Winston. [Reissued by Waveland Press in 1984.]

1974   The Elementary School Principal: Notes from a Field Study. In *Education and Cultural Process: Toward an Anthropology of Education.* George D. Spindler, ed. Pp. 176–204. New York: Holt, Rinehart & Winston. [Revised and reissued by Waveland Press in 1987.]

1975a   Criteria for an Ethnographic Approach to Research in Schools. *Human Organization* 34(2):111–27.

1975b   Fieldwork in Schools: Where the Tradition of Deferred Judgment Meets a Subculture Obsessed with Evaluation. [Council on] *Anthropology and Education Quarterly* 6(1):17–20.

1977   *Teachers versus Technocrats: An Educational Innovation in Anthropological Perspective.* Eugene: University of Oregon Center for Educational Policy and Management.

1980   How to Look Like an Anthropologist without Being One. *Practicing Anthropology* 3(1). [Reprinted in *Classics of Practicing Anthropology, 1978–1998.* Patricia Higgins and Anthony Paredes, eds. Pp. 43–50. Oklahoma City: Society for Applied Anthropology, 2000.]

1981a   Confessions of a "Trained" Observer. In *The Study of Schooling: Field Based Methodologies in Educational Research and Evaluation.* Thomas S. Popkewitz and B. Robert Tabachnick, eds. Pp. 247–63. New York: Praeger.

1981b   Home and Away: Personal Contrasts in Ethnographic Style. In *Anthropologists at Home in North America: Methods and Issues in the Study of One's Own Society.* Donald A. Messerschmidt, ed. Pp. 255–65. New York: Cambridge University Press.

1982a   The Anthropology of Learning. *Anthropology and Education Quarterly* 13(2): 83–108.

1982b   Differing Styles of On-Site Research, or, "If It Isn't Ethnography, What Is It?" *Review Journal of Philosophy and Social Science* 7(1,2):154–69.

1982c   Mirrors, Models, and Monitors: Educator Adaptations of the Ethnographic Innovation. In *Doing the Ethnography of Schooling.* George D. Spindler, ed. Pp. 68–95. New York: Holt, Rinehart & Winston. [Reissued by Waveland Press, 1988.]

1983   Adequate Schools and Inadequate Education: The Life History of a Sneaky Kid. *Anthropology and Education Quarterly* 14(1):3–32.

1984   Ethnographers sans Ethnography: The Evaluation Compromise. In *Ethnographic Evaluation*. David Fetterman, ed. Pp. 177–210. Beverly Hills, Calif.: Sage.

1985   On Ethnographic Intent. *Educational Administration Quarterly* 21(3):187–203. [Reprinted in *Interpretive Ethnography of Education*. George and Louise Spindler, eds. Pp. 37–57. Hillsdale, N.J.: Erlbaum, 1987.]

1988a   Ethnographic Research in Education. In *Complementary Methods for Research in Education*. Richard M. Jaeger, ed. Pp. 187–249. Washington, D.C.: American Educational Research Association. [Also in a second edition, 1997.]

1988b   "Problem Finding" in Qualitative Research. In *School and Society: Learning Content through Culture*. Henry T. Trueba and C. Delgado-Gaitan, eds. Pp. 11–35. New York: Praeger.

1990a   Making a Study "More Ethnographic." *Journal of Contemporary Ethnography* 19(1):44–72.

1990b   *Writing Up Qualitative Research*. Thousand Oaks, Calif.: Sage. [Now in a second edition by Sage published in 2001.]

1991   Propriospect and the Acquisition of Culture. *Anthropology and Education Quarterly* 22(3):251–73.

1992   Posturing in Qualitative Inquiry. In *Handbook of Qualitative Research in Education*. Margaret D. LeCompte, Wendy L. Millroy, and Judith Preissle, eds. Pp. 3–52. San Diego, Calif.: Academic Press.

1994   *Transforming Qualitative Data: Description, Analysis, and Interpretation*. Thousand Oaks, Calif.: Sage.

1995   *The Art of Fieldwork*. Walnut Creek, Calif.: AltaMira.

1996   Peripheral Participation and the Kwakiutl Potlatch. *Anthropology and Education Quarterly* 27(4):467–92.

1999   *Ethnography: A Way of Seeing*. Walnut Creek, Calif.: AltaMira.

2002   *Sneaky Kid and Its Aftermath: Ethics and Intimacy in Fieldwork*. Walnut Creek, Calif.: AltaMira.

2003   A Natural Writer. *Anthropology and Education Quarterly* 34(3).

Preface and Acknowledgments, 1973

The purpose of any ethnographic account is to provide description and analysis regarding human social behavior. Utilizing a fieldwork approach associated especially with the methods of anthropology, the ethnographer selectively records certain aspects of human behavior in order to construct explanations of that behavior in cultural terms. An ethnographic account focuses most often on some particular group of people, such as the Tikopia or the Children of Sanchez, but it may also focus on some special human process, such as communication or divorce.

The account provided in these pages is an ethnographic inquiry into the elementary school principalship. The purpose of the study is to describe and analyze the elementary school principalship from a cultural perspective. The study focuses not only on a particular group of people—elementary school principals—but on the behavior of one specific elementary school principal during a particular period of time. Of necessity, however, attention is also given to those who customarily interact with a principal, such as the teachers, other staff members, pupils, and parents who collectively comprise "his" school; his fellow administrators; his nonschool acquaintances; and his family and friends. This study focuses on those human processes in which the principal engaged that were most directly related to his assignment as a principal. However, an ethnographic inquiry into what a principal does *as a principal* cannot ignore the broader context in which an individual lives and works, and the various ways in which circumstances which appear to be external to his occupational role may actually exert considerable impact. The attention to context and to complex interrelationships in human lives is what makes ethnographic accounts different from accounts written from the perspective of other social sciences. Ethnographic accounts deal with real human beings and actual human behavior, with an emphasis on social, rather than on physiological or psychological, aspects of behavior.

The test of ethnography is whether it enables one to anticipate and interpret what goes on in a society or social group as appropriately as one of its members. To the extent that the account provided here achieves this objective, readers should feel that if they were suddenly to find themselves in an encounter with staff members, pupils, or parents at the school described, or were to attend a meeting with other principals from the school district, they would understand how they might act if they were in the role of the principal. Conversely, if they were to assume the role of some other person in an encounter with the principal, they should feel they would know how the principal might act toward them.

The rationale for pursuing the ethnographic approach was that almost no attention has been given in the literature on school administration to what elementary school principals actually do. That is not to imply any lack of sheer quantity either in educational literature generally or in that special aspect of it that deals with educational administration. Most of the literature of educational administration readily available to the student or practitioner, however, tends to be normative in its approach—it tells principals and would-be principals what they ought to do and remains seemingly unaware of what is actually going on. This characteristic pervades most subfields within education, although there has been increasing attention recently to obtaining accounts of actual behavior for training classroom teachers and school counselors. What little data exist on the actual daily behavior of school administrators depend mostly on self-reporting techniques in which a principal keeps a time-distribution chart of his or her own behavior (see Ranniger 1962). Such data are influenced (and therefore limited) by each subject's ability to recall and to record those of his or her actions relevant to a behavioral study, particularly in light of the complexity and multiplicity of the encounters in which an administrator engages. Bias in self-reporting may also reflect the influence of pervading norms. Administrators tend to be uneasy about the way they actually distribute their time and, therefore, not completely dependable about self-reporting, for they cannot escape a nagging feeling that the way they *do* allocate their time is not the way they *should* allocate it.

To a literature that has dealt almost exclusively with the behavior of school administrators as it *ought to be* or as it is interpreted and reported by the person performing it, the present study adds another dimension: what an administrator actually does as observed by someone else. While the case approach has not been ignored in educational administration, most of the available cases have either been hypothetical or have been doctoral dissertations that, if they dealt in any depth with real administrative situations or real personalities, were likely to have been locked away to prevent circulation (e.g., the restricted circulation allowed one study of the principal's influence on a school by Christiansen [1954]) or to have undergone an almost ludicrous censorship in which proper names were inked out before the study was released (e.g., the interlibrary loan copy of Boyan [1951]). The very nature of dissertation studies in administration has lent itself most naturally to the survey, usually by mailed questionnaire, of ten, a hundred, or a thousand administrators, subsequently tallied and treated with some high-powered statistical interpretation that substitutes one type of significance for another. If the number of such doctoral studies is dismaying, it is even more dismaying to realize that dependence on this limited approach has been the sole basis for so many educational studies.[1]

Apart from case studies undertaken for dissertation topics, few attempts have been made to augment the overpowering influence of the questionnaire and/or interview approach to studying school administration. The combined talents of novelist and school administrator in the person of one individual (see Barr 1971; Rothman 1971) or two (see Hentoff 1966) provide one source of variation. The relatively few anthropologists who have directed attention to the process of administering schools

---

[1] Seiber reports that one out of three educational researchers reporting in journals in 1964 utilized a survey research approach (Seiber 1968: 274). My suspicion is that studies in educational administration would account for a large percentage of these.

have more often directed their attention to the *role* of the administrator (Spindler 1963a), or to specific administrative problems like innovation (Gallaher 1965) or integration (Fuchs 1966), than to the intensely personal accounts characteristic of other settings that have received anthropological attention. Anthropologist Solon T. Kimball has frequently contributed articles to journals read by school administrators (see Kimball 1961, 1965) and has encouraged others to recognize the school as an important arena for anthropological research (Atwood 1964; Burnett 1969; Eddy 1967, 1969; Rosenfeld 1971). A series of dissertations done by graduate students in education affiliated with the Stanford Consultation Service Team investigated various aspects of school administration with anthropological guidance provided by George Spindler (Christiansen 1954; Fishburn 1955; Sharpe 1956; Shipnuck 1954; Tilden 1953). A few researchers from disciplines other than anthropology have employed its methodology in studying administratively relevant aspects of education (see Becker 1952, 1953; Iannaccone 1958, 1962; Jackson 1968; Lutz and Innaccone 1969; McDowell 1954; Smith and Geoffrey 1965, 1968) and have occasionally provided good incidental case study data about administrators within the context of studies primarily concerned with other research purposes (see Smith and Keith 1967, 1971). The body of literature in the whole field of anthropology and education is not extensive,[2] and anthropologists who have turned their efforts to the study of our formal system of education have only rarely addressed more than passing attention to school administration. This lacuna in the literature provided tacit encouragement for pursuing the present exploration as a relatively untapped approach to understanding and analyzing the human tasks in educational administration.

Certain practical considerations gave further endorsement to the project. As a research associate in a research and development center established expressly to study educational organization and administration, I sought an area of inquiry in which my research interests would be compatible with the total program of the center. What school administrators do interests me not only because their behavior affects what happens in the whole complex of formal education, but also because that behavior in turn reflects both the education subculture and the American value system of which educators are part. My academic interests are, however, centered around the study of education viewed as cultural process rather than about the details of managing schools. Administration interests me as it relates to this process, both in how it facilitates and how it hinders the achievement of formally stated educational goals and how it has some unintended consequences as well.

Due in large measure to the influence of Professor George Spindler on my own professional career, I have oriented my teaching and my research to the application of anthropological perspectives and techniques in studying education. In any educational inquiry I undertake, I am inclined to approach the problem as an anthropologist might, taking a "holistic" approach, distinguishing how things actually are from what people say they are or say they ought to be, and sometimes simply making sure that the obvious is obvious. It seemed both natural and inevitable that in the

[2] For reviews summarizing the anthropology and education literature, see, for example, Spindler 1963a; Wolcott 1967a; Sindell 1969; Lindquist 1971.

Center for the Advanced Study of Education Administration I would approach the study of administrators or of administration with perspectives and methods drawn heavily from cultural anthropology.

More recently I have been struck with the manner in which the rapidly expanding body of education research shows a trend toward huge, costly studies that often yield strikingly unimportant data (e.g., that 97 percent of high school social studies teachers talk about politics in class "always," "often," or "sometimes"; or that "44 percent of the teachers in metropolitan areas are satisfied as compared to 35 percent of the teachers in small towns"). Human beings get lost in masses of figures that bury the very subjects of study. The surveys tell us too little about too many, and they tell us more about how the subjects acted during the filling out of a questionnaire than about how they act in their "real" life. So this study also grows out of a personal dissatisfaction and impatience with the present overreliance on data that are quickly and easily obtained but that alone can never provide a complete picture of actual behavior in context regardless of how one increases his or her "N's" or lengthens his or her questionnaires. Questions such as whether principals feel they should or should not smoke or drink in public, whether they should attend church regularly, even whether they feel they should review with their teachers their written evaluations of them provide remarkably little data about the nature of the principalship when viewed from the perspective of an individual principal. The principal of the case study, Edward Bell, happens not to smoke or drink anyway. He was attending church many, many years before he received his first appointment as an elementary school principal; at one time he had even considered entering the ministry. And regardless of how Ed *feels* about preparing annual evaluations and reviewing them with his teachers, it does not really matter whether he thinks it is necessary or whether he enjoys or abhors the task. He does it because school district policy requires it.

In the course of conducting a long-term study, one accumulates a roster of people to whom acknowledgment and a word of thanks are in order. My debt to the "real" Edward Bell will quickly become obvious to the reader. I wish to acknowledge his great perseverance and patience not only in accepting me in my observer's role but in constantly taking the time to express his personal explanations and feelings regarding the situations that confronted him. I feel a similar debt to staff members at his school, to many of his fellow principals, to certain personnel in the school district's central office, and to members of his immediate family. I cannot say that without them the study never would have been possible, but I greatly appreciate the fact that their continued cooperation made it possible to provide the detailed account that I was able to obtain.

I have mentioned the pervasive influence of George Spindler on my professional orientation, but I must acknowledge the special interest he showed in this study from its very inception. He suggested many of the procedures that I followed in the fieldwork and speculated that two conceptual frameworks, the process of *managing encounters*, with the purpose of *resolving conflict*, might provide a heuristic for organizing the ethnographic account. Although I did not pursue the notion of conflict resolution (or a related one suggested to me by economist Barry Siegel for examining the administrative process as the allocation of limited resources), I invite the attention of other students to the possibilities. Spindler also provided helpful comments in his reactions to the first statements which I prepared toward the ethnography and helped me to establish some guidelines for developing the final manuscript.

For help in formulating the original research proposal and in anticipating problems in conducting the fieldwork, I am grateful for the counsel of Ronald and Evelyn Rohner, who were also colleagues during my introduction to fieldwork among the Kwakiutl, and to R. Jean Hills and John Croft, with whom I first discussed this approach to studying educational administration. Throughout the study I had the support of the Center for the Advanced Study of Educational Administration, and I wish to thank its two directors during that period: Roland Pellegrin, who invited and supported the original proposal, and Max G. Abbott, who not only waited patiently for the completion of the project but kept the faith during a long interim. I also appreciated encouragement from a number of colleagues at the University of Oregon, including Richard O. Carlson, W. W. Charters Jr., Philip Runkel, and Brent Rutherford at CASEA; anthropologist Alfred G. Smith; and sociologist Robert Dubin. Professor Dubin virtually insisted that I obtain the time and motion data that later proved so valuable in the write-up.

Max Abbott and Norman Delue plowed through early drafts of the entire manuscript and gave extensive suggestions for improving it, and in subsequent drafts Delue worked tirelessly to help me eliminate repetition and to indicate how the protocols could be shortened to improve the readability of tape-recorded speech. My research assistant, John A. Olson, organized and summarized interview and census data, prepared the maps included in the monograph, took numerous photographs of the school and community, and, along with his wife, Carey, offered editorial help with chapter 4. I received editorial help with chapter 1 from Alfred G. Smith and Max Abbott, with chapter 7 from Ronald P. Rohner, with chapter 11 from Joseph Schneider, and with the epilogue from Robert B. Everhart. The development of the annual cycle discussion in chapter 7, including the graphic presentation of the material, is closely patterned after Rohner's development of annual cycle data from the Kwakiutl fieldwork (see Rohner and Rohner 1970: chapter 2). In subsequent drafts, the manuscript benefited from suggestions made by David P. Boynton, Louis M. Smith, and Richard L. Warren. Readers familiar with the writings of Anthony Wallace will recognize his influence on the development of ideas expressed in the Epilogue. Mrs. Allie Beat did the majority of the typing throughout the entire project and faithfully watched over the developing manuscript.

1 / A principal investigator
in search of a principal

In the lexicon of the social sciences, the person who directs a research project is formally designated the principal investigator. As I prepared the initial research proposal describing the ethnographic approach I intended to take in studying the social behavior of one elementary school principal, I realized how literally my newly acquired title fit the task before me.

This chapter introduces the study by describing how I proceeded as a principal investigator—how the fieldwork was initiated and how the ethnographic account provided in the ensuing chapters was obtained.[1] This review of methodology begins with a discussion of the problems of locating a principal who would be the primary subject of the research. The chapter includes a consideration of some of the real and anticipated problems in conducting the research and of the formal field study methods by which the research was carried out.

A Principal Investigator in
Search of a Principal

Locating a principal willing to participate in this study was clearly a crucial step in its accomplishment. Although I attempted to approach that step as systematically as possible, as I look back on how Edward Bell became my associate in this venture, I can not help but wonder at my good fortune. Before I began my search I identified criteria for selecting a principal which seemed either essential for the purposes of the study, necessary for the relationship between investigator and subject, or compatible with some personal biases of my own. These criteria included: that the principal be a full-time, supervising principal (in contrast to a teaching principal); that he be responsible for only one elementary school; that he not be new to administration or to a particular building at the outset of the study; that, like the majority of elementary school principals, he be male; and that he regard himself as a career principal rather than someone consciously using the principalship as a stepping-stone to a "higher" position. I also felt the principal with

---

[1] Brief accounts of the fieldwork have also been reported elsewhere: "An Ethnographic Approach to the Study of School Administrators" (Wolcott 1970) and "The Elementary School Principal: Notes from a Field Study" (Wolcott, 1974).

whom I would so closely associate during this study should not be engaged in a graduate program at the university where I was a faculty member. I did not want a subject whose success as a degree candidate might in any way be complicated by our research relationship. It seemed essential that the principal chosen for the study approach the principalship with an integrity evidenced by his concern for the role and by the appearance of sufficient confidence in himself to carry it out. I also counted on intuition to help us assess whether we had enough mutual regard that we could survive the projected two-year period of fieldwork.

From a variety of sources I solicited nominations of and opinions about possible candidates among the elementary school principals in the geographic region in which I planned to conduct the study. I spent a few hours at each of several schools with principals who said they were willing to consider participating in the study. I followed them around at school and then explored my reactions to these trial runs for clues about my own feelings. I decided against working with one administrator in part because he wore white socks with a dark business suit; I imagined that in two years his style of dress—one I personally dislike—might come to be as distracting as his patronizing manner with pupils.

I narrowed my choices to two principals with whom I felt the study could be carried out successfully. At that point I turned to colleagues who could provide professional information or personal assessments regarding the two men, the schools they administered, and their respective school districts. The consensus was that while both men were "very representative," Edward Bell, principal of the William Howard Taft Elementary School, would probably be a better choice. If Ed said he was willing to do it, I was told, he would carry it through. My alternative subject had a reputation for displaying an early enthusiasm for new projects that was not always sustained. Furthermore, their two school districts were felt to have different degrees of authority vested in the central office. The Columbia Unified School District, perhaps because of its greater size, was described as one in which principals were given some administrative autonomy, and Ed was recognized by both his colleagues and mine as "not one of the central office boys." The other district, by contrast, was described as highly centralized, with a benevolent but nonetheless authoritarian director of elementary education who "called most of the shots." Since I suspected that principals wield little authority as seen in the context of the organization of a school district (regardless of their apparent power as perceived by teachers and pupils subordinate to them), I chose the man and the district that had the reputation for exhibiting the greater degree of autonomy.

During the period in which I was looking for a subject, the principals whom I met volunteered a number of descriptive titles for my role, such as "anthropologist in residence," "assistant without portfolio," "lap dog," and "shadow." Ultimately the last term became my nickname, perhaps because it simultaneously provided a capsule description of my role, a nickname for people who could not remember my real name or were uncertain how to address me, and an entrée into a joking relationship where no other pattern for behavior existed: "Hey Shadow, how come you're here on a dark day like this?"

Before extending my invitation to Ed to participate in the study, I reviewed the kinds of activities I intended to pursue with him as his "shadow": maintaining a constant written record of what I observed in behavior and conversation; attending formal and informal meetings and conferences; accompanying him on school business away from the building as well as occasionally accompanying him in non-school settings; interviewing "everybody"; and, with his permission, sifting through notes, records, and files.

Up to this point my search was conducted at the grass-roots level. By using this approach I felt I could avoid the possibility of having an overzealous superintendent summarily assign some fair-haired principal to be my cooperating subject or an underzealous one reject the project because he doubted that any of "the boys" would be interested. For purposes of the project my approach has much to recommend it, but it is a tenuous approach in terms of gaining goodwill in school districts. Colleges and universities often place heavy demands on nearby school districts, not only as sites for training teachers, but also as sites for conducting research. Periodically school administrators at all levels show signs of stress at the extent of these external demands. They rationalize their anxieties by anticipating accusations that outsiders may be interfering with the primary purposes of the school or that the research itself may produce problems because the researcher has failed to make explicit what he intends to do, a particularly sensitive area when it entails interviews or questionnaires addressed to students. It seemed urgent, therefore, to solicit official cooperation and formal approval through the school district's central office as soon as possible. Since no one in the central office had been informed of the project, I suggested that Ed first talk informally to fellow principals and perhaps to certain central office staff before making his final decision about participating. I asked him to stress the fact that we were exploring the feasibility of such a study rather than assuming it to be a *fait accompli*. Though I felt I had found an excellent subject for the project, I was in no position to insist on Ed's participation. I asked him to take whatever time he needed to make his decision, to consult with anyone he wished, and to telephone me if he was willing to go ahead with the study. I was delighted when Ed did call to say "Let's go ahead with it."

I prepared a formal request for permission to conduct research to submit to Ed's school district. Matters of liaison with university research projects were handled by the assistant superintendent of schools. I had assumed that all central office staff would be informed of the project once it was formally approved, but I am sure that even if some of them had indeed heard about the study before I suddenly started appearing with Ed they either had forgotten about it or had never considered its implications. After I had been "shadowing" Ed for eight months, for example, the superintendent spotted me one morning at the central office among a group of principals who had been asked to serve as a screening committee for selecting applicants for new principalships that were opening next year. Since Ed had been assigned to that committtee, I attached myself to it also. The superintendent looked quizically at me as he stopped to chat with members of the committee just before it convened. "Say, you're not writing all this down, are you?" he asked. "I write everything down," I replied. I added that if he was interested in the study I would welcome the chance to talk to him about it in detail. He was and I did. My point is that although I was doing an intensive case study with one principal over a long period of time, in a school district of a middle-sized American city I certainly did not come into contact with all the central office staff. Many school personnel with whom I came into contact had little or no knowledge of my project. No one, myself included, had anticipated all the situations in which there might be stresses in having an outsider present as observer.

Ethical Considerations

Ed and I tried to anticipate the ethical problems which this project might engender. For example, it seemed reasonable that I might often be present when Ed talked on the telephone, but it would not be ethical to listen on an extension telephone since, presumably, the other party would not know that an observer was present and therefore he could not possibly withhold his consent. While files and records seemed within the domain of the project, I made specific requests before looking at materials if Ed did not volunteer them for inspection. During conferences between the principal and others our understanding was that I would assume I was welcome unless I was informed otherwise, but that Ed always had the option of excluding me from a meeting. Presumably his basis for doing this was that the purposes of the school took priority over the research project, and the project should never jeopardize the program of the school. The only times this option was exercised were prior to a few conferences with parents which Ed felt might be "touchy" or where he was concerned about the sheer number of school people that a parent would have to confront, since the parent conferences held in his office invariably included the counsellor, one or more classroom teachers, and other school district personnel as well. Ed always made introductions on my behalf if I had not met those present at his meetings, regardless of whether they were second-grade boys being disciplined for misconduct, families new to the community, or visiting dignitaries.

The obviousness of the advantages of preserving as much anonymity as possible in no way contributes to how best to accomplish it. Pseudonyms have been used, but readers close to the school or district in which the research took place probably cannot resist trying to identify personalities or to speculate about personalities where positive identification is impossible. To present the material in such a way that even the people central to the study are "fooled" by it is to risk removing those very aspects that make it vital, unique, believable, and at times painfully personal. I have instead tried to keep the real actors in mind in every sentence I have written, attempting constantly to anticipate whether those actually involved in the interaction recorded here would accept the account as I have rendered it. Whether or not the degree of discretion exercised in reporting has been sufficient, I must leave to the reader to decide. Past experience leads me to believe that those nearest to the scene may occasionally be disappointed at my judgment in providing details which to a wider audience seem not the least bit extraordinary, while the wider audience, in turn, expresses surprise over details which are taken for granted locally. On the assumption that the data can be considered more objectively by readers who are not preoccupied with identifying personalities, the major contribution toward anonymity has been in keeping to a minimum the number of people outside the immediate locus of my observations who knew where the study was being conducted. Few of my colleagues know where the fieldwork was done unless there was some compelling reason for them to know or they happened upon me in the presence of the principal or at his school. Maintaining anonymity was a consideration throughout the entire project rather than only in the write-up. The people "inside" the study were inside before it began; every consideration was given to keep that number as small as possible.

Two other procedures were followed to help preserve anonymity. First, I was the only person who had access to the bulk of data during the fieldwork stage. Journal entries were made in longhand and were not retyped. Only the taped interviews were processed by others during the research period, and those who worked with this material were requested to treat it confidentially. Second, time itself helps to protect anonymity or at least to make identification more difficult. Over time people forget what others said and even what they themselves said. Issues that were critical at certain periods had lost their urgency a year or two later. The continual student and staff turnover characteristic of public schools has also contributed to protecting anonymity by blending the personalities of new pupils and faculty members with old ones. Ego-shattering as it may be for the researcher, even he is rather quickly assigned to the amorphous category of the "gone and since forgotten" in which the few remaining old-timers at school put the endless parade of pupils and other brief visitors.

Feedback, or in this case the absence of feedback, provided another ethical consideration which we anticipated. I intended to confront this problem directly by warning Ed in advance that I would attempt to display no sign of personal approval or disapproval regarding events that transpired. My purpose was to observe and record rather than to judge, and I intended to remain in the background as an observer. This was, of course, a research ideal which was modified in actual practice. It was easy enough to refrain from commenting during conferences and meetings. In encounters of only two or three people I attempted to give such total attention to writing my notes that speakers would exclude me from their interactions. However, anthropologists interested in proxemics (see Birdwhistell 1970, Hall 1966) have observed the importance of nonverbal cues as concomitant communication systems, and I was conscious of the difficulty of attempting to monitor my own nonverbal responses while assuming the role of observer. To fail to register a smile at something humorous, to fail to nod supportively to encourage an informant's account, or to fail to pursue how a decision happened to be made, may provide equally as potent a "message" as when one appears too eager to know certain details to the exclusion of others.[2] Nor was the mask I wanted to wear always the mask that was perceived. As some of the teachers became better acquainted with me they sometimes remarked that I looked "sad" on days I meant to look interested, "bored" on days when I was only tired, "aloof" on days when I could not shake other concerns and give full attention to the immediate situation.

---

[2] See Kinsey *et al.*, for an excellent discussion of the closely comparable interviewer-interviewee relationship (1948:35–62).

On several occasions I reviewed with Ed the fact that the project was not designed to be an evaluative one and that he should not expect me to provide either a general review of how adequately I felt he fulfilled the role of principal or specifically that he had handled some problem well or poorly. Ed was remarkable in his ability to accept this condition. When at times he seemed to approach the limits of his tolerance for doing so and expressed a wish that I could render my opinion or endorse one of his, he was usually quick to add, "but, then, that's not the purpose of this study, is it?"

I decided against attempting to train Ed as an ethnographer, as anthropologists have sometimes done with informants (see Rohner 1969 for a discussion of Boas's use of this technique). That decision was influenced by several considerations: whether there would be sufficient time to accomplish such a goal, recognizing the constant demands for Ed's attention which precluded any opportunity for uninterrupted sessions; whether I was sophisticated enough as a field researcher to train someone with no background in anthropology (although Ed had minored in sociology as an undergraduate and was attracted to participating in part because of the project's anthropological flavor); and whether such training might make him too self-conscious a subject at the same time it made him a more effective informant. There were times, however, when Ed asked directly, "As we were sitting in that meeting, I was wondering just how it would look to an anthropologist?" If I felt the question was not simply rhetorical, and if I anticipated enough time for us to enjoy the luxury of a brief and uninterrupted discussion, such as riding back to school after a meeting, or walking the length of the corridor together with no one in sight, I usually pointed out some facets of what I had observed that might interest him (for example, the use of space in the meeting, circumstances under which such a meeting might and might not occur, and limitations placed by external factors). While my intent was partly to enlighten him by increasing his awareness, I also capitalized on anthropology's holistic approach to draw attention to the whole context in which formal education takes place, hopefully making Ed feel less self-conscious as the immediate object of observation at the same time that his behavior was usually my major focus of attention.

I was conscious that "friendship" could present another nagging problem. In projecting some possible methodological problems which I might confront in the study, my colleague Ronald Rohner reviewed for me the crucial problems which can develop when a fieldworker (in many fields—psychology, social work, or education, as well as anthropology) invests a long period of time learning the intimate details of an informant's life. This is the paradox suggested in the title of Hortense Powdermaker's account of her own anthropological fieldwork, *Stranger and Friend* (1966). How does one develop a close working relationship with his subject without the degree of involvement that has ultimately left some anthropologists unable to continue to write analytically about a people whom they have studied for years? My conscious goal was to establish a role as a warm, sympathetic observer without making all the commitments of a long-term friend.

A corollary of the friendship problem was the possibility of becoming over-identified with the principal in the eyes of all the others who comprised the research setting. At least two undesirable consequences might have stemmed from this problem, particularly regarding relations with the rest of the school staff: either they might perceive me as working so closely with Ed that they would not confide in me about any matter unless they expected it to get directly back to him, or they might misinterpret my close attention to his behavior as a lack of interest in their own. Because my research strategy was an open one (anyone interested in the project was welcome to an explanation), I endeavored to confront this problem by explaining it as one of my key concerns during the one time when I addressed the entire faculty semiformally in a staff meeting. By the confidence some staff members expressed in relating personal concerns to me, I assume that my strategy was at least partly successful. The related and inevitable problem of the researcher's own role in the field setting is discussed later in this chapter.

Field Methods

Anthropologist Arthur Vidich has suggested that the methodology central to this study, participant-observation, is "the strategy of having one's cake and eating it too" (Vidich 1960:356). Lest his comment be misconstrued as an unqualified endorsement of the participant-observer approach, recall the essential dilemma expressed in that metaphor: one cannot do both at the same time. The role of participant and the role of observer are essentially complementary and mutually exclusive; the more perfectly you activate one, the less perfectly you activate its reciprocal. Behavioral scientists, particularly sociologists, have repeatedly described and dissected participant-observation as a method (see Adams and Preiss 1960; Babchuk 1962; Becker 1958; Becker and Geer 1957; Gold 1958; Kluckhohn 1940; Lohman 1937; Miller 1952; Schwartz and Schwartz 1960; Vidich 1960) and have suggested a variety of terms intended to distinguish degrees of participation and observation more accurately. One author, for example, proposed a distinction among such possible variations as the total observer, unknown and unseen; the "observer as participant"; the "participant as observer"; and the complete and total participant (Gold 1958). Recently the term "non-participant observer" has appeared with some frequency, particularly in *in situ* studies of schools and classrooms conducted by researchers of a psychological bent (see Biddle 1967: 338, and studies subsequent to that review conducted by Philip W. Jackson or Louis M. Smith and his associates). One might conduct a study of a principalship by means of a variety of techniques falling within the domain of the participant-observer approach. At one extreme, emphasizing the observer aspects (and momentarily waiving some ethical considerations), one might design a school building to provide access either through the use of electronic monitoring or by constructing a looking-glass school for observers who would never be detected. Or one could take some role which provided maximum access to observing the principal's behavior (for example, a secretary, a vice principal). At the other extreme, emphasizing participant aspects of the approach, the researcher could assume the role of principal himself. As Vidich (1960) has observed, it is the kind of data to be gathered, rather than any standard field practice, which determines how "native" the researcher should go.

I adopted the role that Gold (1958) describes as the "participant-as-observer," a role in which the observer is known to all and is present in the system as a scientific observer, participating by his presence but at the same time usually allowed to do what observers do rather than expected to perform as others perform. Most of the time it was possible simply to be an observer, and during most of the observation time it was possible to write notes. Indeed, one of the unique aspects of employing the participant-observer methodology for conducting research in schools is that although the independent researcher finds virtually no opportunities for becoming a full-fledged participant (see Khleif 1969), the opportunities for observing and recording are limited only by the endurance of the observer. Thus it is not surprising that fieldwork accounts in schools, like the present one, are based on limited but intense and efficient periods of observation rather than the day-in, day-out style of more traditional anthropological fieldwork. But there were times to remember not to take it all too seriously, and I remembered to bring a Christmas present rather than my notebook to the faculty Christmas party.

Supplementary to the journal entries which are the product of the participant-observer's efforts, one customarily draws upon additional sources and research techniques to provide supportive data of a more systematic nature about specific aspects of the fieldwork. I particularly wanted field notes which would later provide census data about the school staff and a chronological record of school events. I also wished to do systematic interviewing. Any one or a combination of these techniques might provide the central methodological approach to a study rather than be assigned a supplementary one, depending, of course, on the purposes of the study, and some fieldworkers insist that the techniques which I have here called supplementary are all part of the standard methodology of the participant observer.[3] In any case, data were gathered through several methods designed to augment my direct observations. Six such procedures provided especially valuable sources of information:

1. Collecting routine distributions of notices. Like the regular staff members at school, I was assigned a mailbox in the school office. I received routine distributions originating from the central office of the school district and from Taft School. Similarly, it was almost always possible to pick up an extra copy of an agenda or of any handout at meetings I attended with Ed, and in my absence he often picked up an extra copy of handouts for me.

2. Collecting copies of school records, reports, and correspondence. The school secretary made an extra carbon copy for me of routine reports and letters. In some cases I was able to acquire a document itself once it had served its intended function. For example, in June Ed allowed me to have the faculty notebook in which written comments and announcements to and by the staff during the entire school year were recorded. The contents of the notebook had no further value at school, but they provided a useful source of chronological data and enabled me to make a content analysis of school messages. Ed also gave me a small notebook

<hr>

[3] Morris Zelditch, for example, has argued convincingly that the participant observer employs three strategies—participant observation, informant interviewing, and enumeration or sampling—and that only collectively do these facets comprise a proper field study approach (Zelditch 1962).

in which he had attempted during one period of several weeks to maintain a personal record regarding certain recurring problems around the school.

3. Noting, at 60-second intervals for blocks of two hours at a time, the activity and social interaction patterns of the principal. This procedure included recording with whom Ed interacted, who had initiated the interaction, where, when, who was talking, and how many people were involved. Over a period of several weeks I developed a set of categories for tabulating these interactions. During one two-week period, the major effort of the research was directed to recording a carefully sampled interval of 12 two-hour periods during ten consecutive school days.

4. Soliciting pupil impressions. From pupils in all the fifth- and sixth-grade classrooms I requested a brief written response to several open-ended statements regarding what they thought they would remember about the principal. The pupils were told briefly that the principal and I were working together to make a study, that I would be the one who would read their papers, and that each of them could choose for himself whether or not to put his name on his paper. I gave all directions myself, assisted with requests for spelling help, and collected their comments. A total of 142 papers were received and analyzed.

5. Recording with a tape recorder. As I originally envisioned the study, the tape recorder was going to do most of my recording, and I was to have an easy job of note-taking. How I would ever have coped with so extensive a record, even had it been possible to make it, I do not know. In any case, I used the tape recorder far less frequently than I had planned. I did make tapes in a few meetings, in a limited number of special situations, and, most importantly, in systematically interviewing 15 members of the Taft School staff.

I will not belabor a review of the mechanical problems of using a tape recorder. Two problems characteristic of institutions like schools add special complications to effective taping: external noise and constant interruption. The high pitched voices of children far out on the playground sometimes seemed to make more of an impression on my taped record than did the carefully modulated voice of a teacher-informant sitting opposite me. Doors closing, chairs moving, school "bells," footsteps and conversations echoing in the corridors, teachers going "Shhh," all provided a background panoply duly recorded by my nondiscriminating tape recorder. I discovered via a tape that the principal's swivel chair squeaked, a relatively unimportant bit of data, but through taping I also became aware of the constancy of interruptions everywhere and anytime in a school. Initially the interruptions were an annoyance in the taping procedure, but when I finally became aware of their omnipresence, I added a new dimension to my observations. Only once in the total of 15 interviews with staff members made at school, regardless of where the interview was held, was the session uninterrupted by an announcement on the intercom, an inquiry or brief visit by a pupil or teacher, or a work detail by a custodian or maintenance crew, even though all the interviews were held in vacated classrooms or offices late in the afternoon.

Making an initial tape recording is less than half the battle. The cost, time, and problems in transcribing tapes are incredible. In the staff interviews which comprised the majority of my taping efforts the interviewees spoke informally and made many references to people or situations which could not be discerned on the tape by someone unfamiliar with school personnel. As a result, I had to monitor each tape before giving it to a typist and, for accuracy, I found it essential to check the final typescript against the actual recording. This meant a minimum of three hours invested on my part for each hour of interview time, and easily three or four times that again for the typists. Only the remarkable frankness which the staff exhibited during interview sessions made me feel the time and effort invested in the tapes were warranted.

For comparative purposes, I guided each of the 15 staff interviews through the same series of open-ended questions, capitalizing on the interview session itself for probing, rearranging the questions, or pursuing some unanticipated topic of possible relevance to the study. The guiding questions included a discussion of each individual staff member's background, what he felt was good and not-so-good about the principal, and how he felt that pupils, other teachers, and parents felt toward the principal. I asked each interviewee how he would describe this year's staff, with whom he felt closest, and the nature of staff interaction generally. I asked for an assessment of my influence on the principal's behavior and whether he acted differently during my visits or during the entire first year of the fieldwork. (The unanimous reaction was that he did not.) Finally, I asked each person interviewed to describe his idea of a good administrator. Several teachers turned "full circle" at my concluding question to end their interview session similarly to the way it had begun: "A good administrator is just like Ed."

In spite of mechanical problems that restricted my use of the tape recorder, tapes did serve as a useful aid. I was able to get verbatim accounts of two faculty meetings. I held three special recording sessions with Ed. One of these sessions was a summary of the opening of school and a forecast for the year. A second was made in my automobile as Ed presented a guided tour of the neighborhood to three new teachers riding with us. The third tape was a personal one in which Ed talked about the family and friends who had been invited to his daughter's wedding.

The tape recorder also helped as a vehicle for another dimension of the study, learning about Ed's personal life from those closest to him. With his help and approval I was able to arrange recording sessions with his wife and his mother. Their insights added greatly to the personal dimensions of his life history, for through their eyes he became son, husband, and father.[4]

6. Designing and distributing a staff questionnaire at the end of the school year in June. This ten-page questionnaire asked for personal census data as well as for data about the classroom and pupils. It afforded an opportunity to poll *everyone* concerning feelings about the principal, since it had seemed neither necessary nor practical to meet with every staff member for a taped interview.

Some questionnaires were returned within one day. However, three of the eighteen classroom teachers still had not returned their questionnaires after six months. I was surprised (and personally a bit disappointed) at receiving less than a 100

---

[4] Although I have not followed what anthropologists call the "life history" approach in the study, I have been influenced by methodological statements concerning it (see Friedrich 1967; Kluckhohn 1941; Langness 1965). I feel such an approach warrants attention in educational research.

percent return. Although I had an 86 percent return from the total staff, the missing questionnaires introduced some systematic bias in my census data. The teachers who had not completed the questionnaires were all older married women. All three were experienced teachers considered "traditional" in their classroom approach; each of them exerted considerable influence on younger staff members, and two of them were virtually the matriarchs of their respective wings of the building. Although the 24 questionnaires which were returned proved invaluable as a source of supplementary data, and I was subsequently able to fill in essential census data for the missing ones, the not-so-random trio who ignored my request to complete a written questionnaire (they were not otherwise reluctant to answer questions or hold interviews) has left me with an uneasy feeling about teacher research based entirely on "substantial returns" of survey-type questionnaires.

Subsequent to the fieldwork, these six sources of supplementary data lent themselves readily to analysis. In each case, except for collecting routine distributions of notices, the data had been gathered according to some systematic scheme readily adapted to quantitative or qualitative analysis.

Prior to organizing and sorting the information recorded on hundreds of pages of journal entries, the research process underwent a long gestation period for reading, discussing, mulling, and weighing alternative ways to excerpt and catalogue the notes. Before converting the stream-of-consciousness notes, a tentative set of categories was developed from which the sections of the completed ethnography were finally organized. The categories guided the selection of relevant excerpts from the notes, and the notes in turn provided an ultimate test of the comprehensiveness of the categories. Each excerpt taken from the journal notes was typed in duplicate on pieces of 5 x 8 inch note paper, with headings to indicate the category, subtopic, and date of the original and complete entry. Only one topic was included on each paper. These data sheets could then be organized by topics, sorted, rearranged, and finally set up as they would be utilized in writing the narrative. The simplicity of the description belies the complexity of a task that took months to complete. I received helpful advice from sociologist Howard Becker during this task when I described to him the trouble I was having with my initial sorting of the notes. Becker suggested that I was probably trying to refine the data too quickly. By keeping the categories more rudimentary, I had less trouble with the initial sorting. Where my categories had tended to become too discrete, the problem of sorting was not only exceedingly difficult but was lending a premature rigidity to the organization of the monograph.

The Observer-Observed Relationship

It is tempting to report that after a brief "period of adjustment" the researcher blended perfectly into the school setting and everyone at school continued about his business totally oblivious to him. Although my presence at the school was not intended to require major adaptations by those being observed, it seems unrealistic to insist that things were just the same with or without me there. Gussow has suggested in this regard, "Ordinarily, in good fieldwork, researchers are not greatly concerned about whether they have disturbed the natural field or not, provided that they can analyze how they affected it structurally" (1964:231). The remarks in this section are addressed to adaptations to the process of observation by those who were being observed.

Assimilation. The social setting in which the predominant amount of the research was conducted was among the adult teaching faculty and the office personnel to whom I refer collectively as the staff of Taft Elementary School. My assimilation into this setting was easily accomplished. My relationship with the staff was cordial and formal. A warm exchange of greetings, on a first name basis, might fool a casual observer into believing that a more personal relationship existed. In fact, except among smaller cliques tending to consist of teachers of similar ages working with the same or adjacent grade levels, most relationships among the staff were of this cordial, formal nature. Beset as the school was by a constant flow of adult visitors, any newcomer was made to feel welcome by a sort of institutionalized cordiality. If I had an advantage here it was that I became such a recurring visitor that everyone could get to know me, but eventually I realized that the cordiality remained at about the same level as on earlier meetings. Nevertheless, being a visitor in an institution which was accustomed to coping with visitors and was intent on extending its hospitality was an advantage.

Probably a more important advantage in terms of acceptance by the teaching faculty was that I had been a classroom teacher. Gussow has reported on the hesitancy of teachers to accept classroom observers whom they suspect might not be "sufficiently understanding of classroom life" (1964:234), or, in short, the reluctance of teachers to accept observers who have not been classroom teachers themselves. I have taught in public schools, and I made frequent references to that fact in conversations with the teachers. That prior teaching is a valuable asset to a school researcher became evident during the year as I was occasionally re-examined with the query, "Did you say that you'd taught?"

A related benefit of my previous experience as a teacher is that I knew the "language" of the group among whom I was conducting my research. A compelling point argued by many cultural anthropologists is that it is essential for the ethnographer to learn and use the language of the people he is studying.[5] In prior cross-cultural fieldwork (Wolcott 1967b) I was obviously at a disadvantage working among bilingual people who could include or exclude me in their dialogue as they wished. In doing research in the schools, I did not face this problem. I know the language of school people. If I was told that someone had "just returned from representing the ESPA at an ASCD workshop at the Hilton to compare SMSG with Greater Cleveland," my only uncertainty was, "which Hilton?"

To a slightly lesser extent than among the teachers I could even provide credentials to satisfy the principals I met, for my own dossier includes a master's degree in school administration and a California Elementary School Administrative Credential. During one of my years as a classroom teacher I also served as the vice-principal in a large elementary school in California. But I believe it was

---

[5] Goodenough (1957), for example, has stated, "It is in the course of learning his language and how to use it that every human being acquires the bulk of his culture. An ethnographer, himself a human being, can hope to acquire another society's culture only by learning and using its language."

my status as a regular faculty member at a university, rather than my administrative experience, that enhanced my acceptance among the school principals and the central office administrators in the district. I emphasize the importance of these criteria which were external to my actual research role for two reasons: one, I felt that I was "accepted" in settings with the school faculty and in meetings among other principals; two, this acceptance was related more to these other "life roles" than to my contemporary role as researcher. That many people do not have a clear idea of research roles has been noted elsewhere (see Mann 1951:341; Olesen and Wittaker 1967:275) and was evident during my field work. For example, I found it difficult to inquire unobtrusively into Ed's home life, and I decided to rely essentially on his volunteered comments plus any natural social situations which allowed me an opportunity to visit at his home (for example, offering to drive him somewhere and arriving at his home a few minutes early). I was surprised when, 14 months after the study had begun, he remarked, "My wife and I have thought of inviting you out for dinner—we could barbecue on one of these summer evenings—but I wasn't sure if maybe that would interfere with the research."

If my presence in *some* role was understood by the faculty, clerical workers, and other administrators, such understanding is probably limited to these personnel only. I do not think the kitchen staff understood who I was or what I was doing. I am certain the two custodians did not by the comments they made to me, sometimes seeking direction, sometimes asking me to relay a message to Ed, sometimes inquiring if I knew where Ed could be found, and always assuring me that it was "nice to see you again." After twenty months the head custodian asked, "Do you have some other schools you look after, too?"

I made no effort to become personally acquainted with the pupils of Taft School. I assumed this would only complicate a difficult-at-best problem of being able to observe how the principal interacted with pupils under different conditions. I was interested in the fact that most children in the school ignored my presence during the fieldwork year. I spent a great deal of time at the school, but my behavior as Ed's "shadow" left them without any clue to my role. At the close of the school year in June, however, when I described to each class of fifth- and sixth-grade pupils the research project the principal and I were doing (I described the study as a joint enterprise because I did not want pupils reporting at home that Mr. Bell was "having research done on him"), many of these pupils who had so assiduously ignored me now took every opportunity to say hello and to call me by name. Like most adults with whom I came in contact in the course of the study, until the children had some idea of why I was at school, they tended formally to ignore me. The children were simply a bit more obvious about it.

Impact. I cannot imagine that my presence did not produce some changes in Ed Bell's behavior, although I am at a loss to give specific evidence of such change. One of his fellow principals joked at the outset, "Ed'll probably be organized better this year than any other year in his career." Yet I do not believe Ed set out simply to impress me. His frequent boasting about the program and personnel at school seemed suspect at first, but I found this was part of his "positive" approach and was not intended for my ears alone. I always wondered about the extent to which he was consciously or unconsciously screening problems from me, but at times he surprised me by voluntarily introducing some of his more delicate problems into our conversation.

Ethnographers recognize that the very act of observing or focusing the attention of inquiry to aspects of behavior can make *any* aspect of behavior a sensitive one. Seldom, for example, is the direct question "Why?" an appropriate one to ask, since it implies that people ought to be able to state conscious reasons for their behavior or that human behavior is innately rational. But the simple act of asking any question, no matter how cleverly couched in prose, may direct attention to behavior that has otherwise been taken for granted. As behavior becomes self-conscious, it frequently becomes the source of concern, apology, defense, or self-ridicule. I do not know how frequently events toward which I turned my attention subsequently became the focus of more self-conscious behavior. That my attention to particular aspects of behavior *could* result in their receiving more critical attention from others, and that my efforts in obtaining descriptive data *could* inadvertently fan the embers of a self-conscious striving on the part of personnel at school to be doing the right thing, are illustrated by the reaction to a question that appeared in my staff questionnaire. The question solicited information about social contacts outside of school among staff members, including social telephoning and social visiting. My intent was to learn something of the sociometrics of the staff and the extent to which the faculty was a social group as well as an occupational one. Four months after I distributed the questionnaire, the principal and counsellor discussed in my presence what they could do to better draw the faculty together as a social group. They explained that they had both "realized" when filling out my questionnaire that faculty members were not getting together enough for purely social occasions.

Motives of the Observed. What were the motives for those who acceded, either officially or unofficially, to cooperating in the study? What prompted the principal and the central administration to approve of it? What motives contributed to the endorsement, or at least acquiescence, of others—like members of the faculty—who were never formally asked to approve the study but who nonetheless were willing to accept the researcher and to help him gain the information he sought?

For those whose approval could only be displayed or denied tacitly, perhaps the major motive was simply a feeling toward the researcher perceived as an individual, as a member of a university faculty, or in some other better-understood personal role. My being a bachelor, for example, provided a basis for banter which sometimes surrounded lunchtime conversation in the faculty room: "Hey, Harry, why isn't a nice guy like you married?" School people also take professional obligations seriously, and cooperating in research is generally perceived as such an obligation. In this study, lending cooperation was easy because the researcher ordinarily made few demands on the faculty other than that he be allowed to be present.

Willingness to cooperate in research was obviously one of the motives in accepting the project by both the principal and the central office of the school district. For the district, the cooperation was part of a formal (although not invariably enthusiastic) tradition of cooperation with institutions of higher learning, a tradition which benefits the school district by helping it maintain an image of being modern, progressive, and up-to-date. In one instance I suspected the superintendent of capitalizing on my research role when he referred to me in a meeting of all the administrators in the district as "our anthropologist." Such scrutiny as he felt I gave the district was apparently not perceived as an unmitigated blessing, for he confided late in the study that he felt that the district had been fortunate in having me carry out the study because "we wouldn't want just anybody to get that close to us." In the very last days of the fieldwork, he finally excluded me from a district-wide administrative meeting. "There are many things on the agenda that wouldn't interest you," he explained. In closing, he added a comment that strikes a familiar note to anthropologists today, "We're thinking of having you fellows start paying for information. You never help us with our problems anyway—you just study what interests you."

In addition to whatever obligation Ed felt professionally, he also expressed a personal interest in the anthropological approach of the inquiry. Perhaps he felt he would absorb something of the flavor of cultural anthropology through his participation in the investigation. Throughout the research and writing I have felt misgivings because I suspected that personally Ed was hoping for a testimonial about the difficulties of the task and the dedication of those committed to it, and I could not imagine that the straightforwardness of the completed ethnographic account would justify itself to him on these counts. On the other hand, he did understand that the study was not to be judgmental, and he responded favorably to its central purpose in providing descriptive data about what the job of a principal is really like. There may have been other, more personal reasons for Ed's willingness to engage in such a venture. Ed's gregariousness, his social nature, the serious regard he has for elementary school education, and the possibility that he finds the administration of a school a lonely role as well as an unheralded one, may have contributed to his decision. I know he found satisfaction in having me experience the range of problems with which he was confronted and the extent which those demands made on his time and energy. I had some measure of his appreciation of my attention and empathy by the number of times he repeated to others comments I made to him after unduly long days. One favorite was my off-hand remark to him as we finally headed to the school office to lock it up at 12:30 A.M. on the evening following a school budget election. "The next subject I choose for a research project," I said, "is going to be someone confined to a wheel chair." He seemed to enjoy any comments I made that referred to my difficulty in keeping up with and keeping track of him during his long and busy hours at school.

The Personal Dimension

Anthropologists who have addressed themselves to the problem of observer objectivity have advised the fieldworker to make explicit both to himself and to his reader what he admired and disliked about the people he was studying, rather than to pretend to divest himself of his personal values (Redfield 1957:56). At the risk of reflecting discrepancies in the ideal world of research, let me describe some important personal dimensions of the investigation from the researcher's point of view. The sheer amount of time involved in making the study sometimes proved to be distressing. One invests a great deal of time in order to live his way into another cultural system, and the yield for any one hour, day, week, or month during the fieldwork may be remarkably low even though it is essential to provide the context for the processes one observes. Two concomitants of the time factor were boredom and effort. It is hardly a revelation for anyone who has been there that life at school can be exceedingly boring, especially when events become repetitive or when their termination is related to the time of day rather than to the accomplishment of a task. The number and duration of the meetings a principal must attend often made the boredom acute for me, although I suppose it was easier for me to observe meetings which Ed attended than it was for him to sit through them. I could use my note-taking as a stimulus for holding my attention, while Ed's various roles in the variety of meetings he attended never included a commitment to consider everything that occurred with equal objectivity and interest. As a result, he felt freer than I did to get involved or to fall asleep during meetings. He availed himself of opportunities to do both.

While note-taking helped me to remain alert to what was going on (a lessening in note writing usually signalled the approaching finale to a productive observation period), the effort required to continue to make notes was constantly threatened by a sense of ennui born of boredom, varying moods of enthusiasm for and faith in the project, and outright fatigue. Occasionally a series of events would occur so fast that only cursory notes were possible at the time, with a fuller account to be written later. My conscientiousness as a note-taker seemed more a burden than a blessing. I made some working rules for myself about notes. One, if I had not completed my notes when I departed for the day, they were completed as soon as possible afterward. Two, I filed my notes in original longhand. This allowed me to be direct and candid without having to screen personal comments or mask identities from those assisting with typing up notes. Filing the original notes also served to allay the risk of becoming dependent upon comments volunteered by or solicited from secretaries regarding the content of my notes during the long period before I would start drawing the data together. Keeping longhand notes freed me from this potential problem, but it did not add to my efficiency. Three, I *never* resumed my observations until the notes from the preceding observation were complete. Nothing was gained by my mere presence as an observer; until my observations and impressions from one visit were a matter of record, there was no point in returning to school and reducing the impact of one set of events by superimposing another and more recent set.

I was interested in the continuity of what Ed did as a principal, and I did not want to set such standards for recording detail that every period of observation would necessitate days and days of note writing. My compromise with that dilemma reflects at least two relatively preconscious phenomena: selective sorting/forgetting, and an internalized cut-off point for the number of longhand pages which I normally completed following any observation period. The sorting/forgetting factor operated very near the conscious level; sometimes an observed act or possible implication would spring back to consciousness several days after the event. My cut-off point in note-making was more subtle. I became curious one day about whether the notes I was completing were unusually long. I found in looking back over my notes that I seldom wrote more than 11 pages of longhand notes regardless of how long or how "rich" the observation had been. By the time I got to page 11, I seemed to have assuaged my work ethic and was able to summarize briefly anything else I had observed. A human observer must use many such cut-off points to reduce the problem of recording the infinite scene. Here was one that I had been using although I had not been aware of doing so.

As an observer I felt that my presence would be less obvious or disruptive if I were introduced with the least credentials adequate to validate my presence in any particular situation. Ed concurred with my strategy. He usually introduced me as either "Harry Wolcott" or "Mr. Wolcott" who is "from the University and doing some research in which I'm involved." The phrase "from the University" was intended to serve a double purpose: one, to validate the research basis of the project, and two, to dispel any idea in the local community that the school district had assigned additional nonteaching personnel to the school. My identification with the university in turn brought an almost reflexive response from many people to whom I was introduced, "Oh, are you doing this for your doctoral dissertation?" The assumption that I was a doctoral candidate revealed an important aspect about the research conducted in schools. Contacts between a university and a school district are made primarily by university staff supervising students in teacher-training programs. Research contacts are almost entirely limited to projects being carried out by doctoral students. The observation that I must be working on my dissertation suggested, by implication, that if I already had my doctorate I wouldn't be doing research in a school building any longer. There are important limitations in the time, resources, and even the motives which a doctoral student brings to his research, and these limitations are reflected in the studies which comprise much of what exists in educational research. I was surprised by the assumption made by so many of the people I met that I must be a doctoral candidate. (I was also surprised at how adamant I was about pointing out that I was not!)

Of the myriad encounters to which I was a party during the year, I think the meetings between the principal and pupils for reasons of discipline and/or tracking down culprits seemed the most unpleasant to me. At such times it was hard to withhold my characteristically American sympathy for the underdog. Sometimes I could barely suppress my admiration for the ability of a seven- or eight-year-old to stand up to an adult five times his age and size who was bringing all the weight of his role in the institution and of the institution itself to put a stop to roughhousing or to learning who ate another child's sandwich. In general, my discomfort extended to any conference in which the principal held sufficient power that the only option for the other party, whether pupil, parent, teacher, or staff, was ultimately to acquiesce. Such options are a condition of the social contacts among human beings, but perhaps I had not expected to see such frequent recourse to ultimatums in the normal routine of the neighborhood elementary school. Previous experience as a teacher had not prepared me for this revelation.

Another personal note is the slight distress I felt as I slowly came to realize that Ed enjoyed having an audience and I was serving as a full-time one. I have a certain regard for reticence, and I feel a degree of panic when confronted by loquaciousness. As an observer my inclination toward reticence serves me well; better, perhaps, than it serves me socially. To find a willing talker is almost a pre-requisite to having someone serve as informant, and in our early months together I was grateful that Ed talked so freely. A year passed before I realized that he talked easily to everybody about almost anything; once I realized how he enjoyed having an audience, I had that familiar feeling of panic. Occurring when it did, I wonder now if the panic was a reaction to months of note-taking and a realiza-tion that I could *never* get the complete story. From that point on I concentrated less on Ed's verbatim statements and watched more for patterns in the content of his remarks, so that this potentially disconcerting trait did not become a problem. In fairness to Ed and to his colleagues and staff, I should point out that long periods during which I kept notes at the school and did little or no talking myself increased my need to be heard in meetings elsewhere in which I was a participant and not an observer.

It was my impression that Ed and I shared interests on a professional plane to a far greater extent than we shared them on a personal one. I sensed a certain air of teetotaling self-righteousness about him borne probably of his long experience in the networks of ice-cream socials with church friends and in work groups dom-inated by middle-aged female school teachers. After a day's work together I was perfectly happy that I was going my way and he was going his. But those virtues that made him something less than a swashbuckling hero in my personal assessment of him were nonetheless relevant and essential for him professionally, and I re-peatedly recorded in my notes examples of his patience and kindness, his serious-ness of purpose, and the qualities of personal integrity he exhibited in the perform-ance of his chosen role. I admired his dedication to and belief in the importance of the public school and his conviction that a principal plays a vital role in that regard. In due time I began to realize that personality traits which seemed at first to be unique to Ed were widely manifested among his colleagues as well.

Comment

In order to present an account of the sort provided in this monograph, the fieldworker himself serves as the key "instrument" in the research. Social scientists, especially those of anthropological bent, have until recently devoted little attention to providing explicit statements regarding their methodology. Yet just as the cul-tural anthropologist seeks to contextualize the human behavior he observes and describes, he needs also to provide his reader with something of his personal biases and with an account of the context in which he has conducted his fieldwork and translated it into an ethnographic statement. By introducing the reader to the study through a discussion of the methodology pursued, it is hoped that he can better achieve an objectivity of his own regarding the descriptive account that follows.

2 / A day in the life

A dark and gloomy Tuesday morning in January, 1967, became a bit darker and gloomier when Ed Bell's car wouldn't start. Ed wasn't really surprised —he'd been having trouble with the old '61 Ford Falcon lately. A few weeks before he was all set to trade it in on a new (well, 1965, and new to him, at least) Mercury. The car dealer had offered so little for his old car as a trade-in that he decided to keep it for travelling to school each morning. Now, just when he was in a rush to get to school after lingering a bit too long over eggs and coffee, the car battery was dead. He hurried back into the house to get the keys to the Mercury. Alice reminded him that he could borrow "her" car but that he would have to get it back home by mid-morning because she had an appointment downtown at 10:45. "I won't forget," he promised, and off he went after another round of good-byes to his two little daughters and his wife.

Half a block from home Ed turned into the busy stream of morning traffic heading toward the city center from suburbs sprawling in every direction along Sandy Boulevard. A few minutes later he turned on to Golden Lane. Immediately after passing the buildings and grounds of East High School, Ed drove into the large paved lot adjacent to William Howard Taft Elementary School. He parked and locked his car and proceeded directly to the school office.

The school doors were closed but not locked. Ed stepped into the main corridor of the building and through the adjacent doorway of the school office, pausing to exchange greetings with the school secretary. In his customary manner he proceeded directly into his own office to check for notes or messages awaiting him on his desk before pausing to hang up his coat and hat on a rack in the corner of the outer office. Then he stepped into the room that served as the social center of the school, a room known variously as the faculty room, teachers' room, or staff room.

The faculty room was part of the front office complex. The complex included the main school office, adjacent rooms for the principal's private office, the nurse's office, a supply room, and a short hall leading past the men's and women's lavatories to the faculty room. The faculty room did not open directly out to the main corridor of the school building and its door was almost never closed. The room served as both the formal and informal meeting place for a great number of adult encounters at school.

At one end of the faculty room an inexpensive set of Danish modern furniture

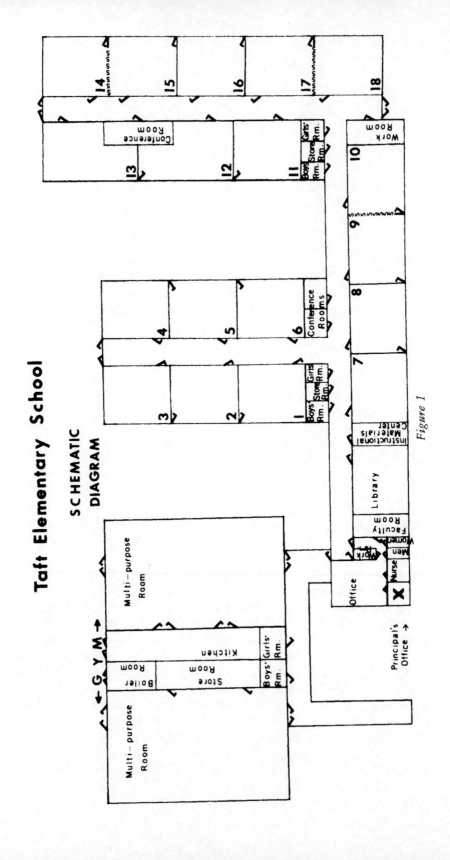

Figure 1

hinted that the room was a place to relax; at the other end a sink, a refrigerator, a stove, and an electric percolator with a usually-dependable source of hot coffee (50–70 cups were consumed each day) suggested the atmosphere of a lunchroom. At one side of the room a large open binder containing the daily handwritten notices for all the faculty, the "faculty notebook," rested on a table. Adjacent to it was a bookshelf containing professional books for teachers. Collectively the faculty notebook and small library gave the impression that the room was a checkpoint for communications as well as a professional resource center. Two long formica-topped tables pushed together in the center of the room revealed that the teacher's room was all these things at once, since the table was usually adorned with copies of recent magazines, the morning newspaper, notices and memos or an occasional card from a former teacher, salt and pepper shakers, a supply of napkins, and a coffee cup or two. Often there were flowers or remnants of a plate of cookies or other goodies if the teacher assigned faculty room "duty" for the week chose to interpret the assignment to include more than merely making the morning coffee and keeping the room tidy.

Most mornings it did not matter too much when Ed arrived at school. He liked to "set a good example" by arriving early, usually around 8:10, but by the time he got to school there were always a few staff members present, and he would have had to get up almost an hour earlier to get to school ahead of Mrs. Edna Willing's customary arrival at 7:20 A.M. to prepare for her class of third graders.

Tuesday mornings were different. Almost every Tuesday the guidance committee met in the teachers' room before school. The guidance committee was one of Ed's pet projects at Taft. The committee formally consisted of a teacher representative from each of the six grades, the school's guidance counsellor, and Ed; any of the other regular or part-time faculty who wished to attend the meetings had a standing invitation to do so. The purpose of the meeting was to facilitate the guidance program at school by providing a forum in which the staff could work together to discuss pupil problems with the counsellor, other teachers, Ed, and sometimes a specialist from the central office. The position of a full-time guidance counsellor at Taft School had been created only the previous year, but the guidance committee meetings were now in their fifth year. On this morning one of the third-grade teachers, Mrs. Troutner, was going to talk about a "problem boy" in her class.

Although it was after 8:00 A.M. when Ed walked into the teachers' room, there were too few people to start the meeting right away; those present chatted while they took seats around the tables. The coffee perked away but was not yet ready for those anticipating it; the moment the perking stopped, several teachers got up to pour themselves a cup. Those present showed a customary deference toward the principal in their greetings and their attention to his contribution to the conversation. On that morning, as often happened in meetings of adults at the school, Ed was the only male present.

Ed raised his voice slightly and turned the conversation to the business at hand, requesting Mrs. Troutner to provide "background information" about the problem boy who was the subject of the morning discussion. At the outset of such discussions of specific pupils, Ed often disappeared into his office and returned with the complimentary set of photographs of all the children at school provided by a commercial school photographer, but this boy and his family seemed to be known by name to all the teachers. To others present who might not know him—on that morning the school district social worker and two university students newly assigned to the school (one a student teacher, the other an intern counsellor)—the picture would make little difference.

Mrs. Troutner's description centered around physical features of her problem boy that distressed her:

> He often wears T-shirts that have holes in them. . . . Once he wore an old pair of shoes and they literally fell off him. I had to call his mother and she took him out and bought him some shoes.

The school nurse contributed excerpts from her conversations with the boy:

> They get a lot of stuff at Goodwill. Not that that's bad, but it seems like it's all from there.
> He told me he makes his own lunch. He also does some of the cooking at home because his mother has some kind of allergy and isn't supposed to work with food. He told me how he can fix hamburgers and things, but I don't think the meals are as good as he says. Not that it's bad for him to help, but then he doesn't get a chance to play.

Ed attempted to guide the discussion toward the boy's progress in school the previous year. One teacher commented that the boy had made a "giant stride" in reading with a teacher who had since left Taft. "I hadn't realized that he did so well," commented Ed.

"I don't think she used anything physical on him," said the teacher.

"She may have taken a pretty firm hold of him at times. She had a pretty firm grip," Ed added.

"What do we know about his home life?" asked the counsellor. The fact was brought out that the boy's parents had separated and the mother had remarried about 12 months ago.

One teacher's comment, "Then the present husband is only a year old," brought some levity to the discussion of a "bad home situation." The reading consultant suggested, "We should make sure that the boy gets satisfaction from school, because that is one place where he seems to get it."

Ed said, "I think we should soft-pedal the idea of sending him home [as a disciplinary measure]. Apparently that is pretty threatening for him."

During the next brief interchange, a buzzer sounded throughout the school. Ed announced, "It's time for the first- and second-grade teachers to go on, now." The teachers began to leave—not only the three first- and second-grade teachers present, but all seven of the teachers who had attended the meeting, including the teacher whose problem student was the subject of discussion. While the classroom teachers departed, the other adults present in the room engaged in light conversation. Ed used the interruption to introduce the new intern counsellor to those who remained in the faculty room, reviewing the schedule of days when she would be at the school as he made the introduction. After the regular signal for school rang at 8:45 A.M. and the teachers' room (and school building in general) had settled down, the principal and five women remained seated to continue the guidance committee discussion over a second cup of coffee. Except for the school counsellor, none of the women present (the nurse, the school social worker, the reading specialist, the intern) was a full-time member of the Taft staff, but the meeting reconvened for 15 minutes as if it had never been interrupted by the departure of the teachers. The counsellor turned to the intern counsellor and said, "Well, from an Adlerian point of view—I've really been brainwashed—this looks like a real power struggle." Ed said he had wondered if the mother was a bit vain, since she always appeared to be well-dressed, even around the house, while the children were allowed to go about in shoddy clothes. The nurse went to her office to see if there were any comments in the health folder which she could contribute. She returned to read an entry recorded by a previous nurse that the mother intended to "take care of things" herself and did not wish the school to tell her what to do.

No one present volunteered any further information about the problem boy. The dialogue turned again to casual conversation which allowed the opportunity for getting acquainted with the new member of the group, the intern counsellor. Ed turned to the social worker to ask her opinion of the guidance committee meetings and what she would like to get out of them.

"Oh, they've been very helpful to me just the way they are," came her reassuring response.

A distraught-looking teacher appeared at the doorway, apparently looking for Ed but hesitant to interrupt the meeting. Ed asked immediately, "Can we help you?" The teacher, Miss Lowe, spoke quietly to him about a problem with the way one of the girls in her fifth-grade class was dressed. Ed said, "I'll come down and talk to her when I get a chance."

The interruption produced a lull in several other conversations which were being held (the surest way to get things quiet in the teachers' room was to attempt to hold a private conversation there). The counsellor capitalized on the moment to suggest the name of a recently arrived third-grade boy who could be the subject of the next guidance committee meeting. She said that the permanent record about this boy had just come from the central office and that the teacher was "having some problems." The counsellor described another boy in the same classroom, a boy in whom the school had been trying to "build up confidence." She related an incident at a recent open house at school where the father had criticized a map made by his son because of its lack of accuracy. "And he's a teacher, too," reminded the counsellor, implying that the father should know better. The intern shook a clenched fist which seemed to affirm that parents are the source of many problems for children. The rest of the group nodded their assent.

Selecting a subject for next week's discussion seemed to signal the conclusion of the meeting. Ed announced, "I ought to get down to Carol's room to see what's wrong—apparently we have a case of too short or too tight pants." He made no actual move to go, but turned his attention to the intern counsellor and asked her if she understood the "role" of the school social worker present at the meeting. When she replied that she did not, he embarked on a description of that position, a relatively new one in the school district. As he spoke, the primary grade teachers began to return to the faculty room for a coffee break during a 9:15–9:30 primary-grade recess. Continuing their conversations which they had begun on the way to coffee, the primary teachers increased the distractions and the noise level of the faculty room. At 9:25, a little more than an hour and a quarter after the meeting had begun, the last of the guidance committee group dispersed.

During the coffee break of the primary teachers, one first-grade teacher started to introduce her new student teacher to others assembled in the room, although she suddenly realized she did not remember the student teacher's last name. Another teacher commented aloud on an unusual number of absences from one of her reading groups that morning. She joked, "I told them, don't any of you Rabbits, or whatever you are . . . Tigers . . . ever be absent."

A buzzer at 9:30 signalled the end of the coffee break ("What, 9:30 already . . . I just got here!") and the primary teachers returned to their classes. The introduction of the new student teacher prompted Ed to go to the faculty notebook and make an entry informing the staff about the presence of the new intern counsellor and listing the four new student teachers and the classroom teachers to whom they were assigned. The secretary entered the room as he was finishing his memo. She looked over his shoulder at the note he was writing and laughed as she told him, "You've written the names of last term's student teachers instead of the new ones."

"Well, hurry and change it before the student teachers see it," he replied, suddenly realizing the error.

Ed was only a few steps from the office when he encountered the custodian coming toward the office leading a dog on a rope. Ed directed him to put the dog in the boiler room for a few minutes and that he would try to locate the dog's owner. Ed returned immediately to the office, turned on the "All Call" switch of the intercom, adjusted the volume knob, and began an announcement heard in every room in the building, "Boys and girls, may I have your attention for a moment. . . ." He paused to allow the school to come to a virtual standstill (one could sense the approach of quiet by the quickly diminishing volume in the characteristic drone echoed throughout the hallway) before continuing his remarks about not allowing dogs to come to school. He described the dog that had just been found on the school grounds and asked that anyone who thought he might know who owned it come to the office to talk to him. He recommended that whoever tried to chain a dog should be careful not to get hurt, that children should always be careful in approaching dogs on the playground, and that dogs were to be kept at home. Before he had concluded his announcement three children had come charging down the hall to name the dog's owner. With a flip of a switch he directed his voice to one classroom and requested a girl to take her pet home.

It was almost ten o'clock when Ed got to Carol Lowe's fifth-grade classroom and asked to speak with the girl reported for being inappropriately dressed. The girl appeared quickly in the hall. She was wearing shorts rather than a skirt. Ed closed the classroom door to speak to the girl in the privacy of the empty corridor. The girl seemed to know why she had been summoned. Ed asked if she was the only one in her class today dressed that way. She told him that two of her friends were also "wearing shorts." He asked her to summon the other girls so he could talk to them together. The girls were all dressed in neatly pressed pedal pushers. The three of them huddled together just outside their classroom door. Ed inquired if they had "teamed up" to wear shorts to school (they had) and then told them, "There's no hard and fast rule, and we don't want one, because we'd just have to change it. But unless there is a special reason, I want you to dress like ladies. Is that OK?" The girls suppressed giggles and nodded agreement to Ed's reminder that they were to wear dresses unless their class was planning to have a lesson in tumbling or was going on a field trip.

Ed headed back to the primary wing of the building to explain a new "innovation" in lunchroom procedures to children in each of the first- and second-grade classrooms. The primary teachers had been complaining about noise and the lack of order in the cafeteria. They had met with Ed the previous afternoon to try to devise a plan to remedy the confusion and had accepted his suggestion to try having children return to their tables after scraping their lunch trays rather than rushing immediately outside as they had been doing. The teachers told Ed that they felt the plan would be most effective if *he* presented it to the children.

Ed went first to the farthest first grade room along the primary wing. He opened the classroom door and asked the teacher aloud, "Mrs. Robin, may I speak with these boys and girls for a minute?" He described the new plan and then asked the children to show him that they understood by acting out the new procedure in their classroom. He told them to form a "quiet line" as they waited turns at scraping their imaginary leftovers into simulated garbage cans. He complimented them on being good actors as they moved through the line and returned to their places in the classroom. He asked if they had any questions. Two children asked about the procedure. The third question was a comment by a first grade boy about a dog that someone in his neighborhood had locked up. It required no answer. Ed thanked the teacher and left the class. "When the questions get that far out, it's time to leave," he commented as we crossed the hall to one of the second grade classrooms.

Ed repeated his announcement and practice session in one second-grade and in two more first-grade classes in the next twenty minutes. At the last of the first-grade classes he joked with the teacher, Mrs. Straight, "I've been in so many classes. I haven't been here yet, have I?"

"No," she laughed. "Don't worry, I'll keep track of you."

As Ed was concluding his directions to the children in that class the voice of the secretary came over the intercom. (She had located him by listening in on classrooms until she had recognized his voice.) "Mr. Bell, can you come down to the office?"

"Yes, I can come right now," he responded. Ed returned directly to the office. He had made his announcement in four of the six first- and second-grade classrooms.

"Your wife just called to remind you that she needs the car *right away* to get downtown," the secretary said as Ed entered the office. Ed turned to me and asked if I would mind following him with my car and bringing him back to school.

By the time I arrived in front of the Bell home Ed was herding his two little daughters across the street where a neighbor had promised to look after them. On the way back to school we stopped at the local gas station so Ed could arrange to have the Falcon taken care of. He started to talk with two attendants at the gas station about batteries, but decided to wait and talk to the manager. Two grades of automobile batteries were available at the station, he learned, one with a 36-month guarantee for $20; another with a 24-month guarantee for $15. "Well, I could use that $5 somewhere else," he explained to the manager. He arranged for the manager to send someone after his car, replace the battery, and deliver the car to him at school no later than 3:30, when he would need to leave for a meeting.

As we returned to school Ed described two meetings he had attended the evening before, a fellowship dinner at his church, and a meeting of the school board. The meetings had overlapped. He left his church meeting early and drove across town to a high school where the board was meeting. He arrived at that meeting after it had begun and left it at 9:00 P.M. after remaining one hour. His interest in the school board meeting concerned a new salary proposal. Ed had been impressed with the way two representatives of the professional association had presented their information to the board, had heard a counter-proposal by the board, and had announced that they would have to take the counter-proposal "back to the teachers to see if it was acceptable." Ed said he had been annoyed with one board member whose attitude seemed to be, "They're lucky to get anything." He said that a neighbor of his who worked for that board member described his employer as "very dictatorial" with his employees.

Back at school Ed found a university supervisor waiting to talk with him about new student teachers assigned to Taft School. Ed said, "This looks like a real good group." Ed reminded him, "We had been hoping you would assign a student teacher to all three of the third grades, so when the three teachers talk about student teaching they could all talk about it . . . but, then, Mrs. Troutner did have a student teacher last term." They talked about last term's students. Ed told the supervisor that one of the girls was offered a contract at Taft, but her husband had accepted a job elsewhere in the state. The supervisor declined Ed's invitation to stay and have lunch at school and left after a brief visit. Ed accompanied him to the office door and then went to the teachers' room.

The primary-grade pupils were finishing their lunches in the cafeteria, and their teachers were chatting in the teachers' room. Ed remarked that he was not too hungry, since his wife had risen early and cooked him breakfast. He poured himself a cup of coffee and joined the teachers sitting together at the table. He seldom ate lunch unless he brought a sandwich from home or anticipated a particular favorite (like roast beef) on the school menu.

Lunch at Taft School was served to two grades at a time beginning at 11:15. The mother of one third-grade boy had joined the boy's class for lunch at 11:45 and then, at the invitation of the teacher, had come into the teachers' room for coffee and a chat. Ed intercepted the mother as she entered the room, introduced her to teachers and student teachers present, poured her a cup of coffee, and invited her to join him in a corner of the room where they could talk. After a few minutes he invited the school counsellor to join them, then he excused himself, explaining that he had to read a story to one of the sixth-grade classes. Afterward, as we walked down the hall, Ed told me that the mother was complaining that her son was getting too much attention from the school counsellor, and she wished the boy to spend less time with the counsellor in the future.[1] Ed had reminded her that everyone in the school was trying to help the boy: "I told her, 'Look, Agnes, we've always been pretty straightforward with each other. Let's face it, this is a home problem, not a school one.'" He did not comment on her reaction to his remark. I noticed that Ed allowed 25 minutes to get to the other end of the building before the sixth-grade children would be returning to class after their noon recess.

During the lunchtime conversation one primary teacher had reported to Ed that a boy had taken a cupcake from another boy's lunch. Another teacher informed him that a second-grade boy had been smoking on the schoolground earlier in the morning. The lower grades had already returned to class from their noon recess, and Ed stepped into the primary wing to look into these two complaints. He remembered the family name of the boy reported eating another's cupcake, but he could not remember whether the first- or second-grade brother had been accused as the culprit. He started out with the older boy; as soon as he realized he was talking to the wrong boy his dismissed the older boy and crossed the hall to ask the younger boy to step into the hall. I recorded the following dialogue:

How are you feeling today?
Good.
Did you have a good lunch?
Yes.
Tummy full now (a gentle touch to the boy's stomach)?
Yes.
Were you pretty hungry?
Yes.
Did you eat anything before lunch—anything from somebody else's lunch?
No.
What did you have for breakfast?
(At this the boy stammered and eventually replied "Potato chips," the same answer given by his older brother.)
How many?
The boy held up his open hand to show: "This many."
You'd never take something out of another boy's lunch, would you? You wouldn't take cake that belonged to someone else and eat it, would you?

The boy admitted eating a piece of cake that morning, but insisted that a fellow first-grader had given it to him. Ed asked him to bring that boy out. The donor agreed that he had told his classmate he could have it, "because I don't like chocolate cake." Ed spoke further to the cake-eater after dismissing the other boy. "If you're ever hungry, you come tell me. Don't take things out of lunches. We'll get you something to eat."

Ed then proceeded toward the classroom of the second-grade boy reported to

---

[1] The addition of full-time guidance counsellors in the elementary schools was a recent innovation in the Columbia School District. The extended services were met with varying degrees of enthusiasm by pupils, parents, teachers, and administrators. Ed was enthusiastic about the program and endorsed it at every opportunity. Most principals felt the same way. However, one of his closest colleagues referred collectively to counsellors as "little head shrinkers," and another principal had steadfastly refused to add a counsellor to his staff.

have been smoking. "I'm not really very interested in this, but it's the kind of thing you have to do something about," he commented. He stepped into the classroom and asked to "see Doug out in the hall for a minute." Faced with the question of whether he had smoked a cigarette on the playground that morning, Doug was quick to volunteer, "Another boy did it too." Ed sent Doug to get the other boy. Together the boys recounted how they had picked up a half-smoked and still burning cigarette and had taken a few puffs. The teacher on duty reported that the cigarette had been flicked near the schoolground by a truck driver making a delivery at the back of the cafeteria. Ed asked the boys if they liked smoking the cigarette.

"Nooo!" they assured him.

"Then next time you can just put it out with your foot." He asked, "Do your parents smoke?" They replied that none of them did. The conversation was brief and casual. Ed made no mention of "rules." After he talked to them we headed down the hall to the upper-grade wing—it was just a few minutes before 1:00 P.M.

The sixth-grade classroom where we were headed was the only classroom at Taft School to change teachers during the year. The first teacher, Mrs. Manning, had begun teaching at Taft the year before, after completing her student teaching at Taft. After the first few weeks of the new school year she resigned because she was pregnant.[2]

The woman who took the class beginning in early November had frequently worked at Taft as a substitute teacher during four previous years on the "sub list." She described Taft as her "favorite school." Her own children were all attending school, and although she had not intended to teach full time she decided to accept the position when Ed approached her about it. On this day her youngest daughter, age nine, had remained home sick and she felt she should go home at lunch-time to see how the daughter was faring. Anticipating that she might be a bit late returning after lunch, she requested that the school secretary ask either the counsellor or the resource teacher to read to her class until she returned. She did not ask the principal, perhaps because his morning schedule had provided no opportunity for her to speak to him alone, especially since he did not happen to be in the faculty room during the mid-morning coffee break for the upper grade teachers. The secretary felt she should tell the principal rather than make assignments to "cover" a classroom, especially after discovering that neither the counsellor nor the resource teacher was going to be readily available at 1:00 P.M. When she told Ed that the teacher was driving home at lunch because her daughter was sick, Ed said he would "cover" the class himself.

Ed explained the reason for his visit to the sixth-grade pupils and asked what story their teacher was reading to them. While Ed struggled with difficult Eskimo names in reading the story aloud to them, the children quietly but effectively communicated with each other in a silent or half-silent language of their own.

---

[2] It had been intriguing to watch the news of her pregnancy spread rather selectively among the staff. I had the impression from my participation at school that Ed had been among the first to guess but among the last to know for sure that the teacher was "expecting." As soon as she shared her news with him, they set a tentative date for her formal resignation to become effective, and Ed began looking for a replacement.

They wrote and passed notes and whispered messages; they passed objects back and forth; some of the more daring even moved from seat to seat, all without appearing to attract their principal's attention. Ed read for 15 minutes, then asked the children to review for him the part of the story they had just heard. He told them he found the story "very interesting" and asked to borrow the book when they had finished so he could read it all. When the counsellor arrived at 1:20 to "take over," Ed was chatting amiably with children seated nearest the front of the classroom. As soon as she appeared at the door, he announced, "Well, here's Mrs. Wendy." He departed immediately.

En route back to the office, Ed spoke with a third-grade boy standing in the corridor outside one of the conference rooms that served as the counsellor's office. Knowing that the counsellor would have to remain with the sixth-grade class until their teacher returned, Ed instructed the boy to go into her office to wait. The boy sat down at a table. Ed asked if the boy knew how to play solitaire checkers. The boy said he did not. Ed sat down opposite him, helped him set up a checkerboard, and began to show him how to play. I chose that moment to make my exit, since I had already spent longer than usual for a continuous period of observation. I had also arranged to join Ed again that evening at a meeting of the local Elementary School Principals Association.

Ed told me later that he remained at school until 3:30 that afternoon. After school he attended two late-afternoon meetings. The first, held at the nearby high school, was a meeting of an advisory committee recently set up by the central office to foster better school-community relations. Two members of Ed's staff attended this meeting, one as the faculty representative, the other as a member of a special district-wide curriculum project on social studies. Ed's attendance at the meeting was optional, but he was interested in seeing the direction the new committee might take and in hearing what concerns the parent members of the advisory committee might express.

Ed left the advisory committee meeting early in order to attend a second meeting, that of the executive committee of the local teacher organization. Ed was not a member of the executive committee but had been asked to go as a representative of a subcommittee on which he served because the teacher chairman of that committee had another meeting to attend.

By coincidence, both meetings that afternoon happened to be scheduled at schools Ed passed on his way home from Taft School, but still he did not arrive home until after 6:00 P.M. He left home soon after dinner to pick up three principals who lived in the same vicinity, and they proceeded together to the monthly meeting of the Elementary School Principals Association. The meeting was scheduled to begin at 7:30 P.M.

The Columbia Elementary School Principals Association was the voluntary professional association of the school district's elementary principals.[3] Their member-

---

[3] One newcomer to the association explained the distinction between what he termed the "day" group and the "night" group of elementary school principals when I queried about the fact that essentially the same people comprised both groups (although not every principal belonged to the association) : "This is the group that looks out for its own interests and does what it needs to do," he explained. "The 'day group' is just an arm of the [central] administration."

ship in this organization linked them in a hierarchy of organizations including the county, the regional association, the state organization, and ultimately to the nation-wide Department of Elementary School Principals (DESP) of the National Education Association.[4] Ed made it a point to attend the meetings of this organization faithfully and to support its activites: "I don't think I've missed a one of these meetings since school started. We don't *have* to go to this one. This one is for me."

The meeting was held in the faculty room of Jefferson Elementary School on the north side of town. Norman Olds, principal of the school and the senior principal of the district, was on hand at the door of the faculty room to greet his colleagues and head them in the direction of coffee and doughnuts. Extra chairs had been arranged in a circle in the room to augment the usual complement of faculty-room furniture. Twenty of the district's 27 elementary principals attended the meeting. Most of them were dressed in the suits or sport jackets and ties which they customarily wore at school during the day; four were wearing sweaters or sport shirts. All three of the district's women principals were present and were dressed in tailored suits. Other persons in attendance included the director of the school district's counselling program, an administrative intern, myself, and the speaker for the evening, a member of the City of Columbia's Police Department.

Ed poured himself a cup of coffee but waited until the break to help himself to a doughnut. He started to settle into an easy chair next to his friend Bill St. Claire, but then commented that he didn't think it would be good for him to get so comfortable, and he moved to a straight chair instead. As it was, he still took some kidding from Bill during the break about having "dozed off" during the speaker's presentation.

A few minutes after 7:30 P.M. the president of the association announced that the meeting would proceed with an hour for a presentation by the speaker and for any questions and then, following a break, half an hour would be allowed for the business meeting. He introduced the program chairman who in turn introduced the policeman who was to be the guest speaker.

The policeman had been urged to "take a comfortable seat" on the one available sofa when he first arrived, and since the group was small and the meeting relatively informal he remained there to make his presentation. He referred to a dittoed page in front of him as he spoke on the announced subject of his remarks, the purposes and methods of interviewing children in schools. Members of his audience appeared to be somewhat in doubt as to the point of the presentation but gave courteous attention nonetheless. The speaker's formal remarks lasted about 25 minutes and included the following major points:

1. Never anticipate what you will hear in an interview. Be prepared for anything, rather than committed to hearing one particular response.
2. Visit the scene of the crime.
3. Ascertain the previous history of the child you are questioning and who his friends are.
4. If you are sure the child is guilty, and he is young enough and naive enough

---

[4] In 1970 the Department of Elementary School Principals became the National Association of Elementary School Principals. Since the change was made after the period reported here, reference is made to the former title of the organization.

—("and we hope they are at this age")—tell him, "All right, we know all about it. Just tell us where you hid the loot." Regarding the place of police interview the speaker stated a preference for interviewing at school rather than in the child's home, but added "we would like to take them all down to our interview booth if we could." He referred to the school as neutral ground for an interview, not as foreign as the police interview room but not as comfortable as the child's home.

5. It is important for the interviewer to dominate the interview. "Don't let him get you on the defensive. If he asks, 'What will happen if I tell you?' he may just clam up when he finds out the consequences. But when he is talking freely, be a good listener and let him talk."

6. Don't make promises, especially like, "You'll probably just get a warning this time." In adult court this can provide grounds for throwing out a case, "and it probably should be that way here as well."

7. Have a female witness present when questioning girls, especially on alleged sex offenses, even if you are only dealing with promiscuous behavior.

8. Let the child be the one to tell the parent. "They'd rather hear about trouble from the child than from the police. Maybe from school people, too."

A few principals prompted most of the discussion which ensued during the question-and-answer period suggested by the program chairman. The administrative intern was the only person who appeared to be taking notes. Mr. Olds, the host principal, sat near the door and got up at one point during the meeting to quiet some children in the corridors attending another meeting elsewhere in the building.

For the next 40 minutes the principals discussed their questions with the policeman. Except for the first question asked ("Is it all right to use a tape recorder?") their questions dealt with the duties and obligations of policemen when they come to school, or with pupil protection, rather than with interrogation. Bill St. Claire asked if it were possible for the police to telephone to a school to announce in advance that they were on the way: "It's always a shock to get back to your office and see an officer there waiting to interview someone."

"What kinds of rights do children have under the law?" asked the president of the group. The speaker explained that at the age of 16 or over children must be advised of their rights under arrest, but that under the age of 16 they are under the jurisdiction of juvenile courts, a civil matter, and a child does not have the same rights. Another principal wanted to know about the rights of the police to enter schools. He was told that no statute in the state requires that parents be notified nor allows school people to restrict the work of a law enforcement officer. He noted, however, that parents are usually notified "as a matter of courtesy." Another principal queried whether a principal should release a child from school to go with a police officer. The speaker advised that a principal should "use his own discretion," but added that if the principal's concern was about the possibility of an accident and lawsuit, an individual riding in an official car on official business is "covered."

"Whose responsibility is it to call the police if there is a case of child molesting while a child is on the way home and the parent telephones the school about it?" asked a principal. The speaker suggested that the parent was responsible. He added, "Of course, the principal might be of some help, particularly if the parent is very excited," but he reaffirmed his answer that essentially the responsibility was that of the parent. "There's a 'gray line' of responsibility there," commented one of the senior principals. Several others mumbled their concurrence.

After almost an hour it occurred to someone that the policeman's description of local police services, of a juvenile department, and of special training he and others had received in juvenile work, applied only within the limits of the city. Many schools in the school district, including Taft School, were located outside the incorporated area of the city. Schools outside the city boundary were not beneficiaries of the special services described by the speaker because comparable services were not provided by the county sheriff's office. "About all I can say on that," said the speaker, "is that each time you have to call the sheriff's office you ought to say, 'You really ought to get a juvenile officer down there.'"

"I called the sheriff's office during this past week to make a report," Ed announced, "and they were very appreciative."

"Every bit of information helps the police," the speaker added.

The president thanked his guest speaker and suggested a brief coffee break before proceeding with the regular business meeting of the association.

Just after 9:00 P.M., the meeting was reconvened. The first item of business was a motion pertaining to a "position paper" on Professional Advancement (i.e., salary improvement) prepared by a committee appointed at the previous meeting. Dittoed copies of the motion were distributed. The motion stated that "the Administration of the School District establish a committee with broad representation to study and make appropriate recommendations of change necessary to the Professional Advancement Requirements of the School District."

The motion was voted and carried. Someone asked what would happen to the motion now that it was passed. "Send it to Dr. Boggs [the School Superintendent] —everything ends up there anyway," quipped one principal. Ed put the idea in the form of a motion. The president commented that he usually preferred to "go slow on these things" but that this particular matter seemed to warrant urgency.

One principal suggested that a new study of professional advancement ought to deal with the extra work done by many principals in connection with special programs conducted by university faculty. Ed commented, "We have all kinds of university people coming to Taft School all the time." (I was under the impression he was referring to the student observers, student teachers, and supervisors constantly parading into the school, but I noticed that at least three principals looked my way and smiled as they nodded agreement.)

The next item for discussion pertained directly to salary—the proposed salary changes for the coming year. As explained, the new schedule advanced an elementary school principal's salary for the first four years to 108 percent, 112 percent, 116 percent, and finally to 120 percent of the top teacher salary. "That means that a beginning elementary school principal gets only 8 percent more than a teacher," someone observed. An alternative salary schedule was described, one designed to place a restriction on top salaries for the principalship, particularly at the senior high school level. "If we didn't put this limit on," explained one principal, "the high school principals would get a $3000 raise."

"If word of that ever got out, the salary proposal would never get through," reflected another.

The actual dollars and cents meaning of the proposed salary schedule was explained in terms of the top salary increases possible: for an elementary principal, a raise of $1635; for teachers, a raise of $1416; for a high school principal, a raise of $1472. "So we're coming out OK on this, dollarwise," was the conclusion. Norm Olds, a member of the committee which had made the proposal, affirmed that the salary increase was a genuine increase. Unlike the procedure followed in some years, he explained, no extra days of duty had been added to the school calendar this time. He also reviewed that the committee had rejected a proposed $1000 "across the board" salary increase for all employees on the basis that it was not an equitable way to improve salaries.

The president called upon a principal who had been asked to get comparative salary data on administrative salaries in a neighboring school district. The principal reporting explained that principals of small schools in the neighboring district earned between $9000 and $11,000. He emphasized that no principal there received less than the top teacher in his school—he got at least $200 more. The range in salaries for the neighboring district, from $9666 to $14,000 was compared with the present high in their own district ($13,000), but it was pointed out that salaries in the neighboring district were based on a 12-month contract.

Comments were made about the need for everyone present to help get the new salary schedule passed. Some questioned whether it was preferable to have principals' salaries linked on a percentage basis to teacher salaries. One principal spoke strongly in favor of keeping principal and teacher salaries linked: "I consider this a good thing in labor-management relations. I consider myself a teacher first, and an administrator second. I don't know if that's right or not, but that's how I feel." Further discussion dealt with how the new salary schedule had been arrived at and, particularly, with how much of its preparation was actually the work of the superintendent.

The meeting had been in progress over two hours. It was becoming more and more informal as new questions prompted personal conversations and casual asides. One senior principal stood up and stretched, joked with those near him: "It's my beddy-bye time," and left the meeting. Another old-timer joined him in leaving.

Apparently sensing the impending disintegration of the formal meeting, the president seemed intent on bringing the salary matter to some kind of official conclusion. A motion was made that the president of the elementary principals' group meet with the head of the secondary school administrator group to compare notes on the salary proposal. ("Who is the head of that group now?" asked a member. Someone jokingly answered with the name of the Director of Secondary Education rather than the name of the group's current elected president. The comment drew some laughter.) Ed spoke against the motion, arguing that the organizations should work through existing channels rather than bypassing them. More discussion ensued before a hand vote was called that narrowly defeated the motion. Ed then made a motion for a vote of confidence and thanks to the committee that had made the proposal. One principal who had sat silently throughout the proceedings cautioned, "We should be careful. We could have been hurt much worse than we were" (i.e., might have received a much smaller salary increment).

"If there is no further business, the meeting is adjourned. Sorry we're so late," said the president. It was 10:05 P.M. Ed and his three passengers continued to discuss the problem of principals' salaries as they exited down the corridor toward the door to the parking lot.

Comment

The day selected for the description in this chapter was not chosen because of its typicality or atypicality as much as for the fact that it was one of the days in which rather extensive notes were made throughout a relatively large proportion of Ed's hours on the job. The day was somewhat unusual in having four scheduled meetings and even more unique in that Ed numbered two of those meetings (the guidance committee meeting at school, and the principals' association meeting in the evening) among the most valuable of all the meetings he attended.

Although this chapter is one of the most purely descriptive in the case study, the emphasis throughout is on description rather than on interpretation. Nevertheless, certain important themes which characterize the principalship have already emerged in the account presented. I would call attention particularly to the absence of a technical language in dialogues among principals and teachers and to the preoccupation with salary (and, indirectly, with status) exhibited in the meeting of the principals' own professional group. This chapter has dealt more with the setting in which Ed works than with him as a person, the subject of the next chapter. It is crucial to recognize the force that the setting exerts on a principal's behavior. Ed seemed to be moved about through most of his day by little problems brought to him or created for him by others rather than by any grand design of his own of what he wished to accomplish.

3 / The principal as a person

EDWARD BELL'S EARLY YEARS

"Don't you think I have a right to be proud of the boy?" beamed Ed's elderly mother, Mrs. Henry Bell. Mrs. Bell may not have been sure of exactly what it was one did as a principal, but there was little doubt in her mind that her son Ed was not only dedicated and happy in his work but was also very good at it. "It was his calling, really," she told me. Since Ed had become a full-time principal, she recalled only once when she had ever heard of his expressing any opinion other than one of satisfaction in the job: "Alice did write me once that when Edward had come home that evening he had told her he believed he'd rather be back teaching fifth grade than he would being the principal."

To his mother, Ed was not only the administrator of Taft School, he *was* Taft School. Her two visits to Taft during the year were not to see the school as much as additional opportunities to visit with her son. The school she saw on those visits was a school which Ed had created. She proudly repeated a comment Ed had recently made to her that may have been intended for her ears alone:

I think Taft School is one of the best schools in the district. And you know, seven years ago it wasn't even here.

Ed's father had died ten years earlier, just shortly after Ed and his wife Alice left their home state of Kansas and came to Oregon. After years of urging, Ed's mother had finally taken his and Alice's suggestion that she come west where she could be near her son. She was in her seventies, and boasted of her four great-grandchildren, but her health had remained good and she remained socially active. Since her husband's death she had occupied and supported herself by living-in with elderly women who required assistance in maintaining themselves and their households but who did not require special medical attention. Shortly after her arrival in Columbia, Ed helped her locate just such a position.

The Bell children had been born and raised on Kansas farms. Ed had one slightly older brother and one sister nine years his junior. Ed's mother's reminiscences about Ed mingled freely with memories of her other son and with her own husband as well:

My boys were mighty good boys, both of them. They had a dad who was a remarkable man. And we had no difficulties with those boys at all. I spoke to Ed since I've been out here. I said, "Ed, I don't think your dad ever laid a hand on you." And he said, "Oh, yes he did, Mother. Two times he gave me a good thrashing."

Of her two boys, Ed's mother remarked that she had always felt closer to him, although in personality she shared more in common with her first son:

The older boy is more like me in make-up. He was shy and backward. Edward is more like his dad. His integrity is unquestionable. My husband was like that.

During our interview, she frequently found herself comparing Ed with her husband:

Ed is very well liked; no doubt you've seen that. His dad had that characteristic, too. He had such a lot of friends. When my husband passed away very suddenly, the florist said, "We've never had as many floral sprays to fix for a funeral before in the many years that we've been here."

Ed has said to me, "You know, I'm quick to think, just like Dad was." My husband had no education, really. His own father was ill a good deal and so he'd get to go to school only one or two days out of the week. But he just didn't need education. He could figure his custom work all up in his head faster than I could with pencil. He had a keen mind. But he just never had the chance to get the book learning. Ed's ability to meet the public is an attribute he acquired from his dad. It wasn't from his mother.

Ed's mother had taught rural school for two years as a young woman—after completing one year of high school—but she was certain that her own teaching did not have any influence on Ed's eventual decision to teach. "I wasn't cut out for school teaching," she insisted. She wondered if Ed's early success in school might have had an influence on his eventual decision to make education his life's work:

You see, Ed really graduated from high school ahead of his years. He took fifth and sixth grade in one year. He had a remarkable teacher who had been at it for years and years. There was this little girl in his grade—it was a country school—and she was just as bright and alert as Ed was. The teacher let them go as fast as they wanted to, and they just raced. They both finished fifth and sixth grades in one year. So that put him ahead of his age group.

Ed continued to live on the farm his father was renting while he attended high school in town. In summer he helped with the haying. During his senior year his parents bought a farm of their own, and they arranged to have Ed stay in town to complete his schooling. Ed graduated in 1938 while he was still 16. The following year, the couple he had stayed with in town decided to go to California, and they invited Ed to accompany them to help with the driving. Ed remained in California for five months. During his stay he visited one of his mother's brothers who had moved west several years earlier.

After returning home to Kansas, Ed spent the next nine years farming with his father. As he explained, "Kids weren't going to college in those days. People would just get married and start raising a family." At the age of 22, Ed followed suit. He courted and married Alice, four years his junior, and brought her to his parents' farm to live. Their daughter Linda was born while they were living on the farm.

World War II did not exert the influence on Ed's life that it did on many of the young men of his age group. His occupation as a farmer exempted him from the draft. Had he been able to foresee the expense and the long period of time it would take him—from the belated beginning of his college career at age 28 until the completion of his M.A. degree in educational administration 11 years later— and had be been able to predict the financial help he would have received as a veteran, his pragmatic nature might have sparked the idea of enlisting early in the war. As it was, he and a group of his other young farmer-friends did decide that it was their duty to give up their occupational deferments and enlist in the navy, but Ed broke a leg in a fall from a horse and his buddies went off to war without him. Yet the war did ultimately exert some effect on his vocational choice, for at its conclusion be began to feel that without the sense of urgency about agricultural production created during the war years, a lifetime on the farm did not hold much promise. Influenced by his wife and by another young couple of their acquaintance, Ed decided in 1947 to leave farming, to enroll in college, and to prepare himself for the ministry.

Ed's mother remembered that Ed's idea to enter the ministry was the second declaration of an occupational goal other than farming which Ed made, not his first. At the time of his high school graduation, she recalled, he first announced that he had been thinking about a different vocation:

> He wanted to go on and study to be a veterinarian. He loved animals. But he had to have five years before he could be eligible to go out on his own, and really, to finish it, seven years—just like an M.D.! And his dad couldn't see it.

Ed frequently commented that "there is still a lot of the Kansas farmer in me." He often related experiences of his farm youth and enjoyed trading stories when he discovered a common corn-belt heritage in a colleague or new acquaintance ("Have you ever husked corn?"). His memories of farming, particularly working with animals, were fond ones. Apparently it was Alice more than Ed who found the thought of remaining forever on the farm a dissatisfying one. In her words:

> I just didn't feel like this could be our home when our children grew up. I didn't especially dislike it, but I just never felt like this was home.

Four years after they were married Ed and Alice moved from the farm to a nearby town where Ed enrolled as a student in Baptist College. As Alice expressed it, Ed had "become a Christian and felt like he might like to work for the Lord somehow." Ed's mother felt that Alice exerted an important influence on that decision.

During two years as a student at Baptist College, the only time in his life when he was a full-time college student, Ed also served as the minister of a small church in an outlying community. He enjoyed his missionary assignment, but he found the work of preparing and delivering sermons extremely difficult. Alice reported that he was under such tension that when he would start to prepare a sermon he would "break out with the hives just dreadfully." "Eventually he sort of got over this," she explained, but during the process Ed came to realize that being a preacher was not his calling.

Reflecting on how Ed happened to turn to teaching as a career, Alice recalled that it was more by accident than by design. The Bell's daughter Linda, then five years old, became seriously ill. She required extensive hospital care throughout the second summer of Ed's college career. At the end of that summer Ed was out of a job (he still worked in the fields each summer) and he did not have enough money to return to school. "Someone suggested he might try teaching, which hadn't really occurred to him until then. So he went to the college and got things lined up so that he could teach."

Ed was offered a job in a nearby one-room country school. He taught there for one year. The following year he took an assignment at a larger rural school nearby. As Alice described the job, Ed was "principal, bus driver, coach, teacher— just about everything."

Ed remained in his "just about everything" teaching position for four more years. The Bells continued to live in town so Ed could take evening classes at the college. Getting Ed through college became a joint enterprise, since Alice did some of the reading required in Ed's studies and summarized the contents for him during spare moments. (Ed described one literature class he took in which the only information he had for writing an exam was the oral summary which Alice had given him at mealtime a few minutes before. The exam received a high mark. Ed said he has wondered ever since, "Now, is that education?") During the summers, while Ed worked full-time as a seasonal farm hand, he continued his college work by taking correspondence courses. Alice modestly acknowledged her part in helping her husband with writing and typing his assignments; Ed stated it even more boldly: "I took my education by correspondence and Alice did the work for me." During those first five years of teaching, Ed completed the requirements for his bachelor's degree. He held his teaching-principal position for one additional year because he could not formally receive his degree until the following June.

With the requirements for a college degree satisfied, with a regular teaching certificate instead of the emergency one under which he had been teaching, and with five years of combined teaching and "administrative experience," Ed was at last in a position to take a speculative long-term look at the possibilities of a career in public education. His experience as a teaching principal had started him thinking about school administration. Alice reported that Ed liked what he had seen of administration and had expressed the hope of someday becoming a principal. He also felt he had gone about as far as he could in the rural schools of Kansas. He and Alice began to discuss alternatives for their next move. At one point they considered so remote an assignment as going to Nicaragua as teaching missionaries for their church. The openings there were in the junior and senior high school, however, and Ed preferred teaching in the "formative years" of the elementary grades.

The Bells considered one other possibility quite seriously—moving to the west coast. Ed's visit to California some ten years earlier had made a lasting impression on him, and the fact that he had relatives and friends there lent further encouragement. Ed sent an application to California for a teaching credential in that state. He also asked that letters be sent on his behalf to several California school districts which customarily recruited teachers from among Baptist College graduates. For good measure he also decided to apply for a teaching credential in Oregon. His certification for teaching in Oregon came through first. Although Ed had originally planned to go to California, when Oregon chose him, he chose Oregon. Meanwhile one of the central office personnel from the Columbia Unified School District in Oregon happened to be in Kansas during a spring vacation and had scheduled a visit to Baptist College, his own alma mater, to see if there were any candidates completing their teacher training who might be interested in teaching in his school district. A satisfactory interview with Ed was eventually followed by a formal letter from the school district asking if he would sign a contract if they sent one. Alice recalled that Ed wrote back immediately, "Just hold it—we'll be out." She added, "So that's it. He graduated on a Sunday, and we left on Monday." The interview in Kansas was the beginning of a long friendship between Ed and his fellow alumnus and their families. Some years later the man confided that he "had administration in mind" for Ed as soon as he met him, but initially Ed was hired to teach in the fifth grade.

Ed's father argued that Ed should take a position at one of several schools near the farm so that the family could remain together geographically. He did not want to see his younger son leave. Ed's mother vividly remembered that on the day Ed and Alice (along with their daughter, their dog, and an automobile loaded to the top with their belongings) stopped by the farm just before beginning their trip west, her husband did not even come to the car to say goodbye. After they departed, she said, he came into the house to put on his work overalls to do the evening chores, and she said to him, "Tom, why didn't you come to bid them goodbye?" "He didn't answer me," she said. "He just sat there and cried like a baby. The tears just rolled down his cheeks. It broke his heart, really."

A NEW LIFE

Now, at the age of 45, Ed has lived in Oregon and been a principal in the Columbia Unified School District for enough years that the first three years he spent in the district as a fifth-grade teacher are fading into the past. Except for occasional comments about specific children who were his pupils in those years (they were now of college age) he made few references to his early days in the district. It had been a long while since Alice had heard him say he would rather be "back teaching fifth grade."

Halcyon days that those first years in Oregon had since come to seem, Ed did recall the growing impatience he had begun to feel about his salary as a teacher and about the apparent eternity he faced before he would ever be promoted. The only encouragement he got was for his patience. The number of men elementary teachers aspiring to the principalship and whom he felt to hold seniority or a more favored position in the eyes of the central office dismayed him. He considered moving elsewhere to improve his salary and his prospects for promotion, and he began writing letters to other Oregon school districts. One of his inquiries was answered with an invitation for an interview and a tentative offer of a $1000 salary increase that amounted to a 20 percent raise. Ed arrived at school the next morning intending to talk about the offer with the principal, Tom Nice, a man whom he had come to feel was a good friend and a reliable counsellor in professional matters. There was no opportunity to talk with Tom before school. By the afternoon of that same day the offer was no longer on his mind, for Ed had reported that morning as a teacher and had been promoted to principal by the time he left that afternoon. The appointment was carefully presented as an interim one, resulting from a temporary reallocation of administrative staff following the heart attack of a principal in another school, but Ed was encouraged with the words, "This puts you in line to be a principal." That fall he was assigned as full-time supervising principal for one of the smaller and older schools in the district. The next year he was reappointed to administer two schools. Three years after his initial appointment he was assigned to open the new William Howard Taft Elementary School, and he had been the principal there ever since. During the initial year of this study he completed his sixth year as principal at Taft.

At 6 feet 1 inch and 200 pounds, Ed presented the image of a big man, and to the younger pupils in school he must have seemed almost a giant. Ed expressed a typically American concern about his weight. He often commented on his propensity toward putting on extra, unwanted pounds, and of his perpetual battle against this tendency. In fact, however, his "battles" were usually of about a two-hour duration—for example, skipping breakfast but snacking liberally during one of several midmorning coffee breaks, especially if someone had baked or bought pastries for the faculty room; skipping lunch, then snacking again in the afternoon, possibly with a cup of Insta-Breakfast. At any night meeting in which refreshments were served, he was back at the snacks again. More than once he proclaimed a diet to try to "get down" to 195 pounds. "Who knows, when I get there maybe I'll just keep going to 185 because I feel so good!"

A full head of gray hair contributed to an air of dignity and of formality about him, and glasses which he had recently started to wear regularly (now with bifocals) served to emphasize an air of austerity about him and led to a tendency for others to overestimate his age by about five years. Ed dressed conservatively, most often wearing a white shirt and selecting suits or sport jackets and trousers from a small wardrobe which served him adequately throughout Oregon's relatively temperate year-round weather. Dark suits, dark stockings (!), dark and not usually polished shoes, and dark ties seemed to provide a reliable formula for a man whose day might begin with a meeting of teachers at 8:00 A.M. and continue almost without pause through a professional or church meeting concluding at 10:00 P.M., with neither the time nor the opportunity to change clothes during the day. A new sport jacket—or even a new shirt or tie—drew inevitable comments and approval from some of the women on the staff who seemed eager to show their recognition of Ed's occasional efforts to introduce variety into his attire. Ed began every day of the regular school year with his jacket on; the nature of his activities plus the weather determined when and if it came off during the day. Once his jacket was off, unless he had to leave the school, it stayed off until he was ready to go home.

The nature of Ed's job, the demands of his family, and the extent of his other social commitments made for days that were invariably busy. At the same time, perhaps because of his own nature, Ed sought consciously to "take it all in stride" and to prevent days at school from becoming frantic. Similarly, he attempted to keep his teachers from perceiving themselves to be in a frantic race with time, particularly regarding the amount of work they "covered" in class. Ed contrasted himself with one principal in particular, a man who had a reputation among teachers for being "a driver" who was "only interested in how hard he can get his teachers to work." Ed commented:

> I think there's more to it than that. My father's barnyard philosophy was, "If that's all you can say about a man, it isn't very much. After all, mules are hard workers."

Ed could come home in the late afternoon, sit in his big new reclining chair, and enjoy just relaxing, although this usually signalled an occasion for his two little daughters to begin climbing all over him. One of the special delights he anticipated in weekends spent at home was the opportunity to nap, just as he sometimes dozed his way through the tedious part of an afternoon meeting away from school. He claimed to have the ability to pause for a minute, to relax, to stop what he was doing, even to momentarily force school problems out of his mind. But he almost never stopped for long, and, particularly at school, his job required him to be constantly available; moments which he intended for a brief respite (for example, a cup of coffee in the faculty room) were more likely to become periods of intense interaction than moments in which he could "catch up." The method he described by which he used to recoup his energy as a young man on the farm still served him, only the naps were no longer as obvious, and the running motor was his own:

> I could work all day driving the tractor and then get cleaned up and go to town. We never did anything without you went 30 to 40 miles to do it. Then with a few hours sleep I'd be back driving the tractor again. But there's nothing so monotonous as driving a tractor all day, and by late afternoon I could barely keep awake. So I'd leave the motor running and just rest my head on my arms. I'd wake up with a start in about five minutes, and after that I'd have a headache for the rest of the day, but at least I could keep going.

Ed could and did "keep going." He accepted his perpetual involvement and activity as part of his self-definition: "Sometimes I ask myself—I wonder just how important is all of this work I do. It's not like bales of hay that you count—or sacks of oats. But I guess I've gotten used to it." In the occupational pattern of Ed's life he could well have "gotten used to" being on the job, for he was proud of the fact that he had not been without work more than six or seven days total since he first sought employment and that, except for a hurried trip east to attend his father's funeral, he and Alice had not had any extended time off since 1957 when they had taken three weeks for a drive back to Kansas.

In spite of some susceptibility to catching colds (he took antihistamine daily and worried about getting too hot and then getting chilled), Ed did not miss a day of school during the year, although late in February he did confess to harboring the idea of taking a day off to rest:[1]

---

[1] Ed's accounting for his "days off" may not be completely reliable. For example, he did "skip," with permission, one day of the administrators' summer workshop in order to drive visiting relatives to the coast, but apparently he either forgot or did not regard this as a day off. The important point is not the accuracy of his account as much as his image of himself as a person who was always on the job.

I've been thinking of just staying home sick—in 17 years I stayed home two days for the flu, four days when I thought I was getting measles, and six days when my father died. Now that my evaluations are all done, I've really been thinking of just "being sick" some day—not to do any reading—oh, maybe a magazine or two—but just to relax.

Ed had never had a summer in which he did not either work, run a summer school program at Taft, or, once, attend a two-month summer session at the university: "I've never had a summer off 'loafing.' That's the old farmer in me." Ed and Alice had dreamed of time free to travel, but such dreams (like "maybe go to Europe") ignored the realities of family finances: "We're planning to go over to the coast and do some more camping. I wouldn't mind just sitting around with my feet up. We aren't going anywhere. It costs too much money."

At least two of the district's administrators in recent years had requested leaves of absence so they could accept temporary positions in government schools overseas. Such an assignment had become one of Ed's favorite ideas, one he had talked over with Alice. In June, 1966, at the end of school, Ed described a tentative plan for his professional future: "I figure I will go about two more years here. Then maybe I'll take a leave and then come back for reassignment. That would be about right. I'd be ready." As things actually worked out, of course, two years and two summers later Ed was right back at Taft School ready to begin another school year, and two years after that he was still there. But the dream sustained him through low points when he became worried that maybe he had been at Taft too long or that he was becoming "a bit stale." And sometimes, at least in fancy, he contemplated changing his vocation completely. After fielding an angry telephone call from a parent one afternoon, he turned to me and sighed, "I think I'll go a thousand miles away and go into business and no one will know I was a principal."

Ed's involvement with every aspect of his school, from the physical condition of the walls to the visit of a university student completing a brief assignment, was a highly personal one. He took Taft's successes and its failures personally. Nothing frustrated him more than criticism, actual or implied, by someone whom he felt "does not understand what we are trying to do here." He bragged about the school, reveled in its successes, and agonized over its shortcomings. To him, Taft remained a successful enterprise which thrived in no small measure because of his leadership and dedication.

THE FAMILY

Ed's immediate family, as defined by a combination of kinship and geography, consisted of his wife, their four children, and his mother. Ed's mother did not actually reside within his household. Since her move west, however, she almost invariably spent Sunday afternoon after church with him, taking that day as her regular "day off" from her duties as a home companion.

A more-or-less automatic weekly Sunday visit by an aged mother—and, for Alice, mother-in-law—is not an unmixed blessing in the typical American family scene. Alice's description of Sunday at home took that into account: "Of course, his mother is always with us. And we sort of feel like we have to entertain her regularly." Alice recalled an agreement reached years before that Ed's brother would be given the family farm with the understanding that he would look after their mother. "Now that all seems to be forgotten," she noted, adding that she had often wondered to what extent Ed's original decision to leave Kansas had been a consequence of his relationship with an older brother who always seemed to have things his way.

Ed's mother, in turn, cast a critical mother-in-law's eye over certain aspects of Ed's and Alice's home life, particularly the late hours they kept and Alice's efficiency as a housekeeper ("That counter and sink can be piled full of dirty dishes and leftover food. And those bedrooms!! If you can find the bed, you're doing lucky."). She did not approve of their permissive approach to child raising, particularly with their teen-age son Jimmy ("Why didn't Ed take the boy out to the garage and give him a right good strapping like he needed?"). At the same time, she said she had tried not to interfere in their household or let things bother her there. She recognized that it had been in their home, of all her offspring, that she had always felt most welcome; her daughter-in-law had always been "a good Christian and the dearest sort of person."

The miles that separated Ed and Alice from others in their respective families (Alice's parents and siblings still lived in Kansas; Ed's brother lived in Kansas, his sister in California) provided an immediate barrier to family get-togethers but in the long-run also provided a rationale which could be drawn upon to justify a visit. For the biggest family event of the year, the December marriage of the Bell's oldest daughter, Linda, the three grandparents were all on hand. Ed's sister and her family also visited in Oregon during the year, and at the end of that summer Ed, Alice, and their two little daughters drove to Kansas for a trip of several weeks, prompted by reports of failing health on the part of Alice's father.

Alice felt that her own family differed from Ed's in some important ways, particularly in the comparison she drew between her own close-knit and easy-going family and the more serious-minded and individualistic members of the Bell family. It wasn't necessarily that the members of the Bell family worked *harder*, she said, but they were "more intense" about everything they did:

> Ed's father was the kind of person that had to have the first of everything in the neighborhood—machinery, appliances, this type of thing. My folks definitely weren't. I think maybe this affects our points of view on many things.

Important as these personality differences may have been in the now 25 years of their married life, Ed and Alice also shared many similarities in their backgrounds. In both Kansas families, mothers who had been teachers married husbands who were farmers. Ed was the second son; Alice the second daughter. In both families many years separated the ages of the oldest and youngest siblings, so that each family literally raised two different sets of children. Ed and Alice subsequently followed that pattern in raising their own family. The fact of the differences in age between the two sets of children was dramatized during the year when their oldest daughter Linda got married and moved away and their son dropped out of high school and spent increasingly longer periods away from home. Ed and Alice found themselves "starting a family all over again" as they realized that life in their household now revolved around their two young daughters, ages five and three. Ed compared himself, with young children of his own at home, to his brother who already had three grandchildren. "Well, I'm my own grandpa," he joked within the family circle.

The two young daughters provided the focus of many family activities. Ed and Alice referred frequently to the fact that the older of the girls would be entering school next fall, and they enjoyed the apparent excitement that idea generated in the child herself. They hoped that her sometimes-intense nature would serve as a positive force in her school success. They conjectured about how differently she might find school compared to her happy-go-lucky little sister. Alice was intrigued by the differences exhibited among each of the children:

> They all have their differences and charms, and it's very interesting to watch them grow. We sort of feel that we should know more now than we did when our older girl was growing up, but I'm afraid we have just as many problems now.

Grandma added a leavening note: "They're both happy little kids. With the parents they've got, they couldn't help but be, really."

One of Ed's major pastimes at home was what Alice called "getting acquainted with the family"—spending time with his daughters and with her:

> He usually doesn't come home from school until about five-thirty or six. From then on, oh, he does a little work around the house, but not very much. I mean, he's not much of a handy-man. And he reads some. And he plays with the girls—they demand a lot of his time when he's not doing something else. We occasionally go to a show, take a drive, sometimes play miniature golf or take the girls swimming. And sometimes just relax.

Ed claimed to enjoy working in the garden, spending many hours there in the spring and summer. Whether he included the task of mowing the lawns among the enjoyable gardening tasks I was never sure; it always seemed that he breathed a sigh of relief when he could report having completed the mowing over a weekend. Evenings that were not preempted by school business often found either Ed or Alice engaged in church activities. Even if Ed had been out late at a meeting, he and Alice usually stayed up for another hour or two after he returned home, talking, watching television, or playing cards (Rook was their favorite) or other games. They both described themselves as "night people."

The Bells lived modestly. Their tastes reflected, in Ed's words, a long experience with "just barely keeping ahead of the hounds." Their home was a one story frame dwelling in which everything appeared just a bit too small for a growing and active family. In 12 years their monthly payments of $91 had earned them a substantial equity in their home. If the decision were his alone, Ed once said, he would have been inclined to refinance the house and invest the money in local property or in the stock market, but Alice firmly believed that anything purchased should be paid off as soon as possible, and a home was no exception. I do not know whether Ed would ever really have taken such a bold step with his money and whether Alice would really have tried to insist that he should not. That Ed even considered this alternative suggested that for the first time in their married lives he and Alice felt that their income was finally catching up with their incessant monthly bills and payments and the rather extraordinary medical expenses they had incurred for Alice, Linda, and the older of the two little girls. Alice commented:

> It seems like we've always been a little bit . . . perhaps not "behind the eight ball," but always hoping that next month will hurry up and get here so we'll have the check. I think we are finally getting to see a breathing space. But it has been hard for me as a manager to always make it go around.

Ed and Alice expressed pride in having "made it" entirely on their own financially. "We never had any outside help of any kind—every cent of what we have is what we earned." Except for occasional and brief periods of seasonal employment, Alice had not worked. Ed's feeling, as Alice explained it, was: "I can take care of my family. My wife is not going to work. She is needed at home." Alice had not shared Ed's opinion in the matter, but as she pointed out, "I guess I've spent most of my life trying to make Ed happy and this was his feeling."

The constant financial press of their family life was reflected in myriad ways in the behavior and attitudes Ed expressed at school. Caught occasionally in a too-blatant demonstration of penny-pinching (for example, having the exact change for a restaurant meal with nothing left for a tip, or "loading up" on a treat in the faculty room but not purchasing a school lunch), Ed sometimes joked about his frugality and admitted he was "cutting down on expenses." Staff members who were bothered by his frugality described it with slightly stronger terms. The dollars-and-cents aspect of every activity he engaged in as a principal seemed to enter into Ed's thinking. It provided a rationale for his spotty attendance at Kiwanis meetings: "It's partly a matter of finances. I don't eat lunch, so that ends up being $8 a month for something I don't need." Feelings of being "put upon" by the school district in having to use his car to attend meetings and to make a 3-mile round trip in order to bank the money collected each school day was a constant source of irritation to Ed (and to his fellow principals as well). He once remarked that by the time one deducted the extra hours and days he put in as a principal and the cost of operating his car on school business he wondered if some teachers at Taft weren't taking home a better salary than he was.

A Daughter's Wedding

The marriage of his oldest daughter marked a significant step in Ed's own life as well as the most important family social event during the year. Linda Bell was 23, a college senior majoring in education and planning eventually to teach elementary school. Linda had initially majored in art, and her later change of a major extended the number of units she needed in order to graduate. She had been a resident student at a small college elsewhere in the state for three years but had recently returned home. She had hoped to complete her course work at the nearby university, but her marriage plans interrupted her student career. During the fall prior to her December wedding she decided not to return to school but to continue with a seasonal job at a local cannery as long as possible to earn money to pay for her wedding. She had agreed with her parents to accept free room and board while she worked and to pay for her own wedding expenses. In that way, her parents explained, she could make the wedding just as plain or fancy as she chose.

The wedding provided a unique opportunity to learn about the Bell family in a formal and structured social situation. After the wedding invitations were sent I asked Ed if he would be willing to hold a taped interview with me in order to describe the invited guests in terms of their relation to his family.[2] I assumed that the wedding list, even though prepared under Linda's direction, would also reflect the kinship and friendship patterns of her parents.

Three quarters of the invitations to the wedding (to 133 of the total of 179 persons invited) were sent by the "bride's side of the family." Twenty-two of these invitations were sent to relatives—primarily aunts, uncles, and cousins—in the midwest who would not be able to attend the ceremony but who nonetheless would expect to receive announcements. Personal friends of Linda's own age group comprised 12 percent of her total list; the balance of the invitations were sent on behalf of the family. The distribution of the invitations sent by the Bell family, as shown in Table 3-1, provides some insight into family social interaction in the

TABLE 3-1   DISTRIBUTION OF WEDDING INVITATIONS SENT
BY BRIDE LINDA BELL AND HER FAMILY

Category	Number of Persons	Percent of Invitations
Church friends	31	23
Relatives	27	20
Family friends	27	20
Neighbors	18	14
Bride's personal friends	16	12
School-related friends	10	8
Other	4	3
	133	100

community. "Church friends" comprised the largest social category (23 percent). The church friends were members of Ed's and Alice's church; Linda and her fiancee had recently been attending a different church and had arranged for the wedding ceremony to be held there. In addition to specifically invited church friends, Ed extended an "open invitation" verbally to all members of his church to attend the wedding. Relatives and family friends each comprised 20 percent of the invited guests; neighbors constituted an additional 14 percent.

[2] A Christmas card mailing list might provide a comparable source of information about family interaction. Although I did not pursue this source, Ed volunteered on December 21 that he and Alice had not yet sent their cards to their list of "over 100 people." They were also considering running off a group letter to enclose with their greeting. One week before Christmas Ed had joked, "We're still about a month away from Christmas, but Christmas isn't a month away from us."

The Bells sent invitations to five of Ed's colleagues in the school district and their spouses. Two of these invitations went to administrators—one to a junior high vice principal who had showed a special interest in Linda over the years, the other to Tom Nice, the elementary school principal who had been Ed's sponsor into administration and who had remained Ed's close professional and personal friend. Three invitations were sent to older female teachers. Two of the teachers were presently on the faculty of Taft School; the third had served on two faculties under Ed's administration. These three teachers had been and continued to be of central importance in Ed's administrative career, exerting an influence that had not gone unnoticed among their fellow teachers or even at the central office. As Ed listed their names, he paused to volunteer this explanation of how certain teachers had been chosen:

> I suppose you might wonder, "Why those people and not others?" I am not sure how to answer that, except that we have just had a closer relationship with them over a longer period of time. It's not practical to invite everyone, and I certainly didn't want to leave out these people.

Wedding preparations occupied much of Alice's and Linda's time in November. Ed enjoyed reporting on the wedding preparations during conversations in the faculty room; several of the female staff pressed him for details. With her mother's help, Linda made all arrangements for the wedding. Ed reported, "It seems to be a common procedure now to hire a wedding consultant to take care of all these details, but Linda just didn't feel it was worth the price." Other than Ed's own brief part in the ceremony as father of the bride and the opportunity to talk about the wedding at school, his administrative routines went uninterrupted except for a brief stop one morning enroute to a luncheon meeting to have a look inside the church where the ceremony was to be held.

For a few weeks after the wedding, Ed gave an account at school following each family visit with the newlyweds, but soon his household settled down with a new orientation centering on the two preschool daughters. As a young married woman, Linda had passed an important rite of passage in her own life. To Ed, she would always be first and foremost his young daughter. Sometimes after conferring with younger female staff members at school, particularly the nurse or secretary, Ed commented on the fact that his staff now included women who were "even younger than Linda." His younger female staff members were in fact sensitive to the fact that although he often asked them questions about the operation of the school, he never sought advice from them as he did from older women on the staff.

A Problem Son

Alice and Ed dreamed of having a large family. Their daughter Linda was born the first year they were married and they hoped for many other children to follow. In subsequent pregnancies, however, Alice inevitably miscarried within the first few months. Ed and Alice began to worry that their daughter might grow up an "only child." After several years they decided to adopt a younger sibling. The boy they adopted was three years old at the time. Now, as a 17-year-old, Jimmy Bell had become a problem. Grandmother had this to say about the boy:

He'd just been shifted from pillar to post in those foster homes. The way I understand it, he came from a large family and they just had more than they could take care of. They just farmed him out.

When they got him, of course, Alice just loved him to death. Whatever Jimmy wanted to do was all right. And you see, he's gotten to a place where it isn't all right. He just never did stick to a job and he don't now. He's not responsible, and he's not dependable.

Alice's comments about her son expressed a mother's hope that everything would eventually work out:

Jimmy is 17. He dropped out of school this spring. He's really been a dropout for many, many years. He has never really been interested in school. He likes to go to school, but he doesn't like to conform to the regulations. He's real good-natured about it, but he just doesn't produce.

Now he's with the State Rehabilitation Program. They are hoping to get him in a school for chefs. This is something he's always been interested in. At the moment we're just sort of keeping our fingers crossed, hoping something good will come from this. He can be a very likeable person if he puts his mind to it. It seems he sort of talks himself into most anything, but then he talks himself out just about as quickly.

An important difference which Alice expressed between Jimmy's influence on her life and that of her husband was that Ed's involvement at school provided him with a respite from problems at home:

We have had a lot of interesting times as well as a lot of grief with Jimmy. We've had him to counsellors, to mental health, to psychiatrists, to special education help. Nothing has seemed to help much. It's been a real traumatic experience for myself.

I think Ed is probably bothered more than he seems to show. But he can go away to school and forget about it. He becomes involved in other problems.

In fact, whether Ed was conscious of it or not, his problems with Jimmy definitely accompanied him to school. Over the years the senior teachers had become well acquainted with the Bell family and had seen them in a variety of settings. One teacher recalled:

One time Jimmy went on a picnic with the staff. All our families went. My daughter has always been real festive about her feelings toward people. After this picnic, she said, "Mama, I just feel so sorry for that Jimmy Bell. He's the saddest boy I've ever met."

The same teacher felt that Ed's problems with his son influenced every situation at school in which a child was having problems:

I don't think he is as sure of things as a lot of principals. Do you know what I mean? Internally he suffers, sometimes. Like when he has to get after a little child or something.

That goes back to the trouble he had with his son. In every little child that has a problem, he sees the father [himself] and son, and he relates to them. I think this hurt, this insecurity, tears him apart sometimes. I don't know what the problem is, but it isn't a happy relationship. He's told me he just can't reach his son.

Other teachers volunteered similar observations during interviews with me. One teacher said:

Ed has seen a son be maltreated by an educational and academically oriented program in school. He has found himself rather helpless to aid his boy. I think that has taken a lot of luster off the sheer academic-drive, competition sort of thing. So he is very much on the lookout for ideas that help him better understand the problems of children who can't perform academically.

The counsellor noted:

I know that he has worried about his son and has mentioned it to me. He has told me that he and his wife wish they had known what we know now about guidance and psychology and what to do with young people when they fall into specific patterns.

Ed was not reticent in talking about the problems he was having or had had in the past with raising Jimmy. Even members new to the staff were taken into Ed's confidence, as this comment by a newcomer suggests:

I don't know all the circumstances behind it, but I do know that Ed's boy in high school has problems. Once Ed said something to me about "not being able to handle my own son." At the time I felt his guard was down somewhat. Whether his policies have any bearing on his son, I don't know. But as I understand, Jimmy Bell does have pretty severe problems in school. Not only in school, but just problems, period!

To some staff, Ed's comments about Jimmy revealed a personal side of him that enlisted empathy in his problem and admiration for his openness and concern. At least one teacher felt that Ed's problems with Jimmy received excessive attention in the professional discussions at school:

Ed becomes emotionally involved in behavior problems and projects his son's difficulties into other cases. He is defensive about his son's problems. I don't think his son's problems should be brought up in staff meetings.

COMMUNITY ACTIVITIES

Church

Ed was involved in the activities of the Central Baptist Church to such an extent that I had assumed him to be atypical of schoolmen in this regard. Yet a comparison with a national survey of elementary principals presented in Table 3–2 shows him to be among the substantial 87 percent who hold some degree of membership in a church or religious body (DESP 1968:93). Ed was serving his third and last year as the elected lay moderator of his church. In a role of major officeholder in his church he was more active than the "average" (modal) principal who reported being a church member but not an officeholder. Yet the extent of his participation as a major officeholder was also characteristic of one-third of the principals surveyed in the national sample.

TABLE 3-2   PARTICIPATION OF A NATIONAL SAMPLE OF ELEMENTARY
SCHOOL PRINCIPALS IN A CHURCH OR RELIGIOUS BODY[a]

Degree of Participation	Percent
Hold major office[b]	32
Active member; hold no office	41
Hold membership; not active	15
Not a member	13
	101

[a] Source: *The Elementary School Principalship in 1968* (DESP 1968:93). Copyright 1968, National Association of Elementary School Principals, NEA. All rights reserved. Used by permission.
[b] Category describing Ed Bell's participation in his church.

While guiding me on a tour of his church building Ed reminded me that one of the practices which characterizes his church is the belief that the baptism ceremony properly requires total immersion. Total immersion also characterized the Bell family's participation in their church. In additon to serving as lay moderator, Ed was also a deacon of the church and a teacher in a high school Bible class. During his three terms as lay moderator he served officially as the "chief executive" of the church. Alice was active in the choir, which required one evening rehearsal a week; she also belonged to a circle, held one special office, was a deaconess, and occasionally attended an adult Sunday school class. The children attended Sunday school. Linda had been active for several years in the choir during her days as a high school student. Alice summarized the usual round of their weekly church commitments:

> We seldom skip Sunday morning services. We go occasionally in the evenings. Then there's usually at least one meeting during the week—sometimes prayer meetings, sometimes business meetings. Right now Ed is on the building committee. There have been quite a number of meetings of this type. Perhaps we attend two or three meetings a week.

From their years of association with the members of their church (there were 295 active members on the church roster in July 1966) the Bells had identified a group of close family friends, a larger group of comrades with whom they shared concerns of their church as a building, a social organization, and a belief system, and an even wider group of acquaintances in a loosely-defined "hello circle." Ed delighted in meeting new people through his church association. During a vacation absence of the pastor he made several home visits as a self-appointed delegate to welcome people who attended his church for the first time.

At the same time that Ed appeared to be very outgoing in meeting newcomers, the behavior he manifested toward long-time acquaintances in the church setting seemed comparable to the behavior that he manifested toward his long-time associates in the school district: overtly informal, cordial without being intimate, supportive of a sustained acquaintanceship without giving any encouragement for increasing its intensity. I wondered if Alice's preferences, especially among their mutual church and neighborhood acquaintances, might be the decisive factor in determining who moved toward the inner circle of their closest family friends. In describing Alice's choir group, for example, Ed explained, "There is a kind of closeness in that group that goes beyond that of just the general run of the church." Similarly, Alice observed that she and Ed were friends with many "wonderful" couples among their neighbors, but that as the housewife she felt that she was closer to them.

Ed's behavior as chief executive of his church seemed, on the occasions when I observed it, a bit less domineering than his leadership style at school. The difference was the sort that one might predict in the behavior of a person accustomed to serving as a formal leader of any group with which he might be associated but cognizant of the appropriateness of different styles in different settings. Within the church body the people he was responsible to were the people who had elected him, and while they expected him to conduct their meetings, they did not necessarily expect him to conduct their business.[3]

Acting in his capacity as moderator, Ed exhibited a preference for achieving complete consensus on issues, with dissenting views aired and worked out individually before a final vote was called. His desire for agreement led him in one meeting I observed to attend inadequately to and to understate the actual number of voters among a small dissenting minority. At the same time, he appeared sensitive about not using his position to be "pushy." Once he made an aside to the pastor, "I never know how far to go with this parliamentary procedure." He accepted a procedural suggestion from the floor with the comment, "It's easy to be moderator of this group; you're all so helpful." He cajoled the membership for a volunteer needed to fill a committee vacancy, but was careful not to put himself in the position of having to appoint someone if no volunteer was forthcoming: "If anyone is interested, you can talk to me after the meeting." Then he added in humorous vein, "The line will form over here. We'll have to find some way to be equitable." Although the meeting was attended by a few young couples, the older people and the pastor did most of the talking. People addressing the chair called Ed by his first name with the exception of the pastor himself, who referred to him as "Mr. Moderator." Ed, in turn, referred to the pastor as "Pastor," although they were on a first name basis and either visited together or spoke on the telephone several times a week, including calls during school hours and even an occasional brief meeting in Ed's office to discuss specific matters of church business. Of church business in general Ed commented, "They always elect a most conservative board, then they have trouble with them approving anything we want to do." With formal channels of conducting church business somewhat cumbersome, Ed and the pastor found themselves needing to keep their own signals straight, particularly before new issues were to be raised at the quarterly business meetings.

Between his preoccupation with other activities and his reluctance to do more

----

[3] As Ed and I were entering the church building one evening for a business meeting, we got to the door just as two couples of about Ed's age reached it. Ed opened the door and held it for them. "Thank you doorman," quipped one of the husbands. "That's a good place for you, Ed."

Afterward I joked with Ed: "There, that one comment makes the whole visit worthwhile. No one says that to you at school."

"No, but they may be thinking it," he countered.

planning than was absolutely essential, Ed's major contributions in time and energy to his duties as moderator and to his other participation in the activities of his church were during the moments he was formally and visibly acting in those capacities, but not in time spent planning or preparing for them. In conducting the business meetings he worked "off the top of his head," with neither an agenda nor a systematic procedure for calling for reports or moving from one item to the next.

Ed's problems with his son Jimmy had affected the organization of the Central Baptist Sunday School. In previous years students in the tenth, eleventh, and twelfth grades had met as one class, following the organizational structure of the community's public schools into senior high schools comprising those three grades. But during the current year, tenth graders had been meeting with the class below. Ed's high school class consisted of only eleventh and twelfth graders; tenth-grader Jimmy Bell and his classmates met with a different Sunday school teacher. "This class is sort of a concession to me so that Jimmy and I aren't together," Ed explained. "We don't get along very well together in the same class."

Attendance in Ed's Sunday school class had been dwindling; on the morning in May when I visited, there were three students. A prayer and offering preceded the lesson. At the time for collecting the offering, Ed remarked aloud, "I'm a little embarrassed for change today. I have a dollar bill. Maybe I'll put that in to make up for some of the other times." The lesson proceeded with questions and comments, with Ed doing most of the talking. The announced theme for the day was "Christian Love," although there was no evidence that Ed was following either a formally prepared lesson from a lesson guide or a previous plan of his own. Questions like "Are there ways we could bring more love into our class here?" or "Do you ever think about our order of worship?" brought a response from one of the students, "You ask the hardest questions."

Other Community Involvement

Ed's own ambivalence about his participation as a member of a local chapter of Kiwanis was reflected in the extent of participation in civic or service clubs reported by principals in the national sample (DESP 1968:Table 73): 50.2 percent indicated some degree of membership in such a group, 49.7 percent did not. Holding major office in a *church* was characteristic of one-third of the principals in the national study; only 13 percent reported holding major office in a civic or service club. Ed's feeling was that he ought to belong to a service club, in part because it was important for him to have nonschool contacts in the community, and in even greater part because he felt it was necessary for the schools to be represented in community activities. At the same time, he expressed the reservation that he did not "have much in common with many of those fellows." Sometimes weeks elapsed without his attending a meeting, and even the urgings of his colleague and sponsor Tom Nice (who had served as president of the Kiwanis chapter and had sponsored Ed as a member of it) were usually met with resistance: "I just can't get away this week, Tom. Maybe next time."

Except for his limited participation in Kiwanis, Ed's other community contacts were generally with local storeowners and others who provided services for his family. The local druggist and gas station operator both knew him by name; the ever-changing clerks and cashiers at the local supermarket did not except for those whose children or younger siblings attended Taft School. Because he had been with the public schools so many years, Ed could expect to run into youngsters and parents who recognized him anywhere in the community. He was known because of the conspicuous public role he held; he could not recognize all those who could recognize him. With the growing, changing, and ever-increasing number of children who had passed through the doors of Taft School he was usually at a loss to do more than return a warm but calculatedly impersonal greeting anyplace, anytime, to anybody: "Hi, there."

A WIFE'S VIEW OF THE PRINCIPALSHIP

By his own definition, and seconded by all those who knew him in the context of his personal life, Ed Bell was "a family man." In the American lexicon this means that he had a wife and children at home; that he provided for them, cared for them, and worried about them; and that he put their well-being ahead of literally any other consideration. In Ed's case, as with perhaps most other "family men," his attention and commitment to the work he did to provide for his family, coupled with the attention he gave to opportunities for professional and social association with other family men, substantially reduced the amount of time he actually spent with his family. His full round of activities created some stress between professional and family obligations. Alice described the impact of Ed's work as principal on her role as principal's wife:

> In a way it's a rather lonesome life. You're involved to a certain extent, and yet you're never in on it. You're very definitely involved in all the problems and aspects of the school, but you're sort of on the sidelines. This is as it should be, I suppose.
> But I think his family life is a little bit wearing, because Ed's a principal first and foremost. He likes school work. There have been times when I have complained a bit or made some remarks and he says, "You know, school has really been good to us." I sometimes feel like his time is taken up so much with his role as principal that it doesn't leave enough time for other things. So many of his nights are taken up that we don't have much social life away from the school or the church.

The degree to which a man should involve his wife in the problems of his work-a-day world is a particularly perplexing issue for husbands whose obligations conflict with the routines of home life or who cannot precisely define the extent of their obligations once they leave the office. Ed's stated opinion was that most school problems could wait until the next day to be resolved. His estimate of the extent to which school matters followed him home was considerably lower than the estimate of his wife. In terms of the number of telephone calls received at home, the disparity in their estimates (Ed's estimate: a couple of calls a term once school had started; Alice's estimate, specifically excluding teacher requests for substitutes: "they sort of come and go in bunches—maybe a couple a day as a guess") may have resulted from different ideas about what constituted a call. Ed apparently disregarded both routine and emergency calls in his estimate. The only calls which he considered to be interruptions or invasions of his home privacy were calls received from irate parents. Obviously he excluded certain categories of calls in the estimation he made, since he preferred that any faculty who were not reporting for work that day make their requests for substitutes through him. On some school mornings Ed might have received two or three teacher calls by 7:00 A.M.

Alice described one telephone conversation which had seemed like the call-to-end-all-calls. Ed's schedule that particular day barely allowed him time to come home, eat a quick supper, and leave again for an evening meeting. Just as he sat down to his meal, the telephone rang. The caller was an angry parent who insisted on talking to the principal. Alice said, "I took the phone to him at the table. He sat there and listened and listened to the lady. And about the time he got off the phone, it was time to leave again. That's a little bit extreme, but he does get a lot of calls."

Telephone calls, plus an occasional brief visit by a teacher wishing to get into the school on a weekend, did not constitute the only ways that school invaded Ed's home life. As Alice explained:

> School is something he can't leave there. It's something that you more or less live with all the time. He has these problems he just can't turn off at the end of the day.

Ed shared many of his concerns with Alice, but she recognized that there were probably some things "of a confidential nature" which he did not talk about:

> In some situations I know he's concerned about something and he says, "Well, this is something that the less you know about, the better off you are." I feel like I sort of live on the edge of this school. I know a lot about it, and I know a lot about the different people he works with, yet sometimes I can meet them face to face and I don't know them, because I don't spend that much time around school.

As the school had grown, Alice had found it more difficult to keep up an acquaintance with new faculty members. Another minor change which occurred in family organization during the year, the acquisition of a second car, freed her from having to vie with Ed for the use of the family automobile but it also eliminated the frequent opportunities she used to have for visiting with the faculty while waiting to borrow the car or to take her husband home after school. She had also given up trying to maintain an accurate calendar of Ed's meetings and activities in order to be able to inform others of his whereabouts. At present she saw her part in the immediate operation of the school as providing "sort of a central clearing house" for messages. Past instances when parents had been upset with her because she did not know where Ed could be reached or because she did not know about certain problems that had happened at school had led her to feel that people expected her to know everything that was going on at Taft School, but she realized long ago that it was impossible for her to do so. "I try to be as kind to everyone as I can," she said, but she restricted her involvement with problems brought to her to relaying them to Ed.

Her husband's role as principal made few demands on Alice socially. She acknowledged one social problem—her trouble in remembering the names of people met briefly at meetings and banquets, people who had an advantage in identifying her because she was the principal's wife: "I meet so many of them that people come up to talk to me and I can't keep them all straight." Such occasions were few in number. Principals' wives are seldom called upon for a command performance. During the year Alice attended two "banquets" held in the Taft School cafeteria. One honored the retirement of a member of the central office staff, the man who years before had been responsible for recruiting Ed at Baptist College. The second occasion was a small banquet sponsored by the Bluebird group which met regularly at school. Ed was invited at the last moment. ("I said fine if I could invite my wife; I called her at home and said, 'Don't start anything for dinner.' She was already dressed up from having been to a funeral. Then she went on to choir practice.") Alice accompanied Ed to the staff "farewell dinner" at a local restaurant in June, but she did not accompany him to any of his other school-related evening or weekend meetings. The Bells did not attend the May "crab feed," the one purely social event of the County Elementary Principals' Association, although they had talked of going and had usually done so in past years. In the Faculty Wives group, an organization in which wives of all teachers and administrators in the district were welcome to participate, Alice was chairman of a literary group charged with presenting programs on books and authors at monthly meetings.

At the same time that Alice Bell sensed an increasing remoteness from immediate involvement with the operation of Taft School, she accepted and supported her husband's involvement in and dedication to his work as an administrator. She had resigned herself to the fact that Ed was also the administrator of their home life:

> It isn't so obvious, perhaps, but Ed is pretty much the dominant one in our family. It's not that he has to have his way, it's just that we sort of live with this. I think he knows what he wants. He's not a selfish person, but it seems like he's sort of the idea man around our place, and I think the family revolves around his wishes.
>
> He wonders sometimes why I don't have more opinions. I think the reason is that occasionally it's easier not to. Perhaps this is why he's in administration. He sees things as he thinks they ought to be and this is the way he works toward getting them to be. I think this carries over into the role of family administration, too.

It was evident that Alice respected her husband's administrative ability and felt that his administrative style was effective. She once asked me if I did not think Ed was different from other principals, and she explained:

> Well, one principal said when he moves to a new school it takes him awhile to get things straightened out and shaped up. But the way Ed administers, he tries to get things more relaxed. He wouldn't go into a school to try to straighten it out.

Alice felt that Ed's very preoccupation with his job sometimes became a source of conflict in his interactions:

> Ed loves his job. He enjoys working with people. He works very hard at it. He has a pretty strong sense of right and wrong. I think that sometimes he

goes at it in a way that alienates some people and this may be a hindrance. He's really submerged in his work.

She felt that the fact that she and Ed had faced problems with raising Jimmy helped Ed in dealing with parents facing problems of their own:

> I think it gives him great satisfaction if he can help parents to see what they're trying to do and different ways of doing things. He does spend a lot of time talking with parents. Of course, having had a real problem child ourselves, I think perhaps he can understand some of their problems, some of the things they're either threatened with or wondering about.

Alice acknowledged that Ed's attempts to offer help, and the extent of his personal concern, were not always met with appreciation, particularly by parents of Taft School pupils. In seeking help in dealing with their own problems with their son, Ed and Alice had similarly rejected the help available to them through the schools. Ed once commented, "As far as anything besides academic counselling or job counselling, the people over at the high school who call themselves counsellors don't know any more about counselling than I do—maybe they don't know as much." Ed and Alice had been receptive to getting "outside help" for their family problems (just as they had been open in talking about them), but they had not considered the school a competent source for obtaining that help.

Alice expressed some concern that the press of Ed's administrative duties was pulling him away from his very reason for being in elementary school education—the children:

> I think probably children are his first love. He likes to be close to the children. I think that as the school has grown, he's gotten more and more away from this type of thing because he's been so busy with administrative duties.

Yet she recognized that Ed derived satisfaction from other aspects of his work, and that his satisfactions were intricately wound into everything that Taft School had become. "He's really very proud of the Taft School group and the staff and the people that work with him." At the end of the school year she commented on how Ed always hated to see a teacher move away or leave teaching ("Well, most always," she added as a qualification), and she described two of the younger teachers at Taft who were planning to stop teaching and begin their own families as people whom Ed had been sorry to see quit. She noted what a good year the present one had been and how Ed had so often spoken of his "great group of people":

> Every year he says at the beginning of school, "This is just the *best* year we've had yet. I've got a great staff." And I always say, "Uh-huh, I know. This is what you said last year."

Is the elementary school principalship her husband's career? Alice thinks that it is:

> He talks about things that he might do eventually. He would like to go overseas—do some teaching or even go to summer school. Or perhaps go to Mexico. We've never really done any traveling and this is something we've always wanted to do. But it will probably be as a teacher or administrator.
>
> He sold real estate one time, and he talks occasionally about doing a little

bit of this or that or something on the side. But things like this aren't likely to go through. He doesn't really have time to do any of these other things. Probably he will always be in the education field.

EDWARD BELL AS A TYPICAL PRINCIPAL

Although certain criteria had been used in guiding the search for a "subject" (see Chapter 1), no great concern had been given to identifying a "typical" principal. The anthropologist generally approaches the problem of representativeness by asking what his subjects are representative of, rather than by trying to identify "representative" subjects before his intensive work begins. As the fieldwork progressed, however, I became increasingly aware of a remarkable number of ways in which Ed Bell both personified the American elementary school principal and reflected characteristics of "typical" principals nationally.

Fortuitously, a nationwide survey of elementary school principals was being conducted during the school year in which the major part of the fieldwork was underway. The survey was conducted by the national organization of elementary school principals, the Department of Elementary School Principals (DESP) of the National Educational Association. The report resulting from that survey, *The Elementary School Principalship in 1968* (DESP 1968), provides an excellent opportunity for comparing Ed with his fellow principals.[4]

The national study was conducted over a 12-week period beginning in February, 1967. The initial mail-out was sent to 2551 elementary school principals in a sample of school systems having an enrollment of 300 or more pupils. Up to five follow-ups were mailed. A 91.7 percent usable return was achieved, a remarkably high return for a mailed questionnaire and itself another source of insight into the manner in which elementary school principals meet their professional commitments. Comparisons in selected categories between the national averages (i.e., the modal response category) and principal Edward Bell are shown in Table 3–3.

As examination of the table shows, Ed Bell and the school he administered reflected the statistical norms of the nationwide sample of principals in a variety of characteristics ranging from his role in shaping the curriculum, or the number of full-time classroom teachers and pupils present in the school, to demographic factors regarding his age, sex, marital status, and formal education. In all, Ed was in the modal category or the next most selected category in 34 of the dimensions on which data were gathered.

Ed's salary as a school principal provided one of the few categories in which he was substantially different (and in this case, "better off") than the typical principal across the nation. Several factors entered into this facet of his representativeness. First, the West Coast, like certain other regions and specific states, usually exceeds national averages in the amount of money spent for public education, including educators' salaries. To illustrate: two percent of all supervising principals

---

[4] An earlier study, "The Biographical Characteristics of Elementary-School Principals," lends further evidence indicative of Ed Bell's representativeness compared with a portrait of the "typical" principal in a national sample (Halpin and Croft 1960:14, 16–20).

TABLE 3–3   EDWARD BELL AS A TYPICAL PRINCIPAL: A COMPARISON BETWEEN PRINCIPAL BELL AND THE TYPICAL (MODAL) AMERICAN ELEMENTARY SCHOOL SUPERVISING PRINCIPAL, 1966–67, IN SELECTED CATEGORIES[a]

Table Number in National Study	Title of Table in National Study	Category Showing Modal Response in National Study	Percent of Principals in Modal Category	Edward Bell Described by Modal Category?
1	Official titles of participants in the survey	Principal	85	Yes
2	Age of supervising principals [males]	35–49 years	55	Yes
3	Sex of principals	Male	78	Yes
4	Marital status of supervising principals	Married	83	Yes
5	Position held just prior to first elementary school principalship	Elementary classroom teacher	57	Yes
6	Age at time of first appointment as an elementary school principal	Less than 35 years old	58	Yes
8	Willingness to become a principal if starting again	Certainly would	56	Yes [inferred]
9	The principalship as the final occupational goal	Final goal	57	Yes
11	Total experience in school work	10–19 years	43	Yes
12	Experience in elementary school classroom teaching	2–9 years	51	Yes
13	Total experience as a principal	10–19 years	34	Yes
14	Total years in present position	1–3 years	37	No. He was in category with second largest frequency, 4–9 years (33%).

15	Number of different schools in which principals have served in the present school system	1 school	60	No, but Taft School had been his only long-term assignment.
16	Highest earned college degree reported	M. A.	80	Yes
17	Major areas of undergraduate study by principals	Social studies	40	Yes [Psychology and Sociology]
18	Major field of graduate work by principals	Elementary school administration	51	Yes
28	Annual term of employment	10 but less than 11 months	51	Yes
32	Average number of hours per week principals spend at school and in school-related activities	48–53 hours	37	Yes [estimated]
43	General administrative status of the elementary school principal in the school system according to principals	Leader	55	Yes
44	The principal's role in the development of policies for the school system, according to principals	Some encouragement	45	Yes
45	The role of the principal in selecting the faculty	Accept-reject among candidates	34	Yes
48	The principal's role in preparing the budget of the individual school	Make recommendations only	42	Yes
49	Number of schools the principal administers	1 school	86	Yes

TABLE 3–3   (*Continued*)

Table Number in National Study	Title of Table in National Study	Category Showing Modal Response in National Study	Percent of Principals in Modal Category	Edward Bell Described by Modal Category?
50	Grades supervised by elementary school principals	Kindergarten–6	44	No. District did not have kindergartens. He was in category with second largest frequency, grades 1–6 (19%).
51	Percent of principals using various vertical patterns in the first six grades of their schools	Graded	Over 83	Yes
52	Percent of principals using various horizontal patterns in the first six grades of their schools	Self-contained	Over 71	Yes
53	Enrollment in elementary schools	400–699 pupils	46	Yes
54	Number of full-time classroom positions in elementary schools	15–24 positions	46	Yes
56	Secretarial help available to principals	1 secretary	58	Yes
58	Availability of full-time assistant principals	Do not have one	90	Yes
64	The principal's role in shaping the curriculum	Modify and adapt	56	Yes
65	The principal's role in the selection of instructional materials	Faculty-principal cooperation	55	Yes
72	Types of student bodies in principals' schools	Some diversity in background	32	Yes

95	Regular salaries of principals in 1966–67	$7,500–$9,999	34	No. He is in category with second largest frequency, $10,000–$12,499 (31%).
96	Principals' income from school employment other than regular salary as principal	None	71	No. Additional pay for attending an in-service workshop plus administering a summer school put him in the highest bracket for supplementary income ($1,500 and over), exceeding the extra-curricular salaries of 95% of principals reporting.
97	Principals' income from nonschool employment	None	66	Yes
98	Total income of principals from all types of employment	$10,000–$12,499	31	No. His total income of $13,040 placed him in a higher income category than 66% of the principals.

in the national sample reported making *less than $5000* as their regular salary, and 10 percent of all teaching-principals reported receiving less than this amount. At the time, this was $1000 less than the salary paid to *beginning teachers* in most West Coast cities. At the same time, 21 percent of all principals reported salaries of $12,500 and over; Ed's regular salary for the year was $11,505. Salaries for administrators in the Columbia Unified School District were based on the district's teacher salary schedule. Principals of large elementary schools like Taft School received 130 percent of the salary they would have realized as teachers for the equivalent years of experience and college units accumulated beyond a four-year degree. Ed's salary as a teacher would have been $8850. The 30 percent additional included a 24 percent salary increase plus an additional 6 percent for the extra days beyond the length of the regular teaching "year" when administrators were on duty after the close of school in June and before teachers reported in August. Ed's contract for the 1966–67 school year specified 205 working days.

Ed's additional income of $1535 from school employment "other than regular salary" exceeded not only 96 percent of the principals reporting in the national survey but also exceeded the majority of other elementary principals in his own school district. The district operated summer school programs in a few elementary schools in the summer. District policy dictated that if a principal's school was selected as a summer school site, the regular building principal had the option to stay on as the administrator of the summer school. This had resulted in an opportunity for Ed to augment his salary by some $1000 for several summers. In addition, a special three-week (12-day) in-service workshop planned for all elementary principals in the district in 1966 resulted in an extra $480 in the salary contract of every principal, a sum sufficiently large to place all the elementary principals in the district in a category which exceeded 70 percent of the principals nationwide in salary earned in supplementary school-related income.

My personal impression lends at least face validity to an assessment of Taft School as a "typical" suburban elementary school and of Ed Bell as a typical elementary school principal. I should reaffirm, however, that by "typical" I mean only that Taft School is representative of a whole genre of schools; the term "typical" can suggest invidious comparison of a sort which I think Ed and most of the staff at Taft might have found disappointing. Some staff members were careful to point out how very *atypical* they felt their school and administrator to be. On one occasion, a teacher summarily evaluated Taft with the statement, "This school is *not* typical," a comment intended as anything but an accolade. More often, however, the staff wanted me to realize how their school and principal were atypical because they were outstanding or special, as the following statements from teacher interviews attest:

> Every day I thank my lucky stars that I'm working with Ed and with his faculty. As I hear others telling me about their problems of working with different principals or teachers, I feel that I'm quite fortunate in that I don't have a lot of problems that they have to contend with. . . . I was thinking about your study, Harry, and I thought well, this isn't really a typical study of a principal because there is only *one in a million* like Mr. Bell. . . . I wish we had more people that would go into administration that have a good educational background and also have this kind of special personality in dealing with people.

He's *such a doll* so many times. I think if I were to describe what an ideal principal would be like, I would just about have to describe Ed. I worry about the time he won't be at this school and this faculty will still be here. In my eyes it would take a pretty big person to fill his shoes. I don't know if I could adjust right away to a new principal unless he had lots of Ed's qualities.

As you said when you came in, Harry, you chose Ed from a number of people that you had gone to interview and looked over a number of situations. The fact that you did choose Ed, I am sure, was a real supportive influence as far as he was concerned. I think all through the faculty there was this feeling of *something special* about our principal. I think that Ed felt this.

To six staff members who were visiting together in the faculty room one afternoon I described my interest in learning how representative a principal they felt Ed to be and how he was like and unlike other principals. Their remarks included the following:

He's more straight-laced. Not in the prissy sense, and not exactly more formal, but very aboveboard in a way that reflects his church beliefs and his whole personal philosophy.

He isn't shady. He never makes off-color comments or flirts or makes suggestive remarks. It's really annoying to work for a principal when you feel you always have to be on your guard.

He's more idealistic, both in his personal and in his educational philosophy.

He feels he is a liberal, but actually he is more conservative than he thinks.

He's not hasty. He doesn't jump to conclusions. He tries to be tactful with children as well as adults. Sometimes he's too lenient, but sometimes that's good because he isn't too impatient. He's real good with children.

He's sincere about everything.

During taped interviews, staff members volunteered a wide-ranging set of opinions about Ed *as a principal*. Their comments form part of Chapter 10, "Behind Many Masks." Comments of staff members frequently included some insight into how they felt about their principal *as a person*. Occasionally their observations dealt with his shortcomings:

Ed's weakest point is his lack of communication and empathy with and for his staff.

One of his weakest points is his insincerity in his friendliness.

Some staff members lauded among Ed's good qualities the very characteristics which others found wanting. Others suggested long lists of his praiseworthy personal characteristics:

I think Ed's respect for the integrity of people—kids and teachers alike—is unique in the school principals that I've worked with. His respect for people is an outstanding characteristic. He has faith that people can work things out themselves and it's OK if they don't come up with the same answers that you come up with.

One thing that stands out is his interest in people as persons. In other words, the academic side of the program is not everything. How people feel about other people, how they are helped to get along, cooperate, and so forth—these things stand high.

He has a really quite relaxed manner most of the time. I don't think there's any time that I've seen him when he was really riled or beside himself and not knowing what's going to happen next. He is an intelligent man. He is usually thinking way ahead of you.

I think that his going to church and being a part of a church body has also given him an added strength in dealing with people and probably given him a lot of insight.

I'm sure Ed is not perfect. Yet I know of no weak points. Ask me after I've taught longer.

Still other staff members attempted to be analytical in their comments:

Mr. Bell is a sensitive person, which is both a weak point and a strong point.

I think he has some little pettinesses, but don't we all. I think he's a little bit what one would term "tightwad." But I think he is an excellent person to work for, extremely understanding and kind. He just has the faults human beings have, and it couldn't be otherwise. I think he's conscientious, a fine man, a devoted husband and certainly a devoted father. And extremely conscientious about his children and about helping children.

If I ever heard of him doing a dishonest thing I'd be very shocked. I wouldn't think it possible for him to do a dishonest thing from what I have observed of him.

If the comments of Ed's staff members do not add much insight into a judgment about his representativeness as a principal, they at least contribute to a developing picture of him as a person. Perhaps teachers are not usually in a position to judge the representativeness of a principal, even though they readily identify traits they do and do not admire in their present administrator, in their former ones, and in their conception of an "ideal" one. I obtained one candid assessment about Ed's representativeness from a professor of educational administration who knew him professionally:

I don't think Ed Bell is very aggressive. He tends to be quiet—maybe even a bit introverted—compared with some of the more outgoing fellows. But he has a wholesome perspective and he's quite sincere.

His school is typical, but it's above average. I'd say he's typical of what I'd call the "more alert breed" of principals.

I was even more encouraged by the observation of one of Ed's fellow principals who said, "I was wondering how you happened to select Ed as your subject. You know, as I got to thinking about it, I thought to myself, you couldn't have picked a better example—he's really typical."

Comment

Through the presentation of perceptions of Ed Bell held by those close to him personally and professionally, this chapter has dealt with two major strands which characterize studies in culture and personality: how Ed Bell is in some ways like no other man; and how he is in some ways like some other men—in this case, other elementary school principals. No personality inventory has been attempted here. I do not find it unsettling to think that the reader may feel uncertainty about Ed's assessment of his personal life and his feelings about being a principal. I feel some uncertainty in this regard myself, and I sense that this may be due to Ed's own ambivalence. At the same time, it does seem apparent that Ed is highly achievement-oriented, a natural consequence of both his personal background and of the prerequisites for upward social mobility characteristic of the society in which his values are so deeply embedded. In the principalship he finds a way to achieve prestige, acceptance, and sufficient ego-gratification to see him through the myriad problems incumbent upon that office that will be evident throughout these pages.

4 / The school and community

About Taft School

Taft School is at 100 Golden Lane, it has 18 rooms. It has a playground with a blacktop and wood shavings in case you fall on something. Taft School is six years old.

From a classroom newspaper

THE PHYSICAL PLANT

When the doors of Taft School were opened in September, 1961, for its first pupils, the building had eight classrooms and an enrollment of 230 children. The next year two more classrooms were constructed, then four more, and finally another four in 1965. When school opened in September, 1966, eighteen classroom teachers, three at each grade level from one to six, were on hand to meet a projected enrollment of almost 500 children. That enrollment projection prepared by the central office proved to be high, an error later attributed to an overestimate of the number of families with school-age children who could afford to live in a newly completed rental-apartment structure. The actual enrollment of 444 pupils on the first day of school climbed during the year to a closing enrollment of 475.

Ed once used the term "conventional" in describing the physical plant of Taft School to a group of visiting principals. The main classroom building was shaped like a giant inverted "F" (see Figure 1 in Chapter 2) with the office and main entrance at its foot and the primary and intermediate grade "wings" each forming one of the arms. Another building immediately adjacent and reached via a covered outside walkway housed a gymnasium, a boiler room, a kitchen, and a multi-purpose room that doubled as the lunchroom at noon and, with its folding benches and tables locked in place along the walls, as an auditorium or recreation area during the rest of the day and on many evenings. An area behind the school provided an ample playground, as shown in Figure 2. However, only a small section of the playground was "blacktopped," and staff members—teachers and custodians alike—complained constantly of schoolroom floors tracked with dirt and mud, especially after a rainy or frosty morning.

To give parents and other visitors some idea of the operating costs of Taft School, Ed once prepared a bulletin board display which showed the projected

66

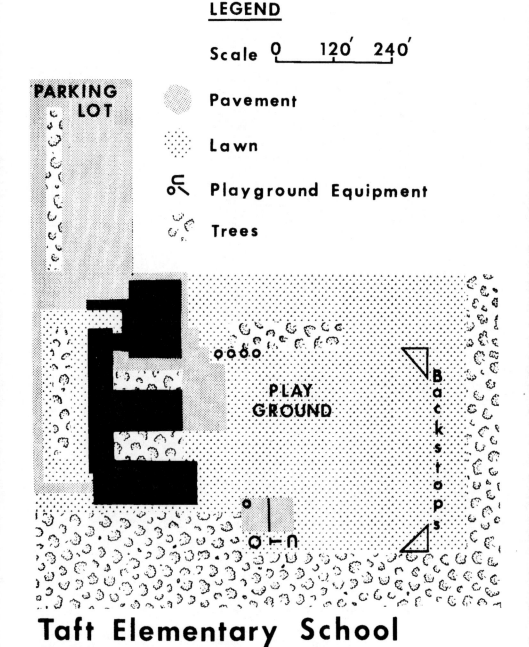

LEGEND

Scale 0   120'   240'

Pavement

Lawn

Playground Equipment

Trees

PARKING LOT

PLAY GROUND

Backstops

Taft Elementary School Buildings & Grounds

Figure 2

operating budget of Taft School for the following school year. He did not provide the grand total of his budget estimate, nor did he give subtotals of major items (the impact of a figure like $200,000 for annual salaries at Taft might well have defeated his intent to enlist voter support), but the estimates regarding operating costs of the physical plant give some idea of its scope:

Custodian's salaries ($6,000; 4,800)	$10,800
Custodial supplies	1,086
Improvement of site	500
Building maintenance	1,736
Heat	2,000
Electricity	2,700
Remodeling	1,109
Water	425
Upkeep of grounds	440

Ed voiced an opinion frequently heard among school administrators regarding the operation of the school plant: "What we need here is a building manager. Someone who takes care of supplies and routine maintenance."

THE STAFF

At the end of every summer vacation each new and returning staff member at Taft School received a copy of the *Teacher Handbook*. Ed had prepared the original handbook years earlier and revised it only cursorily prior to the opening of school each fall. Some sections in the handbook, particularly the section containing the staff roster, showed considerable change from year to year. For example, of the 17 teachers listed in the *Teacher Handbook* in 1964, only 5 were still on the roster three years later. The attrition of the other 70 percent was due to the kinds of changes common to an elementary school: transfers of teachers within the district; teachers being reassigned, promoted, or retired; and, particularly among the younger faculty, teachers moving out of the community or resigning their posts in order to raise a family. Other sections of the handbook remained pretty much intact from year to year. Not a word had been changed for years on the page containing the principal's annual message of welcome to his staff:

Staff Members,

Welcome to the staff of the William Howard Taft School. We trust that you are looking forward to a significant opportunity to help boys and girls make another year of growth in all the areas of their experience which the school program affects.

We will hope to continue a feeling of friendliness and cooperation between the school and the community. We will want to recognize from the beginning that we as a staff are a team, a group which shares its abilities and causes children and adults to feel an equal responsibility to each one. We expect school to be a pleasant place for teachers and pupils as well.

Edward C. Bell
Principal

The full-time faculty at Taft School included a resource teacher and a guidance counsellor in addition to 18 classroom teachers. Part-time professional help was provided by a teacher who supervised two intern (beginning) teachers on a special university teacher training program and by a nurse whose time was divided among three schools. Three specialists visited the school on a regular basis for instruction in remedial reading, speech therapy, and instrumental music. Another special teacher, officially holding the position "Itinerant Teacher of Visually Handicapped Children," worked regularly with a blind pupil who otherwise was a participating member of one classroom. The school also had specialist help available on call from the central office in subject matter fields, in psychological and testing services, and in family problems requiring help from one of two social workers employed by the school district. Noncertified staff members included a secretary, a teacher aide, two custodians, and a kitchen staff of four. This total staff of 35 provided the core of regularly available employees of the school district. The efforts of this staff were augmented by a Bible school teacher who offered religious instruction to Taft pupils on a voluntary basis one hour a week from October through May.[1]

New staff members present at the first opening of school after this study began (i.e., those not at Taft when it had opened the previous September) included nine teachers, the nurse, the secretary, both custodians, and all kitchen staff except the head cook. However, staff change was a more gradual phenomenon than a simple comparison of rosters suggests. Of the nine teachers whose names were new on the opening roster, one had taught at Taft for part of the previous year, two had been at the school as student teachers, and two teachers transferring from other schools in the district had done so in part because of friends already teaching at Taft. Custodial changes had been made during the year rather than at the opening of school. Taft was not considered a school with a high staff turnover in spite of its continually changing roster. The school district boasted an average turnover rate of 14 percent, a rate slightly below the average reported for the state and nation (15–17 percent). Nevertheless, between school district growth and staff turnover, the district's schools absorbed 312 new teachers in 1966–67.

Data provided by 15 of the 18 classroom teachers responding to a staff questionnaire in June, 1967, make it possible to present a brief "profile" of the teaching faculty by describing the range of teacher responses and by identifying the "typical teacher" (modal response category) for a series of demographic questions concerning birthplace, age amount of formal education, and so forth. Such a profile is presented in Table 4–1. The 15 teachers responding included 11 married women, 2 single women, and 2 married men, and thus the profile teacher is referred to below as "she." The problem noted earlier of "systematic bias" in some categories arising from the failure of three teachers to respond to the questionnaire was corrected with supplementary data.

Table 4–1 summarizes many aspects of the typical or profile teacher at Taft School. This "profile" teacher was born and educated within the state. She had

---

[1] Taft School observed a strict and literal separation of church and state in this regard. Although the Bible school teacher herself was at least formally welcomed at school, her instruction was provided in an old converted school bus driven to the school each Monday for the occasion and parked adjacent to but conspicuously off of the school grounds.

TABLE 4–1   THE TAFT SCHOOL TEACHING FACULTY, 1966–1967: A PROFILE[a]

	Range of Responses	Typical Teacher
Birthplace	Same town————East Coast or Canada	Same state
Age	23————58	29 years
Formal education	Bachelor's degree in education————Master's degree plus extended graduate work	Bachelor's degree
Reasons for entering teaching	Income————Altruism	Love children
Professional goal	Stop teaching and raise a family————Become school counsellor	Continue teaching
Number of years in education	1————15	4 years
Number of years at Taft School (including current one)	1————6 (maximum possible)	2 years
Teaching salary	$3,600 (intern)————$8,100	$5,625
Total family income	$5,200 (single)————$21,200 (husband and wife)	$13,000
Family automobiles	1————2	2 automobiles
Dwelling type	Share apartment————Own a home	Purchasing a home ($120/ month payments)
Family size	Single, live with sister————Spouse and three children	Live with spouse; no children

[a] Although the table is based on responses from 15 of the 18 classroom teachers, supplementary data enabled minor corrections to be made so that the profile represents all 18 classroom teachers.

taught a total of four years since receiving her bachelor's degree. For the last two years she had taught at Taft School, and she planned to continue teaching there. She "loves working with children," and she and her husband enjoyed the benefits of a combined income of around $13,000. She and her spouse each had an automobile; they were making payments only on the newer one. They made payments of $120 per month on a home which they were purchasing. They occasionally attended services at their Protestant church but took part in no other formal community organizations. The teacher's nonschool time was taken up with housework and with "outdoor sports and activities," primarily among nonschool associates. Once during the year she and her husband visited in the home of another teacher's family, and once another teacher and her spouse had joined them for an evening of playing bridge.

Although this profile teacher is a statistical creation, the description "fits" at least five teachers at the school. More important, the profile should enable readers to judge the extent to which Taft School is similar to and different from school settings with which they are already familiar. The medians and ranges of teacher responses indicated in Table 4–1 suggest that the faculty of Taft School is similar to many suburban elementary schools throughout the United States.

The teachers at Taft differed markedly in the extent to which they interacted with other teachers at the same grade level, in the same wing, or among the faculty generally. The male teachers, for example, tended to keep to themselves and conducted their classrooms quite independently from the classes of their female colleagues. Teachers at each grade level interacted most frequently with other teachers of the same grade. Differences in schedules and grade levels, rein-. forced by a spatial arrangement that dramatically separated the activities in the primary and upper-grade wings, resulted in a self-consciousness expressed by some teachers that they really did not know their faculty colleagues very well (or as well as they felt they "should").[2] Nevertheless, faculty members appeared unanimous in their positive feeling about the staff as a group. One teacher whose perceptions of the school were greatly influenced by the shortcomings she attributed to its administrator still found words of praise for her colleagues:

> There's so much more openness and sharing and cooperation in this school than in any school I've been in. In a way your first feelings are that somebody has just taken everything away from you and you're all exposed, because of everybody walking through everybody's rooms and saying, "Hey, I like that. Guess I'll do that." But soon you adjust to it. All the teachers in this wing have just been wonderful to me.

Other staff members volunteered glowing accounts of the spirit of mutual dedication and effort which they sensed among the staff:

> The staff is very conscientious, extremely interested in children, happy in what they're doing, and here because they like children and they like to teach. I think it's unusual for a whole staff of eighteen to be that dedicated, comparing it with other places I've been. It shows that they're happy. I think this staff is better prepared, more up-to-date in techniques of teaching and in subject matter than most staffs I've worked with.

> I feel that the staff get along beautifully. It seems to me that the staff communicates and they all work together. This has impressed me in this school. I don't think we have very many petty people here, or *any* for that matter, and this is strange among a bunch of women, isn't it! I haven't seen signs of pettiness. There have been one or two little things, but so slight they're not worth mentioning. I've heard a teacher say, "Well, I want to get in there and get that thing out of the IMC before somebody else does," but this is rare. It would be more likely that she'd say, "I have some of this. You take some. I'll share it with you."

Ed frequently used the term "young" in characterizing the school staff:

> We have a very young staff. The school has been here only six years. Only one of those [teachers] has been here all the time. And she is young at heart.

---

[2] The Staff Farewell Dinner in June provided evidence in this regard. Two of the newer teachers were unable to complete introductions between their husbands and their teacher colleagues because they suddenly realized they did not remember their colleagues' last names.

Comments made at the end of the year by a young teacher who had previously taught in another district revealed a similar enthusiasm toward the dedication and youthful vigor of the Taft faculty, particularly as she compared it with the experience of her former school:

> I think everybody kind of looks amazed around here all the time and wonders, "How can a group of people get along so well with so few gripes." There's very little gossip compared to what I suffered through the year before. There isn't anybody on this staff right now that I could say I really didn't like. I couldn't say that before. I really feel it's a remarkable staff for working together and for getting along together and having fun during the day.
>
> This staff is young in age and young in actions. Progressive. They're really engrossed in children—not just officially, but really engrossed with helping kids. And in compatibility. . . . Maybe one of the reasons we get along so well is because we're all young. Even the older ones are young. I'm not sure that I could converse and carry on a conversation and laugh and be silly with every woman Edna's age or Martha's age. The whole staff really has a sense of humor.

THE TAFT SCHOOL ATTENDANCE AREA

A senior principal attending an evening meeting held at Taft School joked with Ed and a group of fellow administrators, "Things haven't changed much out here. Today it's just like it always was—a bunch of orchards full of nuts." Such levity was reserved for within-group banter. Principals occasionally engaged in such humor when referring to the school neighborhoods of their colleagues, but since Ed, like several other principals, both lived and worked on the Taft School side of town, he would probably not have made such a joke himself. The opinions he *did* express about the Taft neighborhood varied in formality and enthusiasm depending on who he was addressing, which parents he was thinking about, and the recent events in school-neighborhood relations that had probably prompted the discussion in the first place.

Ed's most succinct and formal statement about the Taft attendance area was a one-paragraph description he had prepared for the *Teacher Handbook* several years before:

> Ours is a new community; most of the homes have been built during the last seven or eight years. Community spirit is slowly developing. A large percent of the homes are in the medium price range, some are new, moderately priced homes, and a few others are among the nicest homes in town. The community is composed mostly of persons involved in some type of skilled labor, or in sales work. There are a few professional persons and some mill workers. The community atmosphere is generally favorable for a good school situation. Teachers are encouraged to get acquainted with the community and its resources.

Ed distinguished among the different subneighborhoods within the attendance area according to his estimate of the average cost of houses there. His criterion is implicit in the statement above; he made it quite explicit whenever he had the opportunity to elaborate on his remarks to an interested fellow educator. One visitor to Taft, himself a former principal, gained the impression that Ed was "overly impressed" with the local neighborhood, especially with the small El Dorado area in which the most expensive homes in the attendance area were located:

> Ed Bell seemed impressed with the community in which his school was located. He spoke about unfortunate building zones [zoning laws] in the community which allowed the contractors to build what would be shacks in no time at all, and about the problems of the effect of these shacks on property valuation in general.
> From the community map in his office he could identify the homes in the El Dorado area and who lived in most of them, whether they had students in school or not. He took much pride in this area of his community.

Ed described the socio-economic range of families in the community as follows:

Lowest: Welfare, 10 children in one house.
Average: $16,000 home, 3 children, sales representative or semiskilled.
Highest: Doctor (general practitioner), $50,000 house, 2 cars.

On one wall of his office Ed had three maps of the attendance area: a somewhat outdated map of the entire school district (Taft School was indicated only as a proposed school site), a county surveyor's map showing all the streets and the boundaries of the present attendance area, and an aerial photograph of part of the attendance area given to him by a professional photographer whose children attended the school. The county surveyor's map provided the basic plan from which Figure 3 was prepared.[3]

To obtain a systematic account of how Ed Bell viewed the various subareas which comprised the Taft School neighborhood, I suggested that I make a tape recording of his description of the neighborhood as we drove through it in my automobile. We invited three teachers new to the school to accompany us one afternoon in October. (I hoped that by directing his remarks to new teachers Ed would repeat observations which he had already made to me in the course of earlier conversations.) The tour began, at Ed's suggestion, with a drive along Skinner and Elm Avenues (Zone 2). Our route is noted below by the use of street names and zone numbers which appear on the map.

ED: A fellow by the name of Kent came in here about five years ago and bought this nice land. He chucked as many houses on it as he could possibly get. As you can see, there is no room to park your car. They put in three bedrooms and a bath in most of them and a real small kitchen and small living space and no family space.

TEACHER: It's like postwar housing.

ED: They were selling these for less than $12,000 when it took about $18,000 to buy one that was really adequate for a family. There are some nice fami-

---

[3] The legend and the "zones" were not part of the original map. The map was prepared especially for this study and was based on original fieldwork conducted by my research assistant, John A. Olson, in order to provide a graphic representation of the attendance area and of its various socio-economic components. Olson has reported elsewhere on the general use of maps for organizing information about a school's attendance area (Olson 1969) and specifically on the Taft School attendance area viewed as an ecological unit and studied from the "outside" (Olson 1970) to complement the view presented here of the community as perceived by the principal and school staff.

TAFT ELEMENTARY SCHOOL ATTENDANCE AREA

scale

0   400' 800'

legend

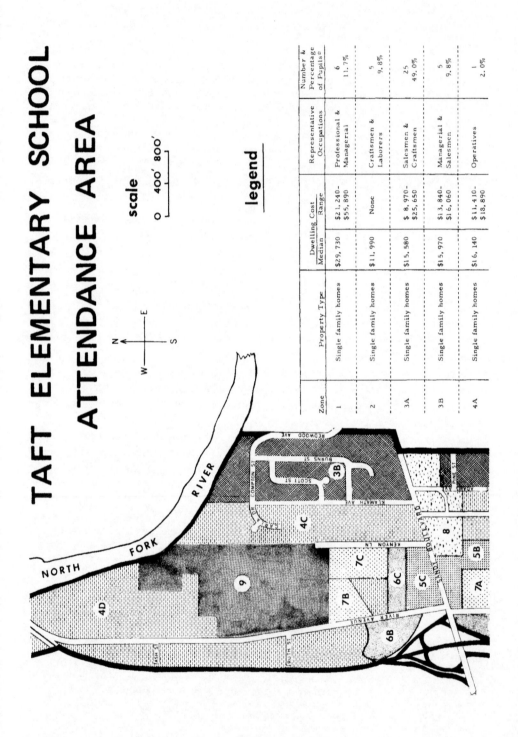

Zone	Property Type	Dwelling Cost Median	Dwelling Cost Range	Representative Occupations	Number & Percentage of Pupils*
1	Single family homes	$29,730	$21,240–$55,890	Professional & Managerial	6 — 11.7%
2	Single family homes	$11,990	None	Craftsmen & Laborers	5 — 9.8%
3A	Single family homes	$15,580	$ 8,970–$25,650	Salesmen & Craftsmen	25 — 49.0%
3B	Single family homes	$15,970	$13,840–$16,060	Managerial & Salesmen	5 — 9.8%
4A	Single family homes	$16,140	$11,410–$18,890	Operatives	1 — 2.0%

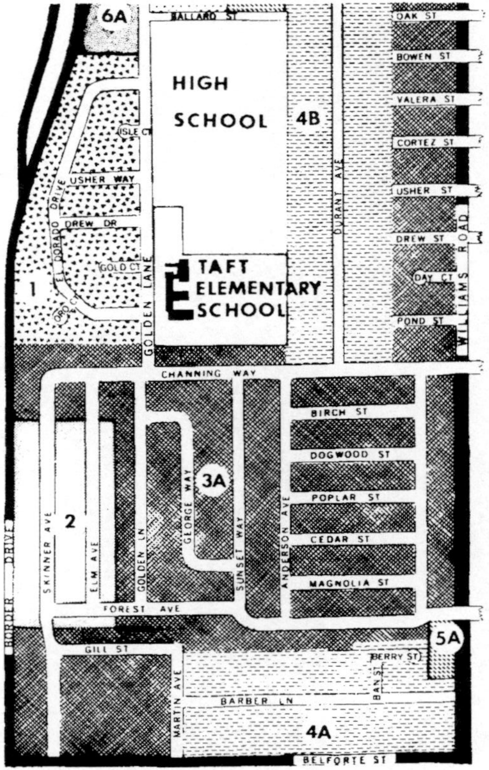

4B	Single family homes	$12,470	$ 9,790- $16,210	Salesman	3 5.9%
4C 4D	Single family homes	$10,230	$ 9,550- $11,500	Foremen & Farmers	
5A	Small shopping center				
5B	Large shopping center National chain stores				
5C	Large shopping center Small chain stores - mostly retail				
6A 6B 6C	Undeveloped com- mercial property				
7A	48 units/rental apts.		$130-$140 per month 1-2 bdrms.	Salesman	3 5.9%
7B 7C	78 units/rental apts. 44 units/rental apts.		$110-$150 per month 1-2 bdrms.	Foremen & Students	
8	Single family rentals Potential commercial & apartments			Laborers	3 5.9%
9	City sewage processing plant				

[*] Elementary school pupils from 10% sample of attendance area.

Figure 3

lies in this area, though. This street [Elm] is so narrow there's not even any place to play. I think people get an awful lot of cabin fever here, especially in the winter time. Mothers live too close to their neighbors. It seems to me they're just making money enough to make the payments, and they don't have money to get out. Well, that isn't all it takes to get out, but it helps. It shows up on the kids.

TEACHER: Yes. You can sense that they are living too close to their neighbors, too.

[We drove to Anderson Avenue, Zone 3A]

TEACHER: Now these are more medium priced. They're not cheap.

ED: Yes. These are medium priced.

[We continued along Durant Avenue, Zone 4B, behind the school district property.]

ED: This is an older area. These lots are all one acre. I suppose the day may come when the taxes and the demand will get such that some of these old time kind of "country people" will have to give up their acre and build on the backs of them.

. . . Here's a little Church of Christ. We have the Lutheran Church over here to our right. Just across the road from the Lutheran Church is the Methodist Church. I suppose that those two probably serve a larger number of our families as far as churches are concerned. And quite a few of them are Episcopal and go to St. Marks Episcopal up on Sandy Boulevard.

[We approached Sandy Boulevard and Zone 8.]

ED: You hear about kids who live on Adams. Well, this [a row of small ground-level apartments] is part of the Adams Courts. These are pretty small and pretty expensive, so you get families that are—well, you have to earn pretty good money to be able to pay $120–125 a month rent.

TEACHER: For that?!

ED: Yes. There are 20 of those units. They're furnished.

TEACHER: You're kidding?

ED: Now this [we approached a large old one-story multiple-family rental unit of light frame construction located right at the boulevard] is the Sandy Boulevard Gables. They are pretty poor, but they are better than they were a few years ago. These are pretty common, but it's surprising, you get fellows like the Corcorans who come in here. They've lived here several years and they just continue to stay on. This is kind of a way of life for them, apparently.

[We crossed busy Sandy Boulevard onto Klamath Avenue and drove through Zone 3B.]

TEACHER: These are pretty nice little houses along here.

ED: Yes, these are. But they are rather poorly constructed.

TEACHER: Yeah, lots of times that's the way it is. They look nice but they don't last long.

ED: Happy Homes, Incorporated, built these. My experience with them is that they tend to put them together very hastily. I looked at one of their cheaper ones when they were opening here. I think they run about $14,000, so I would guess there are some $20,000 homes here.

TEACHER: Those two-story ones?

ED: Yes, those. Do any of you know the Upington family? Well, they moved over to this area. They did like so many of our families have done in the last few years. They moved up from those moderately-priced houses [of Zone 2 and 3A] to these larger, newer homes [of Zone 3B].

[We returned to Sandy Boulevard, passing the shopping center, 5C, and turning onto River Avenue, adjacent to a series of multiunit dwellings, some still under construction, in Zones 7B and 7C.]

ED: You see all these apartments back in here. I think there's 150 units. Yet we only get about three families from here. This is one reason we're getting along as well as we are. You see, they projected us at 496 [pupils], and we're probably never going to make it. We're about 440 now. No one can be sure how many we are going to get out of these places. I understand that those places on the end with the fireplaces rent for $145. They're partially furnished.

TEACHER: Where does Vance [a newly-arrived problem boy] live? Doesn't he live out this way? [We approached the river, leaving the built-up areas behind.]

ED: I'll show you in a moment. This "mansion" on the left is where he lives. [The house is an unpainted two-story one of light wood frame construction, not in good repair. One old car is parked in front.]

TEACHER: Oh, you're kidding!

ED: There's no heat in that.

TEACHER: Is that right?

ED: See the dirty clothes piled against the window there and the window broken out?

TEACHER: And there's no heat.

ED: No.

TEACHER: What do they do in the winter when it's cold?

ED: Stay in bed. When our social worker was in there the other day, the kids had the oven on high and they were running around in all states of dress and undress. The mother was undressed.

TEACHER: Oh, my!

[We returned via River Avenue to Sandy Boulevard at its intersection with the freeway.]

TEACHER: Is Dr. Dale on this street?

ED: No. The Dales live over in that nice part.

ED: One reason this corner [Zone 6A, 6B, next to freeway] hasn't developed is because of the projected overpass. I noticed that the school board is fussing about the road that's going to come off that overpass. It will come right along the east side of the high school lot. I have a feeling our access will be right over Border Drive. Don't hold your breath for that, though. Here's a new lane that's going in [along Sandy Boulevard, Zone 5C]. There's talk that they are going to put a bank in this area somewhere. I'm sure looking forward to that day. [The bank opened 18 months later.] This shopping center has been here about six years. When Taft School began in the fall of 1961, this was just an open field. There were a few houses scattered along, but this shopping center was just an open field.

[We crossed Sandy Boulevard and onto El Dorado Drive, Zone 1.]

ED: This whole Taft area just opened up when I was first here. Golden Lane was just a little road they drove tractors on down through the fields; no houses, no schools. Then three builders came up here and bought this land [all of Zone 1 on the map]. El Dorado Developers, they called themselves. They made it an exclusive area. You couldn't build in here unless you built according to their specifications. It was part of the agreement that they determined the cost of your house and approved the plans. They built many of the houses themselves, but not all of them.

There are a lot of people, including the assistant superintendent, who, when they think of Taft School, or used to at least, think mostly of these nice $30,000–40,000 homes. [The assistant superintendent's brother was one of the original builders who developed the El Dorado area.] But it is a great deal more than that, as I'm sure you've seen by looking at these kids.

TEACHER: Yes. I went through my records the other day, and I actually have only four or five at the most whose fathers are white collar workers.

ED [calling attention to a large home on El Dorado Drive]:   This house has five baths.

TEACHER: Wow!

TEACHER: This gray one?

ED: Yes. The father works in construction, the mother is a daughter of the former president of the Hilldale Bank. I believe that's the way it goes. Anyway they've separated since they built that house. I estimated the cost at $80,000. That's Dr. Meheren's home, right in back of it. And this is where Dr. Dale lives, in the story-and-a-half on the right. One of the El Dorado Developers built the one next to it. He had it priced at $41,000. He didn't get it sold, so he moved into it. They lived there awhile and then he built another one. He moved over there then and sold this one to the von Brockmeiers. Before they moved in there, they put in a swimming pool and a sprinkler system that cost up in the thousands of dollars.

TEACHER: Ummmmm.

ED: So, I estimate this is close to a $50,000 home.

Well, that's about the tour. As you see, we get all the way from expensive ones owned by the doctors to the old places like where the Corcorans live where the rents are about $85 a month and the floors are all buckled.

TEACHER: And then Vance's place. It would take something to live in that place, I would think.

ANOTHER TEACHER: It makes you wonder what you could do instead of sending them home, doesn't it?

ED: Yes, it sure does. That's only the last resort, I assure you.

Except for the comments reported above and made especially for the occasion, Ed customarily referred to different locations within the school attendance area by street names rather than by areas (for example, "They live over on Magnolia."). During the long period of the fieldwork Ed spoke of specific families (or, more often, of specific mothers) on many occasions, but not of entire neighborhoods. He seemed to keep a current mental roster of parents or groups of neighbors who were particularly pro- or antischool (or principal) at any given moment.

Although Ed made few sweeping statements about the school attendance area, the comments which I did record run a wide but rather predictable gamut from hope to despair. Elementary school principals appear universally to be "public relations" conscious, although they are not universally successful in doing much about public relations problems when they recognize them. Ed's approach to community relations rested on the assumption that, like most other school problems, the serious ones would eventually find their way to him as long as he was accessible. As he explained to one parent (see Chapter 6), "I'm not attempting to take the temperature of the community, but the door and the phone lines are always open." At times, however, and particularly during the spring when administrators throughout the school district grew especially public minded because of the impending annual school budget election, he expressed a need to pursue a more aggressive information program:

We ought to be bringing parents along with us on how we believe in what we are doing and are doing it with a purpose. Some of them say they are going to pack up, sell their houses, and move out of the Taft area because they don't go along with us. But others have seen that we are getting results.

Anticipating a difficult time in getting the school budget passed in 1967, the central administration urged principals to pursue some means to alert voters in each school neighborhood, and particularly parents of school children, to the good job the schools were doing. Ed decided to hold a series of evening discussions at school, inviting a different group of parents for each discussion. Anticipating the first such meeting, he told the counsellor, "My main trouble will be keeping my mouth shut and listening. I have so many things to tell them about education." The first group of adults which Ed decided to invite for an evening chat were the parents of eight families in the area designated on the map as Zone 3B, "because they live the farthest from school."

The response to his invitation was a meeting attended by only three parents. Ed dropped plans for calling any further meetings: "It's not worth the time and effort. I'll chalk that one up to experience and not do it any more." Two months later, perhaps with that disappointment still on his mind, he commented one day that the school should be left alone to perform its role:

> I get pretty annoyed by the idea expressed that because a person has a child in school he is an expert about education. The learning process is so complex that parents should leave it up to school people and have confidence in them.

At times the views Ed expressed laid the school's problems directly back on the parents. "We don't meet the needs of children because parents don't want them to be what they are. They want them to be lawyers and doctors." Ed felt that for many parents who were themselves upwardly mobile, this was a serious concern: "The farther up the social ladder the parents have come, the harder it is for them. This is a problem for a lot of people in the Taft area."

At least three times during the year Ed received word of activity in different parts of the attendance area where a parent (mother) had become sufficiently disgruntled to start a campaign to "do something about Taft school" by doing something about its principal. The first occasion was in November. One mother with a child in Mrs. Skirmish's second grade had become annoyed with the newly inaugurated early-late reading program in the primary grades. Finding little satisfaction in talking to Ed, she made two calls to the central office to complain to Dr. Carolyn Goddard, the Director of Elementary Education. Dr. Goodard finally suggested that the mother put her complaints in writing. The mother, in turn, promised not only to do that but also to "get some more names" of other dissatisfied parents. Ed predicted (correctly) that the letter would never be written—he had dealt with the same parent on other occasions—but her complaint gave him pause nonetheless: "I wonder why some people always have to be against the schools. Her family sees the schools on one side, the community on the other."

A second occasion of organized dissatisfaction occurred the following month. Another incident in Mrs. Skirmish's room (to be discussed in Chapter 9) riled a parent who had frequently expressed dissatisfaction with Taft School in recent years. As Ed understood it, the mother, Mrs. North, had been telephoning other parents to arrange refreshments for a classroom Christmas party in her official capacity as "Room Mother," and had used the occasion to learn whether other parents knew about the incident or were interested in hearing her views on it. She was successful in rousing one set of parents to join her in an immediate confrontation at school. The purpose of their unscheduled visit must have been quite apparent to Ed, for he later recounted that when he looked out of his office window and saw the three parents get out of one car in the parking lot and head for his office, he said to himself, "Oh, oh. Here comes a delegation." In private, Ed's opinion was, "I'd like Susan North to know that if she's going to go about stirring things up in the neighborhood, she's going to have to answer to me." In a subsequent telephone call he told her:

> Until we can talk again, I'd like you to do two things. Jot down the things you are concerned about. And I'd like you not to say anything to anyone else about it. You and I should have been talking about this all along. I find you have been talking to at least three other people.

Other instances of organized dissatisfaction did not come to such a climax as this one. In April, the PTA president told Ed she felt she should warn him that there was "a petition going around the neighborhood." She declined to say who had been active in circulating it, but she did suggest the name of one mother who had "kicked them off her place" whom he might talk to. Ed told her he would not bother. If he did eventually learn who had circulated the petition, he never mentioned the incident again. He did have his suspicions, however. The day before he heard of the petition, he had been talking about Taft School's antagonists, past and present, and had identified one person whom he felt was "tops right now." On still another occasion Ed remarked, but without further explanation, "Someone out here has a pipeline to a board member."

Ed did not usually pursue such extreme courses as those presented above—acting as though he could operate the school independently from the parents, or dealing with parents on a threat-counter-threat basis. During the relatively rare times when his faith and optimism ran short, he was more apt to give indications of personal disappointment, resignation, or perhaps futility. Summarizing a day when several incidents had suggested more antagonism than support for schools on the part of both the Taft attendance area and the community-at-large, Ed said, "I just figure, 'What the hell's the use?'"

The annual school budget election seemed to invoke an attitude of resignation on Ed's part, for he considered a vote against the budget to be a vote against the schools, and he interpreted the failure of a Taft parent to vote in a budget election as an unexcusable lack of support for public education. During the two years of this study, budget elections did fail at Taft School and on the Taft School "side of town" just as they were doing elsewhere throughout the state and nation in what was termed a "taxpayers' revolt." After the polls closed at Taft School on one election night, Ed checked the voter list to see which parents had shown enough interest in the schools to come to the polls:

> How much you've helped the kids doesn't seem to matter. Here's the Vincents, who get so much special help here. Or here's the Lampley boy with brain damage—the teacher has done a remarkable job, but the mother didn't bother to vote. The PTA president didn't vote. One of the education professors over at the college finally got registered but he didn't vote.

At the time of the second budget election attempt (it took three attempts to get it passed that year) Ed expressed this frustration during a telephone conversation with the assistant superintendent:

> The thing that just depresses me no end is that we work as hard as we can to develop the best possible program and then have to expose it to people who don't even know who the superintendent of schools is or that we have a [PTA-run] kindergarten program.
> Dr. Boggs told some of us the other day that we are the only state in the union that has to go through this [school budget election] every year. The trampling of the swine! That's the way I feel about it this morning.

The Attendance Area as Teachers Saw It

The teachers at Taft School usually restricted their comments about the homes and backgrounds of their pupils to specific families within the Taft area rather than making generalizations about the entire community. No one spoke disparagingly of any neighborhood area. Only two households of particularly depressed economic circumstances were singled out for prolonged discussion during the year.

Three staff members lived within the school's attendance area, but none of them had children of elementary school age. No classroom teacher lived in the area; the teachers' knowledge of the immediate community was based on limited opportunities for observation (for example, driving to and from school), for meeting with parents at school, and for conversations held with fellow teachers and with Ed. They had scant information about the extent of social interaction in the neighborhood, although they heard occasional suggestions that what went on at school received critical attention and review. One new teacher observed:

> I guess we get talked about more than we realize. One mother said at the Open House, "Well, I guess you're all right. The neighbors say you are."

Whether or not neighborhood women met in regular kaffeeklatches, the teachers were not sure, although one senior teacher felt certain that on at least one street (Anderson) neighborhood gossip was rampant.[4]

The questionnaire presented to the teachers at the end of the school year asked them to describe the socio-economic range of the community as represented by the pupils in their classrooms. Instructions were to identify the most representative family for each of three categories: highest, lowest, and average, in terms of occupation, estimated income, kind and place of dwelling, and parent's education. Several teachers commented that they did not have adequate or accurate information on which to base their answers. One teacher told me, "I'm having trouble estimating socio-economic levels. The parents of kids who live on El Dorado Drive only had a couple of years of college; the people who have the most education are the teachers, and they live in the poor area."

---

[4] In his independent study of the Taft neighborhood, Olson found only one group of women who reported meeting together regularly every morning in the manner characteristic of a kaffeeklatch. The group lived at the end of Golden Avenue (Zone 3A). Olson described the group as "antischool." His general impression from accounts given during interviews was that little house-to-house interaction occurred throughout most of the school attendance area (John Olson, personal communication).

TABLE 4–2   COMPARISON OF ESTIMATES MADE BY NINE TAFT SCHOOL TEACHERS OF THE INCOME AND OCCUPATIONAL RANGE (LOWEST, AVERAGE, AND HIGHEST) REPRESENTED BY PUPILS IN THEIR CLASSROOM.[a]

Estimated Family Income

Teacher	Amount Unspecified (Relief, Welfare, etc.) 1000	3000	6000	10,000	15,000	20,000	30,000	40,000
1	(preacher) 1000	4000 truckdriver			? (business manager)			
2		(disability) 3000	Combined income		?			
3	(occasional employment) ?	3000		10,000		(lawyer) 20,000		
4	(unemployed) ?		Telephone company	10,000 Combined income		? (lumber broker)		
5			(welder) 8000			(manager) 25,000		
6	(welfare) ?		6400 millworker	salesman		(sales representative) 25,000		
7		(millworker) 6000	railroad	10,000			(M.D.) 30,000	
8		(millworker) 4200	6000					(M.D.) 40,000
9	(on relief) ?		6000					(mill owner) 40,000

[a] The data are presented here as given by each teacher. Dotted lines represent estimates based on partial information provided. The purpose of the table is to represent graphically differences in teacher perceptions of the socio-economic range extant in the attendance area.

Nine teachers provided sufficient socio-economic data to allow for the comparison of occupations and estimates of annual income provided in Table 4-2. Differences evident in the socio-economic range reported by these teachers reflected both real socio-economic differences among pupils from one classroom to the next and differences in teacher perceptions. Only one teacher systematically provided all the data suggested (occupation, income, type and location of dwelling, and education) for a representative family in each of the three categories. Teachers who reported data for only one or two categories were more inclined to report on "highest" families; data were omitted almost three times as often for "lowest" families as for "highest" ones. In describing the lowest socio-economic families, teachers were sparing in their judgments ("lives in rental motel," "poorly clothed children," "lives at Sandy Gables Apartments," "very small home"). Their superlatives were reserved for life on El Dorado: "large modern home," "best neighborhood," "cultured family," "excellent home environment," "mansion." Teacher estimates of the educational attainment of parents showed remarkable similarity in estimating parents in "lowest" families at less than high school education, "average" parents as having graduated from high school, and "highest" families having at least one parent who had graduated from college. Among the 13 teachers who described "highest" families, 3 teachers named families of medical doctors. One teacher's description of a "highest" family described the father as "a physician with 25 years formal education."

THE COMMUNITY AND THE SCHOOL DISTRICT

The City

The swath cut through the old orchards where Taft School now stands was only one of the broad ribbons of new development radiating outward from the center of the city of Columbia, a robust "middle-sized" American city experiencing its part in the development of the Pacific Northwest. The old road paralleling the North Fork River had provided a natural path for urban expansion. The growing edges of suburban housing-tract developments and the commercial "strip" along Sandy Boulevard had already moved beyond Taft School. The Taft neighborhood was experiencing problems it had not faced before—traffic congestion on no-longer-adequate arterial routes, actual and anticipated commercial development (rental apartments as well as businesses) along or near the major boulevard, and an increasing turnover rate in less expensive tract homes and in rental apartments (Olson 1969, 1970). Minutes away on a new freeway, groundbreaking for a 15 million dollar shopping center marked the coming of age of the Taft side of town and signaled the end of an era for complacent downtown merchants. Yet city boundaries were expanding slowly, and the Taft attendance area remained totally outside the city limits in an as-yet-unincorporated area under county jurisdiction.

Periodically the school district had published brochures designed to attract teachers to Columbia in order to keep up with a constantly increasing student population already exceeding 20,000 pupils in grades one to twelve. A recent brochure portrayed the city and vicinity in glowing terms:

> . . . a busy, thriving city, full of activity in lumbering, manufacturing, and agriculture.
> . . . population is nearly 80,000 and it has one of the highest growing rates of any city on the West Coast.
> . . . famous for its mild weather, flowers and fruits, and various recreational opportunities.
> . . . an excellent place to bring up children in a wholesome, cultural atmosphere.
> . . . a variety of sports such as golfing, swimming, boating, mountain climbing, camping, hunting, fishing, and skiing are available within easy driving distance.

Generally speaking, the school people liked the community in which they lived and, in turn, felt that they were providing their community with an excellent school system. Teachers who had taught elsewhere made comparisons favorable to Columbia's schools. The elementary school principals, through association with colleagues in other districts within the county and region, constantly expressed preferences for working in their own district. The superintendent of schools was willing to put the district on the line nationally, although in the taxpayer-conscious times of the late '60s, he never missed an opportunity to point out that Columbia's excellent educational system was among the best without being among the costliest: "We're in the upper 10 percent of school districts in the quality of our program—the upper 25 percent in terms of our [per-pupil] expenditure."

The School District

The school district of any city can be viewed as a community within a community. In the case of the Columbia Unified School District, the school district's boundaries exceeded the city limits in all directions, and the school district actually provided services and a commonality of interest to a far larger "community" than the city itself, a characteristic which may be common in areas where the consolidation of small adjacent school districts moves ahead of slowly expanding city limits. Full-time employees of the school district (over 1800) accounted for more than three times the number of employees of the city government.

In terms of the organization of the human beings associated with it, a school district may be thought of as a collectivity of interrelated yet distinct and distinguishable formal systems, further criss-crossed by an intricate network of informal interpersonal systems. It is useful here to identify and contrast two formal subsystems, one encompassing a transient population of pupils, the other encompassing a permanent population of school employees, and to recognize that a principal like Ed Bell interacts with the former system and within the latter one.

Pupils, in their formal subsystem, were organized strictly on an age-graded basis. As six-year olds, they began their participation in their system by forming a new "class" at one of the school district's 29 elementary schools. After six years, they transferred to one of nine junior high schools; three years later they transferred again to one of four high schools to complete grades ten, eleven, and twelve. The graduates of an elementary or junior high school class customarily proceeded together to the next school on the educational ladder.

The other formal subsystem within the school district, that of its employees, was organized on a totally different basis from the pupil system and was designed to accomplish totally different purposes. The pupil system minimized status differences. It was designed to facilitate movement upward through the system without conferring any change of status other than longevity. The employee system, a strict line-staff organization, was designed to maximize differences by identifying each individual's place within a clearly established hierarchy. The locus of the organizational authority was in the central school district office. As far as the rest of the school district's employees were concerned, the ultimate authority within the system resided in the office and person of the Superintendent of Schools. What transpired between superintendent and school board was, literally, his problem. What happened between him and all other employees of the district was theirs.

The administrative organization of the school district placed each principal subordinate to either the Director of Elementary School Education or the Director of Secondary School Education. Each of these directors was in turn responsible to the Assistant Superintendent of Schools for some matters and ultimately to the Superintendent for all matters. Other key central office personnel included a group of other directors (for example, Budget, School Plant, Personnel, Pupil Personnel Services) collectively known as the superintendent's "cabinet."

For administrative purposes each high school, with its feeder schools at the elementary and junior high school levels, was constituted as an administrative unit. The principals of all schools within that unit met together on a regular basis with the superintendent or members of the central office staff. Except for these monthly administrative meetings or a few meetings attended by all administrators, the formal organization of the employees fostered little interaction among those who taught, supervised, or serviced different age-graded groups. As far as working with principals at the other levels, Ed's view seemed to be widely shared among his fellow elementary school principals:

> I haven't seemed to have much in common with them. Even the junior high principals seem to be organization men. They work with classes and schedules, but they don't seem very interested in what goes on in their classrooms.

The formal line-staff organization of the school district, with its clear-cut statuses, procedures, and channels of communication, was interlaced with communication networks established on other bases, sometimes totally independent of the formal organization. These interpersonal networks, comprising what may be called the "informal" system of an institution, provide another dimension for viewing Taft School.

The label of informal system may be misleading for describing the kind and extent of communication networks which linked individuals and individual schools within the district. Kinship ties, for example, provided many communication links between schools and between the formal subsystems of pupils and teachers, and such links are "informal" only from the point of view of the institution, not from the individuals who people it. Taft School was linked through a variety of kinship ties to a number of different schools and positions within the district and also to other school districts. For example, both male classroom teachers had wives who taught at other elementary schools within the district. Four of the women teachers had husbands who were teachers, two who taught at high schools within the district, two who taught in neighboring districts. The sister of another teacher taught at the school where Ed's colleague Bill St. Claire was principal. The secretary's husband taught in a junior high school nearby. The husband of another teacher worked for the district's maintenance department. For several years previous to this study, kinship ties had also linked the Taft faculty directly to two of Ed's peers among the elementary school principals. One of Ed's former teachers was the wife of a principal. Another former teacher was the brother-in-law of a principal who resided within the Taft attendance area. That principal was thus linked to Taft school as one of Ed's fellow administrators, as an in-law relative of a faculty member, and as the father of pupils attending Taft.

Other formal and informal ties, based on participation in community organizations, on formal activities related directly to the school district (for example, the local teacher organization, school district workshops and committees), and on friendships resulting from previous assignments at other schools, created additional interpersonal networks linking Taft School with the rest of the district. Two aspects of school district policy served to increase the extent of the informal networks linking schools. First, a policy had recently been initiated of moving elementary school principals to different schools after they had served at one school for a long (but unspecified) period of time. Several principals had recently been reassigned under this policy. Each administrative reshuffle had a subsequent ripple effect on teacher transfers, particularly among teachers who had been reluctant to leave a school under a satisfactory administration but who had other reasons for transferring when faced with the uncertainty of a new regime. The other factor was related to the steady population increase in the community and the related increase in the number of schools. Experienced principals were customarily assigned to open new schools. Such assignments were made during the spring to allow a principal time to oversee the final preparations for staffing and stocking the new school. Principals transferred to new schools were also allowed to "take" teachers with them and to recruit experienced teachers within the district so that new schools would not be staffed completely with young and inexperienced people. Ed had been permitted to "take" one upper-grade teacher and one lower-grade teacher when he originally staffed Taft School. Thus he moved into his school with what has been likened in administration to an "extended professional family" (Carlson 1962:50) which immediately enveloped the new school into an existing communication network.

Ten members of the Taft faculty were personally linked both to the formal employee subsystem through their immediate participation in it and to the pupil subsystem through their school age children's attendance at other schools within the district. Through dual roles as contributors to and consumers of the school district's educative efforts, these staff members extended the communication network among schools as they assumed roles as parents vis-à-vis the teachers at other schools. One person on Ed's staff vividly illustrated the overlap of commitments. She was a full-time faculty member at Taft and the mother of three children who all happened to be attending different schools. During a discussion about the one organization common to both roles, she recalled: "Last year I had four PTAs."

Comment

From its conventional building plan and its young and predominantly female staff to the predominantly lower-middle class community and the predominantly female clientele of housewives and mothers it served, Taft School was remarkably like many suburban elementary schools throughout the United States. The emphasis in this chapter has been on the attendance area as perceived by school personnel. In a fashion that might be expected among an occupational group that recruits heavily from the lower middle classes, Ed and his fellow educators appeared to be especially conscious of one small "higher-class" neighborhood area that apparently contributed to the social status of the school community far in excess to its proportional contribution (less than 12 percent) to the pupil population.

In describing Taft School's community, I have pointed out that from the cultural anthropologist's perspective, school people tend in their professional lives to serve one community—the geographical one of the attendance area—but to participate more fully in a different community, the cultural subsystem comprised of their fellow educators. This is especially true for administrators because of the ease with which they can circulate throughout a school district in person and by telephone among their colleagues. Although educators like to think of themselves as working closely with the community they serve, the anthropologist finds it equally useful to look at the educator subculture as a relatively closed one, and to view attempts to link school and community as instances of culture contact (see Landes 1965). Often such instances can be marked for their rarity and, from an observer's point of view, for their lack of success. Some of Ed's difficulties in this regard have already been described. The two chapters that follow include further illustrations contrasting the sense of common purpose shared within the educator subculture and the difficulty of communicating that purpose to the community-at-large, a group which educators usually refer to globally as "laymen."

5 / What a principal does: formal encounters

The greatest part of a principal's time is spent in an almost endless series of encounters, from the moment he arrives at school until the moment he leaves. Most of these encounters are face-to-face, tending to keep the principalship a highly personal role. Electronic devices, including not only the telephone but the "intercom" systems widely prevalent in public schools, eliminate this face-to-face aspect of some encounters (about 10 percent of Ed's total time at school was spent in talking on the telephone or the intercom), but even these transactions tend to be held between persons frequently in face-to-face encounters at other times during the day.

In some contexts the term "encounters" is taken to suggest a chance or unexpected meeting, while in others (see Goffman 1961:17–18) it is restricted in definition to include only those interactions in which the participants can engage in an "eye-to-eye ecological huddle." I have employed the term in broader fashion to include Ed's participation in any significant interactive setting (see Goldschmidt 1972), whether as intimate as a private conversation or as impersonal as attending a meeting of the school board or PTA.

During my observations at school I faced the problem of attempting to sort out the multifarious circumstances under which Ed conducted school business, for sometimes in the course of a few moments he had engaged in a series of brief dialogues with several people or had discussed a varied set of topics with one person ranging from personal concern for a sick family member to next year's teaching assignment. This was particularly true of his first few minutes at school in the morning, but was also likely to happen anytime he was "free" and readily accessible (for example, at a coffee break or at lunch in the teachers' room). When I began the "time and motion" study, however, I felt it would be useful to make some distinction among the types of interactions in which Ed engaged. At least three categories of face-to-face encounters seemed warranted by my observations: prearranged meetings; deliberate but not prearranged meetings; and casual or chance encounters. The distribution of Ed's time among these three categories of encounters, as well as the distribution of the time he spent talking to others by means of the telephone or intercom and the time he spent in solitary activities, are provided in Table 5–1.

The first type of encounter, "prearranged meeting or conference," includes not

TABLE 5–1   DISTRIBUTION OF THE PRINCIPAL'S TIME DURING AN "AVERAGE"
SCHOOL DAY, 8:00 A.M.–5:00 P.M. (BASED ON A SAMPLE OF 12
2-HOUR PERIODS OF OBSERVATION DURING A TWO-WEEK PERIOD)

Activity of Principal	Observed Day-to-Day Range (in Percentages)	Percent of Time in an "Average" Day
Prearranged meeting or conference	13–35	26
Deliberate but not prearranged encounter	24–29	25
Casual or chance encounter	10–28	15
Telephoning	7–10	9
Talking on intercom	.6–1.5	1
Alone and stationary (e.g., working in his office)	13–24	15
Alone and enroute (e.g., going to a meeting, walking down the hall)	7–14	9
TOTAL		100

only formally announced meetings (for example, faculty meetings, conferences with parents, meetings held at other schools or at the central office) but also less formal but nevertheless prearranged meetings such as seeing a group of pupils "immediately after lunch." During the period of the time-and-motion study, Ed spent one-fourth of his average day attending formally scheduled meetings. In terms of my observations throughout the fieldwork, this seems not only a reasonable but perhaps even a modest estimate of the time he typically spent in such meetings. The time-and-motion data are based on daytime hours only, from 8 A.M. to 5 P.M.. Had the observations been extended to hours spent on school business in the evening, the portion of his day spent in meetings would have been even greater, since any school business conducted in the evening was inevitably carried out by prearrangement. Ed's participation in social events away from home, focused predominantly on church activities, further increased the amount of his total time spent in meetings; he once joked about "being away eight nights a week." His attendance at six meetings in the course of the two evenings and one day described in Chapter 2 was a rather familiar circumstance, not only because of the total time spent but also because Ed's meetings, like the meetings of anyone whose life is dictated in part by the calendars of others, frequently came "all at once" in the course of a week or month.

The second category, "deliberate but not prearranged encounter," encompasses meetings held without prior appointment at which intended business was discussed. A parent coming to school and requesting "a moment" of Ed's time represents one type of deliberate meeting; so also did any opportunity which Ed took to bring up an item of business during an exchange of pleasantries with adults or children. A walk down the hall for the express purpose of speaking with a particular teacher or pupil, or a talk with a child sent to the office for deportment, represent other examples of deliberate encounters. As Table 5–1 shows, such meetings accounted for another one-fourth of Ed's school day. The combination of formally planned meetings and deliberate but unplanned meetings together accounted for half (51 percent) of Ed's average day at school.

All other face-to-face encounters were considered to be casual or chance ones. Such meetings might seem on first thought to be of the unexpected or unanticipated type suggested by the dictionary definition of an encounter. In fact, however, a principal at school or away from his school on official business does not meet many people who are truly unexpected. The average of 15 percent of Ed's day in which he engaged with others in casual or chance encounters actually draws attention only to the randomness with which he interacted with what was in fact a rather specific and predictable group of "others."

Telephoning provides a special type of an encounter, one that focuses on verbal interaction and excludes the face-to-face relationship characteristic of the other types. For the initiator of the call the encounter is a deliberate one; for the receiver of the call it may be deliberate if the call is purely business, but it can also be casual when the information requested from one person might have been elicited from someone else ("Do you happen to know if anyone is planning to drive to that meeting tonight?") or when no effort is made to call again or have a call returned if the original call is not completed. However, it was apparent that the time which Ed spent in telephoning at school warranted identifying the telephone as a separate category of encounters. During the time-and-motion study Ed spent an average of 3 percent of his total day talking on the telephone in conversations initiated by others, and twice that time, an average of 6 percent of his day, in calls which he initiated. He spent roughly an additional 1 percent of his time talking over the intercom, most frequently in making announcements to the entire school but also in using the intercom in two-way communication to specific individuals within the building. The time he spent on telephone and intercom interactions accounted for an average of 10 percent of his total time during the day.

Ed's gregarious nature probably resulted in his spending less time alone, particularly alone at work in his office, than many principals. Some of his teachers commented explicitly (and favorably, see Chapter 10) that Ed was not an "office sitter" like some principals they knew. The average amount of time recorded in which he was alone and stationary was 15 percent. A separate category for the time he spent alone as a consequence of going from one place to another, whether walking from his office to the teachers' room or driving from school to the bank or to a meeting across town, accounted for another 9 percent of his average day.

Table 5–2 provides further information about the nature of Ed's activity while he was in the company of others. During the period of the time-and-motion study Ed spent three-fourths of his average day at school in the immediate presence of one or more persons.[1] A small part of his total day (6 percent) was spent in the

---

[1] It should be apparent that I considered Ed to be "alone" when I was present as an observer. I suspect that Ed would have spent even less time alone had I not been present, even though he must have been aware that I did not engage freely in conversation whenever I was following him with clipboard and wristwatch. However, I made many trials with this approach before conducting my intensive study, and I had already been "shadowing" him for some ten months. I did not describe my categories to him, and I do not think he was aware of the aspects of his behavior to which I was attending, since my note-making was prompted by the sweep-second hand of my watch rather than by a change in Ed's behavior.

TABLE 5–2   LISTENING AND TALKING BEHAVIOR OF THE PRINCIPAL DURING AN "AVERAGE" SCHOOL DAY (8:00 A.M.–5:00 P.M., BASED ON A SAMPLE OF 12 TWO-HOUR PERIODS OF OBSERVATION DURING A TWO-WEEK PERIOD)

	Observed Range (in Percentages)	Percent of Time in an "Average" Day
Time Spent Alone		
Portion of total day spent alone	20–38	24
Time Spent with Others		
Portion of total day spent with others:		
Without verbal interaction (e.g., previewing material, waiting in a group, "supervising" children on the playground)	5–7	6
Portion of total day spent *listening* to others	28–39	35
Portion of total day spent *talking* to others:		
Giving information	23–27	25
Asking questions	4–8	7
Giving directions	2–5	4
TOTAL TALKING		36
TOTAL		101

company of other individuals but without sustained verbal interaction, such as in previewing curriculum materials (books, a film) with other teachers, reading teacher placement folders, watching or "supervising" children, or travelling with another person in silence. During most (71 percent) of his average day the focus of Ed's behavior was divided about in half between listening to others (35 percent of the total day) and talking to others (36 percent of the total day). Thus, of the total interactions in which he was engaged during an "average" day in which someone was talking, it was Ed himself doing the talking just slightly more than half the time.[2]

Ed's interactions and the proportion of his interactions involving different categories of persons are summarized in Table 5–3. Over 40 percent of his interactions were with professional members of his staff—teachers, the counsellor, the nurse, the special reading teacher, the supervisor of intern teachers, and so forth. Coupled with his interactions with the noncertified staff members—the secretary, teacher aide, custodians, and cooks—interactions with the entire staff of the school accounted for half (50.4 percent) of the total interactions in which he engaged. Pupils accounted for the next most frequently interacting group, with slightly over

[2] It is important to keep this fact in mind in reading the protocols reported throughout this study. Since I did not make wide use of the tape recorder, most conversations were recorded in longhand. While I attempted to get accurate quotations, I could not keep up with entire conversations. Thus, in my notes I frequently summarized what Ed had said—somewhat to my dismay when subsequently searching the notes for illustrative protocols.

TABLE 5–3   WHO THE PRINCIPAL INTERACTS WITH DURING AN "AVERAGE"
SCHOOL DAY, 8:00 A.M.–5:00 P.M., BASED ON ALL INSTANCES OF
INTERACTIONS RECORDED DURING A SAMPLE OF 12 TWO-HOUR
PERIODS OF OBSERVATION DURING A TWO-WEEK PERIOD

Category	Numbers of Instances When Interaction was Recorded (60-Second Intervals)	Percent of Total Time Spent Interacting with Each Category
Teachers, individually	187	16.3
Teachers, collectively	67	5.8
(*Subtotal*, all interactions with teachers, 22.1%)		
Counsellor	146	12.7
Other professional staff	81	7.1
Secretary	49	4.3
Other nonprofessional staff	48	4.2
(*Subtotal*, interactions with teachers plus all other staff, 50.4%)		
Pupils, individually	160	14.0
Pupils, small groups	46	4.0
Pupils, entire class or school	15	1.3
(*Subtotal*, all interactions with pupils, 19.3%)		
Student teachers and cadet teachers	12	1.0
Other principals	89	7.8
Central Office (superintendent or assistant superintendent)	2	.2
Central Office personnel (other than superintendent or assistant superintendent)	70	6.1
Parents	97	8.5
Other adults in community	15	1.3
Others	63	5.5
TOTAL INSTANCES RECORDED	1147	100.1

19 percent of his interactions, most of which were with pupils individually. Principals at other schools accounted for almost 8 percent of his interactions. Members of the central office staff accounted for about 6 percent of his interactions, but during the total 24 hours of the time-and-motion study he interacted with a top administrator (the superintendent or assistant superintendent) for only two recorded minutes. Interactions with parents accounted for 8.5 percent of his time; frequently these were conducted by telephone. The remainder of this chapter deals only with Ed's participation in formally scheduled meetings.

THE MEETING PATTERN

An examination of the time and place distribution of the meetings which a principal attends reveals a remarkable degree of patterning. Given the information that Ed was on his way to a meeting and knowing the hour and day one could almost predict who would be at the meeting and perhaps even make a reasonable guess about the general tenor of business. This predictive quality of a principal's life is due largely to the fact that his own schedule is highly flexible. The presence of the principal is not essential to the routine operation of the school. No one calls a substitute on a day when the principal is going to be absent. At the same time, institutional schedules of every variety, from the time established for school recesses to the culturally patterned "8:00 to 5:00" world of working parents, impose restrictions and conditions on the availability of other people to attend meetings. Thus school administrators call or are summoned to administrative meetings during the peak hours of the school day (9 A.M.–12 noon), assured that their meetings will not conflict with or be preempted by others. They are the only people "free" during these hours.

When the business at hand requires a principal to meet with any group of people (other than pupils) whose lives are intertwined with the activities of the school, the time of the meeting is more likely to depend on their schedules than on his. For example, elementary school teachers are free before school and after it, but they are not customarily free when school is in session unless special provision is made. Such provision *was* made in the school district by regularly sending all pupils home at an earlier hour on Wednesday afternoon. Wednesday afternoons were earmarked for faculty meetings and in-service programs.

When the principal wanted the opportunity to meet not only with a teacher and the counsellor but also with parents in a conference about a school child, the meeting almost invariably had to be set late in the afternoon. Occasionally Ed and the counsellor found themselves at school as late as 6:30 P.M. because of such conferences. Business matters of the teachers' professional association (to which most administrators in the district belonged) similarly had to be conducted late in the afternoon so teachers had time to get a central meeting place after the close of school. Any activity designed to promote school-community relations (beyond involving a small coterie of always-available mothers) had to be called in the evening.

The local and county principal associations also met in the evenings, since they were voluntary organizations independent of the school districts. The monthly meetings of the county association were dinner meetings held at the cafeteria of the host school. Sometimes these meetings entailed such a long drive that principals had to leave directly from school in the late afternoon in order to arrive by dinnertime. Local evening meetings were usually scheduled to begin at 7:30 or 8:00 P.M.; customarily they did not last more than two hours.

The pattern of time and place distribution of Ed's meetings is summarized in Table 5–4. A distinction is made in the table between weekday and weekend activities. School-centered Saturday activities were rare and were on a voluntary basis. Ed devoted a portion of four Saturdays during the year to formal school affairs, one by attending the annual PTA Pancake Breakfast at school, a second by taking his family and joining in a voluntary fourth grade field trip to the coast, a third by attending a two-day principals' association meeting out-of-town which began on

TABLE 5–4   MEETINGS: THE TIME AND PLACE DISTRIBUTION OF THE PRINCIPAL'S FORMAL ENCOUNTERS

	School Days	
Time	*Place*	*Personnel and/or Business*
Before school begins (8:00 A.M. –8:45 A.M.)	At school	Faculty (e.g., guidance meeting)
Morning during school hours (8:45 A.M.– lunchtime)	At school	Pupils, mothers, visitors and observers, personal (rare)
	Central office or other schools	Principals and central office staff
Lunch hour	At school	Brief meetings with teachers
	Other schools	Luncheon meetings with other principals
	Downtown restaurant	Committee or association meetings with other principals; Kiwanis
Early afternoon (lunchtime until primary dismissal)	At school	Pupils (discipline), all-school assemblies and programs
Immediately after school (following dismissal of upper grades)	At school	Teachers (individually and small groups), faculty meetings, in-service program, inter-school sports (rare)
Late afternoon (4:00 P.M. or after)	At school	Parents (mother and father together)
	Central office or other schools	Teacher association meetings, curriculum or other special committees
	Community	Personal and family business
Dinner (5:00 P.M.– 7:00 P.M.)	At other schools, church	Monthly meetings of county principals, school "banquets," church dinners
Evening (7:00 P.M.– 10:00 P.M.)	At school	PTA, Open House, School Fair, Room Desserts (September)
	Central office or other schools	Board meetings, budget hearings, meetings of local and county principal associations
	Church	Church activities (business meetings, evening worship)

	Weekends	
Time	*Place*	*Personnel and/or Business*
Saturday	At school	PTA pancake breakfast
	Away from school	Informal class field-trips, morning meetings at university, 2-3 day professional or church meetings
Sunday	Church	Sunday school, church services
	At school	Emergency only (e.g., meetings following incidents of vandalism)

a Friday, and a fourth by spending the last Saturday of the school year at school during the final teachers' work day. Sundays were free of school obligations, but Ed felt a perpetual sense of responsibility toward the school building. It was not unusual for him to go to the school or to drive by it sometime during the weekend, and occasionally he spent some time on Saturday in his office "catching up on paper work"—that is, preparing written reports. He was called to school one weekend after the sheriff's office received a report that some windows had been broken.

One Tuesday morning as Ed and I drove from school to a meeting of all the elementary principals, we talked about the number of meetings he attended and which of his meetings were most worthwhile. Somewhat to my surprise Ed said he did not particularly like meetings. Of all the regular meetings he attended, he felt the guidance committee meeting at Taft School gave him the most satisfaction. He said he did not like any meeting in which he could not get involved. For this reason he felt that the faculty meetings at Taft School were less effective than the smaller faculty group that met for the guidance committee meetings. Yet size alone was not a sufficient criterion for a successful meeting. Indeed, the meeting attended by the fewest persons among Ed's regular meetings—the monthly meeting with the superintendent, the high school principal and the elementary and junior high school principals of each high school attendance area within the district—was the least favorite of all his meetings. (His criticism of this meeting was that the superintendent usually delivered a monologue about the school district rather than nurture an exchange of ideas.) Of the meetings he attended at someone else's call, Ed felt that the regular meetings of the elementary school principals were "probably the most satisfying," but he was quick to add, "although sometimes it takes us an awfully long time to reach a decision." During my first visit to such a meeting, Ed leaned over and whispered at one point, "It always seems to take us an hour for the first item on the agenda, no matter what it is."

Excerpts are presented in this chapter from four meetings. Each of the four is in some ways representative of comparable meetings of the particular group of individuals present, and each of the meetings has some attributes in common with all of the others. At the same time, each meeting is also unique to the immediate problems at hand; to the particular people present; to the season, the weather, and the time of day; to Ed's own mood or his preoccupation with other problems; and to the extent of his personal concern for the problems at hand. Ed's comment (reported in Chapter 2) while chasing down a report of a boy taking a puff on a cigarette on the schoolyard held true in many other situations in his daily activities: "I'm not really very interested in this, but it's the kind of thing you have to do something about." He endured meetings he was expected to attend and consciously attempted to be patient when the meetings held no interest. Occasionally I observed him dozing off during large meetings attended by his colleagues, but he did not allow himself this luxury in smaller groups. Only rarely did he comment specifically about having to sit too long or attend too many meetings. On one occasion he joked with me, "I sure had TB [tired butt] this morning—we met at 8:15 for that committee on data processing and then we stayed for an elementary principals' meeting that lasted until 12:15 P.M."

AN IN-DISTRICT MEETING OF THE
ELEMENTARY SCHOOL PRINCIPALS

The regular monthly meeting of the elementary school principals had been called for Tuesday morning at 8:00 A.M. at a school on the far side of town. I had proceeded directly to the meeting instead of going to Taft School. I arrived half an hour ahead of Ed. Afterward he explained that he and the two others with whom he was riding were late because "we couldn't decide whether the meeting began at 8:00 or 8:30."

The room in which the meeting was held was a classroom being used as a music room. Six principals were on hand when I arrived at 7:55 A.M. Dr. Goddard, the Director of Elementary Education, had brought two boxes of fresh doughnuts which she was setting out on the counter. The janitor was putting up folding chairs in a large circle. Two principals helped pull small tables in front of some of the chairs to serve as writing desks. For the next few minutes principals continued to arrive and to visit or to take seats somewhere within the circle. The principals were slow in arriving for the meeting. The only principal present from the Taft School vicinity joked, "Is this an all-district meeting?" Another principal responded, "No, just the principals from this end of town."

When Dr. Goddard had originally entered the room, she placed her briefcase on top of the teacher's desk in the classroom. The desk completed a circle which otherwise consisted of about 15 folding chairs. Returning to the desk to start the meeting, she pulled her briefcase to one side of the desk and selected a folding chair adjacent to it rather than take the swivel chair immediately behind the desk. "Why don't you sit behind the teacher's desk, Carolyn?" one of the principals asked her. "If I do, there'll just be some jokes about it," she responded goodnaturedly.

Dr. Goddard raised her voice and addressed the group assembled loudly enough to be heard over their own visiting. "We have some late sleepers. Maybe we had better get started—before some others go to sleep." There was some laughter.

Principals continued to arrive after the meeting had begun until 26 of them were present. When one principal arrived at 8:25, another principal made an obvious gesture of looking at her watch. Ed Bell and his two colleagues arrived at 8:32; another principal arrived immediately after them. The last principal to arrive joked aloud as he entered the meeting, "I almost didn't make it. And I wouldn't have made it at all if I hadn't happened to look at my calendar—about five minutes ago."

The Meeting

The meeting began with an announcement about United Nations Week. Dr. Goddard described a planned telephone call to a school in Korea in which the district would be represented by two elementary school children and two junior high school children. Next she asked if anyone present had read a new article in *The Elementary Principal*. "I think everyone of us has to look at our own conscience. Are we holding the line or are we going ahead? It's the kind of thing you want to read and reread. And while I'm pontificating, I wonder just how much each of us talks with our staff about instruction, not just about scheduling, et cetera. Maybe our discussing schedules and maintenance is just a front so we don't have to talk about instruction."

"This summer we *almost* got to talking," commented one principal. He was referring to a three-week workshop which the Director of Elementary Education had organized in August for all the elementary principals of the district. The workshop theme was "We Live in a Changing Society." A discussion about the summary report of that workshop, a 41 page draft, dittoed and held together by one staple in the upper left-hand corner, containing "15 Position Papers and 3 Special Reports on Selected Issues in Elementary Education" was the major item on the agenda for this day's meeting. All principals had received a copy of the dittoed report prior to this meeting.

8:21   Coffee was wheeled in on a cart from the cafeteria. A secretary entered the room to announce aloud, "There's a message for Mr. Jarvis [a recently appointed principal] to call his school." Another principal quipped as the paged principal hurried out of the room, "He just doesn't delegate responsibility."

Dr. Goddard announced that she had asked one of the principals to design a cover for the position papers which the principals were to be discussing in detail at this meeting and planned ultimately to submit to the superintendent and school board. Then she turned the discussion to the position papers themselves. She asked whether the principals wished to accept the report of each group which had prepared a position paper "by formal vote or by consensus?" When no one spoke on behalf of voting, she concluded, "Well, then, I guess it will be by consensus."

The first position paper was contained on a one-page statement entitled, "Objectives of the Elementary School." Some principals skimmed the copy of the page in front of them, others entered immediately into discussion. The statement of objectives which they had before them was divided into two major parts. The first part defined the objectives of the elementary school in terms of the child. It stated:

> The prime concern of the elementary school is the child and his *behavioral* growth:
>
> 1. To become knowledgeable about the world.
> 2. To acquire communication, problem solving, and social skills needed for productive citizenship.
> 3. To develop the ability to cope with and make positive contribution to change.
> 4. To develop social responsibility.
> 5. To develop an appreciation for the arts.
> 6. To develop responsibility for his physical well-being.

The remainder of the statement described a secondary objective, "the development of an environment in which the child can more nearly achieve the above stated objectives." The statement spelled out staff and community responsibility for promoting such an environment. The staff, it proclaimed, "will" become skilled in fostering good human relationships, extend their knowledge of how children learn, become more proficient in combining talents and resources to guide learners, and develop the ability to use subject matter as a vehicle for capturing the interest of the learner and cultivating the process of learning. The community "will":

> Continue to be sensitive to the educational needs of children.
> Be knowledgeable about the school curriculum.
> Help develop a working relationship between the school and the homes of both preschool and school-age children.

Dr. Goddard began the discussion by asking, "I wonder if the statements here have to do with right now or with the future?" This prompted a discussion in which other principals queried whether the paper dealt with outcomes, goals, ideals, targets, expectations, or objectives.

"Do you want to set up achievement levels or not?" asked one principal. He proceeded to express his dissatisfaction with the vagueness of the statements.

"Doesn't number two [communication, problem solving, and social skills] cover all the rest?" inquired another.

Dr. Goddard invited members of the team who had prepared the statement to "give us your thinking" for developing it. One principal acknowledged that the committee might be a long way from getting the entire group to agree that they had provided a statement of objectives satisfactory to all.

"Since there is no consensus on this paper, I would entertain a motion," said Dr. Goddard. Oblivious to her comment, the group continued to discuss the alternatives of returning the statement to the committee which had prepared it, sending it to a committee for rewriting, or accepting it. Tom Nice recommended that the paper be rewritten to focus more on the *school's* responsibility rather than on the *community's* responsibility. Norman Olds restated that suggestion as a motion. Dr. Goddard repeated the motion and asked if it would be all right to include in it both the task of rewriting and the addition of an introductory paragraph explaining the rationale of the committee. Mr. Olds nodded his assent. Dr. Goddard called for a voice vote of approval and then appointed two principals who had previously worked on the statement, Bill St. Claire and Norman Olds, to continue to chair the committee for this paper. She commended the two on their efforts to date: "They've worked real hard on this."

The next six papers to be reviewed comprised a set of statements dealing with the general subject "Organizing for Instruction." The six papers addressed six specific topics: flexibility, grouping for instruction, cooperative planning and teaching, balanced curriculum, design for change, and Spanish.

The first paper, "Flexibility," posed the question: "How can 'flexibility' contribute toward meeting the needs of children in the district's elementary schools?" The first person to speak raised a question of the amount of repetition in the one and one-half page statement. Another asked about the extent of rewriting done by a special committee that had been appointed to edit the collecion of papers. A third paraphrased one of the stated "facets of flexibility" and asked, "What do I tell a mother who asks what is meant by 'each child should have an opportunity to fail in his own unique way?' I don't want a rationale. Just *what do I tell a mother?*"

Several people commented on the relation of failure to learning. "Learning theory doesn't hold that failure is essential to learning," stated one principal.

TOM NICE added: The term 'fail' has a certain meaning to lay people.

ED: A child who tries to pick up a piece of wood with a magnet has experienced failure.

DR. GODDARD: Would Group I take a look at this paper and have it for us by next week? Is there anything else on this one? Then let's turn to the paper on "Grouping for Instruction."

The next paper posed the question, "What is the most effective method of grouping for instruction to provide the maximum learning opportunities for children?" The question was followed by a brief statement describing nine ways children were presently grouped (for example, according to interest, achievement), a statement of beliefs, and three recommendations:

1. That individual schools use a variety of imaginative groupings.
2. That no one method of grouping be prescribed for all schools or all children.
3. That grouping plans be constantly re-evaluated to see that they meet the needs of the learner.

The paper seemed to provide little basis for controversy. A few uncontested comments like "fine" and "looks good" were taken as an indication of approval. Dr. Goddard turned to the next paper in order, "Cooperative Planning and Teaching." This paper was two pages in length. The second page was devoted to the committee's four recommendations. Three of the recommendations were of a highly general nature (for example, encouraging cooperative planning). Attention was drawn to the recommendation that "time for planning be made available," including a specific recommendation for using the "resource teacher, teacher aides, counsellor, principal and other teachers to relieve staff members for planning." Opinions were offered about where and when planning occurs at present, and whether time for planning itself had to be planned into the school schedule.

NORM OLDS: I don't think it's right for teachers to get a resource teacher to take the class so they can plan.

ANOTHER PRINCIPAL: I once heard Ole Sands [an authority on curriculum] say that no teacher can do a good job if he has to teach 30 hours. He ought to teach for 12 hours a week.

BILL ST. CLAIRE: Some of us have made headway in freeing teacher time at lunch, et cetera. Maybe they plan then, maybe not.

A SENIOR PRINCIPAL: Dr. Goddard, I'd like to take the opposite side. I think teachers need to see kids in the less formal settings. They need to be on the playground and in the lunchroom.

The discussion turned to the use of teacher time in general. Someone asked: How can we go to the community and ask for more time and money unless we show that the time which teachers now have is being used?

NORM OLDS: Could we arrange classes so one teacher in each grade gets time to plan? Is it legal?

WOMAN PRINCIPAL: I'd rather have small classes. Then you don't have the problem of planning for so many.

ED: What does *planning* mean, anyway? A lot of times it just means preparing seatwork for kids the teacher won't have time to interact with. [A principal sitting nearby leaned over to tell me: "That's the best comment Ed ever made."]

ANOTHER PRINCIPAL: I've been listening, for a change. Listening to this group you can really get an idea of what goes on in schools in this community.

A few people were doing most of the talking. I counted nine principals who had not spoken during the meeting. Norm Olds, Tom Nice, and one woman principal had done most of the talking. Carolyn Goddard usually stayed out of the discussions but always made a statement of summary.

9:31 A.M.   Carolyn called a break. Ed headed for the coffee and doughnuts. The principal of the host school asked if anyone wanted to stay for lunch. No one did.

9:45 A.M.   Carolyn called the meeting back to order with an announcement that for future meetings at this school everyone was requested to drive in on the street *behind* the school and to park in the back near the meeting room.

When the room was quiet, Ed commented aloud, "It might sound facetious, but maybe we need another three-week workshop to decide what it is we said the first three weeks."

Discussion turned for the next ten minutes to a position paper entitled "Curriculum." "What is curriculum?" asked one principal. In a pedantic tone Norm Olds made reference to a standard textbook source on curriculum and recited a pat definition. "Page 7," added Tom Nice. Their comments were greeted with laughter.

In the brief (less than one and one-half pages) paper on curriculum the term "needs" (for example, "tailoring the curriculum to individual needs") appeared nine times. A discussion ensued about "meeting the needs of children," directed particularly to a statement in the paper, "Curriculum is designed to meet the needs of the majority."

"That means we're meeting the needs of most children," explained one principal.

"Not *all?*" asked a senior principal.

Amidst a few mutterings of assurance ("Well, we try to!") Dr. Goddard turned to the next paper, "Design for Change." This paper also was addressed to the problem of meeting children's needs:

> Can the school and school day be organized flexibly to meet the needs and interests of boys and girls and still insure a balanced program for them?

The paper provoked no comments among the principals. Dr. Goddard expressed concern with the word "control" in a sentence appearing in the paper: "Certain areas within the instructional program and the school day are beyond the *control* of the teacher." She suggested the alternative phrase, "established by decision beyond the jurisdiction of the teacher," and asked if it was acceptable.

"It's the same thing, but worded better," assured one of the principals sitting near her.

"Yeah. It's a little harder to pin down," laughed another.

The next position paper dealt with the recently inaugurated program of teaching Spanish in all the fourth, fifth, and sixth grades. A question was raised whether the policy statement conflicted with or supported school board policy, since the position paper implied that not all children were profiting from the program and recommended that the effectiveness of the program be evaluated independently at each school. One principal said that some problems anticipated with the Spanish program had not developed. He continued, "Our problem now is the philosophy behind it. Why do we have it?" Another principal commented that the difficulty of the Spanish program was that it might get beyond the teacher's ability even in the third year.

10:25 A.M. The next paper for consideration was entitled "Planning for the Flexible Primary Program." This five-page paper dealt with two problems of special professional interest to the principals, a nongraded approach to the primary grades (i.e., emphasis on many levels of achievement and a de-emphasis on "so-called grade level expectations") and on a "program for five-year-olds." Many teachers and administrators had taken a firm stand on the importance of a kindergarten program in the district, but they had been unsuccessful in winning sufficient public support for the required increase in property taxes. Put to a special community vote in a previous year, the issue of establishing kindergartens in the district had been defeated by a wide margin. District personnel believed the program was in the best interests of the education of children. Tactically they decided to continue to campaign for kindergartens but to give the program a new name to avoid handicapping it with the weight of existing opposition. A new "program for five-year-olds" had been initiated at some elementary schools as a pilot study during the current school year. The position paper lent implicit support to the idea of the "five-year-old program" (the term "kindergarten" was jokingly, but nonetheless effectively, tabooed among the principals). The paper supported small classes (one teacher for 20 pupils) and more integration among grade levels in the primary grades.

As soon as the paper was introduced, one principal spoke on its behalf: "This is the most important paper of them all. It must be brought to the attention of the board. It should be printed on gold."

DR. GODDARD: Aside from printing it on gold, does anyone have any suggestions?
PRINCIPAL: This kind of flexibility shouldn't be restricted only to the primary grades.
ANOTHER PRINCIPAL: It was done that way in order to account for the new five-year-old program. It shouldn't be rewritten now.

Some concern was expressed at the description of "What Exists" as stated in the position paper. The statement consisted of ten points:

1. Expectations of adults are not always consistent with the development of children. Children want to learn but some experience failure in the terms of adult expectations which have become their own.
2. Many times more value is placed on conforming to group expectations than is placed on the uniqueness of the individual. Teachers are faced with the task of dealing with two facets of the child's development:
   a. To help him learn to operate as a member of the group.
   b. To help him become an independent, decision-making individual.

3. Generally speaking, present primary curriculum is skill oriented with concern for immediate functionality in reading, writing, spelling, and arithmetic. Materials and equipment emphasize the abstract rather than the experiential.
4. Readiness is thought of as a level of achievement rather than as a dynamic stage of being. We say, "Is he ready?" instead of "What is he ready for?"
5. In a classroom, one adult is limited in quality and quantity of personal interaction with each child.
6. Reporting to parents is done in terms of a set of standards as interpreted by the teacher.
7. The present primary organization is based on grade level and attendant practices of promotion and retention.
8. Most schools do not meet the challenge of providing for the greater span of experiences, differences, and needs of today's children.
9. Most building facilities are restrictive rather than supportive of flexibility.
10. Alienation often occurs in the child's early years and may be aggravated by his school experience; and yet it may not be easily discernible until later years.

A member of the committee which prepared the statement explained: "Originally we thought of using the term 'generally speaking' in front of each of these statements."

A senior principal stood up to express his view: "Each of these conditions they have described actually exists. These statements should be made just as they are!"

ANOTHER: It seems to me there's sort of a negative tone to the way these are written.
NORM OLDS: We always say we should stand up and be counted, take a firm stand. But now we do have a position to take, and we're afraid we might hurt someone's feelings or step on some toes.

Discussion continued about whether the statements were acceptable as written. Someone suggested that the statements could be softened by using more "weasel words" (for example, "sometimes," "occasionally") but the laughter suggested that most principals were willing to accept the statement as it was. In a tone suggesting that the discussion looked like it might be endless, one principal said rather abruptly, "That's enough talk on this one. I move we accept it as it is." A voice vote was taken and the initial section of the statement on planning for the flexible primary program was accepted. The position paper continued with two major objectives for the flexible primary:

1. Continuous individual development.
2. Promotion of a good self image.

To achieve these objectives, the committee had spelled out 16 characteristics of a program to accomplish them. The term "needs" appeared only once in the five pages of the statement, but the discussion returned to a perennial question which had already been raised earlier in the meeting, whether the schools were "meeting the needs of children."

Tom Nice stated flatly, "The school *is* meeting needs."

A variety of comments revealed several interpretations of the meaning of "needs":

Schools don't meet needs in math.

Schools don't meet the needs of Johnny Warren [a child enrolled at Tom's school but apparently known to several principals].

Are we meeting *cultural* needs?

Do we know what the needs *are?*

If we tell the teacher she isn't meeting the needs, we still don't know how to tell her to change them.

We still are working with teachers who think that what every child needs is a text.

Dr. Goddard called the discussion to order, "We're never going to get the magic thing that will meet the needs exactly."

Tom Nice added, "We are meeting the *challenge* of meeting the needs, even if we aren't always meeting the needs themselves."

11:05 A.M. Dr. Goddard tried to shift the discussion to the last two sets of position papers, but the first principal to speak brought up the topic of the flexible primary position paper again. In order to keep the meeting moving, Dr. Goddard suggested returning the paper to the committee "with some question marks," but the principals continued to offer comments about the paper, the problems it presented, and the importance of taking a firm stand on important issues.

(The meeting had been running almost three hours at this point. I found it difficult to sustain my attention in note-taking. I looked around the room wondering what attention was being given. With the possible exception of one principal who may have been asleep, everyone appeared attentive. However, one young principal had begun nervously snapping an automatic pencil open and shut, apparently without realizing the distraction he was causing. A colleague sitting next to him brought him to attention by saying his name. The principal blushed as he realized what he had been doing. He put the pencil away and pantomimed gnawing at clenched fists in frustration at the pace at which the meeting was proceeding.)

Questions about intended meanings and even about specific wording with the statement continued. There seemed to be some uneasiness about endorsing this position paper in which a particular point of view had been expressed so firmly, not so much for that part of the statement which proposed a solution as for that part which provided an assessment of how things were at the moment:

We have to consider what other people might read into these comments.

Are we just jumping on a gang wagon here?

I think we are meeting the needs of the children at our school. Is this really a problem?

Maybe not in *your* school.

Yeah. Only in the other 27.

One principal proposed mitigating the direct tone of the paper: "I still think this is a very important paper. But maybe we shouldn't highlight it. We could treat it the way the junior high schools did. They wanted to get approval for a free period each day for the teachers, but in the big study of the junior high which they prepared in their workshop, they just had one little comment in there about having a free period. Then when the school board accepted the report, they had their free period all approved." His remark prompted a discussion of "whether *this* group works that way."

Dr. Goddard glanced at the clock on the wall. The time was 11:20 A.M. Seven more position papers, including the position paper which Ed had helped to develop,[3] plus three additional special reports developed during the workshop, were still waiting for review. She said, "I think we've done about all we can do for one day. I guess we better plan to meet again next week and finish this. I had originally planned to invite Dr. Boggs to our next meeting, but since we haven't had a chance to go over these other papers ourselves, I think I'll just tell him to scratch it."

"He'd probably just as soon," someone quipped.

As the principals started to collect their papers and to stand, stretch, and leave the meeting room, Norm Olds made an announcement about paying for the doughnuts which Dr. Goddard had brought to the meeting. "Last year she did this completely on her own," he reminded them, "and she ran out of money." (She made a good-humored gesture of wiping tears from her eyes.) "I suggest that next time everybody bring a buck and we'll put it toward the cost of the doughnuts."

"Now we're meeting one of *her* needs," someone suggested. There was general laughter among the departing principals at the use of the term which had been so frequently repeated during the previous three and a half hours.

FACULTY MEETINGS

Ed Bell stated that he did not believe in or hold faculty meetings on a regular basis. Meetings should be called only for specific purposes, he felt. Routine announcements could be made in other ways.

The meetings Ed did call were almost always announced a day or two in advance, and were usually scheduled at times especially earmarked for staff meetings throughout the district. These times included special teacher "work" days when teachers were at school but pupils were not (for example, the week before classes began in the fall; one day after classes ended in June; and three Fridays during the year which coincided with the end of reporting periods in the district's high schools) and on Wednesday afternoons when all pupils in the school district were dismissed early.

Not all of the Taft faculty recognized Ed's endeavor to keep the meetings to a minimum, and a few were outspoken in complaining about the numerous faculty meetings held and of their interminable duration (see also Chapter 10):

There's these forever meetings, you know. Oh, this [interview] wouldn't be complete without my gripe about meetings. I've never heard of such a meeting, meeting, meeting school.

---

[3] The committee on which Ed served had developed a statement regarding manipulative activities. It stated, in part, "We believe that since the sequence of learning is from the concrete to the abstract, schools should provide additional opportunities for manipulative experiences."

Several factors may have contributed to the complaining about faculty meetings, not the least of which is an apparently universal tradition among teachers of doing so. In previous years, Ed had held meetings more frequently, and his teachers might well have assumed that the current year was to be no different, since a faculty meeting had been held during each of the first five weeks of the new school year. After September, however, only three meetings were held until the Christmas holiday, one of them expressly for the purpose of planning the school Christmas program. After the Christmas vacation one meeting was called in January, two in April, and three in May.

Of the total of 15 all-faculty meetings, 11 were scheduled either on Wednesday afternoons or on teacher work days. Three of the other meetings were scheduled for Thursdays immediately after school was dismissed. The fourth meeting was called on a Friday afternoon; Ed promised in his handwritten announcement in the faculty notebook that the Friday meeting would be "short and important."

Unquestionably the fact that all but two of the teachers on the faculty were participating in an in-service workshop held at Taft School on most Wednesdays was an important influence in limiting the number of other staff meetings called. The pattern of dates on which Ed did call meetings suggests that as long as his faculty was meeting for *some* purpose, he did not burden them with additional meetings, but if no gathering of any sort was planned he was inclined to bring them together at least once in every two weeks. Three of a total of four meetings which featured special consultants were held during the last meetings of the year in April and May after the in-service program had concluded.

On some Wednesday afternoons a broadcast of a taped message prepared by the superintendent of schools was played over the intercom system of each school. On a few occasions, Ed included the message on the agenda of a faculty meeting; at the proper moment the secretary turned on the intercom to interrupt the proceedings while Ed and the teachers sat silently in the faculty room and listened to the broadcast. On Wednesdays when the superintendent had prepared a message but no faculty meeting had been called, the talk was broadcast throughout the school building over the intercom system, the superintendent's voice echoing throughout the corridors while teachers worked in their classrooms.

Taft faculty meetings invariably included a combination of discussions about procedures (for example, announcements and explanations; planning for an open house, school fair, or other program; problems of budgets and salary schedules) and discussions about purposes (for example, the educational "atmosphere" of the school, how much freedom and structure children need). Ed always had a few notes reminding him of items of business, although he did not often have the school secretary prepare formal copies of the agenda. The faculty meetings tended to be specific and well-organized at their outset, as procedural details were discussed, and then sometimes trailed off in a conversation-like manner to discussions of personal philosophies and previous experiences. Such discussions were not received with enthusiasm by all staff members, particularly if the hour was late or the meeting was already of long duration.

The meeting recounted below differs from most faculty meetings in that it was called specifically for the purpose of discussing the philosophy underlying the instructional program. The setting was a meeting of the summer school faculty at Taft rather than the regular faculty. The summer school faculty included teachers from the regular faculty, teachers from other schools in the district, and one elementary school principal who had elected to teach during the summer. In connection with a graduate training program at the university, Taft was serving as a training school for a group of intern teachers who would be assuming full-time teaching duties in the fall. The school was also serving as a laboratory for a group of five visiting teachers enrolled in a university-sponsored workshop on classroom supervision. The visiting teachers from this workshop had asked to meet with the principal to discuss the philosophy of the summer school program. He, in turn, extended the "invitation" to the entire summer school staff. At the height of the meeting there were 27 people in attendance. The meeting was held in the teachers' room.

The summer school program for the children concluded at noon each day. Teachers were expected to remain on duty until 2:30 P.M. Since the school cafeteria was not operating, faculty brought lunches and ate together in the teachers' room immediately after the morning session. With everyone on the same schedule, each noontime provided an opportunity for formal announcements and for conducting any business involving the entire staff.

An air of casualness pervaded the operation of the summer school, fostered by a clientele of voluntary pupils, an easy-going schedule free from bells, casual attire worn by pupils and staff, and a conscious attempt on everyone's part to remain relaxed. The contrast between the summer school and "regular" school provided the basis for the discussion at this meeting. The meeting began at 12:30 P.M. The day was Monday, the beginning of the fourth week of the summer session. With the knowledge of all present, the meeting was tape recorded, although the following account has been abridged.

A Summer School Faculty Meeting

ED: (raising his voice to signal the beginning of the meeting) Those teachers of you who are here have had some contact with this Supervision Workshop Team. They wanted to talk with me about the rationale behind our summer school. So you people are welcome to stay and enter in or not if you like.

INTERN SUPERVISOR: Although we really would like you to, because you've got comments and things and they have positive and negative . . .

ED: I've got a feeling that you teachers probably have a little more to contribute to the answer to their questions than I have. But I don't want you to feel obligated to stay if you have other things that you feel are more pressing. [No teacher left the meeting at this time.]

INTERN SUPERVISOR: I have one more comment on that. It is that we simply just stop at 1:00 P.M. no matter what. You know how discussions go on and on after they say it is over. We've got work to do. So if you feel that you wouldn't like to be in on this all afternoon, why, I, for one, am going to sit down and watch the clock.

ED: Did I receive your direction correctly? You want to know what is the rationale behind the summer school? [Nods of assent.]
        We began talking about it a year ago before summer session. At that time Jim Ross [one of the senior principals] was the coordinator of the program.

So Carolyn Goddard called in Jim and I and others who were interested in setting up a workshop, along with some consultants for setting up summer school sessions. We felt then that summer school had been particularly focused on "remedial" for a number of years. We had some strong feelings that this might not be meeting the needs even of the remedial children, and maybe there were some other needs that could be met for children who did not have any definitely recognized remedial needs.

VISITING TEACHER: Can I ask a question? By remedial, do you mean any child who could possibly be below grade level and would need help?

ED: Yes. We've had remedial reading courses in a number of areas and also some remedial math. So we thought we would operate on the premise that if the children got involved in the learning process and had an enjoyable time at it, that they wouldn't learn any less and possibly might learn more than if we said, "OK. You're the jokers who need to be jacked up a little so you can get on grade level," or something like this, might have a better psychological approach than what we had been using. So at least on this staff, I think, we understand that pretty well and set about to make it a pleasurable experience for kids. I thought we were pretty successful in doing that. I don't know if teachers who were here last year feel we are doing as well as we did last year or not. That's about it in a nutshell. Probably a great deal of elaboration could be offered. If you want, we'll try and answer any specific questions that you might have.

VISITING TEACHER: Well, one question that I have in my own mind is that there seems to be a certain amount of casualness among the students here as far as doing whatever they want to do. Do they have difficulty, say, readjusting to a more formal expectation in a regular school year? In other words, it's sort of nondirective during the summer time, which I think is good, in theory. Do they have problems conforming to the wishes of the teacher in the regular school year as a result of this experience?

ED: I would answer, from my point of view, very quickly, and then maybe the teachers can answer that. I would say that we're . . . this school runs a little more casually than perhaps some schools they might go back to. Anyway, I don't think this is a problem with our students. It certainly does keep them active at other schools.

OTHER PRINCIPAL: I think they read the signs and conform to whatever the expectations are. When they go through the door they know which is winter school. It might be somewhat different.

ED: We have a couple of third grades, well, we had three here in the past year. Those teachers work together real closely. The children go back and forth from one teacher to another. There is quite a difference in the noise tolerance between these two teachers, but those kids don't have any trouble adjusting to them. They walk through the door and they know that these are the expectations here and these are the expectations there. They seem to just turn the dial without anyone saying anything about it. This is a very natural thing. They seem to learn it much more quickly than adults do.

TEACHER: It's interesting how the teachers who were here last year decided that their classes should be more like summer school. Why did they?

TEACHER (from Taft faculty): They felt there was more expression. We felt that with less pressure the kids really came out on top.

ED: Of course, one teacher who was here last summer operates like that whether it is summer school or not.

VISITING TEACHER: Part of this supervision workshop of ours is about taking verbatim data of what we see actually going on. In considerable classrooms there are kids who are continually bothering other students to a point where they distract a number of kids and apparently they are just let go at this point.

Is this typical of your winter program, or do you clamp down on the kid as soon as he comes in the door in the fall? If so, why is he being let go now?

ED: I suppose we have to put the question back to you. What do you mean by "clamp down?"

VISITING TEACHER: Well, would you go ahead and let him disturb any other kids?

ED: I've shared your feelings on this for a long time, but the more I look at it, the more I come to the conclusion that the kid that is being disturbed, say if he is a fifth grader, has had four or five years of this situation where there are these kinds of people around, who lives in a home where the television runs in one room and the tape recorder[4]—the record player—in another one. There is a lot happening, and he apparently is learning well anyway. I don't believe distraction is as important to students as I once thought it was. It is my conclusion that the majority of kids in school would learn something even without us as teachers. To me, clamping down on a kid who obviously has problems only adds to his problems. He needs a lessening of problems rather than an adding of problems.

TEACHER: How do you know that the child is really learning? Say you have someone in class who is distracting everyone else. Well, on one hand, it's worth listening to what the teacher is saying, but we get some feedback from them so we know what they are thinking. But if we have students who are constantly doing the talking, you never get to hear what anyone else is saying. So how would the teacher know what is really going on?

ED: How does the teacher really know there is any learning going on?

INTERN SUPERVISOR: Yes. Because if she doesn't have the chance to hear what other youngsters are saying, but only maybe the one that can yell louder than anyone else, and he is talking while she is taking up most of the time. . . .

ED: I think it would be a real disappointing situation if a child began the year dominating the class, teachers and all, and this continued all year long. This would be too bad. This child who plays the role that you and I are agreeing here is, I think, saying to us very clearly that he needs some help, and you better be getting him that help. But I don't say that the principal, the teacher, the counsellor, are the only ones that can help that child. I would say that his peer group can help that child a great deal, too.

VISITING TEACHER: I was just wanting Larry [the other principal] to comment on that.

OTHER PRINCIPAL: Of course, I'm an . . . as an . . . I would have two points of view. One as a principal, perhaps, and one as a guy in there working with people. And I think that they might be a little different [Laughter].

I like your ideas of flexibility and freedom to operate and move around. I like that very much. But, when I get those little guys there in the morning and they are running me every which way and direction . . . If I could get them all in their seats . . .

Like this morning. Boy, that was a tough fight! [Laughter.] I'd get five of them down and three of them would be up. Finally, I got everybody paying attention and little Ricky got to play with his magnet. He didn't disrupt too much, but I think once I tried to give them about three overall types of discussion lessons, and it was a real problem to do that. I think it's just my own inadequacy in teaching these little kids that books mean more. I think it would bug almost anybody who has an idea he wanted to get across. These

---

[4] This vocabulary "slip" suggests that Ed was distracted by the presence of the tape recorder, although he usually insisted that he paid no attention to it after the first few minutes of a recorded session.

little guys are always involved, every minute, and they will stay in there all recess and come back, but I don't know whether they're learning anything.

ED: Do you know if they're learning anything if they sit down?

OTHER PRINCIPAL: No, this is true.

VISITING TEACHER: Larry, I want to ask you another question now. From a principal's aspect, if you walked into a room and was going to make an announcement to the kids and said so, and, as you were speaking, there were kids looking out the window and playing with clocks and problems and rabbits and whatever else you might have, would it mean anything to you or would you go ahead and make the announcement?

OTHER PRINCIPAL: I think I'd make the announcement. [Much laughter.] That wouldn't disturb me as much as if I was a teacher and we tried to let someone else come in and make a speech. Then I would be a little more concerned.

VISITING TEACHER: What would your concern be?

OTHER PRINCIPAL: Well, the fact that the person would take the time to come in there and say something and we were being a little discourteous and not listening. And it would be my adult feelings of discourtesy, not theirs necessarily. They were involved in something.

ED: Maybe we need a little research on whether children learn more on their seat or on their feet.

I talked to some of my teachers about a wild idea. Or at least I thought it was wild until I tried it out on Carolyn Goddard. She said, "Why don't you try it?" And I haven't yet. Here's part of the plan. Say you are all teachers. You are to plan a program and publish it—make it common knowledge—so people can read it right on the door of your classroom. And we'll say that there is a maximum number of students that you can have in this class, and you don't know what age level there is going to be. You just put out a program that will attract kids. Kids can take first choice anywhere in the building and can go and stay as long as they want to stay as long as there is a limited number within that room. And when they have got their cup full of that room they can move to another one which has room for them and anybody can do this as long as you want to. What would that mean to you as a teacher?

SEVERAL TEACHERS: (speaking at once) Five weeks. . . .

> I'd start looking for
> another job. . . .
>
> I'd think it would be
> really funny. . . .
>
> Let the children plan
> a program?

ONE TEACHER: And plan just any program we want? That would be simple.

ED: Do you think so? How would you say it would be simple?

TEACHER: Well, I'd plan the things that I can do best. I'd attract a certain number of children that would really like to do those things.

ED: What are you going to do when that group gets tired of that?

TEACHER: I don't know. Maybe I'd quit then. Or change it.

ANOTHER TEACHER: Do children get tired of learning?

ED: We've got another situation going there in the summer time and I thought maybe we ought to ask ourselves this question, too. How would you alter it as teachers? This applies to Larry and I, too. How would you alter your program come September if any child who came could leave when he wanted to? What would this do to your plans?

TEACHER: You couldn't do any long-range planning, could you? You'd keep getting new children. You'd never get off the ground floor.

ED: This is what is happening in summer school. These children are here for the most part because they want to be. I suppose there is some parental pressure, but the law doesn't say they have to be here. We have, for a long, long time acted as though when kids come into our school, they are a captive audience; we don't really care much whether we like kids or not: "This is good for you, we have decided it. You're going to be here." OK! We're only kidding ourselves. These kids stay here in body, but they don't stay here in spirit. They leave us. We have a lot of dropouts who sit in a room twelve years. If we don't think so, we just ought to take another look at what happens.

INTERN SUPERVISOR: I want to agree with you. But I really am not sold on the fact that a child can direct. Children really get tired of "do we *have to* do what we want to do today?"

ED: Of course, my theory is a long way from my practice. You've been around long enough to know that. I think you have to be a little more realistic than I may sound at this point. But I don't think there is anything wrong with teachers planning *with* kids. I'm not saying that we ought to just abdicate our will as adults at all. I think we have to be around and play the role as adults, but we need to take a new look at that role, I think. So far we've said, "We're the all-knowing, almighty, and you poor little guys. . . ."

TEACHER: What if they didn't choose any of those rooms? There would be a certain number that nothing appeals to them, all they want to do is just run around the building. Who's going to decide for them where they go?

TEACHER: Well, they could go their whole lives having you decide.

TEACHER: Do you suppose they would ever decide?

TEACHER: Yes, I think they will.

ED: I have a couple of kids down there and we're still waiting. I think we have just not waited on kids nearly long enough. We say they have to do it our way and do it now. The ship's going to leave the dock and let's get on board.

VISITING TEACHER: Unfortunately though, I think you need this kind of experience, too, because life is pretty much this way. That is, the guy who doesn't do what society expects is left out. I can't think of too many things that I've done in my adult life that I've really enjoyed. I've been forced to do them because this is what life expects of me, and once I've forced myself to be exposed to this, I learned to enjoy it. It's like eating your vegetables, and so forth. If Ma let me eat just what I wanted to eat, I'd probably just have had meat, potatoes, and dessert.

ED: Research proves you're wrong, though.

VISITING TEACHER: Is that right?

ED: You give children the opportunity to choose the balance in their diet, you provide and make available the material, and they balance their diet. They may eat all peanut butter for two weeks, but after awhile, they begin to eat something else.

VISITING TEACHER: OK.

ANOTHER VISITING TEACHER: Am I right in assuming that you have established here basically two different programs, two different aspects? The winter program and the summer program being basically two different ideas? Are they the same?

TEACHER: I'm teaching no differently than in the winter.

VISITING TEACHER: In other words, your summer program is just like the winter basically?

ED: Not at all.

VISITING TEACHER: Oh, that's what I wondered.

ED: This isn't true of all the schools in this district. I'm just speaking for this school.

OTHER PRINCIPAL: I think we're all in favor of this theory. Real good!

TEACHER: You know what gets in the way? Parents!

ED: Yeah.

TEACHER: They want them evaluated, graded: A, B, C.

ED: I'm a cockeyed realist. I know you've got to sell a program. You've got to sell a budget each year. And I'm sure this affects the way I talk to people about the school in the winter time. I don't feel that same obligation in the summer.

OTHER PRINCIPAL: Have we had the standard complaints about the way we've run the show this summer?

ED: No. We do get some in winter time, though.

INTERN SUPERVISOR: There have been dropouts, though. There has been feedback that parents wanted them to learn something, and they didn't think they were learning. But that's third hand.

OTHER PRINCIPAL: I think this is the strength of the program that's been run here this year. I've had a large number of kids in my PE program get tired of PE. So they went back into art. Now some of these people have come back, plus a girl and another girl. I don't know if she's in there officially or not, but she has been in there the last couple of days. They seek their own, where they want to be.

VISITING TEACHER: I feel at times we let kids create distrubances that bother other people, and we're really leaning toward the minority instead of the majority. What should we do with the child who continually distracts everyone and everything?

ED: Move him to another classroom?!

VISITING TEACHER: I think that's what we've been doing for years, isn't it? Just send him to someone else.

SCHOOL COUNSELLOR: We say that this child has a need that is not being met, and this is probably the reason he is acting out.

ED: We'd better be looking for what that need is and meet it. And sometimes we've done this. We say, "OK, let the principal, the reading teacher, the psychologist do it. And somewhere somebody is going to push the button, and the student returns as a model student." Well, we found this just doesn't happen. Who is the key to this problem? The classroom teacher!

Sometimes, if you push it back—as we've done with the counsellor here, particularly this year—push it back to the family, you find the child who is not learning but he has the ability to learn, and he comes from a home that is receiving all the help that it is able to receive, and still it is about to break up, and the whole family situation is about to deteriorate into nothingness and this child comes to school, what are you going to do? Force him back on *that home*? Well, if you do, you're just forcing him to the junk pile. So you put up with him, and do the best you can every day. At least that's my premise. As for the point that the world is this way, maybe you aren't as close to these fellows who work as custodians or who work in the mills as I am. A lot of these people prove to us every day that you can do as you darn please.

VISITING TEACHER: Well, I have just one little question and then I'll quit. I'd like to ask the teachers this. I've worked with a summer session that was on a different basis. It was set up for reading and arithmetic, et cetera, for average kids. They didn't necessarily have to be remedial for kids to get in and enrich themselves. As the teacher, if you had a child who could attend either program, which would you send him to? The one that was planned and based on enriching his program, or one which is similar to your own summer program, which is more laissez-faire or whatever you want to call it?

ED: Well, I think you're misreading our program.

VISITING TEACHER: No, I . . .

OTHER PRINCIPAL: I think he means more formal.

VISITING TEACHER: Yeah, where they're actually doing more work on skills.

ED: We have skills in mind, too.

TEACHER: They don't realize they're getting them here.

ANOTHER TEACHER: But the way our old remedial program was—I worked in that one, too—I had trouble with discipline.

ANOTHER TEACHER: Even remedial. The person who needed remedial help, maybe they need it worse.

ED: Why?

TEACHER: Let them unwind. Find themselves.

ED: Why did they need remedial help in the first place? They've already been in trouble with remedial help. Why should they subject themselves to more failure all along the way? If they find some satisfaction and success here, *maybe* they'll go on and they'll do the things they wanted to do all the time.

TEACHER: Send him to the one who accepts him the most as who he is. It will depend on him.

ANOTHER TEACHER: We don't have any questionnaire or background information on who the remedial children are. So maybe he's not a remedial or a problem child here *this* summer.

ANOTHER TEACHER: You know, some of them are even surprised that they did something good. Like with painting a picture, they can't even believe it themselves.

ED: Last year some kids sat around for about three days waiting for teachers to get them a textbook so they could get busy. I don't know—did that happen again this year? There were lots of new students.

INTERN SUPERVISOR: (standing up at exactly one o'clock) I want to say this. Our questions . . . we just needed to say these out loud and have you talk about them. Whatever we say, we really want to come back during this summer. So we don't want you to get the idea that we're critical of the things we see. Now I'm not shutting off anybody, but I have to leave, and I know others have to leave, because several of these people have classes at the university in the afternoon.

The comment by the intern supervisor concluded the formal meeting. Several teachers got up immediately and left the room. Others remained seated or stood up and continued talking together for the next few minutes.

A MEETING OF THE
PTA EXECUTIVE BOARD

Ed Bell frequently expressed the opinion that parents need to be informed about and involved with the school. He felt that the Parent-Teacher Association (PTA) offered the best potential for accomplishing school-community communication.[5] He was an ardent supporter of the Taft School PTA and an optimist about its

---

[5] Ed felt it essential to have some kind of school-community organization "to keep the doors open and to show the community that *somebody* is watching the schools even if everyone isn't." His preference was to have Taft School linked up with the well-established and nationally organized PTA rather than to form an independent Parents' Club. "The PTA has a charter, direction, and organization. It helps parents know what they are supposed to do."

potential. Reviewing with a fellow principal the success of the Taft PTA during one year of the study Ed summarized, "This year it fell flat on its face. Next year it may pick up again. We have a couple of good people. I'm enough of a Kansas farmer to know you can't harvest a big crop every year."

Ed expected his teachers to be active participants in the Taft PTA, particularly through regular attendance at the evening meetings held each month. During a discussion with the PTA president about the eternal problem of getting people to attend the meetings, she complimented Ed on the fact that the teachers were "so good" about attending. Ed confessed, "Well, I do twist their arms a little." To some of his teachers, Ed's obsession with teacher attendance at PTA bordered on the irrational. One teacher expressed the following viewpoint on the subject:

> He has a *thing* about PTA. You just absolutely have to go. You have to have a death certificate in triplicate to get out of it. I was clued in on this immediately, thank goodness, because when teachers haven't been clued in, there have been some repercussions. They asked to be excused and they just are excused, *period!*
>
> But I was clued in—like one time, I didn't know until that very day that I didn't have a baby sitter—just not to show up and the next morning to apologize about it and explain it. It worked beautifully and smoothed right out. As it turned out he'd had a good show [attendance] for PTA and it had been a nice meeting, so he didn't blame me for things not going right.

The faculty did have a high attendance rate at PTA—in fact, they sometimes outnumbered the parents who attended the meetings, especially on evenings of inclement weather or when the announced program seemed to hold little promise. When called upon for the customary greeting and comment by the principal on one January meeting, Ed began his comments by joking to the teachers and the tiny complement of parents in attendance:

> I was tempted to welcome all you fine people to our *staff* meeting. But, seriously, I've long ago learned that you don't measure PTA success by the attendance.

As principal, Ed's participation in PTA affairs extended well beyond attending monthly meetings. He had been the second vice president of the Taft PTA for the previous five years. He probably would have been the nominee for that office again had not one of the recent officers discovered a rule that no officer could succeed himself. As Ed had long since realized, however, he was in effect always the second vice president.

Seven evening meetings of the Executive Board of the Taft School PTA were scheduled each year. Ed customarily attended them all. The meeting recounted here was held on a Monday evening in March. It was the first Executive Board meeting which I attended, and I asked Ed to brief me about it beforehand. He said the meeting would be held in the faculty room beginning at 7:30 P.M. and that there *could be* as many as 18–20 people present if the chairmen of all the standing committees were present. "There are usually less than that," he hastened to add. I asked how long the meetings usually extended. Ed replied, "The meetings sometimes run quite late. Of course, you are free to leave anytime. Just hope that the president has an expensive baby sitter."

The Meeting

7:35 P.M.   Five cars were parked in the school parking lot, but inside the faculty room Ed was talking to only one mother, the first to arrive for the meeting. On the counter by the sink, the coffee pot perked away with coffee which Ed was preparing for the meeting. On the table in front of Ed was an album of photographs of children and teachers taken recently by a school photographer and delivered to the school on that afternoon. Ed was showing the album to the mother and explaining how the teachers went about making room assignments for future grades.

The next mother to arrive, at 7:38 P.M., said, "What, no one here yet?" She did not address the principal or the other parent by name. Ed directed his comments to both parents as he began talking about his staff. He told them he had "the strongest staff ever this year." As he was talking, the president of the PTA entered the room. She waved hello to me and sat down to join the discussion group at the table. Recognizing the class picture of one of her children, one of the mothers announced that she had two children in this school, one in the second grade and one in the fourth. "They argue constantly about which is the best teacher, but according to my children, a teacher who isn't married is best," she continued.

Another mother arrived. Ed made an attempt at introductions but did not recall the names of everyone present.

With a total of four parents present including herself, the PTA president officially called the Executive Board meeting to order at 7:50 P.M. A reading of the minutes revealed a treasury of $509.04 and that the recent Saturday morning pancake feed held at the school had grossed $220.09 with costs of about $90.00. An official treasurer's report was dispensed with because the treasurer was sick.

The president said she planned to eliminate the regular April board meeting. The School Fair was scheduled for the following evening, she explained, and PTA members would not only be attending the fair but would also help by providing food. She reminded the group that the fair would run from 7:00 to 9:30 P.M. In connection with the date for the fair, Ed announced that he would have to miss the regular monthly meeting of the county principal's association. "That's all right. They can get by without me," he assured them. One of the mothers added, "Is that the first Tuesday of the month? Oh! That's my church circle. I *never* miss that."

The president called for suggestions about the kinds of food the PTA might sell at the School Fair. The first suggestions included soda pop, "pronto pups," cotton candy, and snow cones. The president reviewed the suggestions in terms of parents who might be called upon to help provide necessary equipment or assistance in preparing food at the fair.

8:10 P.M.   The discussion about food continued. Ed took out a nail clipper and began to trim his fingernails; he did not take part in the discussion at this point. Two of the mothers left the room at different times to use the telephone in the front office to telephone parents about helping to prepare or to serve food for the fair. Someone recalled that at the previous year's fair the school had been able to obtain a donation of Pepsi-Cola because one of the mothers in the PTA worked in the local Pepsi-Cola bottling plant. Apparently nothing similar had been planned for this year. "Why can't we get someone to donate something every year?" suggested one mother.

8:17 P.M. Ed glanced idly through the new album of school pictures. The four women continued their discussion of which foods to serve at the fair, especially in terms of the possibilities of getting free donations. One suggested calling upon a food store chain which had recently announced plans to open a store in the local area. Ed commented, "I have a friend who is a principal in a town where they have that chain. He says they get a lot of stuff donated from them."

8:24 P.M. The discussion continued about food, including how to keep it hot and how to serve it. The proposed menu had been elaborated to include baked beans and potato salad. Someone asked if it was going to be possible for the PTA to use the school kitchen. Ed answered, "This sale of food at the fair is supposed to be a profit-making enterprise. The district has a policy that if you use school equipment for profit-making, you have to hire a cook. Maybe you're getting into too much with the beans," he added as an afterthought. His remark prompted the discussion of a proposed menu to start all over again, this time with some new alternatives.

8:27 P.M. The president suggested, "Let's leave it like it was, without the beans, the cole slaw, or the potato salad." Everyone nodded assent and there was no further discussion.

The president introduced the next item of business, the selection of a new kindergarten chairman to oversee the voluntary, PTA-sponsored kindergarten program conducted at a local church. The president commented on the "possibility of having Mr. Bell interview the prospective teacher" and then went on immediately to ask the kindergarten chairman for her budget report of the year. The chairman reported: rent, $189; custodial costs, $180; supplies, $100; teacher salary, $1600; total $2446 to run the program for one year. The kindergarten chairman said that she had heard that she was not going to get any additional money from the Taft PTA to cover operating costs for the current year. She described how the kindergarten program "would come pretty close to the line." Two "broken families" in financial straits had withdrawn children from the program, and thus the class was not running with a full enrollment for the last three months of the school year. She reported a strong feeling among parents against increasing the tuition charge for the following year.

The president introduced the next item of business, plans for presenting a movie and demonstration for mouth to mouth resuscitation as the program for a forthcoming PTA meeting.

8:44 P.M. The telephone started ringing in the office. Ed left the teachers' room to go answer it. Out of habit, he put the telephone on "hold" before he returned to the meeting to tell the president that her babysitter was calling for her. The president arose immediately to go to the telephone. From the office she called back down the hall, "How do I get this thing to work?" "Push the lighted button," Ed directed.

While members of the Executive Board waited for their president to complete her call, Ed went to find a catalogue to see if the district had the resuscitation film. When the meeting settled down again the discussion turned to whether the film might be made available for all the children in the school. Ed said they could show it at school on the day the PTA ordered it for their meeting. One mother said, "We still might put on our announcement that children are welcome. Maybe there are junior high kids who haven't seen it."

8:50 P.M. The president said she had only one more item of business, the election and installation of next year's officers. She said she wanted to have an installation at the April meeting. Suddenly she remembered that she had just announced the cancellation of the April board meeting, so there would be no opportunity for the board to review the slate of candidates. She said she intended to "go home and study the bylaws some more" before deciding what to do.

8:55 P.M. The president remarked, "There's just one more thing. I'm not sure whether to bring it up at a board meeting, but why don't we have more playground equipment?"

Ed responded, "I've tried to add something each year. Now we have a tether ball and about eight different climbing pieces. I'd like for us to have more blacktop, and more room for basketball."

"How about tennis?" asked one of the mothers.

The PTA president added, "I still like swings, myself."

Ed answered that he did not think the district would approve of swings even if he put them in his budget. He reviewed some special problems with swings, noting especially the danger of having hardtop underneath them and the nuisance of having older children constantly wrapping the swings over the top bar on the weekends. He continued by discussing other problems of the playground: "We're trying to get as many kids involved as we can. This is something to work for all the time. It's awfully hard to get out enough equipment. If we had one ball for each child, they'd still want more. But this doesn't answer your question."

One mother asked, "Do you feel that it's alright for kids to come here to the playground when it isn't school?"

ED: I do. The community hasn't made any other provision for the children here.

Another parent complained that her children had come over to fly a kite on the schoolground one afternoon and some older children threw rocks at it. Later that day the children returned with another kite and an older girl drove over it with her bicycle. "There's always someone trying to put the kibosh on things, no matter where you go," she concluded.

9:08 P.M. The PTA president adjourned the meeting and stood up to put on her coat. One mother left as soon as the meeting was formally ended. The remaining mothers talked with the principal about the photographs of the children and thumbed through the album. "Who did the pictures this year?" asked one.

ED: The photographer was Charles Roberts. He was the one who did them last year.
ONE MOTHER: They seem better this year.
ED: How do you feel about the price?
MOTHER: $2.75 is *plenty*! Over at the junior high school it only costs $2.00.

Ed continued thumbing through the photo album and made comments about several children with the president and another parent who remained to visit with him for a few minutes. By 9:12 P.M. the last of the mothers had left. Ed looked at the clock and said, "A record!" "But," he added, "I don't really mind these meetings. You never know what may come up."

Later, as we were leaving the school (after a visit with the night custodian) Ed reflected on the meeting: "Funny they would take up something like playground swings. Maybe they figure that's something they know something about. Instead of math curriculum."

A MEETING FOR "NEW" PARENTS

The day was Tuesday, the month, May. Ed had returned to school at about 12:20 P.M. for lunch after spending the morning at a two-and-a-half hour meeting of the elementary principals. The major event scheduled for the afternoon was a meeting planned for parents of children who would be entering school as first graders the following September and for the children themselves. The meeting provided an opportunity to begin registering new pupils (parents were requested to bring proof of age of their children to the meeting); for the parents to be introduced to the first grade teachers; for the principal, the nurse, and the counsellor each to have a few moments for making announcements and answering questions; and for the children to have an opportunity to visit the classrooms and to see the teachers and children with whom they would spend their first year of school.

Plans for the afternoon meeting called for the teacher aide to supervise the formal registration of pupils at a desk in the hall and then to send the parents into the school library for coffee and an informal visit. The children were to be met by sixth-grade girls and conducted to one of the three first-grade classrooms. When the program began, the adults were to be divided into three arbitrary groups meeting in three locations, with the principal, nurse, and counsellor circulating among the three groups and talking with each for about fifteen minutes. Meanwhile the children, also divided into three groups, would move through the three first-grade classrooms, stopping with one teacher to hear a magnet-board story, with the second to have a short music lesson, and with the third to have a brief art lesson in which they would make a construction paper dog which they could take home.

A few minutes before one o'clock a father who had a third- and a sixth-grade pupil in the school arrived at the office. He had already been to see his child's sixth-grade teacher (Mr. Adam) to register a complaint about the supervision of children in the lunchroom. The teacher had suggested they go to the office and include the principal in their discussion. It was not unusual for this father to make such a visit. Another teacher said of him on this occasion:

> He's always coming in with a complaint. He gets all worked up about anything that happens. Usually it's the mother who does that.

For the next half hour Ed, Mr. Adam, and the father talked together in the office. Ed kept one eye on the clock. He still had some last minute arrangements for the fast approaching afternoon meeting. He interrupted the discussion at one point to ask the secretary to "tell Betty [the head cook] to make that pot of coffee for the meeting of next year's first graders." The secretary stepped to the intercom and relayed the message to the kitchen.

"What coffee?" boomed the reply over the intercom.

"She doesn't know about it yet," explained the principal from his office. "We'll need coffee for about 40 people at two o'clock."

An end to the impromptu parent conference being held in his office did not seem to be in sight. Ed explained to the visiting father that he had a meeting to get ready for, and since the father's complaints extended to a problem about his third-grade child as well, why didn't they go down the hall and see if the third-grade teacher was free at the moment.

The secretary had gone to see that chairs and refreshments were in order for the meeting. When Ed returned to the office the telephone was ringing. He stopped to answer it and to take a message for one of the teachers that a meeting of a curriculum committee scheduled for later that afternoon had been cancelled. Just as he hung up the telephone it rang again, this time with a call for the school nurse. He called to her to answer (there was an extension in her office); as soon as she started talking the telephone rang again on the other trunk line, and Ed answered another call for the nurse. He stepped to the intercom to inform the teacher about the cancelled meeting. While he was using the intercom, he decided to make a general announcement. He flipped the button for the "all-call" and announced throughout the school that in just a few minutes there would be some parents and new first-graders visiting in the building but that they would not be bothering any of the other classrooms except for the helpers from the sixth grade. He then hurried down the hall to get a table set up for registering new pupils.

The time was 1:50 P.M., ten minutes before the announced starting time of the meeting. Ed returned to his office and made a frantic but futile search for a clipboard which held the notes that he planned to use for his remarks to the parents. He picked up some extra copies of a little booklet prepared by the first-grade teachers at Taft, *We Start School,* to take to the meeting. In the hall he met some mothers who had arrived early. He directed the sixth-grade girls who were acting as hostesses to begin ushering the arriving children into the first-grade classrooms. He greeted a few more parents and stepped into the library.

The program began at 2:10 P.M. while the last of the arriving children were guided to the grade-one classrooms. The group of parents included one father. One teacher looked at the group and commented to me, "First grade mothers are always so eager." Ed asked aloud if everyone in the group had a cup of coffee. He noted that several older pupils at Taft were helping with the program, the boys moving furniture, and girls acting as hostesses. A few mothers held younger children in their laps. Some mothers appeared to be at the school for the first time, while others were clearly oldtimers at Taft. Ed greeted a few parents by name. He, the nurse, the counsellor and the three first-grade teachers all wore large name tags printed on yellow construction paper.

Ed divided the parent group into three smaller groups and asked two of the groups to accompany guides to other classrooms. He remained in the library and brought the meeting informally to order by raising his voice to ask if there were any questions about the school. One mother raised her hand immediately to ask if the staggered reading program under which some children arrived at school early and others remained later in the afternoon would be continued next year in the first grade. Ed said that it would. She said, "Has any poll been taken of the opinion of the mothers who are now in it?"

Ed answered, "No, I'd have to answer we have not."

The mother said, "Well, from what I've heard in my neighborhood, I'm already dissatisfied with it."

Ed asked which parents were presently in the program. A few of them held up their hands. He stated that the teachers liked the new program. He added, "I think they're one of the most dedicated group of teachers you would find anywhere. We continually ask ourselves 'What's best for kids?' I knew this question about the reading program would be asked, so I asked the teachers, and they said that this schedule gives them more chance for individualized instruction. The teachers feel they can do a better job. Well, there aren't any practices around our school that can't be changed, so if there are problems, please let us hear about your feelings."

A second question was asked about bringing money for lunches and whether the children would continue to bring their money each day. Ed said that there were no plans to do it differently.

Ed glanced at the clock. It was 2:30. He concluded by saying that it was time for him to meet with the next group, inviting parents to phone him any time they had questions about school. He went to another classroom where the school counsellor was concluding her comments with another group of ten mothers. Just as he was about to begin his remarks for the second time, the nurse stuck her head in the door to see if this was the group that she was to address next. Ed said to her, "You belong down in the library." She closed the door. Ed said, "Isn't she pretty? And she's just as efficient as she is pretty."

Ed began with the same comments he had made to the earlier group, welcoming the parents to the school and inviting their questions at any time. He asked if there were any questions which people would like to ask right at the moment. Since no questions were volunteered, he referred to the questions which had been asked at his first session. He said, "I was asked a few minutes ago about the early-late reading program. If we ask your child to come at a time that isn't good for you, we hope you will tell us." He went on to discuss the lunch program, and that the price of a child's lunch next year might be increased to 30¢ (from the present price of 25¢) since the school board had decided to eliminate a $40,000 subsidy of the hot lunch program from its budget.

At the conclusion of Ed's remarks one mother asked, "I know of a child who's quarter for lunch disappeared and he was sent home. Do you do that?"

ED: We never send a child home if the parents aren't expecting them unless we telephone first.

THE MOTHER: Well, in this case the parents were pretty surprised when the child appeared at home.

ED: I knew I should have said, "almost never."

At 2:45 it was time to move to the third group. In this group there were 15 mothers and one father. Ed began by saying, "We probably have the most qualified first-grade staff you could ask for. They are well trained, dedicated people. They like to have fun, too. Just listen to them in the staff room. And they'll enjoy your children, too. At least most of the time. If history repeats itself, education will continue to change and will be changing a lot in the six years your children are here at Taft School."

When he opened the discussion for questions, he was asked when children at Taft School started receiving band instruction. He explained that band instruction started in grade six, but instruction in string instruments began in the fourth grade.

A parent asked about the times for opening and closing school. Ed answered, "Half the first graders come at 8:25, the other half come at 9:15. I think children need to develop habits of arriving at the right place at the right time."

The topic of lunches came up again. One question dealt with how much the lunch would cost. Ed said he had forgotten whether he had already talked to this group about lunches. He explained that each child was to carry his own lunch money to the cafeteria each day.

"How long do children have for lunch?" came the next question.

"Not very long. About 35–40 minutes," Ed answered.

Another mother asked, "Do you think that's enough time for them to run home, eat, run back, and that it's good for digestion?"

"This schedule seems to be working out quite well," Ed answered, "and kids have stomachs made of iron, anyway." (The mother who had asked the question did not seem amused at his response.) There were no other questions. Ed explained that this concluded the afternoon's program. He invited the parents to return to the library to meet with the teachers, to get another cup of coffee, and to pick up their children. He said hello to a few more parents and engaged in a rather long discussion with one parent whom he already knew. By 3:15 most parents had left. Ed continued his talk with one mother. One of the first-grade teachers held a long talk with another parent. Another first-grade teacher sat down at a table with six of the new first-graders and visited with them while they waited for their parents to depart.

Staff members expressed satisfaction after the last of the parents had left that the meeting had been "a success." One first-grade teacher complained in jest about all the children bringing dogs to her class (the construction paper animals they made in their brief art lesson) and then both teachers expressed admiration to their colleague that her art lesson was "so creative."

During that brief visit at school many of the new parents had undoubtedly begun to form opinions about the program and personnel of Taft School that would set the tone for future interpretations of their dealings with members of the school staff. Judging by external qualities such as how they were dressed for the meeting, their interactions with and responses to Ed and the faculty, and the reactions of their children to their first "day" in school, certainly not all parents and children shared identical expectations or reactions.

A specific instance of what the meeting had meant to one mother, the one who had opened Ed's first session with the question about the early-late reading schedule, came to light two days later following another of the evening meetings of the PTA executive board. The major business at that meeting had been to appoint the chairmen of standing committees for the coming year. The process entailed discussion by board members, followed in most cases by a telephone call to see if the person whose name had been suggested would accept the appointment. Some attempt was made to "involve" mothers whose children were about to enter school. The outgoing PTA president had suggested the name of the new mother and had personally made the usual telephone inquiry during the meeting. After the board meeting ended, the president remained at school to speak to Ed privately. She told him, "One of the parents I called tonight is not very happy with you. It's about that early-late scheduling. She was the one who asked you about it at that meeting with the first-grade mothers the other day. She said you should have asked right then how many of them were unhappy about it. She said that she has talked to a lot of mothers who don't like it."

"They're not the group to ask," replied Ed. "The one's to ask are the ones who are in it now, not the ones who are only anticipating it. You'll find that most of them are all for it. And anyway, I had two other groups of parents to talk with in those few minutes. I couldn't take the time just then."

The PTA president said, "Well, I just thought you ought to know about this."

"You're right," Ed answered, "and I appreciate your keeping me informed."

Comment

The four meetings described in this chapter were selected because they illustrate the variety of roles Ed was called upon to play during his formal encounters. We see him variously as participant and member of the firm, person-in-charge, advisor and guide, and mediator. Having attended to the specific and unique aspects of several of Ed's meetings, we need also to consider "meeting behavior" collectively and ask what functions are performed by this seemingly endless pattern of gathering and conferring by which schoolmen appear to conduct so substantial a part of their affairs. I find the concept of manifest and latent functions useful here for drawing attention to the contrast between the stated purposes for calling meetings and the real function that I believe they perform.

The manifest function of school meetings was to facilitate communication and to make collective decisions. As the meetings described in this chapter and in several others (see Chapters 2, 6, 8, 9, 11) suggest, these ideal functions were not accomplished to any great extent. Even in parent meetings, where the formal school organization exerted little control and the schoolman had to proceed with utmost patience and tact, communication tended to be one-way. Participants were generally called upon to concur with decisions already made rather than engage in significant decision-making of their own. Within the formal confines of the educator group, communication was almost exclusively unilateral, decisions more often revealed than reached. Note how the principals devoted one entire meeting to assuring that a document they had been preparing for weeks would not communicate any controversial information upward within the administrative hierarchy.

The latent functions of meetings, especially those within the educator subculture, accomplished rather different purposes. First, they served to validate role—to give visible evidence of being engaged with the "problems and issues" of schooling. Secondly, and more importantly, they served to validate existing status hierarchies and to provide a continuing process for reviewing each person's position in those hierarchies. What actually transpired at any of the meetings was never as important as the underlying issue of who could call a meeting for what purposes, who felt obligated to attend, and what kind of priority was adequate for an excuse.

When the status machinery was working properly, there was no question of who had to attend meetings; one's presence at a meeting served as his acknowledgment of his status. Regardless of Ed's personal assessment of the urgency of items planned for the agenda of a meeting of the elementary school principals, for example, he would never have considered missing one of the meetings. But occasionally there were meetings to which Ed was called, and meetings which he called, where there was evidence of ambiguity about or resistance to the authority of the summons. His virtual insistence on faculty attendance at PTA meetings provides a case in point, for he seemed to be operating at, or perhaps exceeding, the limits of his power by making demands affecting the after-school hours of his teachers. The real issue was not whether PTA meetings accomplished anything but whether Ed's position carried the authority to insist that teachers attend. The same question applies to his other meetings as well, both those to which he was, or felt himself to be, summoned and those to which he summoned others. That the latent, status-validating function of meetings, as suggested here, is, independent of and rather far afield from the content of them may help explain why educators complain chronically of the great number and little purpose that characterizes meetings they are called upon to attend yet faithfully attend nonetheless. As situations and statuses change in the constant flux of personnel they, in turn, call meetings which others are expected to attend and thus proclaim their own positions in the hierarchy.

6 / What a principal does: informal encounters and daily routines

The time that Ed Bell spent in formal, prearranged meetings restricted the time available in his total day at school for handling other routines. The net effect was that the busier a day was with scheduled meetings and appointments, the busier were the unscheduled moments available for handling daily routines. Conversely, on days with few meetings or appointments scheduled, Ed sometimes seemed at a loss about what to do. Thus, the time he spent at the routines described in this chapter was a function of a sort of Parkinson's Law[1] in which the amount of available time was a critical factor in determining the extent of his involvement with the multifarious problems brought to his attention.

The informal encounters and daily routines of Ed's life as a principal, presented in a series of brief statements and illustrative vignettes, have been organized in this chapter into three task areas which required perpetual time and effort on Ed's part: "Receiving Requests and Handling Problems," "Orienting and Greeting," and "Taking Care of the Building." A brief final section, "When the Principal Is Away," considers how the school operated in Ed's absence.

RECEIVING REQUESTS AND HANDLING PROBLEMS

Arriving at School or Returning to the Office

Some problems at school cannot "wait until the principal gets here." Most can.[2] The result at Taft School was that Ed's return to the front office any time during the day, and particularly his arrival at school in the morning or after several hours away from the building, tended to precipitate a flurry of activity in which he caught up with problems and problems caught up with him. The following account describes Ed's first moments at school on a Monday morning in January:

Ed arrived at 8:15 A.M. As he walked through the door into the office the cook, who had just completed making a telephone order for groceries, walked up to him.

---

[1] "Work expands so as to fill the time available for its completion" (Parkinson 1957:2).

[2] The absence of a principal is frequently handled by those left at school in the same way that a father's absence may be treated at home, particularly in disciplinary matters on which action can be postponed: "Wait till the principal gets back. He'll take care of it [you]."

"Mr. Bell, can I talk to you first thing?" She did not wait for an answer but began immediately to describe a problem with the milk:

> You know, we have a new milkman now. He's only been on a few days. I think he's honest. But on Thursday we were short 7, on Friday we were short 8. I think he's delivering the right number, but I don't know who is taking milk without paying for it, the "lunch" people or the "just-milk" people.

Ed asked her if it would be possible to keep a running inventory on the milk supply. The cook explained that she did not think that was possible because of the way the milk had to be stored. She asked him if he could come to the kitchen sometime to look. Ed said, "I'll go right now, if you'll just let me hang up my coat." He accompanied her to the cafeteria, nodded sympathetically as she showed him how milk was handled for storage and distribution and explained her problem again. Ed promised to "give it some thought."

Ed returned to the office and decided to make a brief tour of the building as he often did just before school started. He chatted briefly with Kay Johnson, the "beginning" fourth-grade teacher, while he inspected his pet project at school, a salt water aquarium he referred to as "the farm." (Ed had become interested in maintaining an aquarium at school during a science workshop. He had maintained the present aquarium since the beginning of the school year.) He told Mrs. Johnson that he had hoped to get to the coast during the previous weekend to get new specimens and a supply of salt water, but there were too many other things to do with his family.

He continued down the corridor. He joined a hall conversation between a teacher and the counsellor about a second-grade boy who had bitten another child the previous week. The counsellor suggested to Ed, "Be sure and make a note on it. That's the specific kind of thing the caseworker wants." Ed commented that he thought they already had enough evidence of that kind. He turned to greet another teacher passing by and then walked the length of the intermediate grade wing. A few children had entered the halls and classrooms; the day was clear and most children were playing outside as they awaited the morning bell. Ed poked his head into Mrs. Duchess's classroom to say hello and chat about her weekend, then went across the hall to ask Mr. Adam for his suggestions about the problem of the disappearing milk. Adam said he was aware of the problem and that he intended to "station a student monitor at the 'milk jar'" to assure that children taking milk were also paying for it.

Ed stepped into another sixth-grade classroom just as the bell rang to start school. The regular teacher in that class had telephoned him at home that morning to say she had the flu. Ed had called the central office to request a substitute. The substitute teacher had not yet arrived, so Ed remained with the class. His announcement to the children that they would be having a substitute teacher that day was greeted with "boos." He admonished them to "be good sports about it" and to cooperate with the substitute.

"Who's coming?" they asked.

"I don't know," he answered.

"Where is she?"

"She'll be right along."

He told the class to quiet down and asked if they had a class president who could take charge. The president was absent, so he asked the vice-president to conduct the class and to begin by taking the lunch count. By the time the count had been taken the substitute had arrived. She appeared to be quite young, perhaps no more than 22. She had not been at Taft School before. Ed welcomed her with, "I'm glad to see you." He immediately left the room. As he left, he picked up a chair with a splintered leg which had caught his eye as he entered the classroom. He said he would take the chair to the office and break the leg so that it would not be used again.

On the way back to the office Ed stopped by the resource teacher's room to see how he was feeling. The resource teacher had missed several days the previous week because of flu. Ed also wanted to inform him that the teacher aide would not be at school that day because she was helping in the compilation of a school district census being made at the central office.

When Ed walked into the office for the second time that morning the secretary was talking to a woman accompanied by a seven-year-old girl, "Mr. Bell, we have a new girl this morning for the second grade," the secretary informed him. Another round in the morning's routines had begun.

The Telephone

Through its three telephone extensions and two trunk lines, Taft School was linked with the telephone network of the school district through a switchboard at the central office and, through the switchboard, to the outside world. "Outside" numbers could be dialed directly from the three telephones in the front office (one on the secretary's desk, one in the nurse's room, one in Ed's office) by first dialing a "9" to get an outside line, a procedure which gave children at school no trouble but seemed frequently to confuse their parents. Incoming calls were taken by operators at the central office who transferred them directly to the school.

During most of the day, the secretary monitored incoming calls. She specifically delegated responsibility for "watching the phone" during moments when she was going to be farther away from the office than the teachers' room. Ed did not customarily answer the telephone if someone else was available to do so. If he was preoccupied in his office he avoided responding too quickly to calls even if he could see that the secretary was not at her desk. The ringing of the telephone was perceived as a summons that had to be met, however, and if no one else responded, Ed would answer. His reluctance in answering was probably related to the fact that many calls to school did not directly concern him, rather than to any reluctance on his part in talking on the telephone. Indeed, the time-and-motion study described in the previous chapter showed him to spend an appreciable portion (6–10 percent) of his day in telephoning. He had a tendency to engage in rather lengthy conversations (he reported having talked to one mother for one and one-half hours one morning) as well as to initiate calls purely conversational in intent, particularly to his wife and to certain colleagues among the principals at nearby schools. The vignette which follows provides an example of the kind of telephone call which Ed liked least, a call from a complaining mother.

Ed was in his office working at his desk. The time was 9:00 A.M. on a November morning, and the school had just settled down for the day. The telephone rang. Ed looked up from his desk to see whether the secretary was free to answer it, which she was. "Good morning, Taft School," she said cheerily, and then she paused to hear a long comment by the caller. "Just a moment, please, and I'll see if he's free." The secretary walked to the door of Ed's office and asked him in a low voice, "Do you want to talk to Mrs. Silvera? It's about her boy having to wait outside in the draft in the morning?"

"No," Ed replied. They both laughed as he reached for the telephone to begin the unavoidable conversation. "Good morning, Sharon. I understand you are concerned about your boy having to wait outside before class starts? [Pause for a reply.] Would it be possible for you to time his arrival so it coincides with the start of his class?"

From the conversation that followed, it was apparent that the mother had telephoned to express dissatisfaction with the then newly-inaugurated "early-late" reading schedule in Taft's first- and second-grade classes. Under this schedule some of the children in each classroom arrived slightly before the regular time for starting school, and the balance of the class arrived 45 minutes later. In the afternoon the late group remained at school 45 minutes after the other children had gone home. The early and late periods were used for reading instruction and were intended to give teachers more time to work with individuals and small groups of children. Five of the primary teachers were very enthusiastic about the program. Complaints from parents had come only from families with children in Mrs. Skirmish's second grade, the one teacher who had been opposed to the schedule change. Mrs. Silvera's boy was a pupil in Mrs. Skirmish's second grade.

The telephone conversation continued, and I recorded excerpts from Ed's comments:

Oh no, ... some ... we have some who feel as you do, I guess.
Fifteen minutes.
What do you want to compare it with, the way it was before we started this?
We're far above the *state* [i.e., minimum] requirement.
We're adhering to *district* policy now.
He won't have to stand in the rain if he comes now.
If he gets here at 9:25, he'll be in time and be under cover.
I'm a little surprised at you, Sharon. You take your kids skiing, don't you?
If we say we want them to come at 8:30, then we're responsible then.
What difference is five minutes in the breezeway?
Talk to his pediatrician. He'll tell you the germs that give him trouble come from inside.
I don't care who you get, I'll go with you.
You mean about the lunch time? No, you're the only one [complaining]. I'll be glad to meet with anyone, anytime, in any number. You're good for me, Sharon. I'm not attempting to take the temperature of the community, but the door and the phone lines are always open.
Well, you know now. ...

Based upon what reason, what decision?

Why don't you come over here? I'll read the law with you.

Forty-five minutes to eat their lunch? They have forty minutes from the time they leave the room.

Golly, Sharon, what's the difference—five minutes, give or take. . . .

Well, you come up here and tell me just how you want your child's program and I'll run it *just like you want*. [Ed told me afterward that her response to this suggestion was, "You're being condescending."]

What do you mean? I'm agreeing with you.

Who have I told that you were unreasonable?

Your kids seem pretty healthy to me. I didn't know you were keeping them home with running noses. But they look pretty good. And pretty well educated. . . .

[At this point, the conversation turned to a discussion of the education of Mrs. Silvera's other child at Taft School, a girl in Mr. Adam's sixth-grade class.]

Oh, I know we haven't batted a thousand. . . .

He does more to teach kids to think than anyone else around here. . . .

[Afterward, Ed recalled that her criticism of Mr. Adam and of Taft School in general was, "I think all you're doing is teaching kids to think. I want them to learn some facts."]

He's good for kids. I'm satisfied with him.

All right!

The conversation ended abruptly. Ed hung up the telephone, turned to me with a sigh, and said, "The rainy season has begun." He shook his head, got up from his desk, and went to the teachers' room. He announced aloud to the primary-grade teachers gathered for their morning coffee break, "I've just been raked over the coals by Mrs. Silvera." He described part of the conversation. "She's just generally angry, and this early-late reading schedule gives her something to be angry about." The teachers laughed when Ed recounted telling the mother that it seemed strange she would be so concerned about her boy standing in a draft before school when she regularly took the children skiing. Ed said: "She didn't even answer that."

One first-grade teacher commented sympathetically: "I'd never want to be a principal. Not with my tissue-paper stomach."

Another teacher added: "Me either—I'd cry a lot."

Staff Requests

Staff requests directed to Ed were routine in the sense that he could expect to receive them in almost any form and at almost any time. But the handling of such requests was routine only as a *category* of behavior on Ed's part, since individually each request entailed making a disruption, or remedying a disruption that already had occurred, in the normal routine of the school. Requests for personal favors (for example, leaving school earlier than the customary time in the afternoon, for reasons ranging from self-diagnosed "exhaustion" to an appointment with the hairdresser) were usually made in the relatively casual moments before and after school or during lunch or coffee. Once the children were in class, staff requests directed to Ed usually focused either on the instructional program or on the pupils themselves (discipline, lost lunch money, missing articles of clothing, and so forth). Often—perhaps usually—the requests which teachers made regarding their instructional program did not require the principal's attention per se as much as they required the attention of someone not immediately burdened with the responsibility of supervising a group of children. If Ed was available in the office and not otherwise preoccupied, he might go to the rescue of a teacher to "see what was wrong" with the TV set, the heater, a crying child, missing supplies, the clock, and so forth; he might direct someone else to do it; or he might send word back to "get by as best you can for now and we'll see about it later." He used whichever of these alternatives seemed appropriate or at least adequate at the moment. In Ed's absence, anyone else available in the office who received such requests met them with the same available alternatives.

In the following illustration, Ed responded in person to a routine teacher request. The request was made by a teacher substituting in the first grade, a woman not well acquainted with Taft School. The request was made shortly after lunch, a period which was usually the least preoccupied in Ed's entire day. The following sequence of events covered a period of half an hour:

1. A first-grade child had been sent to the office by the substitute teacher to get a "different" record player. Her pupils were already gathered in the multi-purpose room and waiting to use it.
2. The secretary asked Ed what to do. Ed said he would go see what was wrong.
3. Ed accompanied the child to the multi-purpose room. The substitute teacher showed him a broken stylus on the record player she had taken from the classroom to the multi-purpose room. She had been assured earlier in the day that a machine was always available there, although that had not been the case. She had returned to the classroom to get a player but had been unable to use it because of the broken stylus.
4. Ed said he would get a record player for her.
5. Ed went to the intermediate wing to check with the teacher who supervised the upper-grade lunchroom (Mr. Adam) to ask why the record player that was supposed to remain in the multi-purpose room was not there and to learn who had taken it. Adam told him which teacher had borrowed it.
6. Ed went to the primary wing to get the player that belonged in the multi-purpose room. He had to interrupt another class to do this. As he closed up the machine in order to carry it, he reminded the teacher (Mrs. Skirmish) that the player in the multi-purpose room was not to be removed. She, in turn, explained that she had needed to borrow it this one time because the other players were all spoken for that afternoon.
7. Ed took the player to the multi-purpose room, set it up, and waited to see that it operated properly before leaving.
8. Returning to the office with the broken player, he told the secretary to "type out a work order" for his signature so the player could be repaired in the audio-visual department at the central office.
9. Ed glanced at the clock and realized he should already have been on his way to pick up Bill St. Claire en route to a meeting at another school. He grabbed his coat and hat, hurriedly informing the secretary where he would be and that he would return around 4:00 P.M.

Illness and Accident

The spatial and architectural arrangements made in virtually every large public school provide evidence of a concern bordering on obsession for pupil health and safety. At Taft School the nurse's office was immediately adjacent to the principal's private office. It was larger and better equipped than his, since it contained not only a desk, filing cabinet, and telephone comparable to the stark furnishings of his office but also a sink with hot and cold running water, a medicine cabinet, two built-in bunk beds, and an adjacent private room with toilet and shower. Although the nurse was shared with two other neighboring schools, the position of nurse and the place for nursing were always present at Taft School. The place for nursing was almost sacrosanct; there were only minor exceptions to limiting the use of the room exclusively to its intended function. The telephone extension in the nurse's office provided one exception. The office was a relatively quiet and private place for telephoning and allowed the second trunk line to be used even if someone was talking on the telephone at the secretary's desk. Callers desiring quiet or privacy often used the telephone if the nurse was away. During the "rush hours" at recess and noon the female teachers also commandeered the additional toilet in the nurse's office if the office itself was not occupied.

At the same time that the nurse's office epitomized the school's concern for taking care of the bodies as well as the minds of its pupils, the actual treatment for illness and accident cases was essentially symbolic. District policy regarding emergencies directed that school personnel, including the nurse, do the least possible to provide adequate care. In no case was medical *treatment* (as contrasted with initial first aid) to be given. Tincture of Green Soap and water provided the most popular disinfectant. Children might be allowed a first bandaid for a minor cut, but subsequent bandaids had to be supplied at home. School personnel were not authorized to give aspirin to a child. Even a splinter had to meet special criteria to qualify as an emergency which could be handled at school—the nurse was not authorized to remove a splinter which was completely covered by skin. On one occasion when the nurse was away a child came to the office with a splinter in her finger and asked the secretary to take it out. The secretary told the child,

> I'm not allowed to remove a splinter, and the nurse is not here. But I'm not sure if she is allowed to take out a splinter even if she were here. You go in the nurse's room and wash your hands *good*, honey.

After the child left the office, the secretary looked at me sheepishly and added, "That's pretty silly advice, isn't it!"

The most generous dosages of "medication" were of attention and, except for the budding hypochondriacs, of sympathy. Ed could express such confidence in applying a thin coat of Zephiran (zephiran chloride, an antiseptic solution consisting essentially, according to the label, of its "inert ingredient—water 99.87%") on a thumb that "hurts every time I write on it" that a pupil could hardly doubt the healing properties of either the colorless liquid or the sympathetic and attentive man who applied it. A duo of permanent cold packs stored in the freezing compartment of the refrigerator in the teachers' room was endowed with similar healing qualities when authoritatively applied. If "going to the office" or "seeing the nurse" did not in themselves provoke a recovery, children were allowed and sometimes encouraged to lie down in the nurse's office. For almost any problem the essential mode of treatment, after providing an initial dosage of attention, was to place a telephone call to the child's mother or to an alternate telephone contact kept on a record card immediately on hand in the office. The availability of the nurse or secretary and the vagaries of Ed's own whereabouts dictated the occasions when either the administering of first aid or the task of notifying a parent fell to him. On days when the nurse was present to provide personal attention, the secretary sometimes had an accident report form typed up and ready for Ed's signature before the nurse had stopped the flow of blood and tears.

Ed campaigned endlessly against accidents, particularly those inflicted by children through their own negligence, such as running in the halls or throwing rocks. He kept a special list of rock throwers; first offenders were summoned for a talk in the office, second offenders were sometimes given the alternative of having to go home at lunchtime or wearing a patch over an eye for a day at school "to see how it would feel if a rock put someone's eye out."

On an April day when a rock was thrown that did hit another boy in the forehead hard enough to require three stitches, Ed immediately sent the rock thrower home and forbade the boy to return until an office conference with the boy and both his parents could be arranged. The rock throwing incident occurred during an unusual rash of accidents. On that very day another child had fallen while playing at noontime and had cut his arm badly, and on the previous day a child broke his arm in two places. "Our total will go up this month," Ed sighed, referring to a monthly accident report submitted to the central office by each school, a report on which Taft School usually showed a comparatively low accident and injury rate.

The most dramatic medical emergency of the year was a case in which an upper grade boy went into insulin shock. Ed and Mrs. Duchess, the boy's fifth-grade teacher, rushed the boy to a local hospital in the back of her station wagon. "Two minutes after we got him to the hospital he was sitting up talking," Ed recounted after he returned to school later in the morning. "They shot glucose right into his veins." By contrast with this dramatic race to the hospital, most illnesses and accidents at school provided minor and almost predictable variations in the office routine and were in themselves routine in both type (upset stomachs, headaches, cuts and bruises) and treatment. The following entry from my daily journal notes from a Monday in December serves to illustrate:

> Ed returned to the office at 2:20 P.M., after taking some measurements in the halls to complete a budget item on maintenance. He noted that the secretary was in the nurse's room and went to see what was wrong. She had gotten an ice pack for a third-grade boy who was lying down on one of the bunk beds.
> "He hit his head and now he has a headache," the secretary explained.
> Ed looked down at the boy and asked, "How's your tummy?"
> "Fine," the boy whispered.
> "Better fill out an accident report on this one," Ed instructed the secretary. Then he returned to his office to continue working on his budget estimate.

Office Routines

Office routines at Taft School were handled by a full-time secretary. Customarily the secretary was stationed behind a child-high (29¼ inches), L-shaped, formica-topped counter in the school office. The secretary acted as receptionist for incoming visitors and telephone calls; she kept records on attendance, lunch and milk counts, and bank deposits; she distributed incoming materials and relayed messages; and she handled many of the myriad requests directed to the office during the course of any day, frequently doubling for the nurse, counsellor, principal, or for the generalized "authority" of the front office. Her official territory was bounded essentially by the walls of the office complex. The extent of her authority was a function of the momentary location and activity of the principal. If he was present in his office or immediately available in the building (for example, in the faculty room having coffee) her control was restricted to monitoring who or what messages got through to him. In his absence, however, even a decision on whether or not to make an interim decision could be important in the routine operation of the school (for example, whether to make a classroom assignment for a new enrollee, whether to have a child who had been sent to the office for disciplinary purposes wait in the office or return to the classroom).

For the most part, running the school office was reduced to a routine almost as predictable as the school bell (buzzer) itself: making the correct change for lunch money when the children first entered the building each morning (children wishing to take a hot lunch were required to present a twenty-five cent piece for their meal), receiving slips noting daily pupil absences from each classroom, keeping the permanent attendance record up-to-date, giving the composite lunch and milk count to the cafeteria, preparing routine forms and reports, counting the daily monies received at school and preparing the bank deposit (about $80 was collected and banked each day), typing correspondence and memos, and passing out material sent to the school for general distribution among pupils or staff. "This isn't like a secretarial job," the new secretary explained to me after she had been on the job about three months. "Most of the letters so far have been crank letters to people who sent us the wrong materials. Mostly I fill in reports and forms."

Taft School received two deliveries of written material each morning and a morning newspaper. The regular mail delivery was left in a large, rural-type mailbox across the street from the school office at the curbside, since mail deliveries in the area were made by motorized carriers. Magazines for the school library (over 25 subscriptions) and professional magazines taken for use by the staff (including *Life* as well as elementary school stand-bys like *The PTA Magazine, Grade Teacher, Elementary School Journal,* and *The Instructor*), plus a steady flow of advertising mail, mailed textbooks, and other materials swelled the size of the deliveries. Yet "important" messages arrived by mail so infrequently that the secretary looked upon the walk to get the mail as a break from the routine of her desk work rather than as a crucial moment in the day's events. Occasionally on busy days she forgot about the mail until well into the afternoon, and during inclement weather she wondered aloud (but to no avail if it was a hint for help) if the effort in getting the mail was worth it. Ed's assessment of the mail was that it was "about 90 percent junk."

Of more immediate importance to the daily operation of the school was the morning delivery and pick-up of school-district mail by courier in a route van operated out of the central office. The interschool delivery included record folders of pupils who had transferred within the district (or anywhere within the county); correspondence and announcements to district employees from the central office; and centrally distributed materials such as communications to all teachers from the local teacher organization. The interschool delivery also included the distribution and collection of films and other audio-visual materials for classroom use. Collecting due and overdue classroom films at the office in time for the morning pick-up often occasioned a flurry of last-minute checking by the secretary. Several of the primary grade teachers exhibited an uncanny intuition in sensing when new films had arrived in the office. Sometimes primary teachers were on hand in the office within minutes after the morning delivery, not so much to pick up the films they had ordered as to see what other films were going to be available which they could borrow to show in their classrooms (see Wolcott 1969).

District school mail and announcements originating at Taft School were distributed to teachers and staff in individual mailboxes built into the wall of the inner hallway between the office and the faculty room. Teachers "checked their boxes" two or three times daily through the front office. The secretary carried mail addressed to Ed (or more ambiguously to "the Principal") directly to his desk whenever a delivery was received in the office unless Ed was engaged in a private conference. When Ed was not at his desk, she left mail or messages in the middle of his desk, placing the newly arrived materials on top of anything else that happened to be there. Almost reflexively on his every return to the front office Ed walked to his desk to check for mail and messages. The rather dependable flow of messages onto his desk, many of them written by the secretary on a printed message form, plus the incoming mail from the school district and post, served constantly to reinforce Ed's message checking habit. The secretary further reinforced his habit pattern by referring to the fact of messages awaiting him on his desk. Frequently, she summarized verbally the content of the messages as well: "There's a message on your desk to call Bill St. Claire. He said he's only to be at his school for the next half hour, then he has to go to a meeting.

The content and urgency of messages relayed to Ed ran the gamut one might expect, from double underscored messages about calls to be returned or teachers to see "immediately," to semi-emergencies ("We have opened the next to last can of coffee today"), to the epitome of administrative routine, opening "junk mail" distributed in nationwide mailouts to schools. As Ed was going through the day's mail one morning, he turned to me with a smile as he held up an envelope addressed to "Principal, Taft Elementary School" before dropping it unopened into the wastebasket: "Here's one from Lowell Thomas, Junior, I wonder what Lowell Thomas wants with Taft Elementary School?"

Ed's desk was not usually cluttered, but it was almost never cleared. The essential artifacts on top of his desk included the telephone, a flat monthly calendar large enough to serve as a desk blotter,[3] a three-tiered metal in-basket, a file box of individual cards containing the name, address, and telephone number of each child in school, and a spindle containing brief notes in Ed's own handwriting which he referred to as his "file." At the back of his desk, along with photographs of each of his two little daughters, were a desk pen and a small calendar which showed day, date, and month. The pen and calendar were ornamental rather than functional, since Ed did all his writing with a ball-point pen carried in his shirt pocket, and the mechanical calendar was often a week or more in arrears. Ed possessed a nameplate for his desk with "Mr. Bell" painted on it, but it reposed on a shelf in the corner of the room.

In attempting to order the written announcements and requests which came across his desk, Ed had evolved a system for sorting materials utilizing the three tiers of his metal in-basket and based on priorities for action. At the end of the first month of the new school year, the bottom basket, containing written materials for "immediate action," was full. The middle basket contained materials which Ed described as being "for action, but not so pressing." That basket was almost full. The top basket contained materials "to be filed." That pile was at least twice the height of the other two. Not too many days later Ed wondered aloud, "I wonder when this whole thing is going to tip over."

Ed described his procedure for handling written materials as consisting of three parts. In fact, however, he utilized five categories in his sorting. One category included the recent messages, notes, and correspondence reposing in the center of his desk awaiting an initial screening. Ed usually went through everything new on his desk in a matter of seconds, sorting out top priorities on such bases as the source of the message (handwritten messages from the secretary or personally addressed envelopes from the central office received high priority), often grabbing one or two items and leaving others scattered centrally on his desk. His customary next step was to collect the materials which needed sorting according to his in-basket system into a loose pile at the side of his desk. Advertising mail usually remained unopened in this pile until he was ready to look over each item and make some disposition of it. Each day or two, depending somewhat on the frequency of other interruptions, he opened any still-unopened envelopes in the loose pile and systematically sorted everything in the pile. Each item was either assigned to one of the in-baskets on his desk, marked for the attention of a particular teacher (sometimes with a brief note such as "Bob, do you think we could use this? E.B."), or was disposed of in the wastebasket ready at the far side of his desk. For some items placed in the "immediate action" basket, Ed wrote an additional reminder to himself on a smaller scrap of paper and stuck it on his desk spindle.

Most of the materials which Ed referred to in his office were close at hand and visible on his desk top; bulky materials like the printed forms used within the

[3] Ed recorded many of his appointments and meetings on his desk calendar, but his complete and accurate calendar for both school and personal appointments was a pocket-size booklet containing a month-by-month annual school calendar distributed by the state teachers' association. He literally never left his house without first tucking this calendar in his shirt pocket, a habit shared by several other principals in the district and local region.

school or district were kept in the outer office. His desk drawers were little used, even though he referred to the drawer in which he kept notes for future staff meetings, current class lists, and referrals from the counselling program, as his "often" drawer. In another drawer he collected all materials pertaining to budget preparation. Telephone directories for the local community and for the school district occupied the top desk drawer. Rarely did Ed refer to a metal filing cabinet in the corner of his office. These drawers contained curriculum materials and some records of previous school years. The file cabinet also held personnel folders for each teacher which, except near evaluation time, contained a rather haphazard collection of papers, since the complete file for all teachers was maintained at the central office.

Among the numerous bulletins and announcements, notices of events and meetings, and advertising material that came to school specifically for the attention of the principal, items selected for action were precipitated out rather quickly, not by being put into the "immediate action" basket but by receiving the action required rather than by being incorporated into the filing system. For the rest of it, Ed was inclined to talk about needing to "get at" the accumulation of materials to be filed, but he was not overly concerned with its urgency: "Filing is the *last* thing we get done." The first time in the new school year when he took more than a few moments to systematically go through the in-basket did not occur until the seventh week of school. On the following day, Ed reported:

"Yesterday was the quietest day of my life. Nothing happened."

"What sort of 'nothing?'" I asked.

"No discipline problems. I had a chance to do some reading—mostly by fits and starts. And I had a talk with the secretary about all this filing system. As you can see [pointing to substantially diminished piles in the in-basket] we got a lot of this stuff taken care of."

Several times during the year, Ed waged a similar campaign to reduce the size of the constantly-fed pile of paper on the top section of the in-basket. Occasionally he commented that he wished his secretary did not have so many other things to do so she could keep up with the filing. At such times he also hinted that his former secretary had always "managed to keep up with it a little better."

Pupil Conduct

Disciplining pupils appeared to be a task which Ed did not enjoy but which he could not escape. He gave the impression that in his conception of an ideal school, either the teachers would handle their own discipline problems or the problems would disappear altogether. He alluded vaguely to principals of the "old days" as disciplinarians, and he liked to contrast them with the more enlightened administrator of today's schools. After describing how a mother had recently questioned him about the meaning of having her daughter summoned to the office he commented, "She's of the generation that thinks going to the principal's office is bad. I told her a visit to the office is just like going to see any friend." On the other hand, Ed also acknowledged the responsibility he felt for serving as the school's disciplinarian, expressed through comments like "Of course, sometimes you have to put on that administrative hat" or "When the axe has to fall, I'm the one who has to do it."

In matters of classroom deportment the role which Ed played as disciplinarian depended to a great extent on the role assigned him by each individual teacher. The teachers expressed a range of perceptions about Ed's effectiveness as a disciplinarian and an even wider range of perceptions regarding his personal feelings about being asked to perform in this role. Old-timers like Mrs. Duchess expressed complete sympathy with Ed's position:

> There was a time when I did send children to the office. But I think Ed is right, when they come back, we still have to deal with them, so we might as well learn to deal with them right now. He's willing to sit in and talk it over with the youngsters, but to send them to him to deal with, unless we're willing to go along as a group and sit down and talk it over, is a very poor procedure.

Comments from the three teachers who taught third grade and who worked closely with each other in planning and in teaching illustrate differing opinions about sending children to the principal. The senior teacher in that grade, Mrs. Willing, expressed an opinion similar to that of Mrs. Duchess;

> I never send my children to the principal's office. Ed doesn't want to be a disciplinarian. He doesn't think that's the role of the principal, and I don't either. Who wants a child afraid of the principal? How can you like to go to school every day if you are afraid?

Another of the third-grade teachers felt that Ed's attitude about disciplining had changed, and that she could count on him now more than in the past:

> Last year I got the feeling that he didn't want to have to assume the role as disciplinarian. I think that this is probably why I didn't feel like I should bring discipline problems to him.

The reluctance expressed by the third teacher of the trio in sending children to Ed was based on political expediency—she didn't do it because Ed didn't like it. She felt that she had found a way to bring behavior problems to Ed's attention without risking his displeasure:

> He doesn't like discipline problems. We try not to bother him any more than we have to with behavior problems, because we know he doesn't like it.
> I have personal tricks that I can do in the classroom on my own. Sometimes isolating them and talking with them and so forth. And now that we have Mrs. Wendy, we work with her a lot. She sort of screens out the ones that should go to Ed. So we take them to her first, and if it's something serious she goes to Ed with it, which is fine with us.

A first-grade teacher noted that one of her colleagues consistently avoided sending children to the office because she was dissatisfied with what happened once they arrived there:

> I know that Beverly Straight makes a lot of decisions without taking them to Ed, because she knows that she would not agree with his decision. She just kind of handles a lot of things on her own. For instance, sending the children down to him. She would rather handle it *her* way than have him handle it *his* way.

The teachers new either to the Taft staff or to teaching made more frequent demands on Ed as a disciplinarian and were candid in reporting their reliance on his help. Mrs. Berg, the intern teacher in grade two, considered sending children to the office a "last resort":

> When I went to school [in Canada] the principal was a threat, somebody you really didn't want to have much to do with, because it wasn't going to be very good for you if you had to go see him. The principal that I remember I didn't like at all. I thought he was just terrible, and I didn't ever want to have anything to do with him because he really scared me. Children were strapped very often.
>
> I try not to use the principal as a threat. I feel that if I'm going to have to use a principal as a threat at all, it's going to be very rarely and I want it to *be* a threat. I want to have the child learn something from this experience and that I wasn't kidding. So I think there really should be a little fear there. I'm not saying they should hate him. I think they should respect him.
>
> Twice this year I've taken children down to the office. Both times it was over very bad fights. These had occurred a couple of times before and I couldn't handle it myself. I just had to have help. So I went down to Ed and told him this is the way it was and that I really would appreciate it if he did something about it. He did, and I think it's helped.

Mr. New, the other intern teacher, expressed complete satisfaction with Ed's handling of discipline problems, although he also recognized that Ed might not care for the task:

> I've heard other teachers comment that Ed doesn't discipline the kids like he should. This isn't the problem with me at all. I think that he does a fine job. I've sent kids down to him, quite a few, and he does a good job with them. I'm pleased with the way he handles it. Maybe Ed wishes he didn't deal with them so well, because of the ones I send down there.

Regardless of the opinions expressed, however, *every* teacher appeared willing to share with or assign to Ed some problems of pupil behavior. The less-experienced teachers made more frequent demands for help with classroom problems, but even old-timers brought or sent behavior problems to him occasionally as a result of misbehavior at recess or lunchtime. I had the impression that at least one senior teacher took a delight in reporting children from other classrooms even though she boasted of never taking up Ed's time with the discipline problems of her own class.

Many of the recurring types of pupil behavior problems at Taft which Ed was called upon to deal with are represented in the following series of vignettes. The episodes range from a semitantrum on the part of a "problem boy" to the humor of an anonymous "threatening letter" written to the principal. These incidents are not reported as case studies. Each vignette describes only the immediate encounter as seen from Ed's perspective. The manner and extent to which Ed followed through on procedures initiated in the original encounter with a pupil varied considerably. Since certain pupils (for example, Gary and Tony in the first two vignettes) were often in trouble, both their behavior and Ed's reactions to it were actually part of a long and continuing dialogue rather than limited to the specific incident at hand as they appear below.

Gary, a "Problem Boy"

The time was 2:00 P.M. Ed's office door was closed. Through the window of his office I could see Ed sitting backwards on a chair, facing the filing cabinet. He motioned me in. At first I did not see anyone else in the office, but when I entered the office I saw Gary, a "problem boy" from grade two, crouched into a tiny space behind the filing cabinet in the corner of the room. He was crying. Ed introduced us and I took a seat at the opposite side of the room. Ed was talking softly to the boy, pleading with him to get hold of himself and come sit next to him at the desk. The boy continued to cry and occasionally shouted comments like, "You don't like me," and "You brat, you hate me."

The immediate problem concerned a missing library book. Because Gary had not returned a due book, he had been denied his "library privilege" in the school library a few moments earlier. The boy had shouted at the librarian for her reprimand and had subsequently been sent to the office. Ed said afterward, "It's too bad people like Mrs. Wilson had to see Gary. She's from a day when they turned them over their knee." Mrs. Wilson was one of the group of neighborhood mothers who volunteered a few hours of service each week in the school library.

Gary continued to shout his insistence, as he had apparently been doing ever since he arrived at the library, that he had already returned the book. Ed told Gary he would not allow him to continue his shouting and that he did not intend to talk about the book any further. He changed the subject by asking, "Would you like to see my car?"

Gary screamed, "You're going to take me home!"

The secretary opened the office door to tell Ed, "There's a call for you which you might like *right now*." The call was from Gary's foster mother. Ed explained that Gary was in the office at that moment and would soon be coming home. He hung up the telephone and placed a call to the social worker asking him to come take Gary home. Again Gary screamed that he did not want to be taken home. Ed interrupted his call to ask Gary whether he would prefer to be taken home by the social worker or by himself. Gary said that he would go with Ed if he could "get his paper" first. Ed said that would be alright, and continued talking to the social worker on the phone. The social worker told Ed that under the circumstances he felt he should come out to school anyway. Gary did not realize that the social worker had said he was coming. Later Gary called Ed a "big liar" because Ed had told him that the social worker was not coming to school.

The next scene was another shouting scene, this time in the classroom. Ed accompanied Gary down the hall so that the boy could get the paper which he wished to take home. Ed stepped inside the classroom to wait. When Gary was on the other side of the classroom, he yelled out that Ed was going to grab him. Ed explained to Gary, the teacher, and the other children in the classroom that he was not going to grab Gary. The teacher was able to usher Gary back to the door, and he returned with Ed to the office.

Apparently intent on avoiding another session in the principal's office, Gary darted into the nurse's room instead of into Ed's office. Ed followed him and sat at the nurse's desk. Gary toyed with the telephone. Ed kept the telephone button depressed with his finger but did not reprimand Gary any further. Ed was obviously stalling for time. When Gary turned to the nurse's scales for amusement, Ed asked him if he would like to learn how to weigh himself. Ed and the boy spent the next several minutes working the nurse's scales.

In a rather short time, the social worker arrived at the school. He was a young man, perhaps 23 years old. He greeted Gary by name as he walked into the nurse's room. He remained there to talk with Gary. Ed returned to his office after first contacting the counsellor and the intern supervisor to see if they were available to come to the office for a conference about Gary. Once their discussion began, they were joined by the social worker. The social worker explained that Gary said he needed to go back to the classroom to get his coat. Gary never returned to the office, and the adults agreed that he had probably gone home. Later, Ed called the foster home to check whether the boy had arrived. The mother had the impression that the boy had been brought home and had not realized that he had walked home by himself.

"We're just about at the end of our rope," Ed explained to the social worker. The four adults continued the discussion of Gary's problems and of problems in his home life. The social worker expressed deep concern for Gary and said he wondered "how this will all work out." At the same time, he informed the school people that he would be quitting his job as social worker in two weeks. "Gary has already seen several case workers," observed the counsellor.

Being in the Building at Noon

The time was 10:20 A.M. Ed had summoned four boys, all from one sixth-grade classroom, to the office. Tony Salerni grabbed a chair nearest the desk, commenting to Ed, "I like to sit next to you." The boys had been called to the office for being reported in the building and causing damage in a classroom at noon the day before.

One boy explained that he had only been in the building to wash his hands. Ed excused him after reminding him, "We don't mind you coming in and washing your hands, but come right in and go right out." The three boys who were left in the office were in some way responsible for a hinge being broken on a classroom window during the noon period. Ed addressed another of the boys by name: "Dave, if your mother has to get someone out to fix a washing machine, how much do you think it costs? You didn't use very good judgment. You shouldn't be playing there anyway. Let's think of the classroom as a restricted area. OK, Dave, you may go."

After talking to and then dismissing each of the first two boys, Ed made a brief entry in a notebook on his desk. Then he turned to the two remaining boys and asked each one, "What is your mother doing today?"

"She'll be here for the Valentine party in our classroom," replied one boy.

Tony, the other boy, said, "She is watching the kids and cleaning the house, I guess."

Ed said to Tony, "She could probably use your help. Didn't we talk about suspending you boys if you were in the building again?"

The first boy realized that Ed had him mixed up with another pupil who had received an earlier warning. He explained this to Ed. Ed apologized for having them mixed up, but nonetheless launched into a discourse about the need for school rules, the need for enforcing them, and the importance of giving children proper supervision. He pointed out that children receive proper supervision at Taft School when they are in the places they are supposed to be. "If you break the rules you will have to come in with your parents," Ed concluded, and then he dismissed the first boy: "All right, you may go."

Now only Tony remained in the room. "That's a nice shirt and sweater you have on," Ed began. "Is that what you wore yesterday?"

"No, I had on a suit. My mother didn't have these pants washed."

"But couldn't you have stepped outside. I know what it's like to have limited clothes to wear, but I still expect you to be out on the playground."

Tony answered, "I didn't think that I needed a note just to stay in the building."

"Everyone else does," Ed explained. "It's in the handbook which your parents got. Anyway, it's not my fault. Tony, I wouldn't send a guy home on Valentine's Day. You stop by after school. I'll send a letter home and your mother can send one in return. Goodbye."

The conference with the four boys had taken 20 minutes. After Tony left, Ed wrote additional comments in his notebook. He looked up the telephone number of Tony's home and turned to the telephone to dial, but saw by the indicator lights that both lines were busy. Instead of telephoning, he drafted a letter to Tony's mother, continuing to write uninterrupted for the next 11 minutes. Then he walked to the outer office and asked the secretary to "type this up for Mrs. Salerni, but her name isn't Salerni, she's remarried." He instructed her to leave the letter unsealed, because if he was at school in the afternoon he planned to go over the letter with Tony before the boy took the letter home. The secretary brought Ed's letter back after a few moments. She pointed out some changes she had made. "Fine, I appreciate the help," he commented as he added his signature to the letter. The letter read:

To: Mrs. Sowards
Re: Tony Salerni staying in the building at recess time.

On February 1, Tony was part of a group of boys who returned to the building during recess time without permission. At that time the boys were reminded that they were expected to be on the playground at recess time unless they had a note from home asking permission for them to remain in the building. Yesterday, Tony remained in the building to keep from getting his suit dirty. While he was there he was involved in a scuffle in which boys on the outside of a window pushed from outside and Tony and another boy pushed from the inside. The window was slightly damaged. My main concern is that Tony disobeyed school rules by remaining inside, and might have been injured in the scuffle. I have seriously considered suspending him for a day or more. Since this situation is somewhat different from the previous one discussed, I will only ask that you send me a note to let me know you are aware of the seriousness of the situation.

Please feel free to come see me or call if you have questions.

Sincerely,
Edward C. Bell
Principal

ECB:jy

Stealing

Mrs. Wendy, the school counsellor, came into the office one April morning and asked Ed if he had a few minutes to talk about a problem. She sat in the chair next to Ed's desk and told him that she had just learned about a boy who had stolen two 15¢ bags of marbles from the local drug store in order to "pay back" marbles owed to another child. She asked, "What shall we do?"

Ed said, "Let's get involved. Who is it?" When the counsellor told him the name of the boy, Ed said, "That's not his pattern. I'd better go see him. How many kids know about it? Everyone?"

The counsellor said, "Only one other boy knows."

Ed said, "The moment I go get him he becomes suspect." They agreed that it would be better for Mrs. Wendy to go to the classroom to summon the boy to the office. Ed said, "I'll be in the office when he gets here."

A few minutes later the boy arrived. Ed explained what he knew of the problem. He confronted the boy with the question, "What could you do about it?"

"Don't steal any more," said the boy.

Ed made some comments about stealing. Then he asked, "How do you feel about this?"

BOY: I feel bad.
ED: Your parents don't know about this, do they?
BOY: No.
ED: Would they feel badly, too?
BOY: Yes.

Ed asked the boy what alternatives he saw for making things right. When the boy suggested paying back the money, Ed asked, "How could you pay the store back?"

BOY: I don't know. I don't have any money.
ED: You don't have a chance to do little jobs and earn money that way?
BOY: No.
ED: Right now I'm a little bit puzzled, just like you are. I don't know what to do.

Ed suggested that the boy talk to Mrs. Wendy, because "she's a pretty good listener." He said, "I promise I won't say anything to your mom unless I call you." He sent the boy back to his classroom. Later in the morning when he saw the counsellor again he said to her, "I'm in a real dilemma. If the parents find out about it and learn that I know, they could be real upset at me."

The counsellor said, "I really don't see how you can keep from telling them."

"Well, he's really afraid of his parents finding out. It's like putting him into the jaws of a lion," Ed concluded.

Defacing School Property

In September Ed commented that he had recently had the worst case of having marks and words written on the outside school walls that he ever remembered. As a result, he was "going after" a new incident of writing on the walls which had been called to his attention. He spoke informally about the writing with a group of older pupils at the morning recess, and was given a lead by one of them: "I saw Melody and another girl marking on the walls." The named girl had been in trouble before. Ed chose to speak with the other girl first, a sixth-grade girl new to the school. He went to her classroom and said he wished to speak to the girl in the hall. The girl approached him by asking whether she was in trouble. Ed explained that she was not in trouble, but that other children had reported that she had been writing on the walls of the school building. She appeared to be on the verge of tears and vigorously denied the charge. Ed told her that the adults at Taft School were all anxious to help her. "But," he added, "if you refuse our help, then I'll have to call your mother. I just want to help you, and I think you need help."

GIRL: I told you I didn't do it.
ED: Well, you need help. When you need help, who can you get help from?
GIRL: A teacher, I guess. Or maybe parents.
ED: Then why didn't you want me to call your mother?
GIRL: Because if you called her, she'd think I did it.
ED: Well, I'd like to think you didn't do it. And that's what I do think—at least until I find out otherwise. But I don't think you're telling me everything.
GIRL: We didn't do it. But a lot of kids hate us, so they would say that we did.
ED: Oh, come now. They don't hate you. That's just what some kids say to tease you. But I want to get at the bottom of this business of writing on the walls.
GIRL: (again on the verge of tears) Well, I didn't do it. And if Melody did it, I wasn't with her when she did.
ED: Well, I guess I'll leave you. If you find who did it, you'll come and tell me about it, won't you?
The girl turned away and slipped quickly back into the classroom.

Fighting

Ed was finishing a cup of coffee in the faculty room. It was a Friday morning in March. A second-grade teacher, Mrs. Keppel, arrived at the entrance of the room almost out of breath, paused until she had Ed's attention, and then said, "Are you ready?" She described a discipline problem which occupied Ed for the next hour and a half. After he had rounded up the children involved (seven second-grade boys, in a fight on the playground) he said to me, "About in the middle of all this, those Sisters [visiting nuns] will come. The nice quiet atmosphere of the public schools." Sure enough, they did—but he herded the nuns to classrooms while the boys waited for him behind the closed doors of the nurse's office.

The following comments were recorded during the disciplining session. The seven boys, the counsellor, Ed, and I were present in Ed's office:

BOY: The fight started because one boy called another a clown.
ED: (to boy) You were carrying this boy on your back?
BOY: Yes.
ED: That's not a very good idea, is it? Let's not do it.
ANOTHER BOY: My mom says if somebody slugs me I should go after them.
ED: Is that what your mom does?

BOY: No.

ED: Oh, she has you do something different. What does she do if she doesn't go after them?

BOY: She doesn't do anything.

ED: (to another boy) She [the boy's mother] don't mind if you fight at home?

ONE BOY: (whispering to another) He's going to talk to our mothers.

ED: Mark said all this started because someone called someone else a clown.

BOY: That wasn't it.

MARK: Yes, it was. I just walked off and you came with Bobby and Larry.

BOY: Well, you went to get Eric.

BOY: I wouldn't talk.

ED: Maybe it would help if I called your parents and none of you could leave home until 9:30 each morning. How many of you think you can come early and play without fighting? [All raised their hands.] Well, maybe I should let you talk to your parents today and come back early on Monday without fighting.

The boys wiggled to show their disapproval, becoming a bit silly as they over-exaggerated their motions.

Ed raised his voice to restore order, "Boys, I want you to listen to me!" Immediate silence. He told them he would write in his book that when he called them in to the office he had planned to send them all home, but "since you fellows have handled the situation pretty well, I think I will let you stay in school today. Now, I like you fellows and I like you to be around here, but I don't want you to be fighting."

The boys left the office; the counsellor remained. Ed jotted a note in his desk notebook:

3/31   Fighting before school and at recess.
    [List of seven boys' names.]
    These boys to find better ways to play. Any more fighting and parents are to be called and boys to go home.

He turned to the counsellor. "Well, Mrs. Wendy, I chickened out."

She laughed, "You joined the 'chicken club,' eh? Well, those boys certainly didn't want to go home." Before the meeting with the boys she had stated that in her opinion at least three of the boys involved in the fracas ought to be sent home.

Together they discussed the different points of view which parents express to their children about fighting. They agreed that "up to a point" maybe it is all right to hit back, and that seemed to be what many parents probably advised. "But," Ed added, "the kids don't understand what that point is."

Ed told Wilma Wendy that as long as he was having boys in for talks about playground fights, he had two more boys he needed to talk to: "Maybe I'll send them home." He went to the intercom to ask the teacher who had reported the fight to "send Steve and Bart to the office now." The boys arrived a moment later, seemingly unperturbed and self-consciously making light of the rather obvious reason for their being called to the office. Ed told them he would speak to them one at a time. He closed his office door to confer first with Steve.

"Steve, you were fighting, weren't you? And you know that fighting is against the school rules, don't you? And you know you have to go home when you fight, don't you?" He told the boy to go back to his classroom to get his coat and "some work to do at home," because he planned to have him go home. Since the boy lived on the other side of Sandy Boulevard, "sending" him home actually meant that Ed had to take him home in his own automobile. He had made that particular trip several times in recent weeks.

Steve left the office and Ed summoned the other boy. Ed informed the boy that he was about to be sent home because of fighting at school. He reached for the telephone and said he was going to call the boy's mother. The boy immediately lowered his head and began crying. Ed stopped dialing and put the phone down. He said, "A few minutes ago you thought this was all fun." He talked to the boy about "doing his part" at school and reminded him that everyone was anxious to help him. At the same time, the boy "had his chance," and, Ed explained, since they had been in the office recently for similar infractions, both boys would have to go home. Ed picked up the telephone again and completed his call:

> Mrs. Thorpe? This is Ed Bell at school. We've had a bit of trouble and Bart is going to have to go home. He doesn't understand why he is going to have to go home and some of the other boys aren't, but he has had his chance. You don't have to take any blame for what has happened. We are making real headway, but I think we'd lose ground if we didn't send him home this morning.

Ed sent Bart home after first having him return to his classroom to get some schoolwork. Then he told Steve that he was ready to take him home. The boy dropped back reluctantly as he followed Ed out of the office to the car. Ed told him to hurry along. As the boy walked alongside him, Ed put his hand lightly on the boy's head and said, "I'm not mad at you. I just don't want you fighting at school."

The ride home took only a few minutes. Ed had Steve point out where he lived among the row of ground-floor apartments. He instructed Steve, "Run in and tell your mother we will need to talk to her a minute." The mother came to the door quickly. She had not known the boy was coming home (they had no telephone), but she did not seem surprised to see him or the principal. Ed reassured her that everything was all right *in class*, but that now Steve needed to know that rules of conduct applied on the playground as well as in the classroom. He remained standing just inside the door to the apartment. He told her that Steve had brought some school work with him. "We're making good progress. We'll expect to see him Monday morning," he concluded cheerily.

Lunchroom Problems

Three times each school day the four women who constituted the kitchen staff served a hot lunch in the school cafeteria and readied the kitchen and multipurpose room for the next serving. Most children at Taft School ate in the cafeteria, either purchasing a hot lunch or carrying a lunch from home. During the first period for grades one and two, and again during the second lunch period for grades three and four, teachers of those grades rotated the duty of lunchroom supervision. To supervise the final seating for fifth- and sixth-grade pupils, Mr. Adam had volunteered at the beginning of the school year to take the lunchroom duty position on a permanent basis, in return for which he was relieved of other supervision assignments. At all three sessions, but particularly at those with the supervision constantly changing, there was abundant opportunity for establishing rules and for reporting their inevitable violation. As the year wore on, particularly during winter months, teacher tension about lunchroom behavior increased. Early in the school year, the teachers realized that the same pupils appeared to be causing trouble from one day to the next. They decided to keep a systematic record of pupils who caused disturbances too major to ignore but too minor to warrant a trip to the office. Beginning in November entries were made in a booklet kept in the faculty room; in January Ed began adding notes in the booklet whenever he spoke to the children involved. For example, after a memo listing the names of two boys whose offense was "taking food" Ed had written, "Agreed they should go home upon further trouble. E.B." Sometimes Ed's follow-up entries provided a reinterpretation of an incident. On one day when the teacher on duty recorded eight rule-breakers, six for throwing food (peas provided the major source of ammunition), her description of one boy's offense stated: "spitting bread, crawling under table." Ed's subsequent entry written below it explained, "Laughing caused food to fly into other boy's face. Under table to pick up food."

For serious or repeated infractions, Ed usually arranged for children to eat lunch at home for a few days. Ed liked this approach, since it was not overly punitive—it simply treated eating at school as a privilege instead of a right—and it involved the parents in the school's problems with children. The handling of the following incident was typical.

Ed returned to school in the late afternoon after having been away since early in the morning. He was visiting with teachers in the faculty room and hearing their accounts of the events of the day. A first-grade teacher described a lunchroom problem which had occurred. She had subsequently sent the boy to the office for disciplining, she explained, "Because I didn't know you were gone today." Ed knew the boy as a problem boy; that very morning he had asked the secretary to let the boy into the building early. ("I don't think he can make it out there without hitting someone.") He suggested to the teacher:

> The boy has been warned before. Now let's have him stay home permanently at lunch for awhile. Let's go call the home right now. You stay by and I'll make the call.

As they walked to Ed's office the teacher commented, somewhat patronizingly, "Gee, things sort of fall apart when you leave, don't they." Ed smiled appreciatively but replied, "Oh, not really."

Ed's telephone call to the boy's home was received by the father. Ed said, "This is Ed Bell. Ed Bell at Taft School. We've got a little school problem here. Would you like to talk about it or would you like your wife to?" The father said he would talk about it. Ed explained the problem in the lunchroom that day, concluding that he felt that under the circumstances the boy had better go home for lunch each day for awhile. The father asked whether his son was the only one in the entire school who had broken a rule in the lunchroom. Ed replied:

> Oh, no, but you don't want to talk about all our problems. Let's just talk about the one that concerns you. We think we're making real headway with

him, and the teacher, Mrs. Robin, is here beside me nodding "yes". But at lunch time he isn't always with his own teacher, and lunch is just proving to be a very tough time for him. . . . Be assured, we aren't particularly upset about this week. But this way of handling things seems to be working satisfactorily. We feel he should stay home some more.

The Academic Marketplace

Sometimes the children's recess and noontime activities turned to trading, "playing for keeps" (as with marbles) and even to cash sales of coveted items. While there was no way to monitor all such transactions, there were not many well-kept secrets of children's activities on the schoolground. Such activities are often self-exhausting, but Ed felt he had to show that he was a patient listener to all the stories that came to him and he frequently followed them up with a pupil conference.

In the following case, the resource teacher reported that he had seen two boys who were supposed to be at the school cafeteria returning instead from the local supermarket at lunchtime. Ed called the boys to the office and learned that the purpose of their trip had been to replenish a supply of candy which they were selling to other children. (Although the upper-grade children operated a daily school "store" each morning before school, candy and gum were conspicuous by their absence among the goods which pupils could purchase.)

"We're making a 50 percent profit," one boy explained enthusiastically.

"Do you want us to stop?" asked the other, sensing a lack of enthusiasm on the part of the principal.

"What do you think would be best?," said Ed.

"It doesn't matter," said the boy.

"I think it would be best," Ed suggested. He offered a series of reasons, including reservations about both the health value of the merchandise and the legitimacy of the enterprise:

"The kids don't need all that candy—all that candy isn't good for you." The boys insisted that at their prices no one individual could afford very much.

"If you boys are in business, you need a license," Ed explained; he ignored the counter-question of one boy, "Does the school have one?" When the boys reviewed their profit mark-up, Ed said, "Maybe the school ought to go into the business of selling candy."

"You could be our competitor," suggested the more outgoing of the two boys.

After a brief discussion the boys agreed not to sell any more candy. The same boy pressed, "May I keep my IOU?"

"Was the candy eaten?" Ed asked.

"I think so. Anyway, the label was torn on it."

"Well, in that case, I guess so," Ed conceded.

A Kind Word

As Ed was walking through the primary wing, he saw second-grade teacher Mrs. Keppel and was reminded that he wanted to get a progress check on the behavior of one of her pupils. He asked her how the boy was doing.

He's shaped up very well since you talked to him," she said. "I don't think he needs anything more right now than an encouraging word from you."

The class was just returning from playing outside. The teacher winked as the boy they had been speaking about went by. Ed called the boy aside. He patted him on the head and said, "I've had good reports about you." He bent down lower to add softly, "And how nice you've been to some people at this school."

The boy beamed and continued walking down the hall.

A classmate asked the boy, "What was that all about?"

"Oh, nothing," he replied. He turned back toward Ed and smiled again.

"I Want a Room Transfer 'or Eles.' "

Ed was handed a note by a teacher who said that it had been written by a boy in her fourth-grade class. The note was about moving to another room. It appeared to have been written as a threat, probably in anger over some specific classroom incident. Ed asked the teacher about the author of the note, and she confirmed his opinion that such behavior was "not like him." She could not recall a recent incident that might have provoked the boy to write it. She suggested Ed talk to him sometime during the morning.

Ed called over the intercom at a lull in his morning's activities to ask if the boy could "come have a talk." The boy appeared at Ed's office moments later. Ed invited him to take the chair at the side of his desk.

ED: Why did you write that note? Were you thinking I'd really move you out of that class?

BOY: I guess I really felt mad.

ED: Would you like to tell me how you felt.

BOY: Don god [doggone?] mad.

ED: I'd like to have you read the note out loud to me.

The note read:

Mr. Bell,
    I want a room transfer or eles there will be one less school.
    And I now how to. I now a principle that will pull strings for me and he will.
                                                                                    Room 7

BOY: Boy, I must have been awfully mad. I guess when I get mad, I don't know what I'm doing. I must have been pretty far out to write that.

ED: Do you ever get that mad at your parents?

BOY: Yes, but not as mad as I must have been to write that note.

ED: What would happen at home if you got that mad?

BOY: I'd probably get a lecture or a spanking.

ED: Then I'd like you to write out for me the lecture you expected to hear from me today. Can you do that?

BOY: I guess so.

ED: Have I lectured you?

BOY: Not yet.

ED: Well, I'm not going to, either. Now you go back to your class. And bring me your paper when you finish.

ORIENTING AND GREETING

Among the host of functions which Ed performed at school, the function of host accounted for a substantial part of his time. This section deals with two rather distinct aspects of Ed's activities as the administrator-cum-host of Taft School. The first concerns the continual process of keeping the collectivity of persons who were already part of the daily complement of the school oriented about what was happening or was about to happen in the formal operation of the school. The latter part of the section deals with an activity of a potentially far greater time-consuming nature for a principal, the business of greeting, orienting, and conferring with an elementary school's endless parade of newcomers (for example, new staff, new pupils and their parents) and short-term visitors (such as student teachers and university supervisors, curriculum consultants, "observers").

Messages and Announcements

Keeping Taft School's many and diverse audiences, particularly its 470 pupils, its 335 families, and its staff of 30, informed of coming events and aware of institutional expectations, was a never-ending task in which Ed was variously engaged as a sender of messages which he generated or a relayer or receiver of messages generated by others. The task of orienting the children and staff who were present at school every day was accomplished primarily through verbal means and augmented by written ones. For more remote audiences like parents, routine announcements were dittoed or mimeographed in the school office for distribution "in bulk." Literally tons of announcements must have been circulated through the Taft School office during each school year, since the school not only distributed material originating from its office but it also served as a distribution center for district-wide announcements and bulletins sent from the central office. To economize, or at least to give the appearance of economizing, materials originating at the central office sent to parents via their children in elementary schools were frequently accompanied by a directive that they were to be distributed "one-to-a-family," a distribution which required a special roster at each school.

The type, source, and frequency of material originating from or distributed through the school office in 1966–67 are summarized in Tables 6–1 and 6–2. Table 6–1 describes materials intended for general distribution to parents as well as to staff. Table 6–2 describes materials intended for distribution to staff personnel.

Ed had no regularly scheduled time during the day or week when he systematically reviewed announcements for the two audiences, teachers and parents, who were the targets of most of his written messages. Notices to parents originating from his office were compiled on an as-needed basis, varying in frequency from brief periods during which notices were sent home daily to other times when two weeks might pass without an all-school notice being sent home. Ed used either of two formats for notes to parents, one a letter beginning "Dear Parents," the other an announcement or series of announcements under the banner of "Taft School News." The school year began with a flurry of notes concerning such topics as

TABLE 6–1   TYPES AND FREQUENCIES OF MATERIAL DISTRIBUTED THROUGH THE
TAFT SCHOOL OFFICE INTENDED FOR GENERAL DISTRIBUTION TO
STAFF AND PARENTS, 1966–67

Type of Material	Source	Frequency
Welcome to Taft School	Principal	Once, in fall
Memoranda to parents ("Taft News" or "Dear Parents")[a]	Principal	Daily to semi-monthly
Administrative notices and forms (medical, insurance, etc.)	Central office	As needed; most during beginning of school year
School District Quarterly Report	Central office	Quarterly
Taft PTA Yearbook	PTA president, with help of principal and teacher aide	Once, in fall
PTA Newsletter	PTA president, principal, and others	Occasional, usually to coincide with forthcoming PTA events
Special productions and programs of interest to pupils	Sponsoring organization (e.g., drama groups; local park and recreation district)	For the occasion

[a] Notices and materials were also prepared in the office to special categories of parents, for
example, parents of all third and fourth grade children, parents planning to enroll pupils
in first grade the following fall, and mothers serving as voluntary librarians at Taft.

home-school procedures, optional programs like pupil accident insurance or enrollment in instrumental music, and invitations to the evening series of Room
Desserts. Once the school year was underway, the frequency of announcements
appeared to be greatest immediately prior to any period in which school was to be
closed and prior to forthcoming events important either to Taft School (for example, Open House) or to the entire school district (for example, the annual school
budget election).

Ed was torn between his recognition of the need to keep parents informed about
the school's activities—not only schedule changes but its entire educational effort—
and his reluctance about preparing written statements for wide circulation. "I talk
OK, but I don't write very well," he observed. Sometimes he put off writing (or
completing) a memorandum needed that very day until after lunch. Then he would
hurriedly complete a handwritten draft and present it to the secretary or teacher
aide with the double assignment of editing his copy and rushing to get a stencil
prepared and copies run off for distribution to the first group of primary children
dismissed daily at 1:55 P.M.

The editing job which the secretary or aide undertook often resulted in a substantial rewrite of the original. Ed had particular difficulty, for example, in preparing a letter to parents informing them that he planned to continue the early-late reading program in grades one and two the following school year in spite of some parental resistance. He made a point of asking the secretary to review his original draft and make any editorial changes she considered desirable. She, in turn, asked the teacher aide to help her. The secretary and teacher aide discovered when they completed their editing that they had in fact completely rewritten the memo. They laughed self-consciously as they brought the new draft to Ed and asked him if he recognized any of it. Ed scanned the new draft, thanked them for their help, and instructed the secretary to make copies to send home. Ed's ego-involvement as an author appeared to be restricted to his concern about the final form of messages sent from school over his name, not to the extent to which his own attempts at preparing notices were subsequently revised by others.

Ed's written announcements to the staff were most often made as handwritten entries in the faculty notebook, a loose-leaf binder with a separate page allocated to each school day of the current year. Ordinarily the binder remained open at the page designated for that day to display the messages already written and to receive new ones. Any staff member could write in it to communicate any message to other faculty, and the messages (and rebuttals) at times went rather far afield:

Please note typing error in Wilma's cake recipe. It should read 7 tsp cocoa, not 1 tsp.

Anyone having empty Kleenex boxes please contribute to Room 4 or 5. Thanks!

Announcing: Genevieve ("Jenny") Manning born yesterday afternoon to Sandra [a former teacher]. 6½ lbs. Room 224, Central Hospital.

38 dozen candy canes @ = $36.48
22 people @ $1.65 = 36.30 (.18 left)

Occasionally the notebook provided an outlet for staff humor. For example, an entry signed by Mrs. Duchess, "Does anyone have some colored chalk I could use?" prompted a fellow teacher to add, "No, but I'll be glad to loan you my rose colored glasses!" A block lettered "Y I P P E E!!" appeared on the last day of school. "Kilroy" recorded one visit.

An analysis of the total entries made in the faculty notebook during the regular school year 1966–67 showed that the content dealt most frequently with notices regarding meetings (20 percent). Other major topics included matters of administrative detail (17 percent), announcements concerning the instructional program (11 percent) or instructional materials (9 percent), and notices of staff absences for the day (10 percent). Whenever a single copy of printed or machine-duplicated materials was received from the central office for the attention of all teachers, it was placed in the faculty notebook. By the end of the year the contents of the faculty notebook (without the binder that housed it) had grown to 33 ounces, its bulk consisting of printed matter distributed from the central office, but its essence contained in the handwritten notices added before and during each school day.

The faculty notebook had, over the years, become something of a tradition at Taft School. It appeared to be effective as a communication device without being

TABLE 6–2 TYPES AND FREQUENCIES OF MATERIALS DISTRIBUTED THROUGH THE TAFT SCHOOL OFFICE INTENDED FOR STAFF PERSONNEL, 1966–1967

Type of Material	Source	Frequency	Distribution
Organizational material (faculty handbook, duty rosters, class lists)	Principal	Beginning of school year and subsequently as needed	Teachers and staff
New rules or procedures	Principal (in consultation with staff)	Infrequent	Teachers
Goals of Taft School	Principal	Once, after a summer workshop	Teachers
Agenda for faculty meeting	Principal	Prior to *some* meetings	Teachers
Staff bulletins	Principal	Only when necessary to supplement faculty notebook announcements	Teachers
Announcement of staff socials	Social committee (in consultation with principal)	For the occasion (e.g., Christmas, end of school)	Teachers and staff
Favorite recipes	Various staff members	Seasonal, especially around Christmas	Available in faculty room
Newsletter and other materials	Local teachers' organization	Monthly	Principal and teachers
Proposed salary schedules	Local teachers' organizations; also superintendent's office	Spring	Staff
School board actions	Superintendent's office	After each school board meeting	Staff

Superintendent's bulletin	Superintendent's office	Monthly	Staff
Central office policies and procedures	Superintendent's office	Occasional	Staff
Grade level bulletins and instructional bulletins	Central office staff	Occasional	Principals and teachers involved
Special reports (projects, surveys, workshops)	Central office staff	For the occasion	Principals; teachers
Newsletter	Local branch of state school empolyees' association	Several during the year	Staff
Newsletter	County school office	Monthly	Staff
Newsletter	State Department of Education	8 times yearly	Staff
Notices of money-raising campaigns	Sponsoring group	Occasional	Staff
Lunch menu	Head cook	Weekly	Teachers (one copy for each classroom)

particularly efficient. It was effective because teachers did get the messages in it, either by word of mouth or from their own perusal of the day's page whenever they came to the teachers' room. Entries were made only on the page on the left of the binder rings so that printed materials could be inserted into the rings on the right side of the open book. A note or arrow often helped call attention to them. The book's lack of efficiency stemmed from its location in a corner of the faculty room and, more critically, from the fact that entries were sometimes made during the day after most teachers had already glanced at the book. Ed insisted that each teacher should look at the book "a couple of times a day," probably because he often failed to make his own written entries until after morning classes had begun.

Ed was responsible for about 30 percent (90 of the total of 312) of the handwritten entries made in the faculty notebook during the school year 1966–67. His entries were among the briefest made. They dealt directly with matters of administrative concern, particularly in making announcements or reminders of meetings (or, occasionally, cancelling them) or of changes in the daily program:

8:00   Guidance Committee. Two fifth-grade girls and others who have disturbing home situations.

2:45   staff meeting
Please spend some time preparing placement cards for next year's class lists. We should finalize these in a couple of weeks.

7:30 P.T.A.

9:00 Jr. High School Band here for grade 3–4–5–6

Wilma Wendy is ill—
Five Sisters from St. Mary's School will visit our building on Friday. You may want to prepare some children for the attire which may be new to them.

Ed's longest entry of the year dealt with an occasion in which he had volunteered the cooperation of his staff in having their rooms available for an evening visit by principals attending the county association meetng. Ed had made the commitment to the principals' organization several weeks earlier, but he introduced the news in the faculty notebook one Friday as though he had just learned of it:

Dear Teachers—(Friends So Far)
I learned today that I am to be host for the County Elementary Principals' Monthly meeting. The Group (35) will be served in the multi-purpose room at 6:30 P.M. The custom is for the group to be invited to tour the building at a break time. May I let them in your rooms with this small amount of notice?

The note caused greater dismay among the first teachers to read it than Ed had anticipated, until one teacher called to his attention that he had not included the date of the meeting. The teachers had assumed that the event was to occur that very evening. Excitement was contained when Ed added to his message that the meeting was set for the following week.

Ed tended to conduct business verbally and to avoid having to prepare written communications whenever possible. The time-and-motion study discussed in the previous chapter showed that Ed was a "talker." Even the apparently small portion of his "average" day that he spent on the intercom (1.2 percent) resulted in a cumulative total of over 30 minutes a week conducting business with individual classrooms and teachers and making general announcements heard throughout the school building. Ed expressed reluctance about interrupting the activities of everyone at school (apparently teachers across the nation complain about the number of administrators who dominate their classrooms via excessive use of an intercom), but once he had their attention he seemed to become captivated by the phenomenon of hearing his voice amplified and echoed throughout the building.

Ed's more enthusiastic supporters commented on his "friendly, relaxed manner" in talking to the children over the intercom. The counsellor once remarked, "I had a feeling as I was listening to him one day over the intercom that after he had spoken to the students they probably had a feeling that they would pretty well want to do what he'd want them to do."

Not all adults at Taft School were convinced of the effectiveness of Ed's lengthy discussions and announcements. As one staff member commented:

> I feel that sometimes Ed's interminable lectures to children are valueless. I've heard them say, "Oh, don't be afraid, all he'll do is talk to you." And I think he says too many words. His announcements over the intercom are definitely overwordy. But he may not have the ability to speak.

An example illustrates how Ed's announcements tended to expand into lectures. A neighbor of the school had come into the office one afternoon inquiring whether any child had reported finding a puppy that had strayed away. The secretary said no one had mentioned a puppy to her. She went into Ed's office to check with him. He said he had not heard of a puppy being brought to school, but offered to make a general inquiry on the intercom. He proceeded directly to the intercom's elaborate switchboard, flipped the "all-call" toggle, blew twice into the microphone to assure himself that it was working, and began:

> We have a man here looking for a lost puppy. If any of you have seen a puppy today, will you please come to the office and tell us about it. And while we are on the subject of things lost, there is a girl in our school who is looking for some "lost" records which she brought to school to share with her class. But I wonder if I've used the right word, since they were labeled with her name and were in the conference room. It's too bad that a person can't leave things in our building and feel that they will be here when he goes to get them. And I guess there are many of the 469 of you who wish that, too.

The staggered schedule of pupil arrivals in the morning, and the fact that primary children were dismissed early in the afternoon, limited the period of the school day during which announcements could be made to all the children simultaneously. By the time during the mid-morning when all children had arrived at school and were back in class after a morning recess, Ed was likely to be engaged in some activity of his own. No special time was set for announcements, although they were most frequently made just after classes had begun or just before some group was preparing for dismissal. Occasionally Ed found himself in a race with time to get to the intercom before a tick of the clock would set off an automatic signal for dismissal. Ed's approach seemed haphazard, and there were ritual complaints from some teachers about never knowing what was going to happen next, but the important messages regarding the daily operation of the school did seem to get out.

Ed was aware of another facet in announcement-making, the problem of monitoring the number of announcements made at school on behalf of others. As community message centers, schools are prevailed upon by outside agencies to announce
special events and programs. Taft School was no exception. Ed usually responded
graciously when such requests were made personally by a visit or a telephone call.
Community and personal goodwill was easily worth a few moments of school time,
and if the request was fresh in his mind and promised as a personal favor, Ed
would make it even if it had little relationship to the school program. However, he
had no systematic procedure for recalling announcements to be made on future
days. Such announcements were sometimes overlooked both by accident and design. An entry from the field notes describes an announcement that was "lost":

> *A Friday afternoon in January.* The last bell of the week had rung. Ed was
> in his office sorting papers on his desk. He came upon a request from the high
> school sponsor of the American Field Service Foreign Student Program to read
> an announcement about a spaghetti feed which was to precede the high school
> basket ball game on Saturday night. "Guess I'm a little late with this one," he
> rationalized. "They don't realize over at the high school how far down things
> can get in my in-basket."

Occasionally principals checked with each other on their disposition of "outside"
announcements. For example, each school received a mail-out about having
classes sponsor birds (i.e., contribute $10.00) in a fund-raising homing pigeon
race for a local benefit. One of the women principals had brought the announcement
with her to an administrator's meeting, and at a break in the proceedings she
turned to two male colleagues and asked, "What are we supposed to do with this
thing about homing-pigeons?"

One principal replied, "We have enough going on without that. I just threw it
away." The second principal nodded in agreement.

"Ed gave his copy to me," I informed her.

She frowned, then smiled as she announced, "Well, I guess you can have my
copy, too."

"Showing the Ropes"

Newcomers were oriented to Taft School according to the purposes which
brought them there. One type of newcomer included any person who was in the
employment of the school district (or in the employment of a firm contracting work
for the district) and who was to some extent responsible to Ed while at Taft
School. This category included repairmen and temporary statuses like teacher or
secretary "substitutes" as well as new members of the permanent staff.

Ed did not make explicit distinctions among Taft's various types of newcomers,
but he sometimes used the term "showing them the ropes" when referring to his
part in formally orienting newcomers who were at school as employees. His part in
orienting such personnel was performed casually and, as time permitted, graciously.
At the same time, his comments or directions were more task-oriented and to-
the-point than his sometimes rambling discussions of educational philosophy or
tours of the building reserved for persons not actually reporting for work.

New staff required differing orientations to specific aspects of the physical plant or program. Regarding the physical plant, Ed might be called on for crucial but usually brief moments to show a repairman how to get at some piece of equipment or to help identify possible sources of a maintenance problem. Repairmen from contracting firms required more assistance than men from the school district's own maintenance department, since the latter were usually familiar with the building and always worked under the direction of maintenance supervisors familiar with it. Ed did not often have to single-handedly "break in" a relief custodian totally unfamiliar with the building. In the absence of the regular daytime custodian, he could either request a relief custodian already familiar with Taft or he could call the night man to come in early and in turn instruct his own substitute.

Time was specifically allocated at the beginning of each school year for the orientation of new teachers. Once that official orientation period was concluded, Ed did not devote much effort to showing the ropes to teachers assigned to Taft as "substitutes" during absences of regular teachers. Little time was available for orientation on a new substitute's first day. If Ed was free to do so, he usually provided a quick tour of the office (faculty room, coffee pot, teachers' lavatories) and then guided the substitute to the classroom. If he was otherwise engaged, he might try to take a moment to lead a newcomer to the faculty room or venture as far into the building as necessary to locate a regular teacher of the same grade and ask the teacher to take the responsibility for orienting the newcomer. Sometimes in the absence of either the principal or another teacher to act as host, a substitute could only be sent down the hall to find a classroom on her own with instructions to "let us know if we can help." Of course, no substitute teacher was a total stranger more than one day, and requests could usually be met by the personnel office to send out individuals who "substituted" frequently at Taft or had at least been there before.

From Ed's point of view, the presence of substitute teachers was unavoidable but not desirable. He was cordial to substitutes, just as he was cordial to all visitors, but he had a strong conviction that an effective classroom program was absolutely dependent on the presence of the regular classroom teacher. He never discouraged teachers from staying home when they reported sickness, nor did he encourage them to return quickly from convalescing, but as long as a regular teacher was absent, Ed felt that the children in the classroom could do little more than mark time. "Even if you don't teach them anything today, they will survive," he once assured a substitute. "Just do the best you can for today."

The occasion for which "showing the ropes" most critically affected Ed, and thus the times at which he exerted his most stalwart efforts in this regard, occurred whenever he needed to orient a new secretary. Without having that position occupied by someone familiar enough with Taft routines to handle most of them without assistance, Ed was virtually a captive in his own office. How dependent the operation of the principal's office had become on the secretary was apparent when Ed found himself anticipating the start of the school year in September, 1966, with a new secretary.

From a principal's point of view, the presence of a secretary in an elementary school is vital, although the position is certainly unheralded beyond the confines of each individual building. For most temperaments, the job is not a demanding one, but the pay and occupational status are low. Women who take such positions usually do so for reasons other than purely monetary ones, particularly because of attractive working hours, varied duties, and vacation periods which allow them to be home when their own school-age children are home. Ed's former secretary had been at Taft School for four years. When she announced during the spring of 1966 that she would "stay home and be a mother and housewife," there was little Ed could do to entice her to stay on except to reaffirm the importance of her part in the total operation of the school.

In considering a replacement, Ed's thoughts turned to people who were already familiar with Taft rather than to ways of locating some highly qualified stranger to fill the position. Neither the teacher aide at Taft nor a former aide working at another elementary school was interested in assuming the added responsibilities (the difference in salary between the aide, paid on an hourly basis, and a beginning secretary, paid on a monthly basis, was less than $500 for the year). Ed inquired whether one of the women who helped in the kitchen might be interested. She expressed interest but explained that she had no secretarial experience and was an extremely slow typist. Ed smothered her doubts by assuring her that typing was a relatively unimportant aspect compared to the importance of working with children, parents, and staff, keeping accounts straight, and generally keeping the office "running." He suggested that she spend some time in the office with the secretary whenever she was not needed in the kitchen in order to get an idea of what the job entailed. During the last few days of school in June she did spend some time "learning the ropes." When school closed for the summer, she promised to brush up on her typing, both for the requirements of the job itself and for a proficiency test required by the school district personnel office.

During the summer school Ed had still another secretary, a teacher aide at a different school who had requested summer employment. Although she was not familiar with Taft School, she was familiar with school operations and policies in the school district. In the informality of the summer school operation she acquired the new skills quickly, and since most of the summer school staff was new to the school, she managed easily to keep up with everyone. She had another marked advantage, the primary basis on which she had requested and been sought for the Taft assignment. She was a member of Ed's church, and through that association she and her husband were also close family friends of the Bells. The nature of that friendship and her own out-going personality made it easy for her to ask for information she needed. In the quarterly business meetings of their church she and Ed assumed the same formal relationship they maintained at school, since she was the elected secretary and Ed the chairman of the lay governing board.

To Ed's surprise when he returned from his brief respite between the end of the summer's activities and the start of the new school year, he did not have a school secretary after all. "It all happened on that week I was 'supposedly' off," he explained later. His secretary-to-be had failed to pass the basic typing proficiency test administered by the personnel office, and since other qualified people were available he could not hire her. Being prevented from employing the person he had selected to replace his secretary served to increase Ed's disdain for the personnel office (many principals shared a feeling that the Director of Personnel usurped their authority in selecting teachers and staff), and he decided to try to locate someone on his own rather than have the assignment made for him. He made inquiries among his colleagues to see if they knew of any prospective secretaries living in the vicinity of Taft School in addition to two names he already had. Bill St. Claire had such a recommendation for him. He told Ed that the wife of a young man who had just moved into a rented house in the Taft neighborhood might be interested in a school job; furthermore, she had secretarial experience. Her husband had accepted a teaching position in the school district, and his aunt had formerly been the secretary at Bill St. Claire's school. Ed interviewed three potential candidates on his first day back at school, and talked to three others on the telephone. His choice was Jeri Young, the person recommended by Bill St. Claire.

Mrs. Young later recounted that she had been unable to decide whether to find a new job or to return to college, now that her husband had finally become the major wage-earner of their household. For the previous few years she had held jobs as secretary, typist, dental assistant, clerk, and meat-wrapper while her husband completed college. She had not been in an elementary school since the day she graduated from one.

Ed immediately recommended she be hired—he was ready to put her to work the first day he was back at school. The personnel office could not move quite that fast, but an appointment was made for a formal interview for her at 8:00 A.M. the next day. Afterward Ed gloated that although the personnel office had intended to make her go through their complete screening process, when she produced the official results of a recent civil service test "they just didn't have the gall to make her take even the typing test." Ed's recollections of the difficulties of showing the ropes to a new secretary just as school was getting underway were recorded during a taped interview later in the first month of school.

The day after I interviewed her here she had to report down to the personnel office at 8:00 A.M. She was out here about quarter to nine. We went over what had to be done. Frankly, I learned there were a lot of things being done in the office that had just been done routinely [i.e., without demanding Ed's time or attention]. I knew they were being done, but I didn't realize how much time it took. And I began to show her these things.

My own secretary, in four years' time, had kept up with the changes and knew right where to send anything. And if she didn't know, she knew how to get the information. Mrs. Young was a little bit frustrated by the fact that there is not a clear-cut handbook written which says, "You do this." She says she is going to make one, but I doubt she'll ever get around to it. In the first place, she just won't have the time. And if she did, she'd find that these procedures change often and she'd be writing a handbook all the time.

Most of that week we spent trying to help her get organized so that she knew what she was doing. The teachers came in the next week. All that first day that the teachers came I was out of the office, either in general session or down the hall trying to help the teachers get started. She was kind of on her own that day, and she felt it was kind of a lost day. And it's been that way ever since. She's just now beginning to get caught up and feel she knows how to do things. She's still bothered by the fact that she can't just cut it dry and wrap it up. It's constantly changing, which I think is kind of characteristic of school work.

In addition to orienting one new secretary at the beginning of summer school and another one at the beginning of the regular school year, Ed was faced with having to orient at least three different relief secretaries during the year when Mrs. Young was sick. Unless he made a fervent plea for an exception to existing policy, no substitute was sent out when a secretary was expected to miss only one day at work. On one occasion Ed did make a special request to have a substitute, because neither he nor the teacher aide was going to be able to "cover" the office during the secretary's absence. With or without a substitute secretary, Ed still had to spend more time near the office either explaining procedures or handling them himself. Such days provided evidence of some nagging priorities in operating a school office, such as "covering" telephone and personal inquiries; tabulating milk and lunch counts; accounting for attendance; and receiving and sending materials customarily routed through the office.

Early in the spring Mrs. Young announced that she did not plan to work the following year: "I've worked since we've been married, which is nearly four years now. We'd like to start a family." Once again Ed found himself anticipating the task of having to orient another secretary. He started making casual inquiries and collecting names of women who might be interested in the job, especially those who had experience working in other schools as former secretaries or teacher aides and women who had substituted as secretaries at Taft during the year. He decided to give his former secretary a call, in case she had grown restive after her return to being a full-time housewife and mother. To his great delight, she did ultimately decide to return to Taft. At least for a few weeks in the spring, Ed anticipated that when school opened in the fall he would have almost all "seasoned" faculty and staff members returning, a rarity and, because it relieved him of the chore of showing newcomers the ropes, a delight.

Orienting New Pupils and Parents

The pupil population at Taft School changed slowly but continually during the school year. Teachers reported an average change of six pupils in the composition of their classrooms during the year. Thus the overall pupil population was about 80 percent constant, a figure typical of schools in comparable suburban communities and one that represents considerably more stability than figures reported by schools in transient inner-city areas.

The problem of orienting new pupils and parents was similar to that of orienting new teachers. An orientation period was formally provided once each year, with prior planning to assure its effectiveness, but was planned as though newcomers were an annual rather than a recurring event. Few vestiges of the procedure remained to guide the orientation of a year-long parade of new comers.

Formal periods for orienting new pupils and parents occurred twice each year at Taft. The more obvious one occurred as a natural part of getting school started in September. The first few days of school were labeled "hectic," and procedures and rules for behavior were often overlooked until the school settled into a routine in which pupils understood what was expected of them. Although the schools within the district attempted to publicize early registration for new pupils entering in the fall, each school also anticipated a few new registrations when school opened, and necessary materials for orienting parents and for registering pupils (medical and dental forms, family information sheet) were immediately at hand in the office. Classroom rosters were considered to be in flux until head counts could be made to assure an equitable distribution of pupils among the classrooms at any one grade level. Once this shakedown period had ended, however, formal efforts at collectively orientating newcomers diminished rapidly. Throughout the remainder of the school year, the orientation received by incoming pupils and parents was subject to such vagaries as who happened to be in the office and how preoccupied those individuals were at the moment.

As with the orientation of new substitute teachers, newcomers occasionally received royal treatment: they were introduced to Ed by the secretary only moments after they had come into school, and he personally took charge of their initial encounter with Taft. First, he would examine the up-to-date office copy of class rosters and announce his decision regarding the assignment of a new pupil or set of siblings. Then he would escort the children to their classrooms, calling each teacher to the classroom door to make formal introductions among pupil, parent, and teacher. Then he would accompany the mother back to the office, all the while describing some of the "interesting kinds of things" going on in the school. This entire procedure took only a few minutes, but it lent the tone of cordiality and personal interest which Ed liked to exhibit.

On the other hand, there were occasions when the secretary was the sole person available to greet and orient newcomers. At such times she did not feel free to stray farther from the office than to step into the hall and point parent and child in the general direction of the classroom. The secretary's efforts at orientation were influenced by her own role, with an emphasis on forms and records required in the office, the handling of lunch money, and the daily schedule. In the principal's absence, the secretary also made a tentative classroom assignment, based usually on placing a child in the classroom at the appropriate grade that had the smallest enrollment.

A new pupil in a classroom is not a unanimously welcome event among elementary teachers, although the target of teacher annoyance in such circumstances is the disruption and extra work involved, not the child himself. The secretary's position in assigning new children was a bit awkward in this regard; when possible, she conferred with the counsellor or the resource teacher in making assignments. In any case, it often fell to her either to make the assignment or to announce the decision. This was done via the intercom, the secretary's voice interrupting classroom activities to announce cheerily, "Mrs. ———, there is a boy new to Taft School here in the office and he is going to be in your classroom. May I send him down?" I found myself holding my breath on such occasions, hoping that the teacher would realize that her voice would be amplified back into the office and that a parent was probably audience to the interchange. The teachers inevitably maintained their poise, but faculty room joking at the next break frequently revealed other feelings: "That's it." "No more." "My classroom is closed for the year!" or "Hey, how come? I got the last one, too!"

In the following vignette, the secretary had conducted the initial assignment and orientation of a new pupil. She had been unable to locate the principal, although he was somewhere in the building. (Some schools have a special bell signal to summon the principal, but no such procedure was followed at Taft.) While the mother was completing a brief questionnaire about the child, Ed returned to the office. The secretary said, "Mr. Bell, we have a new girl this morning for the second grade." She introduced the pupil by name.

Ed turned to the adult and asked. "You look familiar. Are you the mother?"

The woman said that she was the aunt of the mother. Her niece's marriage had just broken up, she explained, and until the niece got settled again, she would be looking after the three children, this second-grade child and two children of pre-school age. "The reason that I look familiar is that I have two children of my own in Taft School, one in grade six and one in grade two."

"Well, I thought so," Ed assured her (and himself).

"I put the child in Mrs. Skirmish's room," the secretary related. "Mrs. Berg has the fewest, but this girl's cousin is in that room."

Ed picked up the book containing class rosters and flipped back and forth among those of the second grade. "Under the circumstances, I think we'll put her in room 6 [Mrs. Keppel] instead. You can fill those out later," he said, turning toward the woman. "Let's go down and meet the teacher." Ed ushered the woman and child out of the office and down the hall. He stepped inside the door of the classroom in room 6 and said, "Mrs. Keppel, may we see you for a minute?" The teacher stepped out into the hall.

Ed made his introductions, starting with, "This girl would like to be in your class." The teacher smiled and replied, "Oh, would she?" The girl stood rigidly at attention while the principal and teacher discussed her assignment. "Should she be in the early or late reading group?" Ed asked, and then continued by answering his own question, "Well, maybe you ought to wait for a few days before you decide." (As it turned out, the girl had to take the bus to school because the family lived across Sandy Boulevard, and thus the bus schedule dictated which reading period she would join.) The teacher showed her new pupil where the girls hung up their coats ("If you hang it on this side, it will get mixed up with the boys") and turned to introduce the new member of the class to the other children. Ed and the woman walked back to the office. Ed asked if there was anything the school should know about the child. The woman said she could not think of anything except that she did not know how well the child could do in school. At the office door they encountered Wilma Wendy. Ed paused to introduce the two women ("You probably already know our counsellor, Mrs. Wendy") and to report to the counsellor the news of the new enrollee. The woman excused herself by explaining that she needed to get back home to other children. Wilma capitalized on the occasion to ask Ed if he had a moment free to talk about a guidance meeting scheduled for the following morning.

Parents of children entering Taft School in the first grade had a special orientation event planned for them, an annual program held one afternoon each May. A detailed account of one orientation meeting was presented in Chapter 5. Such meetings were not held at all schools in the district, although each school provided some sort of special program or materials for this purpose. The Director of Elementary Education felt that the orientation of new parents was an especially important responsibility of principals. She included a discussion of orientation procedures on the agenda of one of the regular meetings of the elementary principals, and she called on Ed to describe what she considered to be an excellent orientation program at Taft School. Ed described the program to his colleagues, carefully pointing out how the staff had "felt the need" of the program and contributed to its success. His account gave him an opportunity to repeat one of his favorite observations, that children new to a school orient themselves quickly, while parents are not necessarily so adept: "When parents and children come to school together, I always make sure that the *parent* understands."

Orienting and Conferring with Supervisors, Consultants, and Other Visitors

In the survey completed at the end of the school year the teachers were asked to recall the number of different cadets, student teachers, observers, consultants, and others who had been in their classrooms during regular school hours in the previous year. The results of their estimates of the total number of visitors to their classrooms during the year are summarized in Table 6–3. The table shows the maximum number of visitors in each category recalled by any teacher and the median number of visitors recalled among all the teachers reporting. The median number of total visitors per classroom was 19, with a range from 12 to 36. These figures provide only an approximation, and they do not take into account the fact that most visitors made several (or perhaps even regular) visits. I would assume

TABLE 6–3   NUMBER OF DIFFERENT VISITORS IN TAFT CLASSROOMS DURING THE SCHOOL YEAR 1966–67 (BASED ON TEACHER RECALL IN JUNE; 16 TEACHERS REPORTING)

Category of visitors	Maximum number of different persons in each category visiting any one classroom	Median number of classroom visitors in each category
High school cadet teachers	4	2
Full-time student teachers[a]	2	1
Other university students as observers	3	0
University supervisors	5	1
Number of different substitute teachers	4	2
Other teachers formally visiting as observers	8	2
District consultants, supervisors, etc.	3	1.5
Other Taft staff members (e.g., resource teacher, counsellor, aide, but excluding principal)	5	3
Parents visiting during class hours	15	3.5
Other visitors and speakers	7	2

[a] Eight teachers had no student teachers in their classrooms during the year. However, seven of these teachers were either in their first year of teaching or were new to Taft School. Two of the eight were themselves fulfilling student teacher requirements as intern teachers. The remaining ten teachers accommodated 14 student teachers, some classrooms obviously having two student teachers during the year. Thus the school was "oversaturated" with student teachers in terms of the standard of one student teacher in a classroom per year generally felt to be desirable by both school district and university personnel.

them to be very conservative estimates of the total number of different classroom visitors during the year. They do lend quantitative support to the observation that Taft teachers entertained a constant flow of visitors to their classrooms.

The number of visitors to individual classrooms is only a fraction of the continual parade of adults and children to the building on any regular day. Consultants and faculty with commitments to other schools or tasks (for example, special teachers, the intern supervisor, central office consultants) arrived and departed at school subject to their own personal and professional schedules. Parents, university personnel, and delivery people streamed in and out of the building. A regular staff member occasionally found himself having coffee in the faculty room among more adults whom he could not identify than those he knew by name or could even recognize.

Notes from a Monday morning in January reveal a busy but not atypical schedule of visitors routed through the school office:

1. A parent whose own children were enrolled at Taft came to enroll the daughter of a niece. (This new enrollment was described in the previous section.)
2. Four student teachers from the university spent the day at school.
3. A visiting professor from the State University of New York, accompanied by a professor from the local university, arrived at school in order to observe the student teachers.
4. Two cadet teachers from the high school (high school students contemplating teacher careers who were assigned to Taft School for one period a day as classroom assistants) came for the duration of a regular high school period.
5. A parent came to school in order to bring a selection of paintings from a rotating gallery from which pupil representatives selected a "picture of the month."
6. The food supervisor from the central office arrived to conduct an evaluation of cafeteria procedures and personnel.
7. The Spanish language consultant presented a demonstration lesson to upper-grade classes.
8. The physical education consultant presented demonstration lessons in physical education throughout the day on a request basis.
9. The researcher conducting this study was present from 8:10 A.M. to 1:00 P.M.

It is a custom in all schools and a directive prominently displayed by a sign on or near the door of many of them: All visitors report first to the school office. Of the complement of visitors described above, only the student and cadet teachers customarily proceeded directly to classrooms at Taft School. Whether other visitors would necessarily check with the building principal or not was partly a function of the purpose of their visit, partly a function of who was available in the office to greet them, and partly a function of the mood, preoccupation, and personality of each individual principal. Because Ed enjoyed meeting new people, he usually glanced up whenever a new visitor came into the office, and unless the purpose of the visit was obviously no more than a brief errand (for example, a parent leaving something for a child or requesting permission to take something to a child in class), Ed's behavior often signalled that he was available even if he did not actually come forward to initiate a conversation. At the same time, he usually instructed everyone whose business at school was on a regular basis (student or cadet teachers, special teachers) to "go right on in." Anyone without regularly scheduled teaching responsibilities usually followed the customary protocol of stopping at the office to announce both his arrival and his purpose. It seemed not to matter with whom one checked in at school as much as that one checked in with someone. Visitors were inclined to provide a fuller account of the purpose of their visit if they happened to be met by the principal rather than the secretary.

Many visitors came to school specifically to see Ed or included holding a brief meeting with him as part of their business. Personnel from the central office appeared to move about the building with a freedom inversely related to their status in the school district hierarchy—i.e., the Director of Elementary Education usually met exclusively with Ed when visiting at school and did not customarily venture past the front office; subject-matter supervisors spent a substantial part of their time conferring with Ed and talking informally with teachers in the faculty room; specialists like the coordinator of the Spanish language program proceeded directly to the classrooms to provide demonstration lessons; and maintenance personnel seemed to pop in and out of the building almost at random (except for supervisory-level personnel, who always checked with the office and usually conferred with Ed before proceeding into the building).

Ed seemed alternatively delighted and dismayed at the number of outsiders who passed through the portals of Taft School each week. His gregarious nature often nudged him to volunteer personally to escort adult visitors new to the school. During such tours it was his custom to introduce guests to any and every member of the professional faculty he happened to encounter, a custom which led to some confusion among those staff members who assumed that introductions made at school had some ulterior purpose beyond a purely social one.

Acting the role of host did not have the same appeal to every principal that it did to Ed. All principals in the school district appeared to be conscious of the need for good public relations, but unquestionably they did not all share Ed's affinity (or at least his tolerance) for meeting new people and providing them with a "grand tour." One of Ed's colleagues said he had once informed members of the central office, "I need a greeter—just someone to greet all the people who come into a building." The same principal said that when he finally realized how many new people each new program brought to his school (for example, additional faculty and students from the university, worried or interested personnel from the central office, visitors from other schools and districts) he resolved that whenever he had any choice in the matter he would attempt to keep new programs *out* of his school and keep his school out of the limelight. Ed preferred to give the impression of running a school always receptive to new programs and their inevitable complement of observers, but in private he expressed an ambivalence widely shared by his fellow administrators:

I get the feeling of being overstimulated by having so many people coming in and out all the time. It's nice to have it. But we could use a rest from it.

Conferring with a Consultant

The following notes were made when the physical education ("PE") consultant for the district made a visit one Wednesday morning in June to discuss the plans for the PE program at Taft School for the next school year. Technically this meeting could be considered a formal encounter, since Ed and the consultant had agreed upon a 9:00 A.M. "appointment" for their visit. Sometimes consultants made such appointments, especially if they wished to be sure of time to see Ed; sometimes they merely visited with him if he was available and promised to "catch him later" if he was not. Other than the starting time of this particular meeting, however, it was informal both in its organization and in the fact that Ed was continually distracted before and during the meeting by other details of the morning. The phone had rung eight times in the 15 minutes immediately preceding his conference, including a call from one mother complaining that her second-grade daughter had been choked "practically blue" on the way home from school the previous afternoon by an older pupil. Ed himself had been late to school because the clutch on his car had given out. And he had been almost totally preoccupied ever since arriving at school in searching for a mislaid draft of a teacher memo prepared the day before. The memo had to be distributed that morning. Ed finally decided he would have to rewrite it after attempting to recall and retrace all his steps of the previous afternoon ("I can't find the damn thing anywhere," he confided to Mrs. Duchess) in search of his original copy.

The PE consultant apologized for arriving six minutes late. Ed assured him that "on a morning like this" it hadn't mattered. He asked if the consultant minded waiting "so I can make an important call first." His dialing was interrupted by Mr. Adam, who stopped by the office to introduce a woman from the university who had come to present a story to his class. The introduction in turn set off a round of introductions to the PE consultant and to me. Mr. Adam announced that his visitor would need a ride back to the university later in the morning. ("As soon as I get through" corrected the guest, looking directly at Ed.) After the introductions, Ed returned to his dialing. His telephone call to the (foster) home of the boy who had done the choking prompted a long explanation on Ed's part and a reminder of help available through the school counsellor.

Thirty-five minutes after the time scheduled for the beginning of their meeting, Ed turned to the PE consultant seated in the chair along side his desk. "Well," he said, "we need to talk about PE for next year. I knew you were coming. But I haven't had a chance to give much thought to it." In a conversational manner, Ed described a male teacher he had hired to teach fifth grade the next school year. He talked about the institution where the man had taken his teacher training and the school district in which he had done his student teaching (a community recognized for its enthusiastic support of school athletic programs, particularly in terms of state-wide high school sports) and summarized that his new teacher "probably got more in PE there than he would have gotten here." By contrast, he noted that his two female sixth-grade teachers had not provided much of a physical education program during the current year: "Maybe they don't think it's very important.

About all you can do is give them some ideas. Margaret Elder [one of the sixth-grade teachers] doesn't like to expose herself to outsiders. She'd rather work alone. Adam is the same—he'll want his own program. Maybe the other teacher would work with a fifth-grade teacher." He reviewed the PE programs of the two female fifth-grade teachers who would be returning: "Carol does a good job, especially with tumbling; Mrs. Duchess [always] does a good job." For the rest of the grades the program was "OK," Ed explained. "Many of our staff are younger and recently out of school. I'd go so far as to say that Mrs. Robin, in grade one, is a 'PE-oriented' teacher."

Their visit was interrupted again when a high school cadet who had been coming regularly to Taft School to help in the first grade stopped at the office to say goodbye. This was the last day of her eight weeks of service. The interruption by the cadet prompted Ed to give the PE consultant a brief description of the cadet program. The consultant listened patiently, but when Ed had finished he turned the conversation back to the purpose of his visit.

"Is there any way you'd particularly like me to help with your PE?" he asked.

"No. Just keep on sending around those innovative ideas like you have. And, of course, be available to help teachers when you are asked."

"Well, it looks like there are no problems here," concluded the consultant. "Sorry to have come by when you're so busy."

"We're always glad to see you," Ed assured him. They shook hands in parting.

Conferring with a Student Teacher Supervisor

It was Ed's impression that "The University"—that is, the faculty personnel in charge of the teacher training program at the nearby School of Education—had a favorable impression of Taft School and were confident about sending students there for student-teaching assignments. It was also his impression that the Taft faculty enjoyed working with university personnel and with student teachers, and on behalf of his staff, Ed welcomed requests to "place" students in his school. Taft School also had been part of an intern-teacher program for the past two years, a program which required separate and additional university supervision. The weekly in-service program conducted at school brought still more university faculty to Taft in the roles of consultants and instructors. In general the feelings expressed on both sides indicated mutual admiration between the personnel at Taft and the supervisory staff of the university. The supervisory staff assigned to Taft included women on the university faculty who had supervised several "generations" of student teachers there.

Two newcomers among university supervisors whose territory occasionally included Taft had recently introduced some stress into the historically idyllic relationship. These newcomers were young male faculty members, themselves recent doctorates. Neither had created an impression of himself as the helpful and "supportive" type of supervisor heretofore welcomed at Taft. On the occasion recounted below the two had compounded their lack of popularity when one supervisor had shown up on an afternoon in March (two days before the end of the university's winter quarter) to make the first and only evaluation visit of a student teacher on behalf of his colleague who was ill. The "substitute" supervisor had contacted Ed by telephone to say he was coming. Ed had tried to discourage the proposed visit, reassuring him that the student was "getting along fine." "But he came anyway, and somehow got by the office without me seeing him," Ed recounted later in the day.

Ed had not realized that the supervisor, Dr. Howard, had already been at Taft, had watched and evaluated a lesson, and had departed, until later that afternoon when he was summoned from the faculty room by the determined-looking duo of Mr. Adam and Mrs. Duchess. The appearance of these two in collaboration after school hours signaled an event of some importance, but Ed was at a loss to discern it from Mr. Adam's oblique opening remark, "I'm really concerned about this little girl across the hall I've watched do a grand job and who will make a fine teacher. This just isn't right. . . ."

Ed explained that he was not sure who Adam was talking about.

'Little Patty Wilson, the fifth-grade student teacher in Carol's room," he and Mrs. Duchess answered in unison.

"She's down there just *crushed* by the evaluation she got from Dr. Howard this afternoon," continued Mrs. Duchess.

"Where is she?" asked Ed.

"In the classroom," replied Mrs. Duchess. "Maybe you should come down and talk to her."

The three marched silently through the empty corridor to the upper-grade wing and into the classroom. Having summoned Ed and alerted him to action, the two senior teachers remained at the doorway of the classroom, sympathetically attentive to show their concern but ready to return to their own after-school classroom chores once they were sure Ed had the situation in hand. (I remained inside the room but was not part of the interaction which followed.)

Patty was sitting at the teacher's desk, her face flushed. She was talking quietly with Carol Lowe, the regular classroom teacher. Her sentences were interrupted by sobbing. Miss Lowe was sitting in a small student chair at the side of the desk, listening and trying to provide verbal comfort. Ed's arrival precipitated more sobbing which in turn prompted a series of reassuring comments by Ed and the two teachers who had summoned him: "Isn't this something?" "We'll try to help." "We're all upset at this." "Well, let's hear what it's all about."

Ed seated himself at a student desk. Patty sobbed out her story and answered Ed's questions in part sentences. Dr. Howard had come today for the first and only time because her regular supervisor was sick, she explained, and it was essential that someone from the university make an official evaluation report. The lesson he saw had not gone very well ("It wasn't really *bad*," Miss Lowe assured, "Just 'so-so.'"). Patty explained:

> Oh, he's partly right. . . . He said it appeared to him I never made a student sit down and stay there [sob] . . . but I have. In math.
> The first thing he said to me was, "Say, do you really think those kids were learning much?" And then he said, "Do these students respect you?" I don't know what he expected me to say.
> He said it was up to me whether I wanted another term. He thought that if I had a little more experience student teaching. . . .

At this point Ed interrupted to ask, "Did Dr. Howard actually say that you flunked, or that you have to take another term of student teaching?"

Patty seemed unsure of exactly what had transpired. "I think it's up to me whether I take student teaching again."

"What does that mean?" asked Ed.

"I don't know!" sobbed Patty.

Ed said he would have to find out what Dr. Howard had meant before he did anything, but he expressed his displeasure that anything had been done to upset Patty or make her feel that she could not become a good teacher. He promised to look into the matter and assured the girl that things would work out. He explained to her that many beginning teachers are not sure of themselves at first. He cited Miss Lowe as a teacher who had needed to learn more self-confidence as a beginner. In an aside to Miss Lowe he said, "Howard's advice isn't worth a dime." He turned again to Patty to continue, "You're free to come here to Taft School and get some more experience *on your own* if you like. Of course, it can't be with Miss Lowe. She'll have another student teacher."

Ed concluded with a general comment regarding the two unpopular supervisors:

> Howard told me he is leaving the university. Good riddance, I say. Generally the staff at the university has been very well pleased with Taft School. But I don't think either Howard or his partner is very happy with us. I've already talked to the head of the teacher training program about Howard's partner. I think we'll survive him.

During the walk back to the office I asked Ed if he had been in to observe the girl while she was teaching. "No," he said, "I haven't sat in there for any period of time. But I'm going to raise hell about this one."

At the office Ed happened to see the Intern Supervisor, the member of his own staff who worked most closely with the university's programs and personnel. He briefly related the incident to her, beginning with the statement, "Mr. Howard was here this afternoon. He talked to Patty and flushed her down the drain."

In several ways this incident with a university supervisor was a unique one at Taft School. It is included here because, as an atypical example of a visit by an outsider, it exemplifies what was *not* supposed to happen as a result of a visit. In the first place, Ed had tried to discourage the supervisor from making any visit at all, itself a remarkable behavior in a school so generally open to all "guests." Secondly, the fact that someone within his jurisdiction had been "reduced to tears" seemed to make Ed angrier than any other event which I observed during the fieldwork. Certainly it was the angriest he became as a result of an outsider's behavior, and the intensity of his reaction hinted that someone had exercised excessive authority within Ed's domain, authority that needed to be checked. Finally, the incident was a disruptive one—tears simply were not part of the customary behavior of adults at school—and resources were drawn upon almost instantly to restore the customary equilibrium. One wonders whether Ed found it disruptive not only because the staff was disrupted but also because he personally had not been given the opportunity to attempt to ameliorate the situation before the visitor left the building.

TAKING CARE OF THE BUILDING

The operation and maintenance of a school as a physical plant makes uneven demands on a principal. At best, routines and procedures may be established which free the principal from having to attend to heat, lights, locking doors, fixing windows, collecting paper, and so forth. Such carefree days require, however, that experienced personnel are available to handle routines and that no unanticipated problems arise. Let the routine vary in the slightest and the office and the principal hear about it immediately.

"There's something wrong with the heater. It won't turn off. We're roasting down here."

"How am I going to get into the building on Saturday morning to set up my new unit?"

"Something *has to* be done about that floor!"

Judging by the behavior of groups of principals visiting at other schools, it would appear that at least the men shared a great interest in school building construction, in routine custodial procedures (the argument over the most effective wax for corridor floors will surely wage forever), and in materials and physical equipment for playgrounds and classrooms. The occupational route by which a person ordinarily becomes a principal would not assure expertise or necessarily the least bit of interest in operating the physical plant, although a "country boy" like Ed had lived with maintenance problems both on the farm and in early assignments as a teacher-principal in small rural schools. Upon becoming principals, however, most men seem to develop intense interest in discussing problems and solutions in operating and maintaining the school as a physical plant. At times this collective interest reached such a point that individual principals sounded a note of dismay: "Let's not spend another whole meeting just talking about maintenance problems!"

Given the amount of time that principals *do* spend at matters directly related to the physical plant, it seems surprising to find that no separate category for this aspect of their work is usually included in the time-distribution studies of their job (see DESP 1968). Whether such tasks are deemed to be "clerical" or "administrative" is not clear in the broad categories in which principals are asked to describe their work. One might also wonder whether the attention devoted by some principals to the physical operation of their schools reveals either an escape from other professional responsibilities like "curriculum leadership" or illustrates a need for finding aspects of their work in which some tangible results of their leadership (for example, a cleverly remodeled teacher's work room; a newly developed area within the building for housing instructional materials; highly polished floors) are evident.[4] This section draws attention specifically to three aspects of taking care of

---

[4] In the Taft case, Ed did not appear a likely winner in the battle to keep the school well-polished. His attention to maintaining the salt-water aquarium at school may have served this hypothesized need for tangible evidence of his contribution to the school, however. The aquarium provided an interesting compromise between a contribution to the instructional program and a miracle of maintenance, since a salt-water aquarium presents a variety of practical problems in temperature and saline control, water and animal replenishment, and the like.

the building relevant to the operation of the physcial plant at Taft: the distribution and possession of keys, the perpetual problem of keeping the building clean, and attention to maintenance.

Keys

School keys serve symbolic as well as practical functions. They can be distributed in such a way as to create important distinctions about access to areas within the building. School keys are generally of three major categories: keys for specific doors (classrooms, outside lavatories, special offices), main office and main door keys, and master keys. In some schools every teacher is issued a master key. In others, teachers may be issued no keys at all, so that the responsibility for all locking and unlocking remains under the direct supervision of custodians. In any case, the distribution of keys in any institution, particularly when they are distributed unequally among staff members, can serve as markers to bestow special status or responsibility. Thus while even the most junior of custodians would be expected to have a master key because of the nature of his work, the assignment of one or two comparable keys among the teaching faculty could provide an interesting clue to status differences.

Ed's solution to the key problem avoided any hint of special prerogatives. In the absence of district-wide policy regarding keys, he had chosen a procedure common to many schools: provide each teacher with a key to his classroom, keep the responsibility for locking the building with the custodians, and loan other keys only on an "as-needed" basis. Since the head custodian arrived at 7:00 A.M. and the "night man" did not leave the building until 10:00 P.M., there was, under ordinary circumstances, no problem in gaining access to classrooms, the office, or the gym and multi-purpose room other than the nuisance of locating the custodian on duty. Since one can always get *out* of a classroom or school (school doors can be locked *only* in one direction, so that under no circumstances can a person be locked inside), the building could be "locked up for the night" even while an evening meeting or activity was still in progress.

For the most part, Ed's distribution of keys worked satisfactorily. But there were problems. Occasionally a teacher wished access to a classroom over the weekend. At such times Ed would loan the teacher a key to the main doors of the building. He had two such keys. His rule of thumb was never to loan more than one key at a time, so that he could keep track of it. If two teachers wished to come in on a Saturday, he gave the key to the teacher planning to arrive first.

The policy of loaning only one key resulted in Ed having to make an occasional trip to unlock the school when the designated key-carrier failed to show up. But he knew the difficulty of having more than one key out at a time. He was reminded of the wisdom of his policy at the beginning of school. He had loaned both building keys and then had acquiesced to still another request for access to the building "sometime over the weekend" by Mr. Adam. Ed loaned Adam the master key. Adam returned to school on Friday evening. He left the key in the lock on his way into the building and later could not recall where he had misplaced it. After a fruitless search, he telephoned Ed to explain that the key was lost. The night custodian found the key — but did not telephone Ed about it. Ed and Adam each spent an anxious weekend wondering whether someone had found the key and might use it to enter the building. Ed resolved not to loan his master key again. "Besides," he rationalized, "by locking my office door I indicate to the teachers that comments about them in my files are not open to others. Loaning my master key to a teacher doesn't seem very consistent."

A few times during winter and spring the night custodian "phoned in sick" on days when the central office had no available substitute custodian to send to Taft School. On those days Ed customarily announced a few minutes before classes were dismissed that the night custodian would not be in. He requested teachers to see that their classroom doors and windows were locked, but he attended to locking all outside doors himself.

Problems with getting doors locked or unlocked persisted to the very end of school. All but two of the teachers elected to take the Saturday after the last day of school as their extra "Work Day" rather than return the following Monday. Somehow no one thought about the fact that the custodian would not be at school on Saturday morning to open it. The first teacher to arrive, Edna Willing, a perennial earlybird, realized what had happened and drove immediately to Ed's home to borrow the key, correctly assuming that Ed did not plan to be among the first to get to school. Later that morning Ed recounted to me, "Edna came by before 8:00 A.M. this morning. She caught me in my pajamas. She needed the key to the building."[5]

Keeping the Building Clean

During an interview in March a primary teacher who had transferred to Taft from another school in the district expressed some complaints frequently repeated about the classroom floors:

> Our rooms were getting so dirty. This wing here hadn't been mopped since before summer school and they were used at the time, and so our rooms weren't clean in the fall. They just kept getting worse because of all the winter mud and things that came in. We kept asking—it wasn't just me or anything, it was the other teachers too—if we couldn't have our floors cleaned.
> Ed made a comment to me one day that "things weren't like they are at Woodrow Wilson." Our janitor kept the floors clean at Woodrow Wilson. And at vacation times they were waxed and mopped. We just had two janitors, the same as we have here, and our school was exactly the same number.
> Ed kept saying that a clean school didn't necessarily go along with better education, that physical surroundings aren't as important as the emotional feeling in the classroom. I agree with this, too, but I need to work in a clean room. I don't function very well in a dirty classroom. Maybe it doesn't bother the children, but their clothes were getting dirty and I didn't agree with that. After a few teachers visited some other schools and were mentioning how clean the schools were, we began to have a few things changed. I feel that a physical environment is important toward education as well as an emotional environment.

[5] I laughed at Ed's way of relating this incident and told him that now I could record in my notes that he wore pajamas. "I wanted you to hear my version first," he joked in return.

Taft School had little chance of being known as the cleanest school in the district because a majority of the playing area surrounding the school was unpaved. In the rainy climate of the Pacific Northwest the Taft school grounds often became, in the words of the custodians, the "mudhole of the school district." Ed was concerned lest his school become known as one of the dirtiest, especially since he felt the standards expected on the part of central office personnel remained high because the building was still relatively new.

Taft had two full-time custodians. Whether a school building with 18 regular classrooms required more custodial service than two men could provide, Ed was never certain. At times he complained to the custodians, at times he complained to the downtown office, at times he urged teachers to be patient, but he was relatively powerless to improve the standards of cleanliness within the building except as he could juggle schedules or rearrange priorities on the workload and daily routines which the custodians followed. He tended to overextend the influence of his position when discussing problems with the custodians by making guarantees and promises he could not necessarily fulfill in return for promises of increased effort on their part. For example, he offered to guarantee good pupil behavior in order to get the night custodian to resume filling the soap containers in the upper-grade boys' lavatory after he learned that the custodian had been leaving them empty. The custodian explained that he had cut off the soap supply " 'cause they put it on the floor, the walls, the ceiling—every damn place except their hands."

Ed said, "If you will keep the soap containers filled, I'll get them to use it correctly."

"Is that a deal? Okay, I'll do it," the custodian replied.

Custodial problems at Taft had two major sources, the job itself and the personalities of the men who filled the job. Ed sympathized with his custodians in terms of the amount of work confronting them, although he thought they often lost track of the purposes of a school. He once commented in a faculty meeting, "The custodians' idea of cooperation and mine aren't the same. They'd like us to run school so kids don't get it dirty at all."

In mid-winter, when the problem of keeping the floors clean became most severe, Ed made several requests for authorization either for another part-time custodian or for occasional relief help so the custodians could "get ahead" (i.e., wax or buff one or two rooms in the evening in addition to the regular daily custodial care of the entire building). His attempts to push the night man to get more work done resulted in somewhat of an impasse between the two of them. Ed alternated between laying the blame for dirty floors on an impossible situation and on the fact that he did not feel the night man was trying to cooperate with him. Sometimes he recognized both as sources of the problem. He explained the dilemma in a telephone call to the maintenance supervisor in February:

> I've got custodial problems. I keep pushing these guys to try to get more work out of them. But even if I pushed them all the way we still couldn't keep up. We're not getting the best out of them, but if I push too hard, maybe I just won't have them. Well, the day man would stay around, but the other guy, he's kinda cantankerous. I told the day man to do lavatories in the morning so the night man could buff one room a night. That was two weeks ago. He has

done four and he'll do another one tonight if he can get to it. Now we had a frost last night that brought the moisture up, so today the kids tracked all the dirt and mud back in.

A week after that telephone conversation Ed felt that the problem had gotten worse. He drafted one of his rare letters and had the secretary run off copies so he could distribute them among central office personnel. The letter read:

TO: Maintenance Department, Central Office
RE: Custodial Situation

Our school has now grown to eighteen rooms and has become, more and more, a community center with about a dozen different groups using various parts of the building an average of thirty-five separate times per week during winter weather. The result has been a custodial situation which has lots of heavily used areas to cover, and many interruptions to provide access to groups coming and going. Our two men find themselves so far behind in their work, that they become discouraged about ever getting caught up. The men we have seem to have limited motivation to do a good job under optimum conditions.

I recognize that my recommendation is not new, but I hope it may help you to make others aware of the overall district situation. I would like to see a better wage scale paid to attract men who want to stay badly enough to be sincere about in-service and good use of time. I believe our present situation warrants an additional four hours time daily or perhaps two full days weekly to provide "catch-up" help in such areas as mopping and window washing.

A general appraisal of our situation by the Director of Buildings and Grounds could be helpful and would be appreciated.

Sincerely,
Ed Bell

Ed had occasion a few days later to talk about his request for extra help with the night custodian: "You guys shouldn't have to do the stripping and waxing. Just routine maintenance. Then you could get things like the lights and the windows."

"Them lights haven't been done since last summer," the custodian agreed, and he took out his handkerchief and blew his nose as if to punctuate the point.

"Sounds like you've got a cold," Ed added sympathetically.

"A bitch," replied the custodian. "If it's like this tomorrow, I won't be in."

Ed had several run-ins with the night custodian. After each one he considered having him fired, although his experience in recent years had been that each replacement sent out from the central office was a bit more unsatisfactory than the man before him. As pointed out in Ed's letter to the central office, the wages for custodians were not attractive to most people on the labor market (the night man earned $4,800 for the regular school year in 1968), yet high expectations were held for the work. Custodians, like everyone else working in public school settings, were expected to demonstrate a certain dedication to their work. Once Ed even suggested that one criterion of a good custodian should be his willingness to participate in in-service training, a criterion customarily reserved as a measure of commitment for professional staff.

Ed had recently experienced another kind of custodian problem, one that remained foremost in his mind because it had been a "close call" from an administrative point of view. A previous custodian had seemingly been involved in a series of illicit incidents with some upper-grade girls. Although the precise nature of the incidents was not volunteered (Mrs. Duchess alluded only to the "lurid details" of the affair), Ed did refer to the potential seriousness of the situation, including the fact that the pupils involved were "nice girls from nice families." ("Nice families" can be a source of great administrative anxiety in school districts when something goes wrong.) As soon as word of the activities reached Ed's ears he initiated an inquiry. Mrs. Duchess was called upon to assist in interviewing the girls to learn what had transpired. Ed felt certain that something was amiss. He called in the supervisor of custodians and held a confrontation with his custodian. As Ed recounted the story, he told the custodian, "I have evidence that satisfies me that something is going on. If you want to go into details, all right. If not, we'll accept your resignation *right now.*" The custodian resigned immediately, walked down the hall to get his personal belongings, and left the building forever.[6]

Ed described that custodian as "a good janitor, one who took pride in the school," but as a consequence of the close call he was willing to accept a custodian who was less competent but seemingly a better moral risk. Ed remained adamant about what he felt was a too-casual approach to screening applicants for maintenance jobs in the school district. "We leave ourselves wide open," he warned his colleagues.

Both custodians were relatively new employees when school opened in September 1966. The night man had filled a year-round custodial position at Taft School newly warranted by the continual increase in pupil enrollment. Whether due to the division of labor between the two janitors (the responsibility for maintaining the floors fell essentially to the night man) or to differences in their personalities, Ed often found himself at odds with the night man, and he began to feel that the night man was primarily to blame for the poor appearance of the building. However, with occasional extra hours of help authorized by the maintenance department, the school managed to survive through the winter. A few classroom floors each week—especially those of the primary teachers who made the most frequent complaints—received a special buffing. The night man was rehired for the following year, but he and Ed began the second year at almost the very point in their relationship where they left it. In October, 1967, Ed recounted an argument precipitated over where the night custodian should park his car. Ed said:

> He got so mad I thought he was going to fight me. But I told him I wasn't afraid of him; I'm from the "show me" country, too. We're having a meeting on Monday with the maintenance supervisor. Maybe we'll let him go. This has been building up. He seems to resent any authority. If a teacher asks him to do something, he does it, but if I tell him, he gets all in a huff. We can't keep him around if he won't take directions. It'll be tough on him, too. He's pretty old, and he can't do hard labor. And we won't be able to give him a recommendation.

---

[6] It is interesting to ponder how much evidence a principal is expected to acquire under such circumstances. How does one mitigate between responsibility for the safety of the children and the right of a man to keep his job, particularly when the "facts" are limited to the accusations made by young children? Ed felt some added support for his action in the present case when a subsequent check of police records showed that the former custodian had once faced a similar charge in another state.

Touch-and-go as their relationship seemed, the night custodian did not lose his job. Apparently Ed was able to satisfy his own feelings in the matter with the belief that if things *really* came to a showdown, the man would have to go.

Maintenance

Ed exhibited the interest in the physical plant of his school and in the administrative aspects of building maintenance that characterized most of the male principals encountered in this study. As he walked through the corridors of any school building he automatically noted the condition of the floors, walls, and windows. If the visit was a daytime one, he had already inspected the landscaping and outside of the building as he entered it. Any visit of the principals as a group to a newly constructed school included a tour of the building and Ed inevitably paced off the size of a new classroom (usually with the satisfaction of finding that classrooms at Taft were as large or larger than in schools built more recently), inspected the materials used in interior construction, and looked at features especially pointed out by a host principal such as carpeting, a new intercom, or moveable walls between classrooms. The conversation among principals during such tours usually began with pointing out special features of the new construction, turned next to comparing these features with similar ones in older schools, and concluded with comments and an exchange of problems and remedies in the maintenance of each person's own building.

Aside from some knack for minor repairs (the custodians as often took their problems to him as he did to them), Ed felt a special interest in his school building because he had followed the course of the original construction and had been on hand for all subsequent additions and alterations. He took pride in feeling that he knew more about the building than any other person in the district. He had occasionally talked with the architect and had once invited him to school to point out potential improvements for future buildings. As Taft's newness gradually wore away, Ed attempted to anticipate maintenance problems and to inquire among his colleagues for suggestions about methods and materials, so that he would have an authoritative voice in his discussions with the maintenance supervisor from the central office.

Ed derived some satisfaction from being an "expert" about his school, but the topic of maintenance was essentially a headache because of its perpetual nature and a frustrating headache because of penny-wise economies of the school district. Every requisition and work order sent in to the central office over Ed's signature had to be approved in the business office before it was sent on for action. A state of war seemed to exist between principals and that office. The following vignette recorded in the field notes illustrates Ed's attitude toward the school district's perennial thriftiness:

> Several girls reported that "someone" had been throwing soap balls on the ceiling in the upper-grade girls' lavatory. Ed went down the hall to check, stopping first to ask a pupil working in the resource teacher's room if she would scout whether anyone was in the lavatory. Ed stepped in to verify the wads of granulated soap stuck to the ceiling. He explained that the reason this

had happened was that the soap came out of the dispenser too quickly in this room. He said he had tried to put in a requisition for a fifty-cent sleeve which would fit inside the dispenser and cut down the amount of soap released. The requisition was not approved: "Someone downtown wanted to save the fifty cents."

The combination of a school district's many such economies in the past, the normal wear and tear on a fully-utilized elementary school, and a building just old enough to begin showing signs of its age, kept the business of servicing and repair among Ed's recurring problems.

WHEN THE PRINCIPAL IS AWAY

"I haven't seen Mr. Bell all morning," commented one of the young new intern teachers.

"He's not here. He's gone to a meeting and he won't be back for two days," another teacher informed her.

"Gee, we could just close up school for two days. He'll never know."

Everyone in the room laughed at her intended joke, for even under the changing conditions in today's schools where teachers join and even initiate school boycotts, it is literally unthinkable that a school would shut down because its administrator was not there to assure its continued operation. The question of whether principals should be at their schools at all times when pupils are in attendance is one on which principals themselves seem to be divided (see Foskett 1967:103). However, it would be virtually impossible for a principal to be at the school building all the time and it would be absolutely impossible for him to be equally available to anyone who might need him even if he were.

What does happen at school when the principal is away? Obviously school does not come to a screeching halt when a principal leaves, for if it did, the absences of an "average" principal who was away as frequently as Ed[7] would constantly undermine the regular operation of the school. In fact, routine operations seemed little changed in the absence of the principal except for the lack of immediate authority to substitute in his absence. Messages, problems customarily handled by the principal, and special requests "piled up" awaiting his return, but except for the secretary, members of the staff were often unaware that Ed was away from the building unless he was gone for most of the day. He usually announced anticipated absences in the faculty notebook (for example, "I'll be in Centerville most of the day. Hold the Fort. E. B."). On days when he anticipated a long meeting away from school, Ed followed the custom of many principals of trying to "drop by the school for a few minutes" enroute to the meeting. The intent of such brief visits was not to check up on the staff but rather to see whether any special problems had arisen that required his attention.

[7] The time and motion study showed him to be away about 20 percent of the time in a regular school day. The range over the two-year period varied from occasional days when he never left the building at all to even less frequent periods when he was away for several consecutive days to attend meetings of the state and national principals' associations.

Although the school district did not appoint vice principals in its elementary schools, every school was required to have a faculty member officially designated as the person who assumed responsibility in the principal's absence. At Taft School the resource teacher had usually been the person so designated. There had been three resource teachers in Taft School's history, all males. The current resource teacher, Bob Mason, was officially the "next-in-command." Presumably, the assignment meant that he was in charge of the school in the absence of the principal, although both women who had served as secretaries reported that they thought of the person designated as essentially a disciplinarian for cases of pupil misconduct rather than as an acting principal.

Once when Ed was away at a two-day meeting I asked his long-time secretary what kinds of problems she customarily encountered in his absence. She answered:

> None! I don't even think about it when he's gone. Oh, maybe if he were going to be away for 3 or 4 months, but not for just a day or two. Mr. Mason is here if there is a problem. If it was a broken arm or something, then I would phone the nurse, if she were at another school, and she would come right over. If I couldn't reach her, then I can call the nurse at the high school. And I suppose if I couldn't reach *her*, I'd just take the child to a doctor myself. I don't know if that's right or not, but that's what I would do.

The secretary said she had called on the resource teacher in the past for handling discipline problems, but she felt that even these instances were routine in the sense that discipline cases were among the recurring problems at school. Mrs. Young, in a similar conversation about school operations in the principal's absence, compared the principal and the resource teacher as disciplinarians:

> When Ed has been away at some of his meetings and someone needs to be talked to, I call in Bob Mason. There's a vast difference in the children's attitudes towards Ed and towards Bob. They're both big men. But Ed sits there and smiles at them; Bob uses stronger language and maybe a sterner tone with them.

Ultimately, the telephone provided immediate access to the authority of the school district through a call to the central office: "If there is any other problem we can always call Dr. Goodard." The secretary recalled the only occasion when she did make such a call. A father whose children attended Taft made an unexpected visit to school and requested they be allowed to leave early. The secretary checked with the teachers and learned that the parents had recently initiated divorce proceedings. The teachers cautioned that they "had a feeling" that the children were not supposed to be released to the father. The secretary said, "I telephoned Dr. Goddard for advice. But there was nothing here in writing, and Dr. Goddard said it had to be in writing, so we released them. And we never heard another thing about it, so I guess it was all right. But I guess if a parent really wanted to take his children away all he would have to do is wait for them around the corner." To summarize how the school operated in Ed's absence, the secretary said, "Well, there just haven't been any problems. Maybe if you ask me tomorrow there will be."

Comment

Probably the events described in this chapter come closest to portraying that part of a principal's activities at school most familiar and most closely associated with stereotypes of the elementary school principalship. At the same time, the description has been detailed and specific, focusing on the way one principal handled a wide range of routines rather than providing a potpourri of how a number of principals handled comparable but never quite identical problems. A principal who cannot cope effectively with the range of strangely diversified demands described here would be ill-suited to the principalship. Some principals become meticulous about and obsessed with the details of running a school. Ed's response was to try to elude some detail on the assumption that pressing problems would catch up with him eventually. As this and previous chapters have illustrated, many not-so-pressing problems caught up with him as well. Like his formally scheduled time, his unconstrained time at school was taken up almost totally by demands placed on him by others.

To the extent that an ethnography focussed on an occupational role provides, at least implicitly, a kind of job description, the reader should realize that the description of what a principal does is at this point vitually complete. The next chapter provides an analysis of the sequence of these events, but it does not add to the job description except as it includes attention to regularly recurring events not part of the everyday routine. Later chapters are addressed to system-maintaining functions which provide both explicit and implicit guidelines for principal behavior. They do not tell a principal *what* to do—the job itself provides that. Rather, they set expectations and limits for *how* he should behave regardless of the specific task at hand.

7 / The annual cycle
of the principalship

Anthropologists embarking upon an ethnographic inquiry usually attend to the range of activities that comprise a complete cycle of activities among their subjects. Since they have most often studied small preliterate societies living in close harmony with nature, the natural cycle of events during one year has emerged as a customary sequence in analysis, and with it has come a traditional preference for conducting field work for a minimum of a twelve-month period. This tradition was observed in the present study. The project actually provided for fieldwork extending through a two-year period. The major field research was carried out during the first year, but sufficient participation was included during the second year to allow for placing the first year in perspective, as well as to correct impressions and to fill in gaps in the data.

From the beginning of the study, the idea of attending to the annual cycle also posed an interesting question in thinking about the principalship: When does the annual cycle of a principal begin and end? What would be a natural time to initiate fieldwork? For some categories of people within a school, the beginning and end of the "year" are easily identified. The pupil year, for example, is clearly signaled by the opening of school in September and by the closing of school in June. A shade of ambiguity in reconciling a nine-month academic year with a twelve-month calendar is reflected in the confusion pupils express during the summer vacation about the grade they are "in," since they recognize, at least intuitively, that they no longer are members of the grade they have just completed nor have they yet been incorporated into the next higher one. The annual cycle for the teaching staff coincides with that of the pupils but extends over a slightly longer period, typically beginning a few days before school opens and terminating abruptly on the last day of pupil attendance or on one additional teacher work day beyond it.

Principals do not usually terminate their activities so abruptly in June nor resume their responsibilities so late in the summer as the other members of the school faculty. Customarily they are given longer contracts than teachers. Two-thirds of the supervising principals reporting in the national study indicated appointments of ten or 11 months (DESP 1968:39). The recent trend has been to award even longer contracts; one-third of the supervising principals in the east coast portion of the national sample reported having 12-month contracts (p. 39).

The fact that principals put in more days each year than do pupils or teachers does not of itself make it difficult to identify the beginning and end of their annual cycle. What does complicate defining the cycle is that months before the present school year will terminate, a principal starts directing some of his attention to the school year which will follow. In Ed's district, principals were required to produce their first evidence of planning for the next school year while the current year was only three months underway, with the submission of an estimated budget due the second week of December. As early as February, Ed began talking informally with promising student teachers about the possibility of their joining the Taft faculty the following September. In March he polled the faculty for their grade and room preferences for the coming year and began making preliminary teacher assignments. By April, plans for introducing major curriculum changes of new programs or materials had to be well formulated. During April, Ed reminded teachers to "begin thinking about the class assignments" which they would make for their pupils for the next year. Teachers at each grade prepared the initial class rosters for all pupils in their grade for the following year, a task which Ed liked to see completed early. In May, pupils planning to enter school the following September spent their first "day" at school while their parents received an initial orientation in a newly forming association of parents that for some would be continuous for the next 12 years.

By the time school closed in June, Ed had made tentative assignments for the following September for teachers and pupils. During the summer, preparations for the next academic year continued, although in the two summers of this study Ed's attention was drawn primarily to administering summer school programs and participating in other school district activities. The extended period of the summer brought its own changes and replacements in the plans for opening school as members of the ever-mobile American population—teachers and parents alike—changed their jobs, their residences, or the number of their dependents. On the chance that not every principal might pause during the summer to reflect on his own task and to review the goals he hoped to achieve for the coming school year, even that function was institutionalized by the central office through meetings and workshops called by the Director of Elementary Education or the Superintendent. With the year ahead carefully mapped out, then, and only then, the principal took a respite from school work. By the time teachers reported for the formal beginning of school, the principal was already back on the job and ready for them. But he did not initiate the school year in September, he only accelerated its momentum sufficiently to allow it to accommodate his school's share of the impact of some 37 million elementary school children (1969 estimate) who respond to the sound of the school bell each September.

In sum, then, a principal's activities in relation to each academic year begin not in September, as with teachers and pupils, but as early as the preceding fall or winter. Once a principal initiates his preparations for the coming year, he continues devoting some attention to it throughout the spring and, to a lesser extent, through the summer. His long-anticipated school year springs to life with the infusion of teachers and pupils at the opening of school, and it continues to make demands on his attention until it comes to an abrupt close when school "lets out" in June. By the time that year comes to a close, however, the principal has already been en-

TABLE 7–1 REPRESENTATION OF SCHOOL YEAR "OVERLAP" FOR THE ELEMENTARY SCHOOL PRINCIPAL

Month

	SEPT.	OCT.	NOV.	DEC.	JAN.	FEB.	MAR.	APR.	MAY	JUNE	JULY	AUG.	SEPT.	OCT.	NOV.	DEC.	JAN.	FEB.	MAR.	APR.	MAY	JUNE	JULY	AUG.	SEPT.

Previous School Year

Present School Year

Next School Year

KEY

Period requiring some attention — — —

Period requiring major attention ——————

gaged in the preparation of the next school year for months. Thus although elementary school principals describe their work in terms of initiating and completing a series of identifiable school years (for example, school year 1966–67), their "annual cycle" does not really consist of 12-month periods but is instead comprised of an endless array of overlapping cycles of about 19 months' duration. There is no clearly defined moment at which the cycle begins, and the point at which it ends—perhaps the moment when the final accounting reports are signed and sent in to the central office—is obscured by the activity of the next cycle. In Table 7–1, the overlapping of school years in terms of the attention given by a principal is represented diagrammatically.

In looking back over the time period for conducting the fieldwork, the fact that it was begun in April and was concluded two years later in June might appear to demonstrate superb planning or amazing luck. In fact, however, the beginning date was determined by external circumstances, and I recall my sense of surprise and even mild frustration in finding Ed almost totally preoccupied with his "next year," school year 1966–67, when for purposes of establishing a base line I wanted to learn as much as possible about the year then concluding, school year 1965–66. Apparently Ed's tendency to become too involved in the next year was distracting to his teachers as well. One senior teacher observed:

> Another thing that Ed often does is to get all hepped up about next year at the close of the year. He might as well give up, because teachers are too tired, too involved in the winding up of the classroom, to get very excited about next fall. And it's very boring to the staff that are not coming back to talk about next year's class.

Although Ed had two different academic years on his mind during a great deal of the time, it should not be inferred that during some periods of time his work load was necessarily doubled. Rather, it seems more accurate to point out that during many of his days at school his attention was divided between two school years, the present one and the forthcoming one.

SEASONAL ACTIVITIES OF AN
ELEMENTARY SCHOOL PRINCIPAL

Looking at school years as overlapping ones serves an analytical purpose here; yet in his daily life Ed's activities not only fit into the 12-month annual calendar but, as a school man, were particularly sensitive to it. Instructional programs, particularly at schools attended by young children, are peculiarly responsive to the annual calendar, to the four seasons, and especially to annual secular and Christian holidays.[1] American schools get double duty from every major holiday except the Fourth of July and Labor Day, for not only is the importance of each holiday

---

[1] This responsiveness may be out of deference to the pupils, at least in part, but it is also a characteristic of teachers as an occupational group. Teachers everywhere seem to anticipate and to refer frequently to any forthcoming break in classroom routine, whether it be the end of school, a brief holiday, or even the recurring blessing of Friday, "T.G.I.F." (Thank God It's Friday).

itself validated with a moratorium on school (sometimes with a substantial number of similarly spent days of holiday before or after), but teachers also capitalize on forthcoming holidays as opportunities for introducing variety, relevance, and subject matter into their classroom programs. Christmas is the unequivocal star of the holidays—Taft celebrated it with 19 parties (18 classroom parties plus a staff party) and decorated 20 Christmas trees. Most teachers at Taft capitalized on several holidays in their classroom activities, and the spirit of each forthcoming holiday permeated the atmosphere of the school among adults as well as children.

The extent to which a school principal enters personally into the seasonal activities engaged in by teachers and pupils appears to be a matter of personal inclination coupled with local school tradition. In some schools the principal's involvement in the classroom or school-wide celebrations of Halloween, Christmas, Valentine's Day, St. Patrick's Day, or Arbor Day extends to the full participation involved in leading a school-wide costumed Halloween parade or acting as Santa Claus at a Christmas party. On the other hand, a principal may participate only to the extent of limiting the time or energy devoted to a special occasion, as, for example, Ed's directive in the faculty notebook on Halloween: "Plan to confine parties to last hour of your school day."

By design or oversight, principals and teachers may also ignore many or most of the barrage of special days (for example, Arbor Day, Veterans' Day) and weeks (such as National Book Week, National Dental Health Week) marked for official recognition at school. A favorite commemorative day for administrative oversight, and the basis of some joking among Ed's colleagues, was Frances E. Willard Day. An archaic statute in the state education code directed that every public school within the state provide official recognition concerning the life and works of this educator and temperance leader on a given day in October.[2] The joking followed a pattern like this:

FIRST PRINCIPAL: Isn't Frances E. Willard Day coming along now pretty soon?
SECOND PRINCIPAL: Nope, you've missed it again.
FIRST PRINCIPAL: Well, I know we celebrate it *every* year.

Ed's participation in classroom events associated with the holidays celebrated at Taft was minimal. He usually made a quick tour of the building during a designated party time and he made a point of trying to visit in any classroom to which he had received a personal invitation, but his involvement was brief and formal. The adult staff traditionally observed one holiday-based get-together during the school year, the annual staff Christmas party. This party was held on the last Wednesday afternoon before Christmas vacation. Staff participation was virtually assured, since the party was held immediately after the customary early dismissal of pupils on that day and prior to the hour when staff members felt free to leave the building.

---

[2] "Such portion of the afternoon of the fourth Friday in October of each year, as deemed proper by the teacher in charge of any public school, is set apart for instruction and appropriate exercises in commemoration of the life, history, and achievements of Frances E. Willard. The day shall be known and is designated as Frances E. Willard Day. All public school officials and public school teachers shall carry out the provisions of this section." Source: Revised Statutes of the State, Laws Relating to the Public School System.

TABLE 7–2   SEASONAL ACTIVITIES OF AN ELEMENTARY SCHOOL PRINCIPAL

Duration and Intensity of Activity by Month

Activity	SEPT.	OCT.	NOV.	DEC.	JAN.	FEB.	MAR.	APR.	MAY	JUNE	JULY	AUG.
Orienting:												
New staff												
New pupils and parents												
Student teachers, supervisors												
Meeting:												
Public relations (Open House, room desserts, new parents)												
Faculty and school district												
Regional, state, national												
School-related socials (parties, farewells)												
Pupil Problems												
Teacher Evaluations												
Preparing for Next School Year												
Budget projection												
Interviewing												
Assignments, ordering supplies												
Contingent Activities												
In-service training												
Workshops/Summer school												
Personal vacation												

KEY

Intermittent activity – – –

Intense activity ———

A gift exchange, with each person bringing a present of designated value and receiving one in return, and an ample supply of refreshments representing the candy- and pastry-making talents of women members of the staff, constituted the essence of the party.

The possibility of holding a staff dinner just before the closing of school received favorable response, and arrangements were made to accommodate teachers and spouses who wished to attend the get-together at a local Chinese restaurant. About half the staff attended. A pre-planned "let's all go out for lunch together on the final Saturday [teacher work day] after school" got a bigger response, perhaps because the teachers who had elected to work Saturday instead of returning on Monday already felt in a social and festive mood. Long-time employees of the school district who were retiring were usually feted with farewell "banquets" held at school cafeterias during the final months of the school year. Ed and his wife attended two such functions in May. Ed was the only member of the regular staff to attend either banquet, and he may have been the only person in the school who every had much contact with the old-timers being honored.

The seasonal activities in which principal Ed Bell engaged on a month to month basis are presented. in graphic form in Table 7–2. The table suggests how during the course of the school year, starting with the formal opening of school in September, the emphasis shifts from attention to the present year to attention in making preparations for the forthcoming one. At the same time, many activities require at least some degree of attention as long as school is open. Each of the major categories of activity suggested in Table 7–2 is discussed briefly in the remainder of this chapter, in the order presented in the table.

Orienting   Ed's duties as the host and guide of Taft School were greatest at the beginning of the school year when newcomers among the staff, pupils, and parents were most conspicuous. The influx of newcomers and visitors continued throughout the year, although there were seasonal variations in their numbers. Student teachers and their faculty supervisors arrived at school according to the calendars of their own institutions rather than that of the public schools. Except for two students who spent the first two weeks at school when it opened (thus earning two university credit hours of "September Experience" in their teacher training programs), regularly assigned student teachers did not arrive at Taft until the university term began in late September. Subsequently a new group of student teachers, student observers, and sometimes even new supervisors appeared at the beginning of each new academic quarter and returned regularly throughout the ensuing weeks.

Meetings   The attempt to build or to maintain a close school-community liaison at Taft School was initiated as soon as the school year was underway with a series of Room Desserts. The teachers at each grade level selected an evening when parents of children in that grade were invited to school to meet the teachers and hear about the curriculum and the organization of specific classrooms. Ed liked to see the annual round of Room Desserts begun and completed as quickly as possible, hopefully by the end of September. He made a point of being at school each evening they were held. The next formal invitation extended to parents was for a school-wide Open House held one evening during American Education Week, the second week of November. A spring School Fair, focused around classroom exhibits displayed in the gymnasium, provided another occasion for inviting parents to school. The annual orientation in May for parents of children entering school the next fall concluded one year's formal events by anticipating the next one. Taft School did not formally observe the graduation of its sixth-grade pupils. Ed felt that any activities relating to special holidays should be for the enjoyment of the children, and he did not encourage school-wide programs like the traditional Christmas Program observed in many schools.

All parents were expected to meet on an individual basis with their children's classroom teachers during periods especially designated for parent conferences. At such times teachers reviewed with parents the progress of their children and, in some cases, initiated formal action requiring a change of status (such as promoting or retaining a child in mid-year or agreeing to seek specialist help). Often such problems were first broached during parent-teacher conferences, and Ed announced he would be on hand every afternoon during conference weeks in case a parent wished to call upon him or a teacher needed to. He anticipated that academic problems would be raised at the end of the first report to parents (at Taft the parent conferences were held in lieu of report cards at the end of the first and third 9-week report card periods of school) and noted that there were often a few new problems at the end of each of the subsequent reporting periods.

Ed's involvement in administrative meetings called by the central office began as soon as he was officially on-duty for the new school year; it is a common practice among schoolmen at all levels to initiate (kick-off) the school year with a meeting. On the day the teachers reported after their summer holiday all Taft faculty attended a district-wide meeting at West High School in the morning and returned for an all-staff meeting with Ed immediately after lunch. From that day on, as previous chapters have illustrated, meetings were part of Ed's way of life at school. Not until the very end of the school year did the frequency of official meetings diminish. It was customary for at least one final administrative meeting to be called during the period in June when school had closed but administrators remained on duty.

Ed's professional activities in the county, regional, and state principal's associations[3] were concentrated within the core of the regular school year. The scheduling of these meetings seemed to take into account that principals might not be able to leave school during the first weeks of the new school year, and no meetings were scheduled for that period. The final meetings of the school year were scheduled early enough to allow for widely differing duties and schedules related to the close of school from one district to the next. Thus most of the professional associations were compressed into the periods of relatively stable school routine from late October to early May. The annual state-wide meeting of elementary principals held in October marked Ed's first regular and major (one- or two-day) absence

[3] Ed paid a total of $63 in annual dues in 1966–67 for memberships in seven professional education associations. He attended meetings of each of them except the National Education Association. Locally he belonged to the school district's professional education association and the elementary school principals' association. He belonged to the county, state, and national elementary school principals' associations and to the state and national education associations.

from the school and district. Activities of the regional principal's association included a one-day conference in the late fall (November or early December) and a Thursday through Saturday meeting usually held in February. The meetings of the National Department of Elementary School Principals were held in late March or early April. Ed attended his first annual meeting of the national organization in Portland in 1966. Two years later he attended his second national meeting in Houston, Texas. His way was paid by the school district, and he was the official representative of the regional association of elementary principals in recognition of his services the preceding year as its president. The final event among all his professional associations was an annual crab feed held each May by the County Elementary Principals Association, an event primarily social in nature. Some of Ed's colleagues claimed that they were constantly reminded at home that the crab feed was the only professional activity of any of the associations to which spouses were formally invited.

Pupil Problems   Problems with pupils, particularly regarding pupil discipline, also followed seasonal patterns. They required more of Ed's attention during periods when school ran for days or weeks without some interruption in the routine and when winter rains compounded dreariness and confined the space in which children and teachers moved. As Ed explained:

> During these long periods of dreary weather, the adults, and especially the women, who live in these little houses seem to get cabin fever, and then so do the children and teachers who work with them. Spring really brings the worms out of the woodwork. Then in late spring, in May and June, with vacation in sight, things quiet down.

To substantiate his feeling that discipline problems built up slowly as the school year got underway, Ed reviewed the notes he had recorded of the year's chronic discipline problems: "I see my list of rock throwers began on September 25th this year. But my first real discipline problem wasn't until November 11th."

Teacher Evaluations   One major task which confronted Ed each year was the preparation of his annual teacher evaluations (see Chapter 9). Preparation of the evaluations was carried out under the pressure of a deadline in February imposed by the central office. The evaluation process was a matter of consternation among most, if not all, principals, and once the necessary evaluations were completed, there was a shared sense of relief. In Ed's opinion, the evaluation process (observing teachers at work, writing up the observations, conferring with teachers about each observation, and conferring again about the final evaluative report) "should go on from September until early February." In fact, he condensed the formal aspect of the work far more: "I really get serious about mid-November. And maybe it's January when I buckle down." Ed was one of several principals who returned to his office on a weekend in February to complete his evaluations:

> I came down here Saturday and worked on evaluations from 10:30 to 4:30 and got most of them done. I can't get anything done around here with the interruptions all the time. I need some time to think if I'm going to put down something halfway decent.

Preparing for the Next School Year   The announcement from the central office of a deadline for submitting a budget marked the first annually recurring event in preparing for the forthcoming school year. Ed claimed that he tried to keep budget preparation in mind and to be working on it for five or six weeks prior to its due date the second week of December, but the approach of the final deadline determined when he put forth his major effort. Preparation of the budget entailed estimating the total annual cost of operating the school, including the projection of necessary maintenance expenditures and estimates of the cost of anticipated improvements. Completing the budget proposal provided a brief moment of elation and relief, but the budget submitted by each administrator was only the beginning of an extended annual ritual which pitted him in a duel with the business office to defend or pare down budget items one by one. In 1966 Ed's respite from grappling with the budget lasted only four days; by mid-December he was already looking for ways to trim his original proposal:

> I was in a hurry with it and didn't check it carefully because I wanted to get it in the mail. They called back to say I was over. I've got to trim $100 of fat off of it.

Projection of future staff needs and assignments required not only information about estimated pupil enrollments but also some estimate of anticipated staff changes. Ed gathered information about the future plans of his teachers anytime, particularly through informal comments made by the younger female teachers regarding their husbands' careers and their thoughts about starting families of their own. In mid-March he drew up a list of teaching positions which he knew for sure needed to be filled for the next year. Official policy dictated that if he was formally going to dismiss a teacher, notice had to be given by April 15; even if he was only going to encourage a teacher to transfer (principals confess to trading their problems rather than to eliminating them [Cruickshank *et al.* 1969:5]) the procedure had to be initiated before anticipated vacancies were filled.

Long before he made a systematic projection of staff needs, Ed began chatting with prospective new faculty members for Taft School, particularly student teachers at Taft who were reported to be outstanding by the regular faculty. Whenever he held a formal teacher interview, however, he acted as an agent of the school district. Principals did not hire teachers for their individual schools. They served as a screening committee to interview potential candidates, and they forwarded their recommendations to the personnel director. An interviewer could request that a candidate be assigned to his school, but he could not be sure that the assignment would be made. For vacancies in a staff for which a principal had no particular candidates in mind, he simply took "pot luck" and received the name and personnel folder of a candidate who had already been hired by the district but who was not yet assigned to a specific school. Usually only one candidate's name was made available for each position. The principal could review the candidate's folder or, sometimes, hold an additional interview of his own. As one principal explained, filling a staff position was not a matter of real selection; rather, it was a process of rejecting or accepting candidates one at a time.

Appointments during which Ed was expected to interview possible elementary teachers for the district were made for him by the personnel office on days set aside in advance for that task. Most of Ed's formal interviewing for the district was done in March and April. Early in May, on a specific day announced in advance, all the folders of newly hired but unassigned teachers were made available to the principals in the office of the Director of Elementary Education, and principals indicated their initial preferences among the candidates on sheets attached to each folder. Ed referred to the day as "the grab." After "the grab" and the subsequent assignment of many new teachers, remaining vacancies at each school became clearly defined. A second and smaller "grab" was held later in the month. After that, principals who still had staff vacancies interviewed candidates to fill specific assignments for their own schools. During the summer, interviewing and hiring continued as necessary. In the summer of 1966, for instance, Ed discovered that only one of three intern teachers who had already been assigned to Taft School was actually going to be on hand for the opening of school; one young woman had become pregnant during the summer, and the second's husband was transferred unexpectedly. At the same time, a new program which called for an additional faculty position at Taft had not been funded, so Ed also needed fewer teachers than originally planned. Staffing remained an item of unfinished business until one week before school opened.

Contingent Activities   Certain of Ed's activities during the course of a year were conditional ones or were subject to mutually exclusive alternatives. The fact that on every other Wednesday afternoon Ed attended a two-hour in-service workshop during the school year 1966–67, for example, was due to several related factors, including that Ed needed additional course hours of university work to fulfill a district requirement for "professional growth" and that the course was superbly convenient in time and place (it was held at Taft School on Wednesday afternoon when pupils were dismissed early). Ed encouraged the faculty to regard the in-service workshop as an all-faculty function. The following year few Taft teachers participated in in-service training programs held in other schools, and Ed relied on the more traditional form of assuring staff interaction—faculty meetings.

Ed's summer activities were contingent upon the alternatives open to him for salaried employment with the school district. In his earlier years in the district he had taken summer jobs outside of the school district or had attended summer school pursuing his course in educational administration. In recent years he had opportunities for employment within the school district. During the two summers in which the study was formally conducted, and in the summer prior to it, Taft School was selected as a summer school site and Ed accepted the option to administer its summer program.

The operation of a summer school did not account for much of Ed's time until after the closing of school. Ed recalled having received his first notice about summer school from the central office on March 2 one year. Surely that was as early as he ever thought about it, he explained, yet even as he spoke he remembered having received a formal application for a teaching position in summer school a full month before that. "So I guess you could say I begin thinking about it in March," he said, "but I take it pretty lightly at that point." Ed found little incentive in extensive pre-planning for the summer school, since the central office customarily announced that operating the program depended on the outcome of the budget election in May. One year when a revised budget failed to achieve voter support at a second election held in June, Ed was unsure whether summer schools were going to be operated in the district even as late as the last day of regular school.

The summer school program necessitated attending once again to the problem of orienting new staff, pupils, and parents. Customary school boundaries were expanded to accommodate children from other elementary school attendance areas, and the summer school clientele always included pupils and parents unfamiliar with Taft. The option of teaching in summer school was open to teachers throughout the district, and the summer school population always included teachers as well as pupils who were new to the school. However, the summer program that had evolved at Taft was relaxed and casual, with an emphasis by the staff to provide children with an enjoyable morning experience each day of the six weeks of the session. Few of the time- and energy-consuming tasks characteristic of Ed's activities during the regular session were present during the summer. Meetings were few in number and brief in nature. Parents were welcome but were never formally summoned to school. I never observed a child being sent to the office for disciplinary reasons. Academic problems seemed similarly nonexistent. Ed was not required to make formal evaluations of the summer school staff, so his classroom visits were not perceived as administrative necessities. Technically, Ed was not even called the principal of the school staff in the central office assignments. Instead, he was officially designated the "team leader," although he was never referred to at school by that title except in jest.

The only activity of the regular school year that appeared to become more intense rather than more relaxed during the summer was the use of Taft School as a laboratory for summer programs held at the university. Attending college summer classes has long been a tradition among public school teachers. During its busy summer season, however, the School of Education at the local university was faced with a very limited number of operating school sites to provide education students with opportunities for observing, apprenticing, or practicing new techniques (behavior modification, clinical supervision, and inquiry training were in vogue during the summers of 1966 and 1967). Taft School, like all other local schools which were open, received many requests from the university to accommodate summer school students and programs; during the six-week session Taft easily had twice the number of university-related personnel on hand that it had during the regular school year, and a good deal of Ed's time was directed toward orienting and distributing them (see Chapter 6).

With a summer school operating at Taft, the time available to Ed for full-time participation in other workshops or programs was obviously limited to the one-week interim in June or to the month of August; each of these periods was utilized during the study, a three-week workshop in August for all elementary school administrators during the first summer, and a one-week meeting in June for all administrators of the district at the close of the study. When the summer school program was discontinued at Taft the following year, Ed participated in a district-sponsored curriculum workshop throughout July.

Ed's summer activities had the net effect of keeping him involved with and on the payroll of the school district through part of the summer, thus extending his basic ten-month contract to 11 or more months of actual employment. Whatever his major school district assignment of the summer, he was also available to look after his school, complete the staffing arrangements for September, host visitors, keep an eye on summer maintenance and remodeling projects, and make some effort at public relations in order to gain voter support if the school budget had not yet won community approval.

The time remaining after the regular school year, the summer school or summer curriculum activities, the administrative workshops and meetings, and the contractual requirements of being the last to leave and the first to return in the academic year, constituted Ed's summer vacation. In 1966 his summer vacation period consisted of six working days, and because he remained home and was available by telephone, he was contacted from the central office during this time. He had a longer vacation the following summer when no activities for principals were planned after the closing of summer school.

The amount of time which Ed actually had free during the summers of 1966 and 1967, as in summers previous and subsequent to the study, was less than the average of eight weeks reported by supervising principals nationally (DESP 1968: 39). It placed him within the one-third of the principal group reporting four weeks or less of time available for recreation and study, a group very likely composed of middle-aged principals like himself who had completed all formal educational requirements and who depended on additional summer income, preferably for additional school-district responsibility, to augment their regular salary.

Ed's most complete respites from school seemed to occur not in summer but during the school holidays observed between September and June. During that period the school program was in full swing, ready to be resumed as soon as the school bell tolled the end of the holiday. Such periods found Ed with no anxieties regarding staffing or assignments. The only administrative detail required was for him to help the custodians work out a schedule to get the building cleaned and the floors waxed while the school building was vacant. It was far easier for Ed to plan a trip away at Christmas the first year (to California for visits with friends and his sister's family) or at Easter vacation the second year (for a similar visit), assured that on his return school would be just the way he left it, than it was for him to count on things being unchanged when he took time off in the summer.

Perennial Hope   Table 7–2 does not include perennial hope among the seasonal activities of an elementary school principal, but at least in Ed Bell's case the recurring feelings he expressed in this regard should be noted. As Ed planned for future school years and programs, he liked to anticipate how things might be or would be improved. When summer school drew to a close, for example, he gave this evaluation of it: "It was satisfactory, not outstanding. Maybe in another 20 years, if I live that long, I'll know what it is I want to accomplish."

During both summers, Ed mentioned his anticipation of the forthcoming regular session. Each of the following two comments was addressed to a different school year:

Next year I hope I can get down to some basic problems—to sit down with some teachers and ask, "Now, just what are your objectives?" And, "Do you think you are accomplishing them?"

Well, I already find myself looking forward to September. You just get over one year and you can't wait for the next.

Comment

This chapter describing the annual cycle of the principalship serves a dual function. First, it provides a framework for looking at the sequence of activities which comprise events recurring from year to year. It shows how different activities vie for Ed's attention at different periods and illustrates the overlapping among school years that provides one of the unique distinctions between the professional interests of teachers and principals. Even more importantly, I believe, this chapter sets the stage for chapters that follow in which a somewhat different Ed may seem to emerge, for we turn now from the relatively comfortable setting of the day-to-day operation of the school and look instead at the significant stages and critical points in cumulative years that comprise a *career* in the principalship. We will review Ed's initial socialization into the role of principal and the continuing process of socialization he undergoes to remain in the principalship. It is important to remember that Ed likes the role of principal and intends to remain in it. He will do whatever he feels he must do to protect both the school and his position in it. His decisions from one school year to the next are critical in this regard.

In the chapters to come Ed may seem to exude less decisiveness and confidence, more uncertainty and anxiety than has been apparent in the narrative thus far. Surviving in the principalship from year to year is a different order of business from overseeing a smoothly running school from one day to the next. One might draw an analogy between Ed's work as a principal and a captain of an ocean liner making a hypothetical series of annual voyages. Once such cruise begins each year, captain and crew alike would be committed to making the best of the voyage. But before he embarks on each succeeding voyage, we would expect the captain to profit by all his earlier experience in selecting his new crew, getting his new passengers settled, or setting his new course.

So, too, with embarking on any particular year at school. Once the crew is signed on and the year begun, one senses a certain amount of resignation in accepting circumstances as they are and in trying to make the best of things. Routines are quickly developed to maximize this possibility. But next year, one hopes, things can be even better, and certain mistakes need not be made again. This is, I believe, why Ed could at times adapt so patiently to immediate circumstances that seemed beyond his control and still remain ever optimistic about years yet to come, determined to make them better than any that had gone before. Unlike his day-to-day decisions, his choices for a coming year, especially on such issues as which teachers to add to his permanent crew or what course in administrative "style" to pursue, were of critical importance.

8 / Maintaining the system: the socialization of a principal

This chapter and the one following it deal with processes by which the schools manage to maintain stable cultural systems in spite of the constant change of personnel assigned to their relatively few statuses. The underlying thesis here is that schools, like other cultural systems, are perpetuated through the processes of socializing new members into the statuses which must be occupied. Considering the benign image usually associated with the nation's elementary schools, the processes of socialization occurring in them are at times surprisingly severe, not only for the ever-changing pupil population but also for adult members of more permanent tenure. Since this study focuses on the principalship, attention is drawn in the present chapter to the ways in which a principal is socialized into teaching and administrative roles and, in the chapter following, to his part in the socialization of others holding or aspiring to these positions.[1]

Although I have chosen first to explore how a principal is socialized, I do not mean to create the impression of a neat sequence in which an individual is completely socialized before he himself can act as a socializer. In varying degrees, these processes occurred concomitantly for Ed Bell as the study progressed, although several years had passed since he had experienced the more intense periods of socialization associated with induction into either teaching or administrative roles. Ed's socialization as a professional educator continued not only through the subtleties of daily interactions with his many "others," but also through such direct means as a periodic evaluation conference for each principal held at the central office.

The chapter is presented in two parts. The first, "Becoming a Principal," extends beyond Ed's own experience in what now seems to him to have been his own fairly easy move "up the ladder" by drawing upon studies about other principals

[1] The term "enculturation" appears frequently in anthropological accounts, sometimes used interchangeably with socialization, sometimes subsuming it, and at other times being subsumed by it. The two terms are perhaps best employed as complementary aspects in the process of humanizing individuals, socialization drawing attention to learning how to behave and enculturation drawing attention to the process of acquiring a world view (see Leis 1972:4–5). I believe that calling attention to these complementary dimensions is a signal contribution from anthropology to the study of human behavior. Nevertheless I have here employed only the term socialization, since it has wide currency among social scientists and educators, particularly in the context of learning specific role behavior.

as well. The second part of the chapter describes the continuing process of socialization in "Remaining a Principal."

BECOMING A PRINCIPAL

Any impatience Ed once felt about whether he would ever become a principal in the district had dissipated long ago. Ed laughed at his own impatience in recalling how close he had come to leaving the district after his third year at the time he got his first "break" to assume a principalship (see Chapter 3).

Now, nine years later, as Ed watched the large number of other sometimes-impatient young men obviously anxious to become principals, he occasionally wondered just how he happened to be selected at all, or at least how he had been promoted when he was still relatively a newcomer in the district. "But maybe there just weren't as many fellows available then. And of course, I had Tom Nice supporting me. Tom made quite a bit out of my having prior administrative experience back in Kansas. I didn't really have so much experience as a principal there, but it helped me get to where I *could* get some."

Ed's initial administrative assignment in the Columbia School District was to assume a full-time principalship for the remainder of the school year. A substitute teacher was hired to take the responsibility for his fifth-grade class. Ed's administrative appointment was clearly portrayed to him as a temporary one, but at the end of that year he was assigned to serve as the principal of two small schools elsewhere in the district. Again the temporary nature of the appointment was emphasized, a fact which Ed interpreted as a lack of satisfaction with his administrative style by the central office. "I thought I might end up back in the classroom," he recalled. Instead, he was reassigned at the end of that year as the supervising principal of another elementary school. That assignment was not qualified with the tentative status of a "temporary" appointment.

Whenever Ed talked about becoming an administrator in the district he mentioned how fortunate he had been to receive his initial teaching assignment at Tom Nice's school: "He's the easiest principal in the district to work with." Other principals spoke similarly of how they happened to get their first administrative assignments, typically relating highly personal experiences in which some combination of help from their building principal plus sheer "good luck" accounted for their "break" into administration. As one principal stated:

> I don't think the promotions are based on seniority or on merit. I think it's just luck, catching someone's ear, or being at the right place at the right time. There were other guys who had been around longer than me when they asked me to take my first job as an acting principal.

In their efforts to describe the forces which contribute to upward mobility, social scientists have identified various modes by which new statuses are attained. Two concepts suggested by R. H. Turner (1960), "sponsored mobility" and "contest mobility," seem particularly useful in describing the processes by which teachers become principals. However, I have treated the two modes, sponsored and contest mobility, as complementary rather than as contrasting modes as originally suggested by Turner.[2] To cast these two complementary modes in the jargon of the professional literature of education, I refer to them as "sponsorship" and "GAS-ing." I shall deal first with the concept of sponsorship because it is probably the more crucial of the two processes in becoming a principal generally and it was certainly the more crucial force in Ed's initial promotion.

Sponsorship

In sponsored mobility, as defined by Turner (1960:856), elite recruits (for example, teachers desirous of becoming principals) are chosen by established elites or their agents (for example, the superintendent, or those to whom he delegates his authority). Elite status is *given* by those in authority rather than *taken* through effort and strategy on the part of the recruits themselves. Sponsorship appeared to have been a key factor in the process by which many of the principals in the district had achieved their administrative status. Sponsorship also provided a way for describing the roles they in turn played in encouraging other promising young men to be "thinking about administration" and in their active support of certain candidates.

Not all sponsors are equally effective, and, as a study of sponsorship in the school superintendency showed (Rose 1969), the people who act as sponsors are themselves not always aware of their roles or of their impact. Among the elementary school principals in the Columbia School District, some were consciously and even aggressively engrossed as sponsors, while others may have had more actual impact. One of Ed's younger cohorts consciously and deliberately pursued the role of sponsor. He explained that he had never realized the extent to which the role of principal required him to be a politican, but since the job seemed to necessitate it, he found himself engaging in politics more and more. He described how he had conspired with one teacher at his school to get the young man an administrative position. Their strategy was for each of them to take every opportunity to keep the sponsoree's name "in the fore" by having him named on committees and by giving him assignments that would constantly increase his visibility to central office personnel and school board members. The principal noted, by way of contrast, that Ed Bell hadn't needed to pursue such an aggressive strategy in order to get a principalship: "Ed had just been there when someone was needed."

If Ed did happen to be at the right place at the right time, that was not the only factor working in his favor. Regardless of what his actual responsibilities as an administrator in Kansas had been, he was recognized in the Columbia School District as an experienced principal who would inevitably receive an administrative assignment there sometime in the future. Promotions to principalships in the larger school districts throughout the country are more often made from within the dis-

---

[2] Turner treated sponsored and contest mobility as contrasting, ideal types by which one could compare upward mobility in American and English systems of education, rather than as complementary aspects of the same process. Although the context to which he applied his examination was in formal educational systems, his analysis dealt with upward mobility of students rather than with upward mobility among the permanent school cadre as in the present study.

trict than from the outside (see Elkins 1950; Fleming 1967; McDowell 1954), a policy that was unwritten but nonetheless generally adhered to within the Columbia schools. Thus it was virtually essential for Ed to "work up through the ranks."

Assessing his chances for a principalship after spending almost three years in the district, Ed became discouraged. In the continuing financial press of earning an adequate income for his family, he considered moving to a better-paying district to gain an immediate improvement in salary rather than wait out the opportunity of an administrative assignment in Columbia. At that point Ed's principal, Tom Nice, performed two aspects of the sponsor function, while Ed himself had become resigned, at least temporarily, to remaining a classroom teacher. Tom worked officially to encourage consideration of Ed as an administrative candidate at the central office while he also personally encouraged Ed to complete formal course requirements for the administrative credential at the local university.

Tom's sponsorship did not terminate when Ed became a principal. Ed frequently turned to Tom for guidance while finishing out the year in the school where Tom had been principal, and he had continued to call upon him for advice ever since. The same factors which prompted the initial sponsorship had continued to keep their relationship intact, including shared feelings about the importance of elementary school education as well as similarities in ages and commitments to active participation in their respective churches. The fact that Ed and Tom worked and lived in the same part of town facilitated opportunities for communicaton between them concerning common professional problems as well as frequent arrangements for travelling together to professional meetings. In more recent years, as Ed became thoroughly entrenched as an administrator *within* the district, Tom's sponsorship and personal encouragement had led to Ed's increased activity and influence within the professional associations of principals. With the help of two other senior principals, Tom had actively campaigned on Ed's behalf and had contributed personal funds for printing costs to see Ed elected president of the county and subsequently of the regional principals' associations. Tom expressed personal satisfaction in watching Ed assume responsibilities "beyond the walls of his own school building." In our first meeting Tom explained, out of Ed's hearing, how pleased he was to see Ed becoming "even more involved" in the work of the principalship, by which he meant Ed's recently acquired role as an officer in the principals' organizations.

Although Ed remained in the role of sponsoree vis-à-vis Tom Nice, he also assumed the role of sponsor vis-à-vis certain younger men interested in administrative careers in elementary schools. He had consciously attempted to assist one young male teacher formerly on the Taft faculty to obtain an administrative position. Ed described "mixed feelings" about helping (sponsoring) his former teacher in his bid for a principalship. On the one hand, Ed confessed, he wanted to see capable young men remain in the classroom; on the other hand, he did not want to "stand in the way." Other principals who perceived themselves as sponsors of specific candidates acknowledged facing a similar dilemma and their inevitable and selfless resolution of it. Sponsoring principals did not publicly assume the credit for the successful achievements of their sponsorees. Among his colleagues Ed publicly assumed credit only for "not standing in the way" of the young man.

He did make it known, however, that he had announced his intention to help his teacher in obtaining an administrative positon "when the opportunity occurred." Although Ed and his sponsoree had not subsequently maintained the close relationship that Ed continued to hold with his own sponsor—perhaps because none of the factors which facilitated the frequent interaction between Ed and Tom (age, church activity, geographical proximity of their schools and homes) was shared between Ed and the younger man—they did attempt at least a brief exchange of greetings at every meeting which brought all principals together. Ed enjoyed hearing reports of the younger man's success as a principal, and he reminded anyone who might not have known or recalled it that the man's prior assignment had been at Taft.

GASing

There is some indication in the literature that career decisions about becoming an administrator are made early and that teachers who intend to "move up" exhibit different behaviors and a different orientation toward the authority system of a school and district from the very onset of their entry into teaching. In a study of socialization into the principalship based on interviews with 18 recently appointed elementary school principals in California, Ron Blood noted:

> The bulk of the principals interviewed were actively engaged in the process of becoming a principal from a very early date. Even the *first* year of teaching, for many, is characterized by a strong focus on the system as a whole and on the principalship specifically. The candidates engage in a pattern which at once serves to get the attention of superiors and provides access to the workworld of the principal (Blood 1966:71).

The candidate who aspires to the principalship has already tacitly demonstrated that he recognizes and accepts the authority system of the school. The process of socialization into teaching tends to assure that candidates who survive can live with the educational hierarchy. Advancing up the "ladder" requires more than simply acquiescing to the system, however. One must actively demonstrate willingness and aptitude for assuming greater responsibility. In the parlance of educational administration, such people are sometimes referred to as GASers.

GASing behavior, or *Getting the Attention of Superiors*,[3] describes a style of teacher behavior characteristic of the teacher seeking to move up and out of the classroom. GASing refers particularly to a teacher's taking additional school-related but nonteaching assignments as a strategy to increase his visibility from among the teacher group at large. The consequence of being a successful GASer is that one becomes known to those people who are in a position to make or directly influence promotions or to lend indirect support as sponsors.

[3] The term GASing appeared in a study of teacher mobility in New York City reported by Dan Griffiths (Griffiths *et al.* 1963). Griffiths points out that in a huge metropolitan school district like New York City which used to hold competitive examinations for administrative appointments, it was not the examination which created the pool of potential appointees, as might be assumed; rather, it was the GASing behavior of aspirants. "The examination system validates the GASers; it does not create a pool from which promotions are made" (p. 33).

In the Columbia School District, seriously-considered candidates for principal-ships were known personally, or at least known about, by most principals and central office personnel. No system of examinations existed in the district. Even the technicality of filing a formal notice with the Director of Personnel expressing a wish to be considered as a candidate was not essential for individuals known to be interested in the appointments.

The GASing syndrome appeared to be quite familiar to principals and to would-be principals alike, although the term itself was not used in the district. To what extent Ed had employed such tactics in order to win the initial support of his principal and the eventual support of the central office was never discussed. In Ed's recounting, it was Tom Nice's support which got him the appointment rather than his own effort, although the extent of their shared values, coupled with a possible lack of assertiveness on Ed's part, may have presented Tom with the kind of candidate he preferred to support.   Ed and his colleagues recognized and dis-cussed the GASing behavior exhibited by aspiring candidates among the district's elementary school teachers. Ed was appointed to a Principal Selection Committee to recommend to the superintendent and school board the "best people" among the eligible candidates for three principalships opening up the following fall (Wolcott 1974). During the deliberations of the committee, comments were fre-quently made indicating a sensitivity toward the amount of GASing behavior each candidate had engaged in as well as an assessment of whether the extent of GASing was appropriate for the particular candidate. For example, Ed's assessment of one candidate, a young man who had attained considerable visibility and was suspected of seeking too much power in the internal organization of the school district, was, "I see too many people ahead of him myself." Ed had stated a similar opinion in more detail a few months earlier after attending a meeting in which that teacher had taken a domineering role:

> He's already a resource teacher, and I think this is only his third year in the district. This fellow just doesn't want to wait his turn, that's all. He's trying to get in good with Boggs [the superintendent]. It's not that there is actually a seniority system in selecting principals, but there are a lot of qualified fellows who have been around longer than he has.

Of another candidate apparently not in high favor, one principal's assessment hinted that too little talent in personal dynamics had been exhibited: "I worked closely with him on that big evaluation project. He wasn't loud and forceful, but he did do a good job." Still other candidates were perceived as having tried too hard. The written recommendation of one woman principal reviewed by the selec-tion committee warned that the candidate had done "too much of the business of the local teachers' association" when he should have been attending to his responsi-bilities as the school's resource teacher. Another woman principal expressed concern about a candidate from her staff: "I think his one big problem is relating to people, because he tends to want to move too fast."

Some candidates had apparently managed to exhibit the appropriate degree of GASing. Ed offered this appraisal in support of a candidate whom he felt would be an excellent principal: "He has dealt with some difficult situations very well as a committee chairman in the Teachers Association. He has a real ability to make his leadership felt." The other members of the committee joined in unanimous agreement regarding the candidate in question, capped by an endorsement from the Director of Elementary Education, "I used to think of him as a guy who just 'went along,' but I see him differently now." From the candidate's point of view, her comments could be interpreted as the successful culmination to all his efforts as a GASer, not only to getting the attention of superiors, but to getting that attention to the proper extent and for the right reasons.

Formal Academic Preparation

Complaints about formal graduate studies in "ed-admin" are legion among practicing school administrators. Their complaints provide them with a common bond regardless of differences in the region of the country in which they work, where they pursued their administrative courses, or the types of schools or districts to which they are presently assigned. Often they categorically dismiss all their "professional" training (for teaching as well as for school administration), creating an epithet out of the whole comprehensive field in which they have pursued their studies, "Education courses, aggh!" Less frequently, someone who has experienced both the study and practice of school administration makes his grievances explicit, a sport which appears to be open to all public school personnel and is not unknown among their professors (see the criticism of the preparation programs issued by the 1960 yearbook Commission of the American Association of School Administrators,[4] or suggested in a title like Andrew W. Halpin's "Administrative Theory: The Fumbled Torch" [Halpin 1970]).

During a taped interview made at Taft School, Mr. Adam, the one teacher on Ed's faculty who had experienced both the theory and practice of school administration, volunteered this opinion on administration courses:

> I don't think of administration as being a separate function. For instance, when I think of the presidency of the United States, I can't think of the courses that either Lyndon Johnson or Jack Kennedy or Eisenhower ought to have taken in order to assume those jobs. I can't think of any real courses that I've had in administration, although I've had the three basic elementary administration courses, the three basic secondary administration courses, three basic school district administrative courses, and then the junior college administrative courses. To me it was a dickens of a lot of repetition. Many of the people who taught me were teaching according to what they had learned 20 years before. Good people are apt to do good jobs, they're apt to assume the responsibilities, and they are apt to be flexible enough to find out what they need to know in a hurry.

Ed's own experience as a graduate student in educational administration had been neither bitter nor rewarding. It was simply a fact of life that he had to take sufficient courses to earn an administrative credential if he hoped and planned

---

[4] "The programs appear to be bookish to the ultimate. . . . The mediocrity of programs of preparation comes from the sterility of the methods reported. Instruction is classroom bound; administration is talked about rather than observed, felt, and in these and other ways actually experienced" (AASA 1960:83).

eventually to become a full-time principal. (State law required that the administrator of any school of eight or more teachers hold a valid administrative credential.) Ed had left Kansas as soon as he completed the formal course work for a bachelor's degree, and he realized that he needed to begin the accumulation of units toward a master's degree and administrative credential at once, particularly since his opportunities to take courses were limited to evenings and summer sessions.

Ed's perception of himself was that he was "not much of a student." "I'd rather be doing things and be up and about. And I'm a very slow reader." He found his graduate courses generally disappointing and his major professor in his graduate program "less than no help as an adviser and never prepared as a teacher." Like most of his colleagues, Ed's program at the university terminated immediately upon satisfying the necessary course-work requirements for the degree and credential. The requirements for the master's degree in school administration and the elementary school administrative credential were virtually synonymous, and no thesis was required. Although the degree and credential represented the ultimate pay-off in his graduate studies, the accumulation of course hours beyond his bachelor's degree also had an immediate, practical value, since the school district followed the usual pattern of placing its professional employees at higher increments in the salary schedule with the accumulation of additional hours of study.

Even when he attained the master's degree, Ed's formal education was not completed. A "professional growth" policy of long standing in the district, and widely followed across the nation, not only encouraged continuing course work for professional employees through salary increments but actually required such study ("or equivalent travel or work") as a prerequisite for professional advancement. The requirement could be met in part by participating in in-service workshops and programs offered by the school district and by receiving credit for taking extra assignments (for example, serving on a curriculum project). Not more than eight years could elapse without actually enrolling in coursework offering university credit. Ed did not relish having to take more courses, but he had let the requirement slip by so long that he received a terse reminder from the central office that he had to acquire more "hours." He reacted, "It's true I haven't gotten campus credit for quite awhile, but I've been involved in workshops 'up to here'!" Administering the summer school at Taft precluded an opportunity for him to meet the requirement by attending a university summer session, and neither his inclination nor his daily schedule led him to consider enrolling in a late afternoon or evening university class except as a last resort. Ed was spared from this dilemma when the university literally came to the doorstep of Taft School with a course especially designed for intern teachers but open to any teachers who wished to enroll.

The proximity of the university, the constant exposure to at least a selected segment of its faculty in education, and the continual press for pursuing additional in-service and graduate studies left Ed with an unsettling career question faced by many elementary school principals in similar circumstances: should he go on for a doctorate? The question seemed to be in the back of the minds of several of Ed's colleagues, particularly the younger ones. A few persons in the administrative hierarchy held a degree at the doctoral level, including the four key central office administrators—Superintendent, Assistant Superintendent, and Directors of Elementary and Secondary Education—as well as others like the Director of Counselling and Guidance, and the Director of Buildings and Grounds. So also did some academic department heads in the high schools. None of the principals held a doctorate, although a few had completed the course requirements for the degree or had accumulated a number of graduate course-hours. Ed's ambivalence about the doctorate had seemingly been settled against pursuing such a course himself. "I've thought about it, but I just don't see what good it would do me," he explained. In support of that position, he liked to cite the example of the teacher he had helped sponsor into administration: "Did you know that he completed all of his doctoral program except the dissertation? Yet he has told me he never wants to go back where he can't work with kids. I think he's satisfied where he is, now that he is in administration and getting a better salary than he was as a teacher."

The tangible evidence of Ed's graduate program in school administration was contained in textbooks numbering 7 among a total of 33 books, pamphlets, and journal copies on a shelf in his office that constituted his professional library. Among the 7 titles were several widely read authors in curriculum, supervision, and school administration in the late fifties: Baldwin (1955); Burton and Brueckner (1955); Elsbree and McNally (1951); Hanna, Potter, and Hagamann (1955); Kyte (1952); Smith, Stanley, and Shores (1957); and Spears (1951).[5] Shelved next to these "classics" was a rather uneven assortment of professional pamphlets and single copies of professional journals (for example, *Elementary School Journal, Childhood Education,* three yearbooks of the Association for Supervision and Curriculum Development), a copy of *Webster's New Secondary School Dictionary,* one children's library book (*Island of the Blue Dolphins*), and a paperback copy of what was probably the most widely read book among teachers in the sixties, Jerome Bruner's *The Process of Education* (1961).[6] Since half of the 16 dated pamphlets were from the year 1964, the collection looked suspiciously as though it had last been reviewed during that year or earlier; only one book, the ASCD yearbook for 1965, contained a copyright date more recent than 1964 when I inventoried the library shelf in March 1967. I know of no occasion when Ed so much as glanced toward any of the materials on the shelf (nor candidly am I able to think of any occasion when his library shelf would have contained reference material to which he would have needed to refer).

Ed was not alone in feeling that his formal course work in administration was rather unrelated to his actual work as a school principal. In the national study of elementary school principals (DESP 1968:28), principals were asked, "What type of experience or preparation has contributed most to your success as a principal?"

---

[5] Alfred Baldwin, 1955, *Behavior and Development in Childhood,* New York, Dryden Press; William H. Burton and Leo J. Brueckner, 1955, *Supervision, A Social Process,* New York, Appleton-Century-Crofts; Willard S. Ellsbree and Harold J. McNally, 1951, *Elementary School Administration and Supervision,* New York, American Book Company; LaVonne A. Hanna, Gladys L. Potter, and Neva Hagamann, 1955, *Unit Teaching in the Elementary School,* New York, Rinehart Publishing Company; George C. Kyte, 1952, *The Principal at Work,* Boston, Ginn and Company; B. Othanel Smith, William O. Stanley, and J. Harland Shores, 1957, *Fundamentals of Curriculum Development,* New York, World Book Company; Harold Spears, 1951, *Principles of Teaching,* New York, Prentice-Hall.

[6] Jerome Bruner, 1961, *The Process of Education,* Cambridge, Harvard University Press.

Less than two percent of the total sample of principals gave credit to their college preparation as the major source contributing to their success (see Table 8–1). Perhaps understandably, the major type of experience identified in this regard was on-the-job experience as a principal (41.5 percent of the total sample), particularly among the more experienced principals in the sample. It is less easy to understand why an equally large proportion of the sample (40.9 percent—composed largely of principals with less than five years experience), indicated that their *experience as classroom teachers* contributed most to their success. Classroom teaching may indeed be necessary in order to validate one's claim to, and authority in, the principalship, but it is questionable how classroom teaching contributed to "success" in administration. However, except for 10 percent of the principals who reported that they had first served as assistant principals, vice principals, or interns, respondents were faced with a forced choice between two alternative answers regarding the source of their success—either that their college program contributed most or that their classroom teaching contributed most. Their responses may have been based more on their disregard for the first alternative than on their endorsement of the second one.

Principals not only eschew their formal training, they also look for evidence in support of their intuitive disregard for its utility. A research "finding" popular among the principals in the district and cited by them in discussions of the university's contribution to their adminstrative problems was that "the worst principals are the ones who have had the most courses." The source of this gleefully touted finding is elusive, but, as one study notes, even more modest findings "should give all professors of school administration cause for concern" (Hemphill *et al.* 1962: 340–341):

> The finding of essentially no relationship between amount of academic preparation and performance on the various tasks in school administration that were investigated is consistent throughout. There is no evidence that the

TABLE 8–1 PREPARATION OR EXPERIENCE CONTRIBUTING MOST TO SUCCESS AS A PRINCIPAL[a]

Type of Experience	Total Sample (in percentages)	Supervising Principals (in percentages)
As classroom teacher	40.9	38.8
College education	1.9	1.6
On-the-job as a principal	41.5	41.9
As an intern	1.8	2.0
As an assistant principal	7.1	8.3
In-service programs of school systems	1.5	1.6
By self-study and research	3.7	4.0
Other	1.6	1.8
TOTAL	100.0	100.0
NUMBER	2,304	1,882

[a] Source: *The Elementary School Principalship in 1968* (DESP 1968:29). Copyright 1968, National Association of Elementary School Principals, NEA. All rights reserved. Used by permission.

principal with a lengthier preparation does a more effective job of school administration, from any point of view from which one may examine the data.[7]

Higher Education and the Principalship: Some Paradoxes

In spite of a strong element of ritual in the perennial complaining about their programs of graduate studies, the professional lives of principals are intricately linked with colleges and universities both in their own individual careers and in the complex relationships between the nation's schools and its institutions of higher learning. Colleges and universities perform functions which are at once critical and paradoxical for school administrators. Three of these functions, and the problems associated with them, are discussed under the headings Screening, Sponsoring, and Source of Knowledge.

The essential paradox of the principal-university relationship has already been presented implicitly in the discussion of the preceding pages: although the central objective of their professional lives is to promote the educational attainment of the pupils who attend their schools, principals hold their own formal education, and particularly their most recent experiences with it at its "highest" levels, in low esteem. Their endorsement of the efficacy of education is for education's potential contribution to others. Like Ed, they have generally found their graduate studies in ed-admin disappointing and irrelevant. For the most part they have pursued their studies as a necessary evil leading to pragmatic objectives like improving their salaries or satisfying credentialling requirements rather than in a quest for knowledge.

Screening   One function which higher education serves for schools, a major one in terms of the magnitude of the educational establishment, is to help with the screening of personnel who are either moving *into* or moving upward *within* the permanent cadre of school personnel. These two facets of the screening function affect the principalship in different ways. In the first circumstance, school administrators are consumers who have become highly dependent on having screening services performed for them. At the same time, a would-be principal's career requires a typically prolonged period in which he himself is again subjected to scrutiny within the halls of academe. In the latter regard, principals are more inclined to perceive the screening function performed by college faculties as a hurdle or obstacle rather than as a contribution to their careers. As Ed noted,

> The people at the university are just like medical doctors. Once they get in, they want to make it as tough as they can on the next guy. They aren't all like that, but a lot are.

[7] Lest I am unwittingly perpetuating this "finding," let me add that the authors of the study did *not* accept the explanation that nothing taught in programs of preparation is relevant to being a school principal. In fact, they reportedly did find professional knowledge reflected in the performance of principals. They suggested that their finding of zero correlations between amount of formal education and performance on certain administrative tasks was related to the variable "years of preparation." That variable was obtained by adding *all* the years of post-high school education, rather than allowing for more discrete analyses of special components like graduate preparation in professional education (Hemphill *et al.* 1962:341).

When it came to making assessments of others, particularly in filling staff vacancies, Ed and his colleagues did not appear hesitant about relying on academic achievement as a criterion measure, even though they were critical of teacher-training and graduate education programs. It is hardly surprising that they did depend to a great extent on formal academic performance as recorded in official transcripts and letters of recommendation. Usually they had little other evidence on which to make judgments, particularly if they were not able to observe a candidate teaching or to conduct a personal interview. Furthermore, public school systems place a high regard on academic achievement in awarding status and determining salaries. Certificated personnel (i.e., persons who have met formal educational requirements for teaching, counselling, school administration, and so forth) are clearly distinguished from noncertificated ones; Ed sometimes used "qualified" as a synonym for "certificated" in referring to his professional staff. Central office personnel who held a doctorate degree were formally addressed as "doctor" by those lower in the hierarchy (for example, principals) and frequently referred to each other in the same manner. As noted earlier, professional salaries in school districts also recognize minute increments in hours of graduate study beyond the bachelors' and masters' degrees in awarding salary increases.

Ed demonstrated a deference toward people whose formal academic achievements surpassed his own. He showed a preference for teacher candidates whose academic records were substantial in quantity or outstanding in quality. At least one teacher felt that Ed exhibited a blind faith in relying on college transcripts as a criterion for the selection of new staff and that he had failed to recognize how he had been fooled by academic accomplishment several times before. She volunteered these comments during a taped interview.

> Ed has a tendency to look at some wonderful record of courses the person has taken and be a little overwhelmed by it. Just the other day he was wondering about my student teacher, and he asked my feeling about hiring him for a position next year that has recently opened up in the staff. I said I thought he would be fine and told him why. And he said, "Well, I have two or three possibilities that I have in mind that I would request before I would consider him," and he went on to tell me the glowing record that their files had.
>
> The next day I said to him, "You know, we've been fooled three times in this building by glowing records and lots and lots of university work and extra credits and this type of thing." In one case it was in guidance and counselling, and in the other it was with a husband and with a new program that was being carried out at the university. Ed thought this would be a wonderful opportunity to get some feedback about the counselling program before we had full time counselling here. Well, it just didn't work that way at all. I have the feeling that maybe some of these younger teachers that we see fit into the philosophy of our building of what we're trying to do here work out better in the long run. We shouldn't be too overwhelmed by these wonderful records.

The paradox of screening lies in the dilemma of disavowing the utility and significance of one's own formal preparation but relying on, and having to rely on, the success that others have had with essentially the same system as a measure of their ability. Ed went beyond merely recognizing educational achievement; some of his staff felt he was awed by it.

Sponsoring   A corollary of the screening function occurs because school districts relinquish, as they must, part of the responsibility for identifying, training, and validating candidates moving upward within their own hierarchies. The function of relegating to colleges and universities a considerable portion of the burden of screening and evaluating teaching personnel and those hoping to debut as administrators is performed at the cost of making candidates visible outside the district. Faculty members of schools of education serve as sponsors and recruiters for positions outside the closed ranks of individual school districts. Occasionally they recruit personnel into their own ranks from the public schools.

Those principals in the study who had friends (or felt that they had friends) among faculty members at nearby universities frequently mentioned the personal help or attachment they felt to certain professors in spite of any lack of affection they may have felt for the institutions. They availed themselves of opportunities that arose at professional meetings or during visits on campus to make or renew acquaintances with college faculty. The frequency with which certain professors were invited or suggested as speakers, guests, or consultants among local principals acting in their various organizational roles suggested that some professors may have been perceived as "collective" sponsors or as contact men for the group at large.[8]

This aspect of the principal-university-school district triad necessitated light treading among principals. University contacts provided a valuable resource for any principal or would-be principal anticipating a move to another district or planning to pursue further studies, so at least the younger principals tended not to be outspoken critics of programs or professors.[9] On the other hand, principals did not expect their colleagues to become too closely identified with university personnel in educational administration, since that behavior could signal an intention of moving up or out. This relationship was further complicated by the fact that principals often lacked adequate information for making accurate assessments of the status and power which university faculty members wielded in their own institutions. Opportunities for contacts with senior faculty in the course of a school day were exceedingly rare. Those university personnel whose work regularly took them into schools appeared generally to be of low status—or, in the case of doctoral students recruited for supervising student teachers, no status at all—on their own campus, such as new young faculty or old-timers who had not achieved recognition and full-time campus responsibilities for their academic or administrative prowess. Thus the principals individually and collectively tended to defer to faculty

---

[8] From the point of view of university faculty, to be perceived as a faculty "patron-saint" may have been ego gratifying but it was also threateningly time-consuming. One professor of education confided after an evening presentation to the principal's association:

> I just didn't have the time to prepare for my talk this evening. I took out the material only this afternoon. But you could be out doing this kind of thing all the time and at the university they wouldn't give you any credit for it.

[9] For example, one principal enrolled in a doctoral program had a student teacher at his school whom he felt would benefit by an additional term of student teaching experience. The young lady's university advisor felt otherwise, and his opinion was never challenged. "That same professor happens to be *my* advisor on the doctoral program," the principal explained, "so I don't want to go against him."

who were not necessarily in a position to help them, and in so doing inadvertently contributed to maintaining the *status quo* in their very efforts to change it.

Source of knowledge. School districts generate much of the authority necessary for their own operation, but they do not generate the knowledge that they impart. Knowledge is provided by sources outside schools. Business and industry serve as sources of knowledge for some aspects of technology, but universities are the traditional sources for at least two major categories of knowledge consumed by schools: society's formally accumulated wisdom, which provides the content for *what* is taught, and the accumulated wisdom for *how* it is taught, the institutionalization of education through the operation of schools. Included in the latter domain is the accumulated wisdom, or what some educators refer to as the "knowledge base," of the administration of education. There is a large body of literature on the administration of education. But it does not speak with the level of specificity sought nor necessarily deal with the kinds of problems confronted by the school man faced with a need for immediate decisions. He lives in a time and a society where knowledge is held in high esteem and where scientific research is the process by which the store of knowledge is increased. Yet the daily operation of the school appears little dependent upon any tangible "knowledge base," and for the ultimate questions which American educators have posed (from classic and rhetorical ones like "What knowledge is of most worth?" or "Dare the schools build a new social order?" to Ed's concern for a question like "How does the teacher really know there is any learning going on?") the answers that administrators seek are not to be found.

To reduce the discrepancy between what they felt they did know and what they felt others expected them to know, the principals tended to draw upon the accepted *source* of knowledge rather than on knowledge itself. That source is "research." Pressed by a subordinate for the rationale behind an opinion or decision, Ed often resorted to an answer frequently employed by other principals as well: "I think you will find that studies have shown . . . ," or, in a dialogue quoted earlier, "Research proves you're wrong," without ever making the referent more specific. Among their peers, research findings cited by one principal were sometimes controverted with a claimed knowledge of contrary findings cited by another: "I've seen studies that showed exactly the opposite." The impact of the power of "research" diminished as one used it with those higher in the hierarchy, for unless a claimed reference to research supported a higher-up's point of view, he could always mollify the claim by a remark ambiguous in its sincerity but clear in intent, "I'd like to see those findings . . . someday."

Comments made by principals revealed the ambivalent feelings they held toward the accumulated wisdom of their profession and toward those closer to the sources of knowledge than they felt themselves to be. Ed expressed his opinion about the university as a fountainhead of ideas:

> I wish someone related to teacher education on campus would sit down with me and say, "Let's brainstorm how we can work together to get the best involvement of classroom teachers in the business of training teachers." We should put more time, effort, and even money into getting classroom teachers closer to the university program. Maybe once the university was the fountain-

head of ideas and training for the public schools, but not any more. I'd like to tell that to the dean or the head of the teacher education program. We compromise too much with the university. We just let them take over. We *say* the classroom teacher is so central. We should *do* something about it.

The aspects of "research" with which principals were in most frequent touch—talking with doctoral candidates about their research programs, or overseeing brief research forays made by university researchers into their schools and classrooms—did little to dispel ambivalence about the ultimate value of the work or entice them to become serious consumers of research findings. Ed inquired routinely about on-going "research" projects, as in the following brief dialogue with a doctoral student who was also supervising student teachers at Taft, but the research he heard about did not pertain to the problems he faced:

ED: What are you going to do your thesis on?
DOCTORAL STUDENT: I'm going to study "student satisfaction"—the problems of students who transfer from one high school to another.
ED: Sounds real interesting.
DOCTORAL STUDENT: Well, it's a topic, anyway.

Comments recorded during the study, such as the divergent attitudes revealed in the following two remarks, express something of the disparity between the research efforts which principals actually observed firsthand and the status assigned to those most closely identified with the research mystique:

A lot of this research is just some guy coming out on a doctoral program and asking kids about apples and writing it up.

Bob Gardner ought to be qualified. He has a Ph.D. in elementary education.

Most references to research were verbal and informal. Therefore they did not require the precision that might have been required for written statements. During the preparation of the series of position papers (see the discussion of them in Chapter 5) in the course of the summer administrative workshop, the principals exercised caution and restraint in their written references to or inferences about research by beginning their statements with terms like "We believe . . ." or, "Experience has shown. . . ."

The position paper which Ed and his group prepared contained a statement which began, "We believe that research indicates that. . . ." When that paper was subjected to collective review, one principal read that sentence aloud and commented, "That looks like a tremendous weasel statement to me." The chairman of Ed's group could not restrain a smile as he explained, "We thought if we stated it any stronger, we'd have to cite the studies."

Thus in their process of becoming, principals learn to eschew the formal system of education even as they come to realize that in their chosen careers they can never escape its influence. At the same time, it is their steadfast belief in the importance of formal education for others that gives them their highest professional purpose.

REMAINING A PRINCIPAL

In recent decades the role of the elementary school principal has tended to become more of a career position in its own right and less of a "stepping stone" to secondary school administration. In the national survey, over half of the supervising elementary school principals (57 percent of 1873 persons responding) reported that in the principalship they had achieved their career goal (DESP 1968: 16). Among the minority of principals who reported that the principalship was not their final goal, far more indicated career objectives immediately related to elementary school education, such as supervisors and directors of elementary education (43 percent), than indicated aspirations to administrative roles like the school superintendency (25 percent) or the secondary school principalship (6 percent); the remainder expressed goals ranging from getting out of the field of education altogether (4 percent) or becoming college teachers (16 percent) to returning to full-time teaching (3 percent) (DESP 1968:17).[10]

The meaning of the term "career" as used by school principals differs from the meaning assigned the term in some sociological contexts (see Gouldner's [1959] cosmopolitans and locals) and even in the way the term has been applied to the school superintendency (see the "place-bound" and "career-bound" typologies suggested by Carlson 1962, 1972). In the latter case, "career" orientation is presented as the alternative to being place-bound. That is, career commitment for a school superintendent implies a willingness to change districts in order to keep moving "up." In the principalship, at least among Ed's colleagues, career commitment was generally taken to mean a commitment to the position of elementary school principal and to one's school district as well. Ed's assessment of the situation nationally was that there were more career principals than persons using the principalship as a step up; among his fellow principals he knew of only one person who might possibly have his sights set elsewhere. The principals in the Columbia School District shared a perception of their administrative group as relatively stable, one which lacked the internal strife that could result if some principals were trying to push their way ahead of others either directly via obtaining a position in the central office or indirectly via studying for a doctorate. As one principal expressed it, "The principals in this district are free-wheelers. They've 'arrived.'"

Whether or not they were conscious of their efforts to maintain group equilibrium, the members of a committee of principals assigned to serve as a preliminary selection committee screening potential candidates for principalships were successful in eliminating applicants whom they suspected might "use" the district rather than commit themselves to it (see Wolcott 1974). Their stated objective in this regard was a consideration for the long-range interests of the district, rather than in the preservation of the *status quo* in their own group. As one principal explained:

[10] Dissatisfaction with the position of *teaching principal* as contrasted with *supervising principal* is suggested by comparing the ratio of respondents in each group who reported that their ultimate goal was to get back into classroom teaching in the elementary school: 26 percent of the teaching principals versus 3 percent of the supervising principals.

I would have ranked one candidate higher, but I think of the elementary principalship as a career. He's a stronger candidate than some of the others, but I just don't think he's going to stay—he'll stay about four or five years and use us as a stepping stone.

The real world is replete with examples in which there is a marked difference between the behavior necessary to achieve a new status (such as president, spouse, parent, professor) and the behavior appropriate to maintaining that status once it is achieved (see Benedict 1938). The principalship appears to be no exception. GASing behavior, getting the attention of superiors so that one would be identified as someone special, was precisely the kind of behavior a career-oriented principal wished to avoid once he had achieved his administrative niche. Virtually no advantage accrued to a principal for having his school in the limelight if the principal himself was already established in his career position. If getting the attention of superiors was due to special programs or successes, principals found that the glory of recognition was quickly eroded by the demands of increased visitors, observers, and specialists anxious to introduce other new programs or criticize existing ones.

The alternate way for a principal and school to gain the attention of supervisors was even less desirable—to have attention drawn to the school because someone else's attention, particularly some dissatisfied person or faction in the community, was focused there already. The way to "live and let live" was to run a competent and efficient school program, one that would keep such a wide and disparate group of "customers" (employees, parents, pupils, voters, the school board, university professors, special interest groups) satisfied at best or, at worst, not so dissatisfied that they would organize and stir up trouble. That there would be individual malcontents was generally acknowledged; one parent with children at Taft School had lodged so many complaints over the years, and the complaints had been so well circulated among administrators, that Ed was routinely asked, "How's *that* parent of yours?" Given the inevitable variations among the schools' many customers, principals are less inclined to try to achieve greatness and more inclined to watch instead for signs of any mounting level of discontent. I believe that Ed's effort and anxiety in his work as a principal were to a considerable extent aimed at preventing an event which never occurred during the study: a phone call from the superintendent asking or telling him what was wrong at Taft School. We cannot ignore the significance of such nonevents in the organization of human behavior, events which have sufficiently undesirable consequences that individuals act so as to assure that certain things will *not* happen. Once one had achieved the position of principal, getting the attention of superiors had little potential for contributing toward remaining in that position.

The term "autonomy" was often heard when principals in the district discussed their role or compared the principalship within the district with what they knew or had heard of the position in other school districts. Their feeling was that they enjoyed as much or more freedom to run their schools as other principals throughout the state. The principals who had visited schools in other states felt that their state was above average nationally in the degree of autonomy principals exercised in their schools. Ed once explained to me, "Most of us don't want to give up our autonomy for the sake of conformity. I'm high on that list."

Candidates appearing before the principal selection committee provided further views on autonomy. The following exchange occurred with a candidate who was a principal in an outlying district:

CANDIDATE: I guess I'm just the kind of an administrator who likes autonomy.
INTERVIEWING PRINCIPAL: Why do you say you like autonomy?
CANDIDATE: I like to be an individual—just like you do.
ANOTHER INTERVIEWING PRINCIPAL (ED BELL):   Do you like your teachers to be individuals, too?
CANDIDATE: Yes! As a matter of fact, I encourage it.

Another candidate had been a vice principal in the Midwest before accepting a position as a teacher in the district:

INTERVIEWING PRINCIPAL: How did your previous school district compare with this one?
CANDIDATE: The principals here have a little more autonomy in the selection of staff.
INTERVIEWER: Is this autonomy a good thing?
CANDIDATE: I think this situation is good.
ANOTHER INTERVIEWING PRINCIPAL: Why do you?
CANDIDATE: So a staff can develop its abilities to the maximum. For example, maybe one staff can do more with flexibility than another.

It is difficult to discern from these comments the extent to which autonomy meant anything beyond the absence of a feeling that the central office was breathing down each principal's neck or that the overt indications of a rigid and oppressive hierarchy were absent (see Waller's classic description of the school: "despotism in a state of perilous equilibrium" 1932:10). In any case, the way which principals achieve "autonomy" appears to be universally recognized and practiced: keep to a minimum the dissatisfaction that might threaten it. A researcher conducting a study made of the principal's role in a metropolitan school system several years ago concluded, "When fewer complaints are relayed to the principal's superiors by parents, interested citizens in the school's subdistrict, and teachers, the principal finds that his autonomy increases with his individual school" (McDowell 1954:370). There are several strategies which principals employ for keeping complaints to a minimum. The one attributed most often to schoolmen is to do nothing that is controversial. Ed often explained any hesitancy about making change because he was "afraid to rock the boat too much." That was not his only strategy, however. He had discovered another strategy which usually had been successful: "Now we just go ahead with the program without making a big issue. We used to announce it, but then everybody started shooting at it." The case in point was related to introducing some aspects of sex education into the curriculum at Taft, but the procedure had more general application.

In the strictest sense, every aspect of the principal's role, every encounter an individual makes while occupying it, every nuance he acquires in his almost lifetime socialization into role occupancy in the school organization contributes something to the sum total of what a principal must be or become in order to remain a principal (see Blood 1966). In the remainder of this section, attention is drawn to two especially influential categories of socializers affecting the role of the principal, central office personnel representing the formal authority of the hierarchy, and peer group influence exhibited by fellow principals.

It is important to realize, however, that in a role as public, ubiquitous, and visible as that of the school principal, virtually anyone may exert some influence toward the continuing process of his socialization, whether it is the dropout who lashes out at the injustice of a former principal, a voter who declares himself opposed to a school tax election because he feels the district's administrators are overpaid, a **reporter whose newspaper account makes a principal's comments seem inane, or the anxieties which principals themselves generate in acute self-consciousness about their role (see Chapter 11). No matter who "starts shooting" first, principals feel that they are the ones who inevitably get caught in the crossfire.**

Central Office Personnel as Socializers

Persons at the top of the school district's administrative hierarchy did not merely sit idly in their offices waiting for emergencies. They took many opportunities to remind principals of their obligation to keep them informed of real and potential sources of trouble. The first reminder from the central office about the preparation of teacher evaluations which would be due later in the year provided a very explicit example in this regard: "Please keep us informed all along instead of waiting till it is too late to salvage someone."

Whether Ed was better or worse than most principals in the district about keeping the central office informed I do not know, but it was my impression that he was fairly candid once he made up his mind to let "downtown" know about a budding problem. His preferred professional confidant in the central office was his immediate superior, Dr. Goddard, the Director of Elementary Education. He referred to her telephone number as the "hot line." Although her telephone may have been the hot line to him, his alternatives to it were even hotter: the telephones of the assistant superintendent and the superintendent. In some cases the Director of Personnel had authority to hear a problem and make a decision on it, but Ed's preference was to restrict his discussion of problems to the two administrators who were immediately "over" him (Director of Elementary Education; Assistant Superintendent), and they were the people he called for problems of any consequence. I have no record of his calling the superintendent or of the superintendent calling him, although calls were sometimes exchanged between Taft School and the superintendent's office (i.e., his secretary) concerning the preparation of reports requested specifically by the superintendent.

Ed's personal feelings about each of these four administrators also influenced his choice of who to call, particularly in this preference for working with Carolyn Goddard. The following excerpts from comments made throughout the course of the fieldwork leave little doubt about Ed's personal feelings:

Of Dr. Carolyn Goddard:

Isn't that Carolyn something! Even when I might want to react angrily to something, she reacts pleasantly and finds something positive that can be said.

And she is always stimulating, and always encouraging of new ideas—even if they aren't any good.

Of Dr. Floyd Prince, the Assistant Superintendent:

He and I have never gotten a long too well. . . . I think he wanted this place (Taft School) to be a showplace. He wanted to put a more sophisticated guy out here. But, then, he could have.
Floyd doesn't think the elementary school principalship is very important.

Of Dr. Samuel Boggs, the Superintendent:

I've never known how he felt toward me. Maybe he wasn't sure of what I was doing. And maybe I'm just wondering for nothing. I guess I don't know exactly how he feels. . . . He's the only official I worry about, and I'm not sure just how worried I am about him.
I guess it sounds like I'm anti-central office. Well, maybe I am. I do respect Sam, although I don't particularly like him. He is interested in new ideas. He knows what is going on across the nation. That's where he's so different from Floyd. Floyd is so conservative. . . . We've been riding the crest ever since Sam came here.
I think Boggs is a pretty smart guy. Oh, there's a bit of farmer in him, but he's pretty alert. I just get sort of tired listening to all his talk at times.

Of the Director of Personnel:

He's next to nothing. If he wasn't Sam's man [the Superintendent had brought the personnel director with him from another district] he'd have been bagged long ago. . . . He doesn't know what's going on in the schools.

Information filtered to the central office (and back) via myriad formal and informal channels. The superintendent explained, "Information just comes to us, in all sorts of ways." Those scholars who look to the "communication problem" in schools and school districts perpetuate a myth in the belief that the remedy to school malfunction is so simple as merely to get school people talking to each other. There are indeed problems in assuring that the messages intended are the ones received, but no one can ignore that information is constantly being exchanged in schools and that for most purposes the channels of communication are exceedingly effective, even when the content of the messages is not especially welcome (see Smith 1968).

Ostensibly to foster the "upward" as well as to facilitate the "downward" flow of information, administrators in the central office had established several regularly recurring meetings in which key personnel met with groups of administrators. Such groups were usually divided on the basis of geographical boundaries or school levels. Monthly "area" meetings held by the superintendent at each high school were attended by the high school principal and principals of the junior high and elementary "feeder" schools. The stated purpose of these meetings was to "keep lines of communication open," but the superintendent had a reputation for dominating any conversation, and the principals looked upon the meetings as a two-hour monologue with compulsory attendance: "It's the same every time. That guy never says a damn thing." The monthly meetings of all elementary principals held by the Director of Elementary Education seemed to allow for a fairly easy flow of information both "up" and "down" of those items of interest to the elementary principals collectively. These formal meetings also provided informal opportunities for exchanging information with members of the central office staff.

One special event of the year in terms of principal-central office interaction was a formal "principal's evaluation" conference held between members of the central office staff and each school administrator midway through the school year. A form letter sent to all elementary principals by Dr. Goddard stated that the evaluation conferences were being held "in accordance with the school board request." Ed did not express undue concern when he received the notice. He recalled a similar evaluation procedure three years earlier:

> It was favorable. I expect this one to go even better. They did say something about losing my temper, which is still a problem. Also, Floyd said I was too dependent on one member of my staff. I didn't agree but I didn't argue.

Ed's conference was scheduled for 8:30 A.M. in Dr. Goddard's office on a Tuesday in February. Ed accepted the appointment hour given to him, although the time chosen happened to be when he would otherwise have attended the guidance committee meeting at his own school, the meeting which he described as the most important one he directed.

Ed's evaluation conference provides an excellent source of information regarding his continuing socialization as an administrator by central office personnel. An account of the meeting is provided here in some detail, although it is not presented verbatim. Those present at the meeting were Ed, Dr. Goddard, Dr. Prince (the assistant superintendent) and myself.

ED'S EVALUATION CONFERENCE
AT THE CENTRAL OFFICE

Ed and I arrived at the central office about ten minutes before the time scheduled for his appointment. Ed suggested we walk through the halls while we waited. As we walked, the idea occurred to him of stopping at the personnel office to ask which substitute had been sent out in place of a Taft teacher who had "phoned in sick." Ed was still early for his appointment when he arrived at the office of the Director of Elementary Education, but she bade us come in and be seated while we waited for the assistant superintendent to arrive. Until he arrived, she continued working at her desk. Ed and I visited. As soon as Dr. Prince arrived, he, Dr. Goddard, and Ed arranged themselves around a small table; I sat some distance away to facilitate note-taking and to minimize the distraction of an outsider. After the meeting Ed said that he had not felt restricted by my presence, and he doubted that it had restricted the others.

DR. GODDARD: (turning to Ed and indicating the beginning of the conference) We'll let you start and we'll just chime in. What is the emphasis in your school?

ED: The emphasis at Taft School is toward the individual child. Our philosophy is in the direction of the nongraded school, although we aren't in a position to offer this. I think this year is an all-time high. The children are feeling a greater responsibility for their own education, that it's up to them. We're there to help.

DR. GODDARD: How do you work with your Instructional Materials Center [IMC]? Is it always manned?

ED: Yes, our teacher aide is always there. And Bob Mason, our resource teacher, is there sometimes. I'm still not satisfied with the amount of materials.

DR. GODDARD: Is there any place where youngsters can work in the library?

ED: Not much. We do have a conference room in the new wing. Ideally, we need to make Room 7 into an IMC. I'm not satisfied with it as it is. It's too far from the resource teacher.[11]

DR. GODDARD: Bob [Mason] isn't really too interested in instructional materials, is he?

ED: Oh, yes. He has a good working relationship.

DR. GODDARD: Does the intern program fragment the staff?

ED: Somewhat. Our in-service training program plus having intern teachers have kept us pretty close to how much teachers can do.

DR. GODDARD: If you were going to plan this year over again, would you still have the in-service program?

DR. PRINCE: Who actually made the decision about having the in-service program?

ED: Well, the whole staff. I made the final decision.

DR. PRINCE: How committed does the staff feel?

ED: They are committed to it. At least, all but a couple. Wally Adam hasn't come; neither has our new teacher we added during the year.

DR. PRINCE: How is Wally doing?

ED: He'll finish his dissertation this summer.

DR. GODDARD: Does he still resist authority?

ED: Yes. The people around him are not always comfortable and neither am I. But he is a very stimulating person to have on a faculty. He has a very effective way of working with parents, and he has many supporters. Last month he had the father of one of his sixth-graders come in to help with math. I hadn't seen that particular father around before, and I haven't seen him since.

DR. GODDARD: Wally is just one of these off-hand people. He doesn't fit in and he doesn't want to.

DR. PRINCE: As far as his working with children, do you have any problem with him?

ED: No. If anything, he overdoes it.

DR. PRINCE: Is his class bedlam?

ED: No, it depends on what they are doing. When he's ready to go, they are with him. But he doesn't expect children to sit around like puppets.

DR. PRINCE: And they don't! Well, it proves that there is more than one way to teach.

ED: I guess you could say he's not much on the "housekeeping" chores.

DR. GODDARD: I've never observed a particular problem there. Maybe it has only been when I wasn't there. How is Sally Jensen doing with her first grade? Is she holding up all right?

ED: Yes. I finally had to step in and say "no" to her. The social studies consultant wanted her to work one afternoon a week helping to develop more curriculum materials.

DR. PRINCE: While we're talking about staff, do you have any other staff problems?

---

[11] I failed to recognize the significance of this comment at the time. Ed was beginning to lobby for a major improvement he wanted at Taft School. Two years later Room 7 had been converted into an IMC.

ED: Yes, I do.

DR. PRINCE: Well, let's discuss them.

ED: Alma [Skirmish]. I've already talked to Carolyn about her. You might say she's a little selfish. She puts other things ahead of school.

DR. PRINCE: (apparently aware of the problem) She knows our calendar. She better take some other kind of work if she wants to attend conferences with her husband.

ED: She also had a little trouble with Santa.

DR. GODDARD: (to Dr. Prince) She told them there wasn't any Santa.

DR. PRINCE: Oh, no, she couldn't have.

ED: Well, they asked her a direct question. She is a *good* classroom teacher. She just makes some errors in judgment.

DR. PRINCE: Who else is a problem on the staff?

ED: Margaret Elder. She has wonderful rapport with kids, but the children in her class just aren't making the progress the other children are.

DR. PRINCE: How experienced is she?

ED: She's an older person, with lots of experience. She's the kind of person I just can't get to know. She's very pleasant, but she seems aloof. I just haven't gotten to know much about her.

DR. GODDARD: I'm interested in your comment that she's aloof. She seems quite talkative.

ED: She's friendly enough, but she doesn't say something like, "I wish I knew how to do such and such."

DR. GODDARD: I wonder if Margaret and your other new sixth-grade teacher could develop some plans for teaching cooperatively. Maybe the two of them could work together. And they could also work with the intern supervisor— if she could do anything in a calm way.

ED: But the intern supervisor doesn't do anything in a calm way. I had a long session with her and Ellwood New last night until quarter of six. It was the same kind of problem she had with one of the interns last year, although I thought it was his fault at the time. I'm really worried about her intensity, overwhelming *fellows*, especially.[12]

DR. PRINCE: (to Dr. Goddard)   Maybe you ought to have a heart to heart talk with her. There are so many things it could be.

ED: I've said to her, "You don't have to prove yourself. You don't have to work so terribly hard at it to prove yourself to me."

DR. GODDARD: I thought that maybe interviewing interns would be a specific kind of job that she could do. Something's not right.

DR. PRINCE: Has she really told you what's bugging her?

ED: No. I thought it was that mother-in-law situation, but after that changed the problem was still there.

DR. PRINCE: I know that she's had some tough problems in her personal life. Maybe you need to sit down and have a long talk with her. Do you think you could have that kind of a talk with her? [Ed nodded in the affirmative.] Some women just shouldn't work with men. I can say that here in front of Carolyn.

   We're running out of time. I'd like to ask about "community." What are you doing to encourage community relations?

ED: We used to have a parent committee, but they depended on me too much

---

[12] En route to the central office that morning, Ed had discussed recent friction developing between the intern supervisor and the male intern teacher, Ellwood New. "She doesn't seem to know enough to lay off when someone has had enough. She has to keep going until *everything* is settled." The next chapter deals with the process of socializing teachers new to the school district or to the Taft faculty, a process in which the central office was particularly interested, as these questions and comments attest.

to provide everything for them. So we don't have that. We have a very active PTA right now. They just had their big pancake breakfast last Saturday—from 6:15 to 11:00 A.M. They made over 120 dollars.

I think the community feels free to come and ask. But they don't as much as I'd like.

DR. PRINCE: What does the Taft community need that your school could provide?

ED: The building is used a great deal. There are about 35 activities a week. The community is a bedroom community. The fathers and mothers both work in many cases. They don't have time to do much with kids.

DR. GODDARD: These parents, more than others, may need to know that kids elsewhere have the same problems as theirs.

ED: I think this community is quite upwardly mobile. These parents are trying to go beyond their backgrounds. Many are living beyond their means, on a prayer and a promise.

DR. GODDARD: Maybe in your community you could use ideas about child rearing. Put them in the Newsletter or something like that. Maybe these are the kinds of things we should be getting for parents.

ED: I'm sure many people look at the Taft School community as one with pretty high expectations.

DR. GODDARD: Like along El Dorado Drive, where the Princes [the assistant superintendent's brother, one of the developers of the El Dorado area] live.

DR. PRINCE: And also the von Brockmeiers. And Dr. Meheren [a former school board member]. What has concerned me there is the condition of vandalism in that whole junior high area. Not just Taft School—I see some of it in the Jefferson area—Norm Olds has some of it. I wonder if parents are aware of what their kids do.

ED: I'm wondering if the kids at East High have somewhat lower goals and whether the vandalism reflects this.

DR. PRINCE: I'm not so sure—maybe West High has more problems, but we don't see it because of the scholars at West. For example, I know of one family whose kid went to West High. That family had tried to keep the reins on their kid from when he first entered school. Then suddenly they got a call from the police to come get their boy at the police station.

ED: I'm interested in the feedback you people get about how the schools are doing. I had a talk with John Robinson, an active PTA father at Taft, on just how he felt about schools. He told me quite frankly.

DR. GODDARD: The little feedback I get is that this is a restless time. I don't think it's done [getting parental feedback] through PTA—but more in informal activities, like coming in to help in a class, or coming to have lunch.

ED: I think I have an advantage there in having such a good counsellor. She moves slowly but surely, but she is making headway.

DR. GODDARD: You give a somewhat austere impression. There is a certain dignity about you, but people need to see your smile. Sometimes when I come into the building you seem so formal, but I know you aren't that way.

ED: I know what's underneath. But you have a point there.

DR. GODDARD: You may find yourself getting irritated on a little point that may not matter in the long run.

ED: I appreciate your saying that.

DR. PRINCE: Maybe they need to know you have empathy with them.

[Dr. Prince departed, explaining that he needed to make a telephone call, and that he would leave Dr. Goddard to review with Ed a rating sheet which they had prepared earlier. Dr. Goddard explained to Ed that he had been rated higher in "staff relations" than in "community relations."]

DR. GODDARD: You run a smooth ship there.

ED: That's not one of my goals.

DR. GODDARD: No, but you are effecting change, and it is comfortable. The general overall evaluation of you would be good. Now this may or may not be true: getting new ideas for meeting educational problems is not your forte, but when it comes to putting ideas of others into practice, you are effective.

ED: What you say is true. I'm not particularly an idea man. This is why I like to have people around like the intern supervisor, or Sally Jensen, or some of those university supervisors and bright graduate students. This is why I want people to feel comfortable in my school.

DR. GODDARD: I think you have organized it so everyone's ideas can get out.

ED: Yes. I know of easier ways to run a school, but I want ideas to get out.

DR. GODDARD: If you personally can relax a little more, then do it.

ED: I think I feel more relaxed in the building than in these other places where you see me.

DR. GODDARD: (smiling reassuringly) I think you've done a good enough job so you can feel comfortable at school and not worry.

Dr. Goddard stood to signal the end of the conference. Ed also stood, and they proceeded to the door together. In the outer office another principal was awaiting an evaluation conference. Ed stopped in the hall for a drink of water before we left the building and walked out to his car.

As we rode back to Taft School, Ed commented on the conference. He said he felt the meeting had gone well and that in general his evaluation had been favorable, just as he predicted it would be. "But I thought I'd come out on the check sheet better than I did." He described his difficulty in determining what the ranking meant, since he was given no comparative information about how the other principals had been rated:

I suppose that people like Angeline or Norman [two of the principals with reputations for being highly organized] come out the highest on the evaluations. In some ways I run circles around them, but these ways don't show. For example, the other morning when we were riding to that meeting with Norman, he was telling me how on that morning one of his teachers had come to him in tears because of the number of memos she had received from him the day before.

Recognizing that some of the misgivings he had about the way he had been evaluated were probably the same misgivings teachers at Taft might be expressing about his evaluations of them, Ed concluded philosophically, "These conferences are a good experience for those of us who have to evaluate teachers."

The secretary, the counsellor, and several teachers were having a morning coffee break when we arrived back at the school. A teacher who had not seen Ed during his brief visit at school earlier that morning joked about his easy job getting to school so late in the day. Several others laughed good-naturedly to share the joke. "Go easy, girls! I've just been evaluated," he countered. In the brief pause that ensued, he added as an afterthought, "But I came out pretty well."

One of the tasks awaiting Ed's return to school that morning was to investigate a complaint turned in by a school bus driver about a fifth-grade boy who had broken a bus rule. Ed's talk with the boy was very straightforward: "Do you want to ride the bus?" "Have you been in trouble with the driver before?" "What happened?" (He had changed seats while the bus was moving; he thought it was about to stop.) "I'll sign this citation and put a note on it that you are not going to cause any future problems." The boy returned to his classroom as matter-of-factly as he had conducted himself during their brief exchange. Apparently musing on his interview earlier that morning, Ed turned to me and said, "I think Carolyn would be surprised to know how unafraid the kids are of me. And how unafraid the teachers feel that the kids are."[13]

Ed did not refer again to his evaluation conference in my presence, and I remained in doubt about whether he really felt he had come out "pretty well" or, in terms of the successful year he perceived this one to be, if he was disappointed in the tone of the evaluation. The fact that each staff member with whom I held a taped interview in the days following Ed's conference brought up the subject of his evaluation suggests that he did continue thinking and talking about it and that, on further reflection, he had felt some misgivings. It was characteristic of Ed not to turn such thoughts inward but to let others know how he felt.

Mrs. Wendy, the school counsellor, gave this account of Ed's conference:

He said he was going to be evaluated last week by some people down at the main office. When he came back, he said of course he wasn't evaluated as high as he would have liked to have been. But I think this is good. I think that we all need to set our goals high and then if we don't achieve them we shouldn't feel that we are inadequate. I don't think he is really that disappointed. I think he was just thinking about himself in terms of how he saw himself.

Mr. New, an intern teacher, explained:

Ed told me that he didn't do too well on the evaluation that Dr. Prince gave him a few weeks ago. Or at least he didn't feel that he was satisfied with the wording of the evaluation. He didn't have to tell me that. But he was just being honest with me. We were talking about *my* evaluation—I think that is how it came up.

Some attempt was evident among the principals to make light of the evaluation conferences both in anticipating them and in subsequently referring to them. For example, a principal who had the earliest conference scheduled one morning later told Ed and others that he "got the first ride on the donkey" that day. However, I was not privy to any discussions or joking references by the principals regarding the *content* of their individual evaluations, nor were the conferences themselves taken lightly. The principals responded to their individual summoning as directed, even ignoring prerogatives which some of them exercised in other settings, such as arriving late for meetings. The Director of Elementary Education reviewed the conferences with satisfaction: "Everyone has kept on time, and we've not run over by more than ten minutes."

---

[13] In my field notes I recorded my personal feeling about Ed's reaction to his evaluation:
  I guess this charge of being *formidable* bothered him. Personally I think it is probably a fair observation. What Ed confuses is his wish to be a good pal under most circumstances and his frequently over-bearing approach with a few kids when things go wrong. Maybe this is linked to C. Goddard's and F. Prince's suggestion this morning that he not let occasional little things bother him.

Living within the Hierarchy

The evaluation conferences served to emphasize the formal hierarchical nature of the school district's organization, but there were other ways, both intended and inadvertent, by which principals were reminded constantly of their station in the professional hierarchy. The policies, directives, regulations, and traditions which a school district develops are designed to clarify lines of authority and responsibility and to introduce consistency into the system. Principals have lived with such procedures all their professional lives. No principal in this study was ever heard making a categorical rejection of policies and directives, and many, perhaps most, of the tasks which they performed in compliance with decisions made by others were accepted as being "all in a day's work." At times ultimatums which were handed down or requests which were made were received stoically or accepted as challenges. But there were other policies, directives, and procedures which rankled, perhaps because they encroached on "autonomy" or served as too-candid reminders of restraints on the power invested in the principalship. Often the specific instances of this sort were minor, and an observer could not assess their cumulative effect.[14] Other practices were singled out as whipping boys, providing the principals collectively with evidence of what was "wrong" with their position. A few such practices are described here.

One policy that threatened the feeling of autonomy required principals to have permission from the central office if they were going to be away from the school district on school business during the day. Permission was to be obtained *in advance* and *in writing* and was to be signed by Dr. Goddard or Dr. Prince as well as the Director of Personnel. With Ed's sometimes helter-skelter organization, the occasions when he complied fully with the policy and had his official away-on-school-business form filed in the personnel office before the absence itself were the exception rather than the rule. At the beginning of the drive to one out-of-district meeting, Ed boasted in jest: "I *already* have permission for today's trip." If he did not have a completed permission form on file, he was careful to notify the Director of Elementary Education or, in her absence, the Assistant Superintendent, before actually leaving the district for any extended period of time. I heard of no cases in which permission was denied or in which any principal made a request that tested the limits in which it might have been, although midway through the study the superintendent did announce a new policy of allowing a maximum of one day of professional leave to attend meetings for each fifty school days. Thus actually securing permission was a routine matter. It was, however, the bureaucratic and paternalistic kind of routine which characterized the way persons at each successive step throughout the hierarchy customarily handled the group below it. Like a pupil raising his hand for permission to go to the toilet, the demeaning aspect was

---

[14] For example, the head librarian of the school district once telephoned Ed about a book order he had submitted for additional reading materials for "slow readers" at Taft School. She informed him that one of the books on his order could be purchased but it would have to be placed in the professional library of the school rather than be put on the open shelves. The restricted volume was *Little Black Sambo*.

not the nature of the request (which is typically, but not invariably, honored in schools) but that the request had to be made at all.

Another whipping boy among the principals did not affect them all, but those who *were* affected by it did not attempt to hide their sense of annoyance at the picayune logic that had worked it out. By starting summer school before the district's elementary administrators had completed the regular service stipulated in their annual contracts, the district found itself paying some administrators for summer employment while they still had three full days of service remaining on their ten-month contracts. The resolution of the problem was that principals who were employed in the summer program were asked to prepare a written statement describing how they planned to "repay" the district *in time* for the 24 working hours covered by the overlapping contracts (8 hour day x 3 days). The principals were assured by Dr. Goddard that any way of working out the problem would be acceptable and that no one was going to "check up" on them in carrying out their commitment. Ed submitted a plan for remaining at his school each afternoon from the official termination of the summer school day at 2:30 P.M. until 5:00 P.M. for the number of days required to make up the time. Most of his colleagues followed the same procedure. By the time the summer school actually opened, the principals involved had ample time to work up strong feelings against being required to make up extra hours. The story was circulated that Dr. Goddard had become so annoyed during a telephone discussion on the topic with one of the principals that she had hung up on him midway in their conversation, a behavior that seemed almost unbelievable to the collectivity of principals who admired her remarkable composure. ("They're still good friends, though," Ed hastened to explain.)

The matter of "repaying" time to the district remained a sore point reviewed intermittently in private conversations for months. Almost a year later I recorded an incident where a principal gently goaded the Director of Elementary Education by declaring that if a new program she proposed was going to keep him at his school later in the day than other principals he wanted to be paid for it. "Or else," he suggested, "you could still use it to make up that week we were dubbed [docked?] if we held summer school." The following summer Dr. Goddard anticipated the recurrence of the problem and issued a memorandum early in June acknowledging the "nitty little problem of overlapping duty periods." At that time she polled each principal to learn whether he "had plans to work later in the summer" to complete the duties of his regular assignments.

From the point of view of the central office, neither of these procedures was probably intended as more than an attempt at organizational efficiency. In fact, however, such measures had a net effect of severely detracting from the image of the principal as an autonomous leader of his school, emphasizing instead his place as a functionary in the hierarchy of the system. That it was even thinkable on behalf of the central office personnel that they should have proposed, albeit gently and even "permissively," that each summer school principal remain an extra two and a half hours "on duty" at his deserted school building until he had accumulated 24 extra hours of duty, epitomized to the principals how oblivious central office personnel were to their actual work week. Having heard the facts themselves, they mused whether those personnel, and specifically the Director of Elementary Education, were really serious about the proposal. Lacking any way of knowing for sure, each principal made his own separate peace. Ed hedged both ways; he felt no qualms about leaving early after the long hours he had put in all year at school, yet he did not wish to go back on his word. Since he lived near his school, he sometimes meandered home after summer school, changed clothes, and returned to school to putter around or "do some filing." But the "nitty little problem" of the total hours he spent at school and the apparent lack of appreciation for the fact was not easily dismissed:

> I have some ideas for helping out with our many problems. But I won't do anything until they tell me from downtown that I don't have to spend every daylight hour in this building, and until they give me some help. Unless I give up my family and just do this job day and night.

The hierarchy was reinforced through formal procedures as well as informal ones. "Voluntary" contributions solicited from school employees provide an instance of the former. Attaining the financial quota for the community's annual United Appeal Fund produced a situation in which formal statements had always assured that the amount of an individual's contribution was "a personal and individual matter," and those were the words that appeared in the letter sent from the central office to all school district employees. At the same time, if the quotas assigned to the school district and distributed among the schools failed to be met, past experience suggested that additional encouragement could be expected. Three principals compared strategies for collecting the money:

FIRST PRINCIPAL: I told my teachers that with $11.50 from each teacher, $20 from the principal, $5.00 from the custodian and secretary, and $1 from all the other employees—do you know that some of our assistant cooks only make $600 a year—we can make our quota.

SECOND PRINCIPAL: The resource teacher [a GASer] and I just make up the difference in our quota each year.

ED BELL: I put mine in first. I don't intend to make up any deficits.

After the drive began, Ed was queried by principal Norm Olds about whether he had subsequently received any special word regarding the amount contributed at Taft School:

NORMAN: Say, did you get a letter from Sam on United Appeal?

ED: No. Not yet, anyway.

NORMAN: The quota for my school was $290. When they called on a survey from downtown some time ago, my secretary said, "Oh, I think we have collected around $200." So I got a *personal* note from Sam. Not a form letter. It said, "Norm, don't you think we could do a little better?" Well, when it gets to that point . . .

ED: When I get so that's my only contribution, I'll start thinking differently.

NORMAN: I wrote across the note, "Collections are now $260" and I sent it back. On the other hand, I know a guy at the bank who has cut down his *monthly* contribution from $10.00 to $9.00. That's still more than some teachers give for the *year*.

ED: Those boys in business and industry are really under pressure from their bosses.

NORMAN: (turning to me) Not that this isn't a good thing, Harry....

Three months later, the teacher appointed to take charge of the United Appeal "campaign" for the school asked Ed if she could make an announcement about it during a Taft faculty meeting.

TEACHER: We were $28.00 short on United Appeal. We thought that if every teacher gave another dollar, we'd almost make it.

ED: Has Dr. Boggs called you?

TEACHER: No.

ED: He didn't call me, either. I understand he *did* call some of the principals.

Contributions (totaling about $18,000) the following year put the district "well over the established quota" during the course of the initial drive for funds. A notice in the monthly *Superintendent's Bulletin* commended all personnel: "This is a very positive indication of appreciation shown by school district employees for the improved benefits that have been provided for the current school year budget."

Peers as Socializers

The major emphasis for the continuing socialization of principals into and by the hierarchical structure of the Columbia School District occurred via formal modes. The socialization which occurred among the principals themselves, by contrast, was carried out predominantly by informal means.

The "conventional wisdom" of the elementary principalship, in contrast to its formal body of knowledge, is carried about in the minds of its successful and experienced practitioners. It is transmitted verbally and, for the most part, informally, to succeeding generations. It is an oral literature. Younger men turn to their more experienced colleagues when they wish to draw upon the accumulated wisdom of years of practical experience. Like teachers, school administrators derive satisfaction from a shared perception that no one can really understand what it is like to be a principal until he has been one himself.

An accumulated wisdom based on years of personal experience lends itself to an oral literature for many reasons. For one, the average principal appears not to be an avid reader, and thus an oral tradition is more expedient than a written one. Certainly the average principal is not a writer, so those considered to be in the know are unlikely to have the time or inclination to make their knowledge a matter of written record. Those who manage to get some part of it written down typically are outsiders, students of administration rather than practicing administrators. An oral tradition allows for essential slippage between one man's experience and another man's problem, for no two administrative problems are exactly alike. The elusiveness of an oral tradition provides some minor protection for the principal from critical attack by outsiders, including those among his daily contacts—teachers and parents alike—whose numbers invariably include individuals who feel they could administer a school twice as effectively with half the effort.

An accumulated body of wisdom presided over by the elders may also provide a certain amount of satisfaction and comfort as a younger man envisions himself coming to hold a more exalted rank among his peers as he accumulates years of service. The senior principals in the group were treated with deference by the younger members. To illustrate: as the principals were gathering for an evening meeting of the local principal's association, one young and recently appointed principal encountered Norman Olds, a senior principal, and the following dialogue ensued:

YOUNG PRINCIPAL: Good evening, Mr. Olds.
SENIOR PRINCIPAL: Let's just use "Norm."
YOUNG PRINCIPAL: Oh, it's just out of habit, I guess. I've been calling you that for a long time.
SENIOR PRINCIPAL: I know. But it doesn't sound right. You even did it at a meeting in front of a lot of teachers the other evening.

A useful distinction can be made between the different kinds of information which school principals control and use. Major attention has been given in this chapter to the task requirements of their work, both in terms of the limited "knowledge base" of school administration and the extent to which the real "know-how" for survival, the wisdom of the role, is transmitted orally. Complementary to the accumulated wisdom or "know-how" of the principalship is an aspect which might be called "know-who." By reason of their long tenure in the school district, the senior principals controlled a great deal of interpersonal information about their superordinates, their peers, and other long-time employees. They could unfold a complex interpersonal professional network, with the name, rank, and professional history of each of their cohorts. The extent and complexity of the network bore resemblance to the extensive kinship systems which anthropologists have often collected from informants during field studies. Principals knew who among their junior peers had formerly served their senior ones, whose careers had been blocked or enhanced by present and former central office personnel, how each person had come through the ranks, and even what his likely prospects were for the future. The principals perceived and talked about committees, schools, and offices in the central administration building in terms of who occupied them. They referred to a school as often by the name of its principal as by the name assigned to the building. They out-guessed, second-guessed, and critiqued personnel changes and new appointments. Whenever a new committee was formed, their interest was directed to its constituents rather than its purposes.

Ed Bell was accumulating this body of information, both by living it and through hearing stories recounted or questions answered by his "elders." In turn, he could recount some parts to those principals who were junior to him. Such knowledge of how people had come "through the ranks" was not only of passing interest. It was useful in dealing with peers and with central office personnel, and it could prove invaluable in knowing how to work with administrators in other districts, professors of education, and personnel in the State Department of Education, particularly in identifying the extent of their experience in and their commitment to the elementary school principalship. For example, the Director of Elementary Education in a neighboring school district was esteemed among principals throughout the region for his commitment to the principalship: "He's real popular. He came up through the ranks. He was very popular as an elementary principal." This man had continued a close association with the principal group after becoming a central-office administrator. He was an active member of their associations. Wherever he appeared away from his district on school business he was always accompanied by several of the elementary principals with whom he worked.[15]

Principals in Ed's district contrasted the background of that administrator with their own Dr. Goddard. She had served as an elementary curriculum consultant and supervisor but had never been a supervising principal of an elementary school. Perhaps because of her personable nature and remarkable poise, she seemed well accepted by the elementary principals. Ed often commented enthusiastically on his appreciation of the way she performed in her administrative role, and even one of his more pessimistically-inclined colleagues conceded, "She has only been a head teacher before, not a principal. But none of the administrators objects to her." Because the principals accepted her personally, they interpreted her lack of experience in her favor: "She *knows* she hasn't been a principal before, so she doesn't tell us how to go about our work." Customarily, lack of experience at the elementary school level was heralded as the central cause of problems between principals and the typical central office administrator or superintendent. One principal noted (see Chapter 11) "I *never have* worked with a superintendent who really understands the role of the elementary school administrator."

If there was one obvious means by which principals exerted some audible degree of social control over their colleagues, it was in their institutionalized use of humor. I do not mean by this that principals are especially humorous men in terms of great wit or an uncanny knack for seeing the "funny side" of every situation. Rather, like most schoolmen, principals appreciated and encouraged the efforts of those among them who helped to keep school business from becoming unnecessarily serious and pedestrian. The light vein of give-and-take banter which they maintained while discussing school affairs, particularly in meetings restricted to themselves and Dr. Goddard, sometimes served as a screen for venting pent-up feelings of tedium or of opprobrium at too-blatantly-authoritarian statements made by colleagues or central office personnel.

Ed Bell was certainly not a humorist, but neither was he humorless. He liked to laugh—or at least to smile broadly. Like the majority of principals, he enjoyed hearing a good joke or an account of a humorous incident, and he enjoyed holding the attention of others with a joke or a true experience from his own youth or from his years as an educator.[16]

In the form of joke-telling, principal humor simultaneously reached its perigee and apogee at professional meetings of sufficient attendance to warrant enlisting

[15] At the same time, outsiders generally felt that his close association with the principals resulted in tight controls over their actions, and that the elementary schools in that district were virtually administered as a single unit from the central office.

[16] Ed's most often told story at school was the apocryphal one about an exasperated rural school teacher who finally decided to write a note home concerning the unpleasant odor of one of her pupils. She wrote: "Johnny smells bad. Could you please do something about it." The next day she received a note in reply, "Don't smell him. Larn him!"

someone—not necessarily from within their own ranks—to act as the emcee of a formal program. On such occasions the jokes seemed designed for one purpose only: "keep 'em laughing." The principals applauded the efforts of every program chairman to accomplish that goal even if the number or quality of jokes proved to be a test of audience patience. The pattern of beginning county, regional, and state meetings with "a few jokes" seemed less related to the purposes of those organizations than to a patent formula for surefire public speaking success learned long ago in elocution classes and never examined since; start off with an attention-getting device to make sure you have your audience with you. Perhaps schoolmen fall back on such a formula in dealing with their colleagues in voluntary associations because under more routine circumstances most audiences a principal addresses in the course of his daily work are captive ones. For his all-call announcements over the office intercom or his comments at faculty meetings, attention need not be diverted from the business immediately at hand.

Some patterned humor was a consequence of the fact that principals frequently found themselves among professional colleagues with whom they were not sufficiently well acquainted to be able to engage easily in personal conversations. Their greetings and informal introductions often included joking references to incidents where a colleague had achieved an administrative coup or to humorous circumstances shared in common. For example, the meetings of the principals were usually of long duration and the termination of a meeting inevitably saw a rush on the nearest men's lavatory. This situation provoked an equally inevitable set of comments by those present on the uniformity imposed on them from within ("That meeting ended just in time") or, as a result of school architecture, from without ("That's a nice bunch of backs, there"). Occasionally jokes were made at the expense of someone higher in the hierarchy: "Say, who's been writing to Dr. Boggs here on the wall?"

The serious functions carried out in the guise of humor accomplished such purposes as maintaining uniformity in the amount of time and effort expended at particular tasks, giving or testing information about the limits of acceptable behavior, or bringing some individual or part of the group back into line. The maintenance of uniformity of effort worked two ways. Through joking about how they were progressing in the preparation of reports, meeting deadlines, and so forth, the principals had some idea of the range of behavior deemed appropriate by their peers. At the same time, the chronic "rate busters" and early-birds could become, or even volunteer themselves to be, the butt of mild joking which relieved some of the tension which might otherwise have developed. Certain principals, for example, were felt to be almost too adept in getting what they wanted for their schools, especially in "scrounging" equipment and materials from the central office. An exchange of banter such as the following provided an opportunity for a socializing note of constraint on the part of one administrator and an acknowledgement by another that he was pressing the limits of acceptable behavior:

FIRST PRINCIPAL: Did you get those tiles this year?
SECOND PRINCIPAL (Tom Nice):   Yes.
FIRST PRINCIPAL: You son-of-a-gun. How did you get them?

SECOND PRINCIPAL: Well, I've worn out one pair of pants just from walking on my knees every time I'm at the central office.

Exchanging information about the expectations of professional behavior was effectively accomplished through humor. For example, most principals subscribed to the idea that it was desirable to know the names of all the children in their school. Whether an individual principal could actually achieve this, however, depended on external factors like school size as well as on personal adroitness in learning names. Ed was not particularly good at remembering names except for those children who were highly visible from the office's point of view. He claimed to have known each child by name when the school was smaller, but he had not been able to keep track of all the pupils in recent years. Bill St. Claire, at a neighboring school, claimed to know the names of all of his students. A principal of a new and rapidly growing school mentioned one day that he had enrolled his 630th pupil, and he and Ed chided Bill that if he had a school of that size he would not be able to keep up any longer. Tom Nice overheard the conversation and added that although *he* could not remember all the names of the children at his school, he did have a secretary who knew them. The principal of the large school chuckled at Tom's announcement and made a joke of the secretary's behavior: "You see, that's all she does. No reports or anything. She just sits there all day long memorizing names."

Although the major socializing influence of Ed's peers seemed to be in the direction of keeping principals "in tow," the formal structure of their professional organizations did provide a channel for politically mobile career-oriented principals who wished to remain in their present professional role and still achieve greater visibility and power. Two routes "up and out" of the principalship have already been described, one via a direct promotion into central office administration based on success within one's own district, the other via academic success and outside help in obtaining a new administrative position or a post at a college or university. A third alternative was also possible. A principal could become active by seeking offices in his own professional organizations. In recent years, with the sponsorship and encouragement of Tom Nice and others, Ed had pursued this latter alternative. His views were mixed about whether to maintain so active a role in the principals' associations. Early in the study, he said:

> You might call me a reluctant participant. I think you have to do something to help these organizations or else keep your mouth shut. Eventually, I'll probably get involved at the state level.

After four straight years in office, and recognizing some major differences between politicking among acquaintances at the regional association and as a stranger in the rest of the state, Ed was not so sure that he wanted to seek office beyond the regional organization. Whether or not he actually does so will probably depend a great deal on the kind of encouragement he gets from his peers in this regard.

> Well, as vice president and then president of the County Association of Elementary School Principals, and then as vice president and president of the Regional, that's four years, and I'll be glad to stop. I have no further aspirations along these lines.

Comment

Socialization as discussed in his chapter has been taken to include not only the process by which one learns to occupy a particular role but the continuing process by which his behavior in that role is appropriately channeled or kept in check by the influence of others. Anthropologists focusing attention on groups of people customarily describe efforts of the latter sort under the broad rubric of social control. In a case study focused on one individual, it has seemed useful to employ the term socialization, thus emphasizing the reciprocal nature of processes of social control. Socialization provides the nexus between the present chapter and the following one in which Ed is presented in the complementary role of socializer, watching over the incorporation of others into the educator subculture just as he has received the brunt of many of the efforts described here. If, in the light of his effort to do a good job as principal, Ed's own evaluation at central office seemed unexpectedly harsh, it may be of interest to the reader to compare how in the next chapter Ed assumes a similarly critical stance toward (some) others for whom he plays a key role as formal evaluator-socializer.

9 / Maintaining the system: the principal as socializer

Ultimately we are all Zuñis who are forced to wear the mask of omnipotence in order to do the world's cultural work.

Weston La Barre, *The Human Animal*

Entry into teaching, generally that period from the beginning of student teaching to the completion of one's first year as a regular classroom teacher, is the most crucial period in the professional life of a teacher. The success of that period is also crucial to the continued "life" of the institution which he has chosen to serve. Only recently has this process of "socialization into teaching" received much attention in terms of what actually happens to beginning teachers (see studies by Eddy 1969; Fuchs 1969; as well as firsthand accounts like those of Kaufman 1964; Kozol 1967; Ryan 1970) rather than what is supposed to happen. The present chapter is concerned with socialization into teaching in terms of the role which Ed Bell played as perceived by himself and by "his" teachers.

Taft School provided an excellent setting for looking at the principal's role in the induction of new teachers. New to the staff were three "beginning" teachers, one of them on a regular first year contract (Kay Johnson) and two serving as intern teachers (Mary Lou Berg, Ellwood New). There were five other newcomers who were experienced teachers but new to Taft School. These five included two classroom teachers who had transferred to Taft from other schools in the district (Shirley Robin, Alma Skirmish), two teachers who had recently been teaching part-time in the district but had not had prior full-time classroom assignments there (Margaret Elder, Joanne Jenkins) and one teacher who had never taught in Columbia's schools (Mary Brightside). The presence of so many "new people" made everyone among the returning staff conscious of the process of inducting new members, since each grade level except third grade had at least one newcomer in its teaching trio. But not all these new people were being inducted simultaneously into careers as teachers and into the professional life-style of the Taft School faculty. School people make subtle but important distinctions between beginners new to teaching and experienced teachers new to a school. Correspondingly, this chapter has been divided into two sections, the first dealing with the socialization of beginning teachers, the second dealing with the socialization of experienced teachers new to Taft School.

227

One teacher's reflections on socialization into teaching as she had experienced it raised an interesting point: is it possible for the process to occur while the administrator remains totally ignorant of and oblivious to it? The process of teacher socialization as she had experienced it during her own induction into teaching, and as she had observed it subsequently, had remained entirely in the hands of teachers:

> I have been in three other schools, and in each instance there were several older people who were very set in their ways. They were not very open to new methods of teaching and were not interested in learning anything different. They were very subject-matter oriented. And in some cases these older people tried to take over the younger ones and tell them "What we've always done in this school *all these years* is . . . and this is the way it shall be done."
>
> Possibly the principals in these cases should have been more aware of what was going on and seen to it that this didn't happen. I think, in this case that I'm referring to right now, the principal was an office sitter. He wasn't very aware of what was going on.

Whether there are principals totally unaware of how teachers are socialized into their schools seems to be open to conjecture and interpretation. My experience with teachers suggests that among the more than one million of them in elementary schools one could easily find a number who would be willing to sign affidavits that they have at some time worked with principals who were oblivious to *everything*.[1] Yet the fact that an administrator fails to intercede in a process cannot be taken as proof that he is unaware of it. Indeed, even if he feels that what goes on is extremely unfortunate or inappropriate, he may not only allow the process to continue but may aid and abet the socializers in order to maintain his own position. In any case, Ed did not abdicate his role in the socialization of either beginning teachers or teachers new to Taft School.

THE SOCIALIZATION OF BEGINNING TEACHERS

Ed Bell was sensitive to the problems of the beginning teacher and formally committed to seeing that each beginner at Taft had a successful experience. Through comments directed to his beginning teachers he attempted to reassure them of his faith in their capabilities and of his personal support of and belief in them. He probably thought of himself more as a person who cleared the way to provide beginning teachers with a sense of freedom rather than as someone contributing to a period of intense socialization. Statements made by the beginning teachers suggest, however, that their socialization into teaching and into faculty status at Taft was conscious and thorough, and in their perception, Ed's part in the process was critical, both in terms of their direct encounters with him and because he represented the ultimate authority of the school even in those cases where other faculty or supervisors were assigned or took more active roles as socializers.

[1] "I think they looked under rocks to find the principals in our district," one teacher informed me when she learned I was conducting a study about the elementary school principalship.

The concept of "cultural compression" suggested by George Spindler[2] (1959) provides an excellent way for looking at the process of socialization into teaching. During the compression process, the boundaries of acceptable behavior for a new teacher become narrower and narrower, starting at the moment he or she receives an initial student teaching assignment. The process continues, and the boundaries tighten, through the progression of taking more and more responsibility for managing the classroom of a supervising (or "master") teacher. Finally the tyro-teacher is assigned a class of his own. This is a period of the teacher's development, to follow Spindler's conceptualization, "when the norms of his group and society bear in upon him with the greatest intensity" (1959:39). At the end of that first year, assuming that the beginning teacher survives it and chooses to continue in teaching, he acquires a new status, that of experienced teacher. From this point on, he finds that his one-time socializers turn their attention to a new group of inductees, and he may become aware that restraints which he once perceived as limiting his behavior are suddenly more relaxed, expectations less rigid. Whatever anxieties exist for some teachers during the period of status limbo until they are accepted as "experienced teachers" and achieve permanent tenure in a particular school district (awarded explicitly or granted implicitly with receiving a teaching contract for the fourth consecutive year in most urban school districts), they are never again customarily subjected to the degree of attention that is built into the initial period of cultural compression. Perhaps not all teachers recognize their own arrival into the "experienced" status. One Taft teacher's account revealed how she had failed to realize when she accepted a second teaching job that she was accepted as an experienced teacher, even though her first teaching assignment, in a different district, had been for only half a year:

> It was sort of funny, when I look back on it. I was [still] inexperienced. I had a lot of ideas to try. I used to make these appointments with the principal to go to his office and go over my whole program. That poor principal! I'd sit down for about an hour and I'd go over my reading program and all the things we were doing. After about two session of this he sits there and says, "Yes, I think that would be fine. Yes, that sounds like a good idea." I decided that whatever I did would be okay with him, and I never bothered him again.

Ed's overt role in the socialization process was not as great as I had anticipated it might be, particularly in his day-to-day involvement. He devoted very little time to the student teachers assigned to Taft. Although he spoke often of his belief in the importance of the student teaching experience and was careful in securing the cooperation of teachers whom he felt would be effective in working with them, he seldom observed student teachers actually performing at teaching tasks. He was often uncertain about their names. He was, however, quite certain about who on his staff had the responsibility for overseeing their classroom work. Unless a student

---

[2] Spindler described cultural compression as "any period of time in the life cycle of the individual when he encounters a culturally patterned reduction of alternatives for behavior" (1959:38). Spindler suggested that cultural compressions may be detected in the life cycle of any society at a number of developmental stages. Although he did not specifically single out entry into teaching, he noted that in our society induction into the working force is a period of cultural compression.

teacher was reported by a regular faculty member as exceptionally good or exceptionally bad, Ed might have little more personal information about each of them than a general impression weighted heavily by appearance and any pronounced personality trait exhibited in brief encounters in the teachers' room. This was especially true of the students assigned in the primary grades, due to the different daily schedule and the all-consuming involvement with activities in the primary wing which characterized that group of teachers and apprentices. Male student teachers, and female student teachers who taught in the upper grades, were easier for him to identify and get to know through conversations in the faculty room during the regular noon hour.

As noted, there were three "beginning" teachers at Taft, one teacher on a regular contract, the other two on a special program as intern teachers. The persons immediately responsible for their socialization differed, and, coupled with the uniqueness of their individual personalities and backgrounds, each of the three beginners experienced a rather different year.

A First-Year Teacher

Mrs. Kay Johnson, a beginning fourth-grade teacher, had done her student teaching at Taft the previous year. She had been a success as a student teacher. Her enthusiasm for teaching, her wit and energy, her maturity, and her stability in the community as a wife and the mother of two junior-high school children, made her seem desirable as a permanent addition to the staff. While she was serving her apprenticeship, Ed asked her if she would be interested in returning to Taft as a regular teacher the following fall. She was delighted with his invitation.

Kay Johnson remained as enthusiastic about Taft School and about Ed's administration of it during her year as a beginning teacher as she had appeared during student teaching, and she conveyed her enthusiasm in a variety of ways throughout the year. Late one Wednesday afternoon in September Ed recounted to me:

> When Kay Johnson left this afternoon after the faculty meeting, she said to me, "This school is different."
> I told her, "Thanks." I don't know why I said that to her. It's her school as much as it is mine.

During the fall, when it was necessary for her to miss a few days of school, Kay sent a note to Ed which contained a reaffirmation of her enthusiasm: "I don't just want to teach. I want to teach at Taft School." She provided space in her classroom for Ed's coveted instructional project, the saltwater aquarium, thus making it easy for him to drop by her room casually (in the course of his daily check on the tank) to see how things were going without appearing to be checking on her in a formal supervisory capacity. Throughout the year Ed conveyed to others and to Kay his confidence in and approval of her work, with such comments as one made to a fellow principal in February, "Kay is a dandy. She's a real crackerjack first-year teacher."

In June, after completing her first year of teaching, Kay Johnson remarked of Ed's evaluative visits, "I know of no formal evaluation visit that Mr. Bell made to my room. He was in and out several times a week—perhaps more at the first of the year." Ed held the one evaluation conference he was required to have with her during the year about her teaching. He formally recommended that she be advanced to second-year probationary status. Kay's feeling was that Ed had an adequate basis for evaluating her as a person, although she noted, "perhaps more formal evaluation would have been helpful to judge my teaching abilities." In addition to Ed's evaluation, Kay also reported that she was visited four times during the year by a special consultant from the central office assigned to "assist" first-year teachers. After each of those visits the consultant reviewed with Kay the lesson she had observed.

Whether Kay's apparently "happy year" challenges the idea that beginning teaching is a time of severe cultural compression is subject to interpretation. If cultural compression is taken to mean that the individual must conform to styles which are alien or adverse to his cultural nature, with an assumption that the process must inevitably be a time of painful relearning, then her case seems to suggest that the notion is inadequate or inappropriate. It seems plausible, however, that Kay had no problems with the socialization process because she had internalized the norms of the teacher role and had acquired the necessary behavior patterns before she ever entered the portals of Taft School. She was motivated in part by forces external to the school in her efforts to improve her socio-economic status. Her term of student teaching the previous June had completed her requirements for a bachelor's degree at age 36, and her new salary boosted the family income by 60–70 percent. She was personally motivated to become a "good teacher." More than once she wondered aloud among other staff members whether after several years she might *really* be a teacher. She constantly expressed the pleasure she derived from teaching and especially from being a teacher at Taft School. In her responses to the staff questionnaire at the end of her first year, she wrote:

> I am interested in children and learning processes. I enjoy the daily challenge of teaching. I enjoy close involvement with children and adults. I enjoy being my own planner.
> A school (staff, administrator, building) has an atmosphere that either fits, or does not fit, yourself as a teacher. Taft School fits me.

The Intern Teachers

Mrs. Mary Lou Berg and Mr. Ellwood New were the two other beginning teachers at Taft School. Both were intern teachers simultaneously completing a special university program leading to a master's degree and, in a closely supervised program, learning to be teachers by assuming responsibility for their own classrooms before completion of their formal university training. Theoretically their year as intern teachers was offered in lieu of student teaching, and thus they were not expected to be as experienced as their fellow beginner, Kay Johnson. In fact, however, Mary Lou Berg not only had done some student teaching but, like Kay, had been assigned to Taft School for that experience. Mary Lou had elected the intern program because of its accelerated means to acquire a master's degree rather than for its acceleration into full-time classroom teaching. Although she and Kay both had experience in classroom teaching at Taft, Mary Lou's position as an intern emphasized her status as a student. The responsibility for her supervision and for her "development" as a teacher was assumed at least in part by university personnel, including an intern supervisor who shared an academic appointment between the school district and the university. Kay Johnson, on the other hand, was no longer involved with an academic institution as a student. Her "success" was the responsibility of the school district.

The comments which Mary Lou Berg and Ellwood New made during taped interviews reveal aspects of the socialization they experienced at Taft School. Ellwood's experiences, as will be seen, were in marked contrast to those of Mary Lou. The following excerpts from a taped interview in April provide an idea of Mary Lou's perceptions of socialization into teaching as a combination of forces resulting from the expectations of others (fellow teachers, her supervisor, Ed, her university professors) and her expectations of herself (a person who can maintain a sense of humor, a person who needs to have things—and people—orderly):

Mary Lou Berg: An Intern Teacher in Grade Two

> Generally I don't consider myself a person lacking in confidence—I really felt confident that I could do the job—but I was still quite scared when I first came into the classroom.
>
> The intern program is set up so that you have a great deal of help. The Intern Supervisor did help me a great deal, to start out, as did the whole staff at this school, especially my colleagues in second grade. I don't think I ever could have done this year without them. Especially Mrs. Keppel, who had gone through this [intern program] last year. She knew just what I was going through and could empathize with me. It really relieved a lot of the pressure.
>
> I feel a lot more confident and a lot more at ease now than I did at the beginning of the year. This staff, my intern supervisor, and my university class in clinical supervision, were a great help to me. Because I'd never really taught on my own. I was a student teacher here before, under supervision and with quite a bit of help.
>
> All of a sudden, there I was with these children and I had to plan the whole day. Because you haven't had a lot of the methods courses and things, although I'm not saying they necessarily tell you what it's going to be like. I don't think there's anything like getting right in and doing it. There were certain areas where I felt I was weak and had to do a lot of preparation. I would lug my books home every night and work for a long time at these specific things.
>
> Discipline was one area that I felt somewhat pressured in. I hadn't encountered anything like this before, in any kind of work that I'd done with children or in my student teaching. These children were quite a bit different. Very immature—very egocentric—and very demanding for attention and for their own way. There were two little boys who had pretty serious emotional problems which I know I cannot handle. They are getting professional help.
>
> I did not feel any pressure within the school. I didn't feel "not accepted." I just felt like one of the staff right from the very first day, although I didn't really know anyone very well. I knew Ed and some of the teachers from student teaching.
>
> Ed was constantly reassuring me that he was sure I was doing the best that I could, and that he knew I was having some problems. In his attitude he gave me confidence that I was a professional person, and that I could handle them.

I think the other second-grade teachers had similar problems, and so I didn't feel I was alone and that it was necessarily a function of my behavior in the classroom, but I was having days when I couldn't handle the children. They're only seven-year-old children and they do have certain things—like when they can't sit for so long—that I'm aware of.

Ed has dropped in to my class. He dropped in even more frequently at the beginning to see how I was doing. He always made a point of commenting in some way, that he'd enjoyed a music lesson or that he'd enjoyed this or he liked that. I can't remember exactly the words he used, but he always made me feel nice, since it was just my first year here and I really did want to do a good job. He'd let me know that this was my room, and that just because I was an intern he considered me in no way in an inferior position to any other first-year teacher. I never felt that Ed was talking down to me or treating me any differently than he would treat the others.

I don't think that he visited as much as I thought he would. I'm not sure exactly how much he's supposed to visit or what the rule is. I'd say he's been in here at least a half a dozen times or more. For a couple of times he sat for a fair amount of class time.

And then, he's kind of popped in and out. I thought he would be in more. The Intern Supervisor was in a lot of times, and so I don't know if that meant she could talk to him about it or not.

He's seen me teach. And he saw me teach in my student teaching—he sat for a whole class that I taught once. I think he knows what I'm like when I teach. I think possibly he could have been in more times to make a true judgment on what I'm like as a teacher.

One of the things that has been a problem to me, that I think I'll be able to handle better next year, is the type of standards that I set right at the beginning of the year and the expectations that I have for a class. My expectations were too high for this group of children. My standards were too loose for any kind of a happy functioning to occur. I wasn't happy and I don't think the children were happy.

What I had to do is something I didn't want to do, because I was warned against it, and that's "tighten up" after you've been nice and easy. But I did. I think that it was better for everybody concerned that I did. I probably don't run as free a class as I would like to and as "children-run" as I would like to. But with this particular group of children it is the only way I think anybody can function. Maybe it's very selfish of me, but I have to be able to live with these children, and the only way I can do it is by setting fairly tight standards as far as discipline goes and as far as what we do at what time. But I still retain my sense of humor, so we seem to get along OK.

Ellwood New: An Intern Teacher in Grade Five

The third beginning teacher, 28-year-old Ellwood New, was also an intern teacher, and thus the responsibility for his success was closely tied in with the university's intern program. There were important differences between him and the other beginning teachers, however. One was experience. Where both his cohorts had virtually completed their formal university training in teaching, he had only begun taking the courses he would need to meet certification requirements. Where both of them had prior supervised classroom experience, he had none. And probably the most crucial, a factor that permeated every aspect of the status and personality differences which he described, Mr. New was a male being socialized into a work-world consisting in large majority (roughly 85 percent of elementary school teachers nationwide) of women.

Mr. New's perception of the socialization process he was undergoing is presented here as he described it at the end of February. His account provides a brief case study of the possible strains which can occur in the complex network of interactions and values in which socialization into teaching takes place, for Mr. New's indoctrination into teaching was a struggle for him, for his university supervisor, and for Ed. Part of the struggle arose from Mr. New's own personality, especially his self-conscious search for identity, although this avenue is not explored here beyond the presentation of Mr. New's own reflections. But his struggle also derives in part from the social setting, and his observations of one aspect of this—the role of the male teacher in the elementary school—provides an appropriate point at which to introduce important sex-role distinctions made in elementary schools as these affect teachers and principals. It is evident in the protocol that Mr. New saw Ed Bell as a source of strength and support in helping him to work out difficulties between himself and his pupils, his female supervisor, and the feminine majority among his co-workers.[3]

Selections are presented from a long (one and a half hour) taped interview made in February with Mr. New. Subheads have been added to help focus on aspects of his remarks particularly germane to socialization into teaching and to the special problems of the male teacher in the elementary school.

Prior Experiences with "Education"

While I was an undergraduate I became interested in education and took several courses in it. But the courses changed my mind. "Magnification of minutiae" is a good way to explain it. There was a lot of magnification of things that weren't important at all in the classes I took. The things that I felt were important were being completely ignored. There was a lot of emphasis placed on how to put a bulletin board together and how to display things and nothing on the development of personality or how a person becomes a human being.

So instead my undergraduate work took a focus toward psychology and sociology. I think this accounted for my interest in probation work. I managed to get into court counselling just as I graduated from college. I got a job with the probation department. I found the kind of thing that I was looking for there. There was more emphasis on people and not on details and planning and the little things which seemed to me to be so insignificant.

My wife finished her requirements for her credential and her degree and taught during this period of four years, so it kept me in contact with what was going on. I was still interested in teaching, in spite of the things that happened to me as an undergraduate in education classes.

Last year I got interested in education again. I decided maybe the intern program was a way to get into education. I've never felt that I would lose con-

---

[3] Mr. Adam taught in the same wing as Mr. New, but their different grade levels, different schedules of extra duties, and mutual tendency to go their own way precluded extensive communication between them. In speaking specifically of his interaction with Mr. New, Adam once observed. "I'm about the only one he can talk to." Adam reported that his counsel was that New should endure patiently whatever had to be endured in order to get through his year of internship: "I feel free to talk with Ellwood about his teaching and his teaching methods. To encourage him, for instance, to see this year through and then to operate on the level *he* would like next year."

tact with the things that I thought were important as a teacher in the classroom. It was the barriers that I had to go through to get to them that were the problem. I have always felt that I have something to contribute to kids in the classroom and to the total school program. But I never felt like I could get there till I heard about the intern program.

I went over and talked to the professor in charge of the intern program at the university. He told me that next year would be as soon as I could get in. Then he called me on the phone and told me that there was an opening and he wanted me to apply. So I did, and in three weeks I was an intern teacher.

I feel that the kind of attitudes and feelings that I have belong in education. But I'm not so sure that they are acceptable to educators, and I have felt a lot of pressure to change. Both external, real clearly presented pressures, and pressures that are more subtle and under the surface. Pressures among fellow teachers and some from administration, although not as much as I anticipated.

A Favorable Reaction to the Principal

The principal here at Taft, Ed Bell, is the only person who fits in a pretty much administrative or evaluative capacity over me this year that I've been able to feel comfortable in working with. There are many others who sit in the same position because of my contact with the university and because of my first year of experience here and being an intern teacher. I have a lot of observers and a lot of evaluators.

Ed is the one person I've really felt comfortable in relating to. He can come into my classroom anytime and it doesn't bother me. I feel very uncomfortable when other teachers or evaluators come in, because I don't think they know what I am trying to do. They don't understand what's going on here. And even if they did, they wouldn't approve. I don't feel this is true of Ed. I didn't from the first day that I met him. I realized very quickly that Ed was a different kind of school principal. I have worked with many school principals through my court work, and I kind of got the stereotyped idea of what a school principal was like. Ed didn't fit the pattern.

I hadn't made up my mind whether I wanted to go into the intern program when I came to have that interview with Ed. From the beginning I decided that if I couldn't get into education the way I wanted, and be the kind of person I wanted, I didn't want to be any part of it. I didn't want to be phoney. I started the interview by telling him as honestly as I could about my feelings, my goals in teaching, the kind of person I was, my experiences. And I was just as honest with him as I am being here. In the past I had found out that if you're this way with educators you're not always acceptable.

Ed encouraged me to be as honest as I could in telling him about these things. Wonder of wonders, after we got through he still thought that I would be an asset to the staff here, which kind of surprised me. I honestly didn't expect it. So from the beginning we got off on a good start. I didn't have any need to put up a defensive front (which I have had to do since—not with him, but with other people in the education field and here in Taft School) and so I think this has had something to do with my working relationship. I've felt that I can always be honest with him. I have nothing to hide from him and nothing to defend from him. He knows what I am trying to do here. He may have a question about some technique once in a while, but he can never have a question about what I'm trying to do because he knows.

With other people that I've tried to work with since I've been here, I tried to do the same thing in the beginning as I did with Ed. I was honest. They said this was fine, this is what education needed. But it hasn't worked out that way as we have gone along. When they see in practice what they agreed with in theory, they don't agree any more. They think that I'm wrong, that I should change, that I need to make some adjustments. It has caused me a lot of sleepless nights and a lot of concern. If I've got to be different, this is not where I want to stay. The only reason I'm here is because I think that who I am, and what I am, have something to offer. And if I have to change that, then all I have to offer is a teacher's guide, and anybody could do that. Ed has supported me in these times when I have had disagreements with other people who've been evaluating me. I feel that Ed has understood these disagreements and that he has been very fair in arbitrating them.

A Philosophy of Educational Change

Ed seems to me to be unique in his understanding of where education is going. I have appreciated this in him. I have felt since the first time I was conscious of education as a professional field that education is going to have to change because *it's not meeting people's needs*. It's been a kind of a battle from the educational field against people. It seems to me that people are becoming more aware of their own needs and aware that they can have them met. They don't have to put up with institutions and old ways of doing things which don't meet those needs anymore. They can change them.

I think that education is going to change. Ed agrees with me. The direction we think it is going to change is pretty much the same. This helps me work with him. He doesn't see the changes coming as fast as I do. He sees them coming a little slower and a little more peacefully. I think that if the attitudes about education which I'm seeing in teachers here continue, then there's not going to be any peaceful change.

As I see the kids in my classroom, they're demanding change *now*. I'm trying to be some kind of a tightrope walker and straddle the fence and keep as much as I can of the institution and the profession while trying to meet the needs of the human beings in the classroom, too. But I'm finding difficulty in doing it. Because of the formalized system that we have, you either go to the extreme and forget about the needs of the kids and uphold the institution, or you do something else.

Ed agrees with this idea. I haven't presented it to him in these words, but in other ways we come about it. He's agreed with me that we *are* making changes. We've *got to* make changes. We've got to make them just as fast as we can and, as he says, as slowly as we must, but we've got to move. And I think that he's talking about the same kind of things that I am and I felt comfortable with him because of that.

I think we have to recognize that no two people are the same. Though we shoot in the classroom for the seventy-five or eighty percent and try to keep that group moving together, we've got to recognize that even though they may all work together, they are not the same and they don't have the same kind of needs. We're not going to meet their needs by keeping them in a large group. It seems to me that the problems we are creating for ourselves in education are caused by conflict in that individuals, the kids themselves, have a large number of needs that we can't *ever* meet in the large group of 20 or 30. The problems that we have, the discipline problems, control problems, are caused by that very situation. The kids need an individualized program. And that means individual attention from the teacher.

I would like to see us set up a situation where the teacher could have as few youngsters as possible to work with at any time. Let the teacher work with them through what I call "relationship," through all the things that are involved in one person dealing with another person. Not in a "I know and I'm going to tell you" kind of role, but rather "Let's learn together and I know some ways to learn that you don't know yet and maybe by watching me you can see them, too."

What I would propose as a change in education is a complete departure from all the standardized and structured kinds of learning situations that are going on. I think that we should do away with everybody being assigned to classrooms and being one of that group of 30. I think we need to change all the rigidity that exists. It ought to be real easy for anybody in the classroom to change their mind, to start on something altogether different, even if it means wasting materials or getting the floor dirty. We need to do away with all these formalized structured inhibitions that kids feel in school. They are products of the system and have nothing to do with the way people develop or the way that you meet people's needs. These are inherent because we have too many people trying to live together in a school situation.

The thing I'm suggesting isn't very efficient. But I think that the kinds of people who would come from this sort of an unstructured, no grade-level, no report card, no classrooms, the relationship-with-other-people-who-are-learning-too, kind of an experience, would be people who were at peace with themselves. People who knew what they were and who they were. They would accept their limitations and work up to their capabilities. They would be more mature individuals than what I see coming out of schools now. I don't think Ed would argue with any of those things. He's superintendent and administrator of a building and has a niche in the system, but at the same time he's not sure whether that's the kind of thing he wants to see going on. I think he would like to change it.

I've heard the president of a local college suggest a *complete overhaul in education* from the very foundations on up. This is the kind of thing I'm talking about. Almost revolutionary, I suppose. I wouldn't feel disturbed if we wake up tomorrow and all our teachers and administrators are dead and we have to start all over again. I think we could develop some more realistic programs than what we've got now.

Pressures toward Conformity: Preserving the System

I'm talking about the destruction of a system that most of the people that I work with are dedicated to and have given their lives to. They are fighting very hard to preserve it, and that's where the conflict comes from. I feel conflict from other teachers. As a group they are kind of threatened by somebody who does things too much differently. It's not even a question of whether it's a success or not, its just that you shouldn't do anything too different. You should be aware of what everybody else is doing and then fit in and be one of them and not be too individualistic. That's what I'm fighting. We need to get away from this idea of a mass society where the direction we are going is more important than any individual. It's ridiculous to consider that the society itself is more important than an individual, because people make up the society. If it's more expedient for society and society can make more "advances" in space or better weapons or whatever else, we go that direction. We don't need to worry about individuals, just worry about advancing "society." That's what is happening in school.

I don't like to be one of the group and do things just the way everybody else is. I like to experiment and try some things and see if they're good or not and make my own decisions.

I feel pressure because of noise. We get noisy in here sometimes and I feel uncomfortable about it. Even if nobody said anything, I think I would feel uncomfortable, because the classrooms all around me are quiet. Noise stands out as being different. Whether it is good or bad, it is *different*, and you feel uncomfortable when you are different. I'm uncomfortable anyway. I always feel that someone is looking at me to see how much I'm worth and to put a price tag on me. Either through a report card, or a conversation over a cup of coffee, or something else, I feel like I'm being evaluated and judged. My worth goes up and down like the Dow, Pierce, Fenner and Smith averages. Right off the bat, because of a paranoid feeling on my part, that causes me to feel uncomfortable. There are things that people say to me, there are facial expressions that are given to me occasionally, which tend to make me feel even more uncomfortable.

I feel pressures to have my group of kids do things the way other groups do them. That's a pressure I don't want. For example, when we use the library and somebody who was in the workroom tells me that so-and-so did this-and-that while they were in there and would I please do something about it, or that so-and-so ran down the hall when he came back from the library and would I please take some kind of punitive action to see that this is straightened out. Or somebody comes into the classroom, another teacher, and looks around and sees something on the board or on a desk or in the back of the room and then there will be a comment like, "Is that all your kids do in here, is play?" Then there will be laughter, you know, there will be kind of a joke. But I don't feel it's a joke. I feel that my kids receive a lot of correction from other teachers that they shouldn't be getting. I don't say anything, because I don't want to bring in all these feelings that I'm talking about right now. I feel very uncomfortable in talking to other teachers about it.

Pressures toward Conformity: The Influence of Older Teachers

Most of the pressure I feel is from the older teachers. I feel some pressure from the younger teachers, but I can talk to them. I visited some of the classrooms of the younger ones here a few weeks ago as part of my intern training. I really had a good feeling after I visited Sally Jensen's first-grade classroom and had a talk with her. I liked the way her classroom was operated. She was able to take them somewhere, but at the same time she was able to relate with them as one human being to another. Even if she felt that there was something wrong going on in the classroom, she was not critical of the youngster. She would get them to fit into the group in a noncondemning, nonjudgmental way. I've never seen a classroom like that. The kids were happy. And they were learning, too, learning through this "relationship" that I talked about.

I think maybe there is some difference between how I feel about the older teachers. At least I can talk to the younger ones. That's an interesting point, thinking about the teachers here in terms of older and younger. Maybe it's this business of flexibility. The younger teachers are more like me in that they haven't really decided everything already. They are still looking around and trying some things and being flexible. It's not true of the older people and I know it, and I would just as soon avoid them. I don't even want to *talk* to them.

[I asked Mr. New the extent to which his problems related directly to his interactions with Mrs. Duchess, the senior teacher of the fifth grade and the informally acknowledged senior teacher of the upper-grade wing.]

Martha Duchess had been here longer than anybody. You get the feeling sometimes like it's Martha's school and Martha's library and Martha calls the shots. I think Martha is the major source of irritant for me. I avoid contact with her as often as I can. There are irritations that are caused by the people who are supervising me from the university, too. Maybe it's age difference. I don't know. Maybe it's male and female difference, too. Plus they don't know what I'm trying to do, and they're trying to defend a system that I want to see changed. So we don't talk. There is no two-way communication.

Either they are talking and I'm listening, or else I'm talking and no one's listening. There is no communication. I just avoid that as often as I can and try to be agreeable and pleasant. If it comes to a consultation about anything, I just back down and avoid it. I can't see that I'm going to make any changes anyway, and it is just going to cause hard feelings. I swallow my pride and forget it.

Being a Man in a Female-Oriented Institution

It's kind of a degrading, humiliating experience for a man to go into elementary education. There is a lot of "putting down" of your ego, of your pride, and, I suppose, of your masculinity to be able to teach. I think as a society we have thought elementary education is the baliwick of women. Any men who were involved in it, people will turn their eyebrows up at you and look kind of askance: "Oh, you're teaching fifth grade, huh!"

In the institution itself, women seem uncomfortable with men around. Maybe it is because men haven't been here in great numbers before and they just don't know how to act here. And men are uncomfortable because they feel that this is a women's profession and that they are trying to fit into it. I feel uncomfortable because of it. I think that Wally Adam feels defensive, too.[4] Maybe it's just something to do with being a man in a female-oriented institution, I'm not sure. I know he feels uncomfortable, and he does something about it. He takes the offense much more often as a result of his discomfort and his feeling that he is being judged, too.

When my wife complains about teachers at her school, it's very seldom that she has much to say about the women. She may be very upset about something that some *man* said at the faculty meeting, either a coordinator from downtown or one of the two men teachers at her school. She's very sensitive to anything that a man at school has to say. I think that this defensiveness which women feel with men here has something to do with how they work with men and I think it interferes with the man, too. This is what is happening with me, both with the older and the younger teachers, particularly the older ones. Whether they think that I'm right or wrong doesn't matter. It's *different* when it's brought up by a man. Maybe they are trying to preserve that part of the institution because it has been a women's profession for so many years, and maybe that's another act of preservation that they're going through.

Ed is aware of the conflicts that a man has in education, because he's been one for a long time, but he's not going to step in and try to solve the problems for me or anybody else. He's letting people work it out themselves. That is one of the best things he does around here.

Going It Alone

I feel I have the approval of the administration to go ahead with what I am doing in this classroom. If other people aren't pleased with it, well, that's their worry. I would like to work with the other two teachers at this grade level. But if I can't, I can't. We do *very* little together now. I never know what

---

[4] Wally Adam had, in fact, made some observations about the feminine environment of the elementary school in an interview taped the preceding week and subsequently may have discussed his views with Mr. New. Adam's comments included the following:

Elementary school is overwhelmingly oriented in the direction of providing a female teacher with an environment in which she can work. This is true not only of the basic program, but even the professional orientation is in this direction. It's a good-housekeeping operation and things tend to fall into neat patterns.

The idea of putting a wolf into this china shop is one that can be threatening to other people. I think that perhaps if I do have any problem, it is the threat that I pose for other people.

they are doing and they never know what I am doing. The only time we did work together at all was at the first of the year. We got together and we grouped for math. That's gone on since the first of the year, and I'm sorry we did that.

Next year I'm not going to teach fifth grade again, although I do plan to stay here at Taft School. At least that's what my plans are now. I'm supposed to finish my master's degree this summer. If I do, then I'll stay here. I've talked with Ed about it. I'm not in competition with the other two teachers. I'm not trying to show them what I can do and compare with what they can do, which I think they might feel because of this defensive male-female business again.

I think there are some really good teachers here. I mean they're human beings first of all and that they have learned some good teaching skills too. I know that Ed thinks that it's a fine faculty and that tends to make me think it's a fine faculty. Because I have a lot of respect for what he thinks, as he does for me, because I'm a person, I'm an individual, worthwhile. Yet I hear comments that make me wonder. I hear a lot of emphasis on control and classroom management and also on manipulation so you can keep everybody grouped together doing everything at the same time, which I don't like. But that's one of the things that I learned to live with in education. I think that I'm kind of going around in a lot of directions because of my lack of contact with the rest of the staff.

I think that Ed does a fine job. I have sensed enough to know that everyone doesn't think that Ed is the best principal the school could have, but I don't agree. I think he's fine. I really do, and I mean that honestly. I haven't worked under any other principal, but if I had, then maybe I wouldn't be teaching right now. I don't know. Because *I don't have to teach. I can do other things.*

At the time of this interview, Mr. New still had three and a half months to serve in his internship. During the spring, his faint optimism that he and the system could come to terms disappeared. By the end of April he and his supervisor from the university had reached an informal truce in which he was free to finish out the year with less of her "help" but with the tacit understanding that he would not continue to teach at Taft School. The supervisor related to Ed that she had told Mr. New, "I'd like you to find out for yourself if teaching is for you, without all this turmoil around you that has existed this year. After all, teaching isn't right for a lot of people. It's no reflection on you." Ed's response to her was "I don't think it has hurt him or education this year."

In June, Mr. New submitted a resignation to the Director of Personnel stating simply that he would be unable to satisfy the necessary credential requirements during the summer. His real reasons for resigning were more personal and more complex. He explained to me:

I'm just not a teacher. I don't share the same values and opinions they do. I'm uncomfortable as it is, and I'd have to change too much if I was going to continue. Some of the same questions that kept me out of teaching before are still unanswered. I guess you just can't have so many unanswered questions if you are going to teach.

The problems of teaching, as Mr. New saw them, centered around two issues. The first was the lack of consensus about the purposes of teaching. The second issue stemmed from the first: if the purposes of teaching were not clearly agreed upon, how could anyone presume to evaluate teacher effectiveness? The first question seemed the more important to Mr. New, but in the course of his socialization at Taft he had come to realize the immediacy of the evaluation question for those in authority and thus for his survival as a beginning teacher. He volunteered his view of the evaluation procedure after the closing of school:

> I have some serious reservations regarding the entire evaluation procedure for teachers. How can anyone say what is "high caliber" or "low caliber" teaching? What criteria is fair when no one is really sure what teachers are supposed to be doing? Do you use classroom control as a measure? Do you check performance of the youngsters? How? Tests? Daily work? How do you know these things can really measure their growth? Are skills the only thing teachers are concerned with? What about personal and social development? What about moral precepts? Can you evaluate on the basis of, or the lack of, parent complaints, comments by other teachers, etc.?

Mr. New felt that he had been victimized by the procedures used in evaluating him as a teacher. Further, he felt that many of the internal problems of schools could be traced directly to the over-emphasis on and the inadequate means of teacher evaluation. He believed that the teacher-child relationship, the teacher-parent relationship, and even teacher-teacher contacts suffered from constant pre-occupation with it. Although he insisted "I don't mean to be bitter," he summarized his remarks with a critical review of the Taft faculty and staff:

> I have never been in association with any group (including a long-time membership in a narrow protestant church) where so much gossip, back-biting, criticizing, belittling, and phariseeism goes on as I have seen in my past year's teaching experience just concluded.

I find it instructive to think of Mr. New's socialization into teaching as "successful," although it was not successful in the way that school people like Ed or the intern supervisor use the term. In an analytical sense, however, and looking at Mr. New's case from the point of view of maintaining an on-going cultural system, the socialization process was successful because it socialized *out* of teaching an individual who resisted being socialized *into* it. Mr. New did not really have the option to "go it alone." He wanted to believe that he had that alternative, and he did so in his initial assessment of Taft School and in his enthusiasm for the philosophy of its principal, but the experience of the year did not sustain his hopes. By the end of the year he had begun to realize some limitations on the "loose structure" of the school. In response to a question asked on the staff questionnaires, "I think Mr. Bell's strongest points are ———?" he wrote: "He lets people try to work things out themselves (as long as he can)."

Ellwood New probably did not have the whole-hearted support from the principal which he imagined or hoped, especially as the year progressed. Early in the school term, Ed seemed optimistic about Ellwood, as suggested in the following comments he made in September:

> I just like his philosophy of life and education both. He didn't have much philosophy of education, but I liked his philosophy of life. He has the finest rapport with his kids, and that's the place to begin. There'll be plenty of teachable moments if you just have the rapport with kids.
>
> I've encouraged the intern supervisor to stay out of the way of our two interns, to help them only when they need help. I think they're off to a real fine start, both of them.

During the first weeks of school Ed and the intern supervisor discussed their mutual and growing concern for the way Ellwood New's class was progressing under his comparatively nondirective approach. In November the class had a discipline "blow-up" which came to the attention of Ed and the supervisor. The supervisor immediately arranged a four-way conference involving Ed, the school counsellor, Mr. New, and herself. Ed's advice to Mr. New during the conference was, "I like the [nondirective] role that I think you want to play, but these children . . . I mean . . . Maybe I should say it more directly. I think you were pushing too rapidly [i.e., being too nondirective] when this happened. Let's say your direction is good, but take it slowly." During the meeting, the university supervisor echoed the opinion that Mr. New should be "more directive" although her comments were addressed to Ed rather than to Mr. New: "Of course, I recognize that I am more directive than Ellwood," or "Ed, I once heard you say that your son at some particular point needed someone to say 'No.' "

For his part, Ellwood explained his growing concern for attempting to meet the emotional needs of all of his pupils, and how he was "getting torn up" by having to confront so many children. He said he had begun thinking that perhaps schools should attempt to meet the socio-ego needs of pupils rather than to be so concerned with subject matter. The university supervisor argued that in her opinion "content" was essential, since there had to be some focus on what went on in a classroom. Ed reinterpreted her comments in what appeared to be a defense of Mr. New's position:

> You should know that if the university supervisor or the counsellor or I come into your classroom and it's supposed to be math, and instead of math you're talking about what's happening to us as people, we won't mind a bit.

"You don't know how happy that makes me feel," responded Mr. New.

As his own account has already suggested, Mr. New's "classroom situation" did not improve. By the end of the year he had decided that classroom teaching was not for him. At about the time that Mr. New decided not to continue his teaching career, Mr. Adam informed Ed that he, too, would probably be leaving at the end of school to accept a teaching position in a nearby college. In light of Ed's frequently expressed view about the need for men in elementary school teaching, his reaction to learning that he probably would be losing his only two male classroom teachers at the end of the year was not the reaction I had anticipated:

> Adam has probably made his contribution to this faculty. If he is here another year, I doubt that he will make any more of a contribution. It will be the same. And Ellwood hasn't been any great joy to me.
>
> Losing these two fellows doesn't particularly bother me. As a matter of fact, by losing the two men on the faculty I can make a pretty good case to Dr. Goddard and Dr. Prince that my staff will need some men.

"There's Always a Shortage of Male Teachers"

"Our school district usually interviews about three times as many teachers as it can hire," Ed explained during an interview with a male candidate for a teaching position in the Columbia School District, "but this isn't true of males. There's always a shortage of male teachers." Not only Ed but all of his fellow principals voiced concern about the female-dominated atmosphere of the elementary school and echoed a long-touted slogan, "We need more men in elementary schools."[5] They exchanged information about the number of men on their faculties and, like Ed, they assumed that whenever the number or ratio of male teachers at their schools grew too slight their "bargaining position" for getting another male teacher was enhanced. They also expressed optimism in regard to a growing ratio of male to female teachers in elementary schools generally. In describing the faculty at Taft School during an interview with one young woman candidate, Ed observed: "There are only four men on the staff, including myself. I would like to have 50 percent. Maybe that day will come." He explained how within the past few days he had interviewed four *good* men candidates. "And that is a hopeful sign."

Although Ed indicated little dismay at the possibility of losing the two male classroom teachers on his own staff, he did become dismayed at stories he heard about other male teachers new to the district who were leaving teaching because of "unhappy situations" in their first-year assignments. In May he wrote a letter to the Director of Elementary Education suggesting that the district might be more effective in keeping its men teachers if more attention was paid to their inital assignments:

To: Dr. Carolyn Goddard
Re: Placement of men teachers new to the school district.

I was pleased with the promising, yet limited number of young men hired last year. I now note that at least two of these fellows will not be returning next year. There may be no way to avoid this turnover, but I would like us to consider every possible means to hold all these fellows. I believe we might be wise to give more consideration to the needs of the men to be placed where they feel they are most able to grow in the profession. Placing them in small schools with a minimum of staff interaction, or in schools with a deprived clientele may cause some potentially good people to look elsewhere for the satisfaction they expect in the profession. The need of the teacher may demand more consideration than the need of a particular school for the beginning year.

Please accept this suggestion in the light of the limited observation I have made.

Sincerely,
Edward C. Bell

There is an apparent disparity between Ed's stated preference for increasing the number of men teachers in elementary schools and actual behavior on his part which lent no particular support to the men he already had. This disparity was made more explicit in a comment which Ed made immediately after interviewing a young woman interested in a position at Taft School:

---

[5] The concern was reaffirmed nationally by the appearance of an article in the national journal of elementary school principals, "Should You Employ That Male Elementary Teacher?" (Tolbert 1968). The author pointed out that at least as far back as 1908 educators were being warned that their policy of "feminizing" the schools was "influencing and abetting maladjustment in the young male learner." Although Tolbert reported the lack of empirical research supporting the need for male instructors in early schooling, he nonetheless concluded, "Men are needed in elementary schools to serve as models for sex role identification and to lend their masculine influence to the curriculum and child" (p. 43).

Of course, I'd rather get a man. I would always take a man teacher if I could.

I interviewed one man yesterday. He was a couple of years younger than I am. I wasn't too impressed. Too old [laugh]! No, seriously, I just wasn't impressed with him.

To say that he would "always take a man teacher" in one breath and to state in the next that he did not intend to hire a man he had just interviewed does seem inconsistent. An explanation of this behavior that fits with the observed and reported behavior of principals in this study is that they universally endorse the *ideal* of staffing a school with male teachers, but they do not necessarily endorse the males who actually occupy the role. Perhaps principals expect the occupants of the ideal role to be ideal men. When the occupants fail to measure up, the principals turn their efforts as dramatically toward getting particular male teachers out of their schools, or out of teaching entirely, as they turn their energy toward recruiting males in the first place. In Columbia's elementary schools several principals, including a few men as well as all of the women administrators,[6] had reputations as principals who were invariably "tough" on male teachers. I was told of one principal who had "made trouble for at least a dozen guys" who taught under his administration.

Ed did not appear to hold strongly negative feelings toward his male teachers, but, at least in the case of Ellwood New, neither did he provide extensive support. Among the male teachers who had been at Taft School, Ed had promoted two to the position of resource teacher, the first step toward an eventual principalship for them both. He had helped or encouraged male teachers and student teachers who wished to transfer into or out of Taft School. There was some disparity in accounts given to me about whether or not Ed had ever actually requested or insisted that a teacher leave Taft School, although there were cases in which Ed acknowledged he had "not been sorry to see a teacher go." At least one such case had involved a male teacher:

I didn't ask him to leave, but I wasn't sorry to see him go. I think he had problems. Well, I kind of suspected he was homosexual. We don't need that kind around here.

In the eyes of most of the faculty, Ed was exasperatingly patient with Mr. Adam, the one regularly credentialed male classroom teacher on the faculty. The teachers probably would have been surprised (and in some cases pleased) at Ed's personal feeling that the possibility of "losing" Adam was no cause for dismay, even though

[6] In a separate paper (Wolcott 1973) I have suggested that although men predominate in the administration of elementary schools to almost the extent that women predominate in the teacher ranks (85% of the elementary school teachers are females; 78% of the school principals are males), women principals may exert a far greater influence on the principalship as *gatekeepers* to the office than they do in their minority position as female administrators. The influence of female principals as gatekeepers is heightend by the greater-than-chance assignment of male teachers to schools administered by women in the continual and self-conscious attempt on the part of educators to provide adults on a school faculty with whom male pupils can "identify." Women teachers serve in similar capacity as gatekeepers for men entering teaching. Sexton (1969) has provided a further discussion of the male-female division in schools.

Ed had also related that if Adam's college teaching assignment did not come through he could always return to his position at Taft. "No one else would want him," Ed explained. "He's too controversial." Ed had some evidence that this was true, for Adam had come to Taft School at the beginning of his second year in the district after a one-year assignment at a school administered by one of Columbia's female principals. Although that principal had recommended he be rehired, Adam was aware that her evaluation of him as a classroom teacher was something less than enthusiastic. Adam talked with her about transferring to another school. She, in turn, suggested he confer with Dr. Goddard. Adam was transferred to Taft School. Adam felt that his independence had been a "real threat" to his woman administrator. Whether his manner was also unsettling to Ed, neither Adam nor apparently even Ed himself was certain. "I like working for Ed," Adam observed during his third year at Taft, "but I'm not so sure Ed likes having me around."

THE SOCIALIZATION OF EXPERIENCED TEACHERS

Never again in the normal course of events does a teacher receive the attention that he receives while he occupies the status of beginning teacher. After the constant and intense adult interaction which characterizes entry into teaching, the absence of attention, evaluation, and help may produce a "withdrawal" phase in which second-year teachers find themselves relatively isolated from other professional contacts in the course of carrying out their teaching responsibilities. In the context of this professional isolation, visits of other professionals like the principal become more conspicuous regardless of whether they are frequent or rare occurrences. The teachers at Taft had widely varying opinions about whether Ed made sufficient visits to their classrooms (see Chapter 10). Whatever their perceptions of the extent of his visits, however, they were quite aware of any occasion when he did visit and were sensitive to the fact that every visit had implications for the inevitable administrative evaluations.

Teacher Evaluation

Ed needed two kinds of information about his "experienced" teachers. First, and the more immediately formidable, he needed to be able to prepare the formal annual teacher evaluation for the central office. Second, he needed to know in a more global way which, if any, were his teacher problems and his problem teachers.

In managing an ever-increasing cadre of permanent and probationary teachers numbering more than 1000, administrators in the school district followed detailed policy regarding which teachers in any given year were to be evaluated and what form the procedure would take. To assure systematic reporting, each principal received an annual notice from the personnel office giving the names of the teachers for whom evaluations were to be made that year, the purpose for which each teacher was to be evaluated, and the deadline date in February for submitting all evaluations to the central office. District policy required the completion of a formal evaluation report for every probationary teacher (i.e., an evaluation of every teacher during his first, second, and third year in the district) and a report once every three years for tenured teachers. Every school received an ample quantity of official pink forms, "Classroom Performance Observation Summary," and a smaller number of official green forms, "Final Evaluation Form." For each teacher to be evaluated, a principal was expected to make three formal classroom observations. Each observation necessitated a subsequent write-up on the pink form (classroom performance) and a conference with the teacher about the visit. The three completed observations provided the basis for preparing the green summary form, "Final Evaluation," which, together with the final evaluations for all teachers evaluated that year, was forwarded to the central office.

Judging by the comments and jokes revealing apprehension in preparing the evaluations and submitting them on time, Ed was not alone among his colleagues in his disdain of the evaluation task. Although every principal knew which of his teachers had to be formally evaluated before school ever opened in September, most of them followed Ed's custom of waiting until the deadline was only a few weeks away before assigning the evaluation procedure a priority for attention. When Ed realized that the deadline was fast approaching he apologized to his faculty that he could only "give it a lick and a promise this time and hope to do better next year."

Several factors can be identified which appear to contribute to the lack of enthusiasm for the evaluation task. For one thing, a conscientious job of evaluating, with three classroom visits and write-ups, three follow-up conferences, preparation of the final form, and a conference about the final form for each teacher to be evaluated, was no little task. The difficulty of the task was compounded by having to write evaluations acceptable to both the central office and to the teacher being evaluated: "It's a real problem to get it all written up and to write it up so you can talk to a teacher about it." With the large number of new and probationary teachers on his faculty, Ed had to submit 12 evaluation reports in February 1967; some of his colleagues had to prepare even more.

The observation and evaluation process produced considerable apprehension among teachers as well as among principals. No teacher at Taft could ignore the feeling that Ed's classroom visits in January and early February lacked their usual casualness. Among their colleagues, the principals expressed the discomfort they felt in performing a task so judgemental in nature, one which conflicted blatantly with the ideal of democratic administration in which most principals preferred to present themselves among their teacher colleagues as a first among equals. The evaluation procedure emphasized the hierarchical position of the principal both in terms of the subordinates whom he evaluated and the superordinates who held him responsible for completing the assignment. One principal referred to the preparation of teacher evaluations as the "most impossible" of his many duties:

> It's impossible to get people to do a good job for you when you are supposed to write evaluations about them 'with some teeth in it,' and that is what THEY expect you to do.

Perhaps the most perplexing aspect of the evaluation procedure was the unstated (and perhaps unrecognized) fact that for all the work and apprehension associated with them, the evaluations themselves served ritual functions far more than real ones in the sticky business of getting rid of a teacher. Ed once commented in this regard, "There are a lot of ways to get rid of a bad teacher. There are a lot of subtle ways that are effective." The public nature of the evaluation form (it had to be signed by both teacher and principal before it was complete) precluded the making of offensive or libelous remarks about an undesirable teacher. At the same time, no teacher expected to have a "perfect" report lacking in recommendations for ways he might improve his effectiveness. The consequence was that the format of both the evaluation form and the ritual ceremony during which it was discussed necessitated a delicate but predictable combination blending strong points with suggestions for improvement couched in sufficiently ambiguous language to allow for flexibility in interpretation and "reading between the lines." Yet in a school like Taft where the administrator consciously attempted to make the staff comfortable, explicitly negative comments and even implicitly negative ones recorded on an evaluation form had the potential for creating deep and lasting impressions on teachers for whom impending decisions about tenure required favorable administrative review.

For two teachers on probationary status, the evaluation process was particularly critical. Both were older women (Mrs. Elder in her late fifties, Mrs. Skirmish in her late forties) who had recently returned to full-time teaching. Since they were "experienced" teachers, neither was subjected to the close surveillance given to beginning teachers in the building, even though both teachers were new to Taft School. Thus the formal evaluation process provided virtually the only official appraisal of their teaching which either of them received during her first year at Taft. Each of them had, in fact, described her year as being somewhat "lonely," in striking contrast to Mr. New's constant parade of evaluators. As a result of Ed's observations and subsequent conferences about their classroom work, both teachers felt they were reviewed negatively. Until late in the spring, each felt that she had been singled out as the only teacher in the building who had been given a "poor" evaluation. A sense of relief seemed to be shared between them (and extended eventually to Mr. New) when they discovered they were not alone in the uncomfortable position of being out-of-favor with the principal.

The complex process of socializing experienced teachers into Taft School is revealed through the specific cases of these two teachers, Mrs. Elder and Mrs. Skirmish. As with every teacher new to the school, each of these two teachers brought a unique personality and personal history, and each precipitated a unique set of encounters with Ed during the rather extended course of her socialization. Along the way Ed, too, was socialized, particularly since he was dealing not only with teachers but with people who otherwise were peers in statuses like age, experience, family and community position, and, in one case, personal friendship, as well as with the individual personalities of two strong-willed professional women.

Postponing a Decision: The Socialization of Margaret Elder

Excerpts from an interview made in January with Mrs. Margaret Elder reveal her reactions as a new member of the faculty and her reaction to Ed's first classroom observation and follow-up conference with her. As she explained, the fact that she had expected to be assigned a fifth grade, the grade level at which she had taught most often, and had suddenly been changed to a sixth grade at the last minute, had made her initial adjustment to Taft School more difficult than she had anticipated:

> I feel a little at a loss yet. I'm getting my feet on the ground to some degree. At this grade level, where there are three teachers, you might say I'm the newest one in camp. I have no communication with the others. Mr. Adam put me fairly straight within the first couple of days that his plan was to work with the young woman teacher who was assigned to the other sixth grade. So I said okay, and I sort of carried my own banner here for this one sixth grade. I felt a bit like an orphan. Yet I have self-confidence enough so that I know that I'll pull through some way or other.
>
> My main experience has been in the fifth grade. I asked for that grade in this district and was told by the main office that's what I would have. I came out in May or June to talk to Mr. Bell. Then I didn't see him again until about the last week in August. I called one day and asked if I could come out and bring some things and he said yes, that he wanted to talk to me. And the first thing he said, and this came as a surprise: "I've changed you from a fifth to a sixth." I wondered how long this change had been made and if it might have been possible to let me know ahead of time, because I had been planning on this and most of my materials were for that level. I didn't have much chance to make any plans. And I was taken back a little bit. But he said that with my experience I could no doubt handle it.
>
> That, plus the fact that there was two other sixth grades which were going off of other ends, made me feel kind of alone and wondering, "Am I going to hack this or am I not?"
>
> Actually, I've come along pretty well. I have good rapport with the youngsters. We do things without interference or interferring with other people. We're moving along fine.
>
> I would prefer that this closeness existed with my superiors. I never have worked where I didn't feel real free to go in and state my problems and ask what did they have to talk over with me. And I don't feel that here.
>
> I've had one evaluation conference. The thing I think is that it was hasty. I had an appointment at quarter after four. I had the coffee duty that week, so I was in the faculty room changing the coffee. I think the counsellor was talking to me, telling me about something she wanted me to see her about the next day. Mr. Bell came in and said, "Can I see you in the office for a few minutes?"
>
> I said, "Yes, just as soon as I get the coffee pot going."
>
> So I went in, and he said, "Couldn't you give me a little time?"
>
> I laughed and said, "About 20 minutes."
>
> He said that this business [of making classroom observations] was one of the things he had needed to do and he had started doing, and so forth.
>
> It was just hasty. I felt that if he had said, "Let's meet tomorrow evening after school," or "How about such and such a time?" it would have given me a little time to calm down, so I would know what it was about.
>
> In another district where I taught, I worked on a committee on teacher evaluation. We did quite a bit of research—the other members more than I— and I was the guinea pig when they ran the first teacher evaluation. My principal called me in and said, "Okay, Margaret, shall we have this evaluation lesson, say, on Wednesday afternoon? Would that be alright?" There was no specified time, but the *day* was specified, at least, so you had a little bit of an idea. I was unaware of the time he came in that afternoon. He was in the room

at least 15 minutes before I knew he was there, and he left about ten minutes after that. Then we met on it the next morning. It was a little more systematic, a little more personal, a little more of what you are really getting at.

When I was evaluated here, the principal stayed for a bit, then I think maybe he came back again that same morning. He sat in on a high reading group of 8 youngsters. We were doing some oral reading about Louis Braille. There was a little article in their reader and the last part of it showed examples from the Braille alphabet. I had asked that lady who teaches the little blind boy here at school if she would come in and talk to them about Braille subsequent to this. So we were just reading this orally to catch up on some ideas, and to see how they had come out on their vocabulary, and to discuss generally what they had read.

I don't too often have that group read orally, but we just happened to. In his evaluation, Ed asked me why this was done. And so I told him. And he said, "Well, then, that is a case where I was too hasty. I didn't know that was the plan or what was the objective," and so forth.

At the same time that Ed formally recommended Mrs. Elder for "Advancement to Second Year Probationary Status" he conveyed to her his reservations about her traditional approach to teaching and the conditional nature of the recommendation he had given her. Long before the submission of his first evaluation report, Ed conveyed some of the initial reservations he felt about Mrs. Elder's teaching. In the period of time from the beginning of school to the submission of his formal report, he substantiated with classroom observations an assessment that had initially been an intuitive, personal reaction. She simply was not the kind of teacher he preferred to have on his faculty. Remarks which Ed made over the period of a year and a half and presented here chronologically suggest the changing content of his rationale.

In September, after three weeks of school, Ed said (during a taped interview):

Margaret Elder was a little unhappy about being placed with the sixth grade when she thought she was going to get fifth grade. Adam and the other sixth-grade teacher had gotten acquainted last year and had agreed to do some cooperative teaching in their sixth-grade classes. They didn't feel like taking in another person that they didn't know and that didn't know their way around the material and so on. So Margaret did feel a little left out in the sixth grade situation.

I have a feeling that she may have some personal problems that stand in the way of her really getting hold of a task and going to work.

She is an experienced teacher and has taught quite a few years. She taught part time in the district last year, and the principals that worked with her recommended her quite highly. But I've been a little disappointed with her.

---

⁷ Ed seemed strongly swayed by an "individualized" approach to reading and opposed to "traditional" methods of group instruction, including the practice of having pupils take turns reading a story aloud. He drew upon the fact that he observed both of the older probationary teachers using oral reading in support of his assessment of them as traditional (i.e., old-fashioned) teachers. His bias is reflected in the brief entries he made following his visit in Mrs. Elder's reading class: *Discipline*: "Good"; *Development of Mental Processes*: "Seemed lacking."

Ten months later, beginning his next annual round of evaluations, Ed again observed a reading lesson in Mrs. Elder's class. His brief written comments were virtually the same: *Discipline*: "No problem"; *Development of Mental Processes*: "Not seen." Ed added a summary comment the second year: "An atmosphere of quiet rapport was evident. The work seemed routine and lacking in challenge."

Maybe she will come along right now. Martha Duchess has been more than great to help her. Martha knew a lot of the kids that Margaret Elder has now because she worked with them as fifth-graders last year. She has a lot of reading material, and she's been helping her to understand the new math.[8]

Ed tried to sustain some optimism through the initial weeks of the school year. In November he commented, "I'm real pleased with Margaret Elder. She is getting along fine." By February, however, his optimism had waned. During Ed's own evaluation conference at the central office, two weeks before he submitted evaluation reports for his teachers, Ed alerted the Director of Elementary Education and the Assistant Superintendent to the fact that he considered Margaret one of his "problem" teachers. His remarks about her included the following (see Chapter 8):

> Margaret Elder has wonderful rapport with kids, but the children in her class just aren't making the progress the other children are.
> She's an older person with lots of experience. . . . She's very pleasant, but she seems aloof. I just haven't gotten to know much about her. . . . She's friendly enough, but she doesn't say something like "I wish I knew how to do such-and-such."

That Mrs. Elder did not ask "how to do such-and-such" eventually became a clearer issue in an important but obliquely stated comment Ed made that Margaret had been teaching too long to be amenable to change. Margaret recounted the comments Ed made directly to her:

> You have an exceptionally good rapport with children. They like you. Parents like you. But I feel you don't allow them to do enough and varied things. . . . Your older tricks may need "retooling" with summer courses, et cetera.

Whatever his reservations, Ed eventually decided to have Margaret remain on his staff for the following year. As soon as he made that decision, he again became more supportive in his assessment of her and optimistic in his prognosis about her teaching. In April, speaking to a parent, he said:

> **Mrs. Elder is going to be here next year. And I agree that she is firm. She's pretty organized in her approach. But she has a lot of empathy, too.**

Margaret taught sixth grade again during her second year at Taft School. For her part, in spite of some reservations of her own about remaining at Taft, she felt it was better to stay in one school for two or three years since she was "re-establishing" herself in the state after having resided and taught in another state for the past several years. She spoke of feeling more confident about her classroom teaching during the second year. But she had recognized a basic difference between her

---

[8] Margaret Elder's own perception of Mrs. Duchess focused on Mrs. Duchess's status within the school rather than on Margaret's need for "help." Like many other teachers, Margaret felt that Mrs. Duchess acted as the unofficial vice principal of Taft School, at least for the upper-grade wing, and that probably Mrs. Duchess's appraisal of Margaret's teaching had been an important influence in Ed's evaluation. As Margaret explained:

I feel that Ed throws lots of responsibility to Mrs. Duchess. That is all right if you recognize who that person is who has the responsibility. It's something that you sort of gather after a bit. It isn't pointed out to you at the beginning who this person is who *would be* the assistant principal if there was one.

own classroom approach and the "loose structure" which Ed advocated. In Margaret's words:

> This school operates on the premise that children learn more from an environment permitting a maximum of freedom and permissiveness with a minimum of demonstrating responsibility for one's own acts. For those of us who believe that freedom comes only after one *earns* it, this becomes a problem.

The problem was more than a mere difference of opinion. Ed felt that Margaret approached her second year of teaching at Taft in the same "traditional" manner as her first year. Once again he became uneasy about the thought of having her remain permanently on his staff. A second recommendation for rehiring her would be taken both by Margaret and by the central office as an implicit statement of his intent to recommend her for tenure. In Ed's eyes, Margaret's second year only confirmed the existence of problems and shortcomings he felt he had recognized from the beginning. In January he drafted a memorandum to Dr. Goddard stating that he did not plan to recommend that Margaret stay on in the school district:

> Mrs. Elder is teaching her second year with us. Last year I indicated to her that her program needed to be more challenging. I felt she should be aware of some of the newer teaching techniques in areas of Science and Social Studies. She took an in-service course with our staff which emphasized the inquiry method and others. I have not seen any evidence that she has tried any of these ideas. She attends classes in Spanish and Social Studies and yet shows no signs of deviating from the traditional textbook approach. Earlier this year I suggested that she seek help from Bob Mason, our resource teacher; and from the Language Arts consultant in the central office. She likes to watch while Bob teaches her class. She did visit with the consultant on an occasion I initiated, but did not invite him to return.
>
> On at least two occasions, parents have complained to me about some physical rough handling of children. I have arranged a conference with parent, child, teacher, and me in each case. She has minimized the situation and given assurance of her respect for the child.
>
> Her carefully structured classroom situation has been helpful to some children. She provides an adequate program in music, art, and an unimaginative presentation of the skill subjects. She is well liked by other members of the staff. My own personal relations with her have always been comfortable.
>
> I do not consider her a poor teacher, but I feel she has not shown the capacity to grow to be the quality teacher our district demands. Therefore, I plan to recommend her contract not be renewed.
>
> Some weeks ago I asked that she give me a general outline of long-range plans for teaching Social Living. This she has not done.

Ed put the handwritten draft of his letter in Mrs. Elder's file in his office. He decided to review his notes in a few days after he had "cooled down," for the draft was written in a strong and direct tone. Later he decided not to send the note after all. The original draft of the letter remained in Margaret's file at school without further action. The following month Ed recommended her for promotion to third-year probationary status: "I thought of not recommending Margaret. She is so traditional in her ways. For awhile, I thought I should not recommend her. But I will recommend her." By the end of school Ed had decided that he would "probably" keep her on the faculty: "She is doing better and there is no problem now." In any case he postponed his final disposition until the next and, for Margaret, the last possible evaluation period:

> I think I'll probably stick with her. I have until February to make up my mind. I never did send the letter to Carolyn, although I talked to her about it. Margaret hesitates to ask for help. She will ask the resource teacher to do things for her, but she won't ask for help in what she should do.

Ed never had to make a final decision. Although Margaret Elder was scheduled to return to Taft School again in the fall, she resigned her position during the summer and took a teaching assignment in another district, one in which she had taught previously and where she felt that her teaching had been highly regarded. Ed held marital problems responsible for her apparently sudden decision to leave Taft. Perhaps personal problems did account for her decision; perhaps her intuitive suspicion that Ed might not support her candidacy for tenure the following year also played some part in her leaving. Possibly she never intended to remain at Taft, for she confided to at least one staff member during her first year that she only planned to stay one more year. In any case, her decision to leave Taft School precluded Ed's having to make a decision which might affect whether she would remain in teaching at all.

"Trading" Problems

Principals are said to "trade" their problem teachers rather than "eliminate" them. Margaret Elder provides a case in point. Ed was reluctant to argue that she was a "bad" teacher, even though his initial assessment of her was negative and he was never satisfied with evidence of much improvement. But his concern was whether or not to keep her at Taft School, not whether she should continue in teaching, and it may have been his rather apparent ambivalence that led her to resign. A nontenured teacher confronted with the possibility of being denied tenure, and any teacher confronted with a threat of dismissal, is customarily encouraged or "persuaded" to resign rather than be fired (see Warren 1968:14). Had Margaret been a tenured teacher in the district, Ed's apparent ambivalence about her effectiveness would probably have posed less of a threat to her. If Ed had felt strongly about getting her out of Taft School in that case, he would have gone to more effort to find a rationale for suggesting that she consider a transfer—for example, by finding a vacancy in a school nearer her home, by finding an opening in a grade level or new program that seemed attractive to her, or by appealing to her professional integrity to find a school and administrator more compatible with her own personality and teaching style.

The process of teacher reassignment within the same school district has not been totally ignored (see Becker 1952a, 1953), but data are scarce regarding either the cumulative effect of reassignment and "trading" of professional personnel from building to building or the complex interpersonal situations which must lie at the root of many such transfers. Central office personnel, the people who compile and release statistics, customarily report figures which affect the district as a whole, such as net gains or losses and the number of new people hired. Such data obscure the internal transfers which directly affect individual schools, staffs, and principals. Yet even if the numbers of internal transfers were reported, it would be difficult to obtain accurate information about why teachers move out of some schools and how they happen to select others. The sometimes highly personal reasons for which people actually request trades are easily hidden behind routine explanations (or what one teacher referred to as "legitimate reasons") like "want a school nearer home." One teacher new to Taft School but tenured in the district explained how the reasons she had offered for a transfer varied even between what she told the principal of her former school and what she told Ed:

> I'd been at my other school for three years. The two first-grade teachers that were in the school were very nice to me, but they worked all by themselves. They didn't care to plan together. I wanted to try things like individualized reading and the new social studies. I had no one to work with. That was one reason. Then we moved out in this area, so it was closer for us. It was a ten or fifteen minute drive before, and now it's just five minutes. Another teacher who had moved out in this area told me there was a first-grade opening here at Taft.
>
> I talked to my principal and told him that I would like to change because we had moved, and he said fine. I came over and talked to Mr. Bell that day and he called downtown and I had the position that afternoon. For two reasons, then, because I felt I needed a change and because I wanted to work more closely with my co-workers. And it was closer to where I lived.

Even before construction was finished on the initial eight-classroom unit that was to house the new Taft School, Ed had begun looking for teachers who might be interested in coming to a new school and whose reasons for wanting to leave their present assignments did not unduly arouse his suspicion. A candid statement that a teacher was dissatisfied with the principal in his present assignment, at least if used with some astuteness, could provide a legitimate reason for desiring to transfer to another school, for Ed was no less vulnerable than most administrators to the suggestion that *his* was the kind of school a teacher had been looking for. Thus to be uncomfortable in schools administered by colleagues with whom Ed felt his own philosophy to be at odds customarily produced a sympathetic note and sometimes elicited an offer of a position at Taft.

In addition to considering teachers anxious for reassignment, Ed was given the authority to invite any two teachers he wished to bring to the new staff whom he felt would be an asset in creating a new faculty. Mrs. Duchess commented in this regard on her transfer to Taft School:

> Mr. Bell came in as principal of the school where I had been teaching. I taught that year with him. Then he was transferred to this new school. He gave me the opportunity to come over here in the upper elementary as one teacher that he would know, had been familiar with, and had worked with. And, of course, this made about a ten minute drive from home for me. I've been at Taft School ever since it opened.

From its opening year to the time of the field study, the Taft teaching faculty had tripled in number, and Ed's major personnel problem had been the recruitment of new teachers. Recently, as the pupil population as well as the Taft faculty had begun to stabilize, Ed could afford to take a more critical look at the staff already on hand. Occasionally he found himself offering encouragement to certain of his teachers who hinted that they were thinking about transferring. In some cases, he may have helped plant the idea to "look elsewhere" in the first place. A senior teacher reported an instance of a teacher who had been one of the original teachers invited to Taft School but whom, in her words, Ed had eventually "outgrown":

Ed outgrew Priscilla Edmonds. I mean, professionally he grew and she didn't. They were real good friends, and they worked together for years. When Ed became the principal here, he asked her to come with him because, like anyone, when he goes to a new job he likes to have someone he can depend on. She helped him. I'm sure there is a list a mile long of things Priscilla Edmonds helped him with. And he appreciated it.

But after a certain point, he was ready to stand on his own two feet. He didn't appreciate this help any more, because it wasn't good for the rest of the staff members. Even I resented it. [Laugh.] She didn't really have any special relationship with him, but she led everybody to believe it. She would say, "Ed said this," or "Ed and I talked about this." She would always start out that way.

I think when Ed saw this happening, then he . . . well, he wasn't always nice to her. He wasn't rude or anything, but he just kind of went the other way. That hurt her, because she is a very insecure person. She always has to feel she has someone she is helping. Well, he didn't need her help any more. So she went over to another school. There's a young new principal there and I'm afraid she is doing the same thing there.

There was considerable variation of opinion at Taft regarding the extent of administrative persuasion in several recent cases where teachers had transferred out of their school. The staff also varied in their perception of the relative extent of staff turnover at Taft School and of the "real" reasons behind the transfers, as comments volunteered during taped interviews suggest:

We've had a tremendous turnover in staff this year. Some of it might be due to the way things were last year, but I think very little of it. I think most of the staff people had other legitimate reasons for leaving. I don't think there is a single staff person this year that would be leaving because of feelings where Mr. Bell is concerned or a feeling where the philosophy of our building—the way we try to handle children—is concerned. I'm almost positive.

I think that Mr. Bell intimated to one former teacher [criticized for too-rough handling of children] more than once that he really shouldn't consider trying to stay here. I believe he was a tenured teacher.

I know of only one staff person, other than this one, that he asked to leave, which is pretty good, percentage-wise. We had a woman teacher one time—she was not tenured—that he did ask to leave. He just asked her to shift to another building, because she simply couldn't go along with the philosophy of this building. She was much more traditional and came from a completely different set-up. She wasn't about to change or roll with the punches.

I think the fact that only two people are leaving, because their husbands are being transferred, says something with the staff that's here this year. Last year there was more of a turnover. I know that several people last year left because they did not agree in philosophy. I can think of two that left because they wanted to work under a different administration.

The teachers don't always agree with Ed's ideas. I feel that last year this was one of the primary reasons for our large turnover of teachers.

We had a lot of people transfer last year—Mrs. Edmonds, Mr. White, Mrs. Tupper, Mrs. Campbell. It wasn't that they didn't like Ed. They all liked Ed. They just weren't comfortable working across the hall from Wally Adam. It's too noisy. They used these other excuses—they wanted to "get to a school closer to home" —but really, that was the basis.

We had a couple of teachers leave last year, but I think it was mainly because of living closer to other schools. I don't think it was because they were necessarily displeased with the way things were. They may have been happier in a different system under different conditions. Generally speaking, I think this would be the kind of school that teachers would want to transfer to if they were in this living vicinity and it was as accessible as any other school. I can't see any reason why anybody would not want to, myself.

The professional term for moving staff personnel from one school to another was "transfer," and principals were careful to use that term in the presence of their teachers. In their own circles, however, they also referred to the process as "trading teachers." The offhand manner in which such remarks were made suggested that anyone advertising a "trade" was actually signalling that he was having problems with a teacher rather than that he seriously expected anyone to take him up on the offer. Only twice did I record Ed referring directly to "trading." On one occasion, the subject was brought up by another principal during a meeting in Ed's office attended by several principals and intern supervisors:

VISITING PRINCIPAL[9]:   Does anyone have any duds he wants to trade? I've got one teacher who doesn't relate very well to the staff, although she does a fair job in the classroom. She's strictly "self-contained."
ED: I've got one that almost sounds like her. But I don't want to trade. Anyway, this person [Margaret Elder] isn't on tenure.
VISITING INTERN SUPERVISOR: That's the kind of person you should get rid of. She's just waiting to get on tenure.
ED: Yeah. I shouldn't *trade* her [i.e., I should get rid of her].

On another occasion, Ed received word from the central office of the assignment to Taft of a man teacher new to the district. Ed's initial reaction to the assignment was negative—he had not been favorably impressed with the candidate during an interview earlier that spring. He commented, as he reached for the telephone to call Dr. Goddard about the assignment:

He's the least likely of the bunch [among the available new male teachers]. But maybe he's good trading stock. There's still a little of the old horsetrader in me.

Ed got a busy signal on his call. As he hung up, he said, "Maybe I ought to sit tight awhile." He did not make the call again, and the assignment remained as originally made. Ed's subsequent references to the new teacher took a more positive turn. In this case, the busy signal cast the decisive vote by calling off the trade.

Resolving Differences: The Socialization of Alma Skirmish

Alma Skirmish came to Taft School as an experienced teacher and a long-time personal acquaintance of its principal. Her career had begun with an assignment

---

[9] During the ensuing conversation, this principal remarked that in his school (of about the same enrollment as Taft) he had had 64 different classroom teachers in the previous six years.

to a one-room rural school teaching eight grades, and she had taught for nine full years in three different states. In recent years she had been on the "substitute list" for the Columbia schools, preferring to teach occasionally rather than hold a full-time teaching position while her own children were young. She had met Ed not long after he had moved to Columbia, and when he had been promoted to his first "interim" principalship, she was asked to take his class for the remainder of the year. Even before that assignment, she and Ed had discovered many shared interests: both of them had grown up on farms and had received their formal education in the Midwest, both lived lives focused around family and church activities, they lived in the same part of town, and they each had a child in the same grade at school. They were also of about the same age, although Alma admitted the possibility that she might be "just a little bit older" than Ed. Alma shared an interest in music with Ed's wife. The two families had often visited together in the past.

During Ed's first full year as a principal, he had often called upon Alma to substitute for absent teachers. When a vacancy occurred in the faculty of one of the two small schools which he administered, he asked Alma to accept the responsibility of staying on with the class until the following June. Since they lived in the same part of town, they often traveled to school together. As Alma noted:

> I would ride to school and back with him. This was a good chance to visit. So he knows a lot about the background of our family. Sometimes we talked over such things as our ideas about bringing up children. We differ on quite a few of these things. We've been able to allow each other to differ, so far.
>
> Anyway, *up until this year*, I didn't know this man could get upset about anything.

Alma had continued teaching as a substitute teacher for several years: "Each time I taught, they've asked me if I would go on in the fall again, but I wasn't ready to teach full time." She felt that Ed had been one of the people who had especially encouraged her to return to full-time teaching, and she had finally decided to do so. She taught for one year at another school in the district, and then asked Ed if she could take one of the second-grade openings she had heard about at Taft:

> I remember Ed being real kind in the criticism he would give and his recommendations. He was trying to encourage me to go on teaching full-time and telling me that he felt I was needed. He liked the way I related to the kids and the way they related to me. And I thought, "Well, it would be real good to get over to Taft School and teach under him."

Alma's formal reason for transferring was the customary one: to teach in a school closer to home. She also hinted at some personal misgivings about the principal in her first assignment that may have played an important part in her wishing to go to another school:

> He's a very austere, quiet, reserved man. And just so particular about details. You itemize every little pencil you take out of the supply room. He was very supportive of his teachers, and you could feel like he was really behind you, but you'd better know just why you used anything for what you did.
>
> Until I got to know this man, I feared him. I thought I was working under pressure, because he wasn't one to visit with us casually or anything.

It was important for Alma Skirmish to be assigned to a school where she would receive a favorable recommendation for the next two probationary years. Her husband and family were long-time residents and permanent members of the community; if she was going to teach, she was going to teach in Columbia. Certain factors which militated against the possibility of her receving tenure in the Columbia School District—advanced age is not generally esteemed in hiring elementary school teachers, and Alma's many years of experience made her a high-priced addition to the payroll—would only be multiplied in adjacent districts by a failure to get tenure in a home district in which she had been teaching intermittently for years. She assumed that at Taft School, with her long acquaintanceship with Ed Bell, she was virtually assured of a successful teaching experience and favorable recommendation. For his part, Ed must have seen a chance to fill one of the many vacancies in his staff with a mature and experienced teacher of excellent character. If he had any professional reservations, they were overshadowed by obligations to grant a personal request from a long-time acquaintance and friend of the family.

What happened during that year, and particularly during that part of the year between the opening of school and the completion of Ed's evaluation report in February, must have been the very antithesis of either of their hopes. In the many incidents which I observed or which were reported to me, Ed and Alma seemed to be caught in what is described socially as a "personality conflict." Their conflict had to be rooted in feelings much deeper than could be aroused by any of the single incidents in what became a flood of minor issues on which they invariably ended up in opposition to each other. Almost any interaction between them seemed to find them at loggerheads, each lacking the charity of conceding an alternative explanation or point of view, each in turn attributing such myopia to be the basic shortcoming of the other.

Her second year of full-time teaching in the district was a critical one for Alma if she was to be successful in winning tenure. Three transfers in three years would in itself be an indication that something was wrong. Alma's second probationary year was also critical in terms of her permanent assignment in the district. For whatever the reasons, if Ed did not want Alma to remain on his faculty, her first year at Taft was the only year in which he could get rid of her, since after recommending that she be rehired for a second year in a row, it would look strange if he reversed himself and declared her ineligible for a third. And once she received tenure at his school she was likely to become one of his permanent teachers, for if his perception of her as a possibly unsatisfactory addition to his staff was correct, she would be almost impossible to trade once she had tenure. Principals in the district seemed remarkably aware of who constituted "dead wood" on the faculties of their colleagues.

Several months after her evaluation conference with Ed, Alma volunteered a long account of her view of the events of her year at Taft, particularly the events relating to her evaluation. To provide a context for excerpts from that account, it seems appropriate first to present some data concerning the types of issues and incidents which had arisen in the six months prior to the evaluation conference itself.

1. In September, as Ed summarized the beginning weeks of school, he said of

Alma's class: "We have a problem boy in her class. Alma is from the old school. She figures, 'Well, this kid has got to learn something today. He's got to, simply because these are the rules and I'm bigger than he is. He has to do it this way.' We're really having as much of a problem right now with the teacher as with the child . . . I've been in there probably eight or ten times. But don't get the idea that I spent eight or ten hours. Just visits."

2. In October, Ed encouraged the six first- and second-grade teachers to adopt, on a trial basis, a "split reading" program in which half the children in each classroom came early for reading instruction and the other half remained later in the afternoon. Alma alone was vehemently opposed to the idea from the first suggestion of it, and she remained opposed to it after it was adopted. In November she reported to Ed at lunch one day that the parents of her pupils had been complaining about the program during her conferences with them: "The parents are really upset about this new reading. Practically every one of them complained about it." Another second-grade teacher joined the conversation: "Oh, really! I just love it. I didn't have any complaints. The parents think it's fine."

3. In November, just before the hour when the first parent conferences were to begin, Ed checked in the halls to see that teachers had put chairs out for parents awaiting their appointments. No chairs had been placed outside Alma's door. Ed stepped in the room to remind her. She answered that she planned to sit on pupil chairs at a table. Ed said, "You'll want these big [adult] chairs for your conferences, won't you?" Alma repeated that she planned to use the small chairs, if that was all right. Ed nodded, then carried a big chair to place outside the door.

4. In November, prior to the first Teacher Work Day of the school year, Alma told Ed that members of her church had approached her about the possibility of her meeting her Sunday school class during the Work Day, since she would not actually be teaching at school and the children would be available for religious instruction. Alma asked that she be allowed to do it, offering to make up any hours owed to the school district before or after school on other days. Ed told her that she belonged at school on that day. Her reaction to his decision, as he later described the incident to Dr. Goddard, was, "I'm disappointed in you, Ed." He added, "If that's her judgment, I'm disappointed in her." [I know of no other single statement made to Ed in the two years that rankled him any more than Alma's comment on that occasion, "I'm disappointed in you, Ed."]

5. In December, Ed wanted to find a primary-grade child during the noon recess. He went out to the schoolyard. No teacher was on duty.[10] Some children came to him as soon as they spotted him to report a boy throwing rocks. Ed returned to the office via an outside route to check the playground supervision schedule to see who was supposed to be on duty. It was Alma. Meanwhile, Alma had gone to the playground via an inside route through the building. Ed had not

---

[10] Failure to be present during assigned periods of supervisory duty appears to be a universal and surefire way for teachers to induce administrative displeasure. The legal responsibility for providing proper supervision at all hours of the school day is the immediate rationale, but there are often moral overtones of "being reliable" and "taking one's job seriously" as well. It is not the kind of mistake one overlooks or forgives in a teacher already out-of-favor.

seen her, thus setting up the following exchange later in the day: "I didn't see you on yard duty at noon." "That's funny! I was there."

6. In December, Ed suggested in casual conversation that with such a strongly-felt religious commitment Alma might be happier in full-time work in Christian education rather than in the secular setting of the public schools. He commented afterwards, "I'm not sure if it took or not." It was his first attempt to communicate to her his hesitancy about her continuing to teach in the public schools.

7. Just before Christmas, in a classroom discussion about that holiday, a child in Alma's class pressed for a direct answer to the question, "Is there really a Santa Claus?" Her explanation included that there was not. Word of her pronouncement spread rapidly. Before the impact of the episode had faded, three parents had constituted themselves an investigating committee to come to the principal and ascertain why such matters could not be left to the home. Alma reported her admiration for the way Ed handled the problem and came to her defense, although she seemed oblivious to the cumulative effect such incidents might have on his overall assessment of her as a teacher:

> He was absolutely great. He just carried the ball. For one thing, he kept assuring them, "There's no religious issue here." Which there wasn't and he was right. And he kept saying, "When they asked her a question and wanted a 'yes or no answer,' you wouldn't want her to lie. You wanted her to tell the truth. What else could she do?"
> And then he told me about the mother who was making this problem—that she had been a problem through the years and that she kind of always bugged him. And I thought this was a closed issue entirely.

8. In January, Ed learned that Mrs. Skirmish customarily included a prayer of thanks in her classroom during the midmorning snack of milk and crackers. He asked her to recite it for him and advised her not to continue using it. She questioned how as a good Christian he could say such a thing. He responded, "This is no place for any minority to press its view. This is a public school, not a parochial school. I'm in it because I think I can make more of a contribution here without compromising my beliefs. I don't think you should even use the word 'God' in a classroom moment of thanks. Just say 'Thanks' and let it be as deep as each child wants."

On this occasion Ed asked once again if Alma had given serious thought to full-time work in Christian education. She asked why he kept making the suggestion. He replied, "You feel a compulsion to witness in a day and age that brings us pretty close to conflict between church and state." Alma reminded Ed that she had only talked to the counsellor and to him about these things. She suggested that perhaps she simply should not have brought the subject up with him. Ed softened the exchange by concluding, "Maybe you and I are just more sensitive than others about the religious issue."

9. At noontime one day in February, Alma entered the faculty room after supervising the primary lunch period in the cafeteria. She shook her head in exasperation and announced to everyone present her concern over the behavior in the cafeteria. She reported that many children had not eaten their meals. Ed retorted, "This is what I think about kids and food: a kid will eat what he needs." Alma

immediately disagreed; she insisted that the noise and excitement in the cafeteria caused children to eat less. Speaking to no one in particular, but effectively terminating the exchange, Ed commented that if there was less noise and commotion in the faculty room he would probably eat more, precisely what he did *not* need to do.

10. In February, Alma requested two days of leave in order to accompany her husband to a national church meeting. Ed felt strongly that she should not make such a trip during school, so strongly that he told her to take the matter up with the Personnel Director. Later, Alma reported to Ed that she had talked with the Personnel Director and that he had not shared Ed's reservations about taking the leave: "He was very nice about it. He said they are happy to do this as long as it doesn't interfere with the children, and he didn't think it did." The following dialogue ensued:

ED: I'm not very excited about your going. I think you got that the other day.

ALMA: Yes. I hate to lose a friend over it. I would like to talk to you about that. If you feel it makes you uncomfortable, it's not worth doing.

ED: I have a feeling that if you worked for the telephone company I don't think you'd take it off. You'd take it during your vacation.

ALMA: No, if it was the telephone company, I wouldn't care. It's because of the children.

ED: My position is this. It would be a real administrative problem if all teachers did it. Let's see, with twenty teachers, times four days . . . you're really taking four days, but two of them happen to fall on a weekend. . . . Oh, well, maybe I'm just superdedicated!!

ALMA: Yes. Maybe you can't expect us to be that dedicated. But if you feel it would hurt our relationship, I just won't send it in. It doesn't seem to matter to you how the Personnel Director feels about it.

ED: He's so far removed from the classroom. And you're just a name on a list.

ALMA: Do you think it would hurt the classroom?

ED: It's hard to say.

ALMA: With that classroom? What about the time you had a chance to go on your church board, with four meetings a year?

ED: I never asked. It bothered my conscience too much. When our church held its national meeting in the state, I only went on Saturday and Sunday.

ALMA: You don't need to send this in if you don't want. I respect you as a principal. But I kinda have this feeling that, well, first of all you're an individual. And I'm an individual. We have individual needs.

ED: As school people, we have an obligation to show that we are willing to give our best to the job. We ask for special compensation because ours is a subjective job. We have a special obligation to say at all times that we put forth our best efforts for this group of children. Teachers being absent from children isn't good for children.

ALMA: Well, maybe it is. They need change. I don't mean to push this. You don't know how much I've thought about this. I told my husband you take this very seriously.

ED: I think from a Christian point of view we have to show that this doesn't give us special privileges. . . . I'll sign this and send it in. But I think that in another year we'll have to look at the calendar.

ALMA: If I thought school had to be the most important thing, I might want to transfer to another school where it wasn't the only thing.

ED: Well, I see it as a contract. I think you and I have a greater obligation to meet our contract. . . . Go ahead and go. I'll send it in.

ALMA: (with a sigh of relief, and attempting to end the discussion on a pleasant
note) I hope word of this doesn't get out. I'd hate to have all twenty teachers
come in and ask!

After reconsidering, Alma decided *not* to take the time off from school.

The following week, Ed called her in for her formal evaluation conference. When
she entered his office, he handed her the written evaluation form for her to read
and sign. She read it over, apparently taken aback by its negative tone. Yet with
her second sentence she immediately engaged in the counter-socialization that had
characterized their relationship from the beginning of school: "This is just about
the opposite of my other recommendations. They'll wonder just how this fits in
with those."

They discussed what Ed had written on the evaluation form sentence by sentence. "Maybe you ought to think about transferring across town where there are
no problems," Ed offered as a general solution to their item by item disagreement.
Alma asked for examples, offered new information, rationalized problems, pointed
out typographical errors (Ed: "This wasn't the secretary's best day. She went home
sick, you know") and contrasted Ed's observations with those of her previous
administrator. Halfway through their conversation Ed assured her: "I think you're
a more-than-adequate teacher, and very intelligent. Maybe I have violated the basic
rule by not putting down more of the good things." Yet he also defended the statement as he had prepared it: "I think I am reading the situation accurately."

Toward the end of the conference, perhaps feeling sensitive to presenting Alma
with so negative a statement and somewhat overpowered by her firm resistance, Ed
made a summary remark that seemed to completely alter the course which he had
been following for almost six months regarding Alma's remaining at Taft School:

ED: I'd be happy to see you at my school next year at second grade.
ALMA: Well . . . I'm not sure you really mean it.
ED: Yes. And I'll want to retype that evaluation. I don't want to be unfair. There
are some misspelled words. And there are certain terms I may need to change.
ALMA: I'm real thankful for the chance to go over this. Of course, it seems
strange after the recommendation I had last year, which was so good. But we
need these experiences, too. They are humbling. These are learning
experiences.

Ed explained later that he went home with "real misgivings" that evening. The
more he had thought about it, the more certain he felt that Alma should either
transfer or resign, for it was obvious throughout the conference, as it had been
throughout the year, that the two of them never saw eye-to-eye on anything. Although he felt he really ought to get her to resign, he said that he was inclined to
"take the coward's way out" and get her to transfer to another school. He believed
that part of Alma's problems at Taft were due to community problems not related
to school. He pondered how to go about rewriting the recommendation.

Mrs. Skirmish had her own perceptions regarding the evaluation process. She
discussed her views of the evaluation procedure and of subsequent events during
her first year at Taft in an interview taped in May.

Excerpts from an Interview in May with Mrs. Alma Skirmish

I think this year has been tremendous for me. I really believe that in future years, no matter where I teach, I'll look back and say, "Well, I really learned things here."

The year was going along just fine, as far as I knew, until evaluation time, and then, BOOM! I've never gone through anything like that in my life, and I wouldn't like to do it again!

I could *so* easily be wrong. I probably am anyway. If I'd be the only one that would see it that way, then I'd realize. . . . I thought, "Have I all the time had good references and recommendations, and everything has been fine up to one point, and then for some reason everything is all terrible!" Oh-h-h! I just didn't know if I'd live through it.

After I read the evaluation, I said to Ed, "So you're going to try to stop me from teaching by saying such things as, 'I expect that ten years from now you'll be teaching the same way you're teaching now.' On what grounds can anyone say this? Why, I wasn't teaching the same as I was a year ago, and certainly not ten years ago." Like I told him, with teen-age children in my home and everything, you can't stay in a rut.

I thought that was a real unfair projection, with nothing to base it on. I felt *the whole thing was unfair*. Things that he mentioned as weaknesses were mainly what my last principal had mentioned as strengths. It was very interesting—"Acceptance of all the children and giving them opportunity to express themselves,"—the very kinds of things which the other principal had put down as pluses. I had a real excellent recommendation from him. And he was a man who was very serious-minded. He came in and sat down and took notes and was in several times.

Ed told me himself he had recommended one teacher not to return who he felt was just "totally inadequate" or something. He told me, "She was much worse than you." He said that in the school where she was now teaching she was elected outstanding educator of the year. And he said, "Now this could say that I was wrong in my judgment. But I don't feel I was." That told me that there is no way to convince him of anything different.

One meeting I had with him earlier this month about my teaching was *really bad*, because he told me that day, as he had talked to me a couple of times before, "You just don't see any of the things that I mention. You're just so defensive." At the time he said that it had come to the point where he didn't feel he could recommend me for third year probationary teaching. And he said a strange thing. He said, "If you would teach someplace outside the district—go to some other district to teach—I'll give you a good recommendation." This really bothered me, because I thought, "Well, you're just being inconsistent within yourself." I thought it was so strange, because here he professes to be a Christian man and over and over again these were the things he was bringing up.

He had come to this point where he felt like maybe he should just not recommend me to be rehired. I think I'll forever have feelings that I could never fathom before for people who get fired from jobs. He told me that he had talked with another principal about my becoming a counsellor, and this principal had agreed that I shouldn't be. And so I said, "So you've talked to another principal, too."

I asked if I might talk to Dr. Goddard. I did. It was very interesting. Dr. Goddard said that Ed had talked to her. She said to me:

> He told me some of the same things that you tell me: that you respect this person, that you admire him as a person. He said that about you. Otherwise

I'd think it was a personality thing. But there isn't a thing I can tell you that's specific. Everything is just vague. I'm sorry I can't help you know what he's wanting or what's wrong.

Then she asked me, "May I come out and visit your room?" And I said, "Please do!" She never has come. Maybe he has told her that it isn't necessary now.

At my Evaluation Conference he said he didn't have the evaluation formally typed up, but he had this feeling that he should recommend that I shouldn't come back. So I told him that this was his privilege, but that I would probably have to pressure and push on this and go to someone else about it. Because right now we could live at home on my husband's salary. But the time may come, if he weren't in the picture or something, when I may need to go back to teaching. And then [it would be serious] to have been put out of a job without one tangible reason that I could know *why*. I tried to be understanding, but I couldn't. I am sure to this day that I would have gone as far as to the school board or anything. I would have hated to, and the reason I would have hated to is because Ed had much more to lose than I did. I'm just a teacher, but he is an administrator, and I'm sure it would have been really bad for him. And I guess this bothered me more than anything else, because I don't want to hurt him.

When he told me all this, I thought the bottom had dropped out of everything. All the next day I was really wondering. I was to come in and see him after school. He was going to have this written up. You see, we don't have to sign them until we accept it. If I wouldn't sign it, I don't know—he'd have had to sign it and send it in himself. Because it was the deadline, the very last time for sending it in. I think he had more trouble from me than anybody on the staff. I know it gave him a hard time, and I think he lost sleep over it. I know I did.

Anyway, the next day I came in and he handed me this paper [rewritten evaluation] and everything was great! I just couldn't believe it. There was nothing bad on it except: "She doesn't seem to have the same respect for the school calendar that I do," which was referring to this idea that I was willing to ask for some time off, and would like to have had some time off to go for these— two days it was, I think. Other than that it was a very fine evaluation. And what he said to me that day was more like the Ed I had known.

It seemed like all of a sudden this man had become some kind of a monster that I was afraid of. This is emotionally how I felt. That day I came in and he gave me this paper, and I read it and I couldn't believe it. I just looked at him and didn't know what to say, because here all the negatives were taken out. And then he said something about "Don't you want to sign it?"

I said, "Well, I'd be happy to, but what do you really mean?"

He said, "Well, let's forget the whole thing. I'm just sorry it happened. It's all going to be fine. I want you to stay on here next year, and I see no reason why there should be anything different . . ." and so on. "Let's just forget it." Ohhh boy! Now you see my position.

Dr. Goddard made one suggestion when I saw her. She said:

I think it's a communication problem. Why don't you stop in Ed's office—I suggest every week or two weeks—from now till the end of school and just say, "How are things going? Is there anything that you'd like to point out to me that I might do differently?" That way you can give him the opportunity to tell you, so that nothing can ever come up without being caught real soon.

So, after the first couple weeks, I stopped by his office and told him why I'd come and that she had said this. I think this hurt him. I felt sorry that I had done it, but I was doing it on her advice. I tried to do it in a real kind way. He said that if I were going to do that, he would feel like we were just being bugged by an old problem which he had asked that we forget and that we completely obliterate. He said that he would tell me if anything came up, but he said there's no point in rubbing salt in an old wound.

He's been great since. I think he's gone out of his way to be friendly and to include me and so forth. He'll find things that he reads that he thinks I'd be interested in. He brought one out to the playground today and sent this magazine home with me to read—something that he feels that I and a couple of other teachers might be interested in. I kind of feel like he's treating me as a person again.

As far as I know I'll be back here next year. But I sure have misgivings, because I think, "Can I ever totally trust this man, or might I run into this again?" Of course, with my counselling background, I've tried to analyze why he does these things. I can't figure him out. I feel there's a tremendous breakdown in philosophy in this school. He feels like teachers and students are all on one level. If the kids plan what's to be done, it's just as great as if the teachers do. I go along with this to a certain extent, although I don't know where kids growing up into this are going to learn the proper respect for law and authority. But anyway, that breaks down totally when it comes to principal and teacher. He's real friendly when you see him and everything, but—boy—he's probably making judgments and deciding and categorizing you or something and really going to be hard about it.

I think it's inconsistent of him to be so terribly particular about the fact that we shouldn't leave the building until a certain time, when you can do anything you please anytime *in* the building. We sit down there and chat all the time after school until we go home at four o'clock, and that's perfectly fine.

I like the fact that he isn't around checking up on what we're doing and so forth. I think he does follow enough of what is going on in school. I appreciate it when he says things are well planned and organized and presented. I think he knows enough about what's going on.

Maybe it's because I'm an experienced teacher and an older teacher, but I think that he prefers to work with younger people who don't have their minds made up or don't have a philosophy of their own, so that he can just totally mold them and make them the way he wants them. Therefore, I feel like I don't really fit here.

Up to the time of the evaluation, I had felt very relaxed in this teaching situation. That's why I was enjoying it so tremendously. I'm sure I've done the best job of teaching that I've ever done this year. I tried to go along as much as I could with "permissiveness" and "more freedoms" and everything. Still, I was relaxed, because I felt like that was the atmosphere here.

He was in here so little, that he really couldn't possibly know what's going on in here. The longest he ever spent in here was probably 15 minutes. He was in two times that I can remember. Once as I was giving out an assignment, just handing out a paper, when he said that I didn't give the children opportunity to answer. He wanted some samples of what they needed on the blackboard— short and long vowels. Anyway, that day he was in here for about 10 or 15 minutes just as I was starting the afternoon's work. Then another day he was in about 10 or 15 minutes and sat in on a reading group, where we still were concentrating pretty much on group reading and vocabulary and so on. Otherwise he has come in on an errand to put something on my desk or to call for some child. I always wondered when he was going to come around for evaluation. But, I figured he must think he knows enough about it.

I think possibly to get a feel of the classroom, the feel of the relationship between students and teacher and what's going on in a classroom, that he would have to spend a block of almost an hour at a time. I think that this should be spaced at different times during the day. Probably three times or so before the evaluation. That would be a real minimum. Of course, you're going to figure, "If he has to spend so many hours with every teacher, and he has all these teachers to evaluate. . . ." I wouldn't like to be an administrator. I feel that they have a hard position. I think he does less organizing than any other administrator I know. He holds onto everything more loosely. With him, I think it's more a case of "however it happens to come out." I don't think he's the type of person who needs to know everything right down the line and keep track of things like some of us do.

I haven't dared to talk to other teachers about my problems here. I thought that if I said anything, I would just be exposing things, and that would neither be good for me nor for my principal. I don't want to hurt him in any way. I don't think that would be professional or ethical.

Last week I finally *dared* to probe kind of casually to see if anyone else went through this horrifying experience that I did. After that evaluation I thought I was the only one. I've always wondered how much other people knew and whether he talked to them about me. Somehow it came up and I found out that a few other teachers had felt this. All of a sudden they, too, were given a *black evaluation*. And they hadn't been aware of anything along the way.

I know that the school secretary is well aware of it. In fact, she was telling me the other day that she was just about ill over these things as she was typing them up. She thought that they gave her some of her physical problems for awhile. As she and I were casually talking, I became aware that I wasn't the only one. Somehow the load started to lift just a little bit. I haven't even talked to Mrs. Elder. I don't know if she knows [that other teachers received critical evaluations]. Someday I hope to talk to her.

When Elwood New came in one morning, as we walked down the hall, he mentioned something about having been disillusioned about teaching, that it wasn't what he expected it was going to be. I told him, "Don't give it up after one year at Taft. This isn't the whole story. This school is not really typical. You shouldn't put public school teaching aside because of one experience, especially in a school that is so far out."

I don't think I quite fit here. Yet one of the staff told me real recently "We need people like you here." To get some balance, maybe this is true. I don't dare say anything, but at least I'm still around. Personally, if I didn't have this problem of shifting schools one year and another year, I think I'd be more comfortable in another school next year. You see, I shifted over here on my own request. It was so much closer to home and everything. And I should stay here. It looks better on your records if you spend more than one year in a place.

As far as everything is concerned, I'm staying here. Though I did tell Dr. Goddard that I would be willing to move if she feels this would be good for either me or for Mr. Bell. Especially if there's any way in which it is hard for him.

I don't feel that our previous friendship or knowing him before has made any difference. That was one of the problems when I came to talk to him about coming here. He said, "Do you think it will make any difference?" I said, "I feel I can respect you the same as I would any principal. It will make no difference to me." I have checked with people on this, and unless he has told them, no one has been aware that we've known each other so long. The counsellor told me that she has been constantly amazed that there's this teacher-principal relationship just as with anyone else. In fact, she thinks there's probably more of a breakdown between us than with some of the others, because they are free to dare to say things to him and kid around. This is probably true.

It's just that I don't want to go through an evaluation of that type again next year. I felt it was so unfair. I'm not just sure how I will ever know along the way whether everything is really all right.

The evaluation which Ed Bell submitted to the central office midway through Alma's second year at Taft School recommended she be rehired and advanced to tenure status. In preparing his final evaluation, Ed drew upon comments such as the following notes which he had written after a classroom observation during her second year at school: "Shows a continued interest in developing good teaching procedures," "Relates well to all persons," and "No problem apparent in any occasions of flexibility." He described his rationale in the matter of her recommendation:

> I put her on tenure. She really seemed to listen to the things I had to say last year. She runs her classroom like a classroom now, not a Sunday school class. And she pays attention to each child, not just a few special ones. They say you can't change human nature, and sometimes I'm inclined to agree, but in this case I really did see a change. I feel those talks we had were worth it.
>
> She's doing a much better job this year. She has a good group—not necessarily smaller—it may even be bigger, but she's doing very well with them. Maybe next year I'll regret it. But right now I feel I'm right.

The Principal as Socializer: Some Further Observations

Socialization as a Two-way Process   Socialization occurs as a function of human interaction, not merely the unilateral action of a single individual. The socializer socializes, but he also is socialized in the process. Sometimes in the course of inducting newcomers into the Taft faculty it was Ed who "applied the brakes" to keep the process from becoming unnecessarily severe; at times he defended or encouraged the very teachers who were otherwise receiving the brunt of his efforts to socialize them if he suddenly became concerned that others or even he himself might be evaluating them prematurely or too critically. As he explained to Mrs. Skirmish in this regard, "Maybe I have violated the basic rule by not putting down more of the good things."

Except in those instances where Ed specifically acknowledged a remark or incident, as in his reaction to Alma's expressed "disappointment," it was not possible to assess whether he was oblivious to the sometimes rather blatant attempts of staff members to socialize him or to counter his attempts to socialize, or whether he simply preferred to ignore them. But it was quite apparent that such counter-socializing efforts were made by staff members. At times these efforts seemed intended and even premeditated, as in most of the verbal exchanges between Ed and Alma Skirmish. Sometimes the efforts were subtle and perhaps unconscious, as the following illustration may suggest. The fact was circulated among at least a select group of staff members that the school secretary, with the aid of her family doctor, had traced an attack of severe dizziness which occurred at school one morning to her feelings of distress regarding the content of certain of Ed's teacher evaluations as she typed them in preparation for his final conferences. Whether the possible association between her dizzy spell and the task she was performing had occurred to Ed or not, I do not know. On the day in question when he asked her to type his three harshest evaluations, he mentioned that he had originally intended to type those particular reports himself. He had not found the time, however, and he needed the completed forms immediately, one for a conference scheduled that very afternoon with Mrs. Skirmish. Later that day, he did refer to the fact that the secretary had gone home sick. The secretary provided the following account of the incident:

> One time did bother me a great deal. I was going through this business with my neck after I was in that automobile accident. And I was having this dizziness. It left me so emotional, I was almost out of control. One day when I got this severe dizziness, they took me right from school to see the doctor. And I guess he's an advocate of mental health. He started asking me all sorts of questions: Are you happy with this or that? Do you fight with your husband? Do you hate your mother? So on and so forth, until he got down to this business of my work.
>
> Well, it turned out that day I'd typed some of these evaluations. I was kind of upset with them, because I didn't feel they were entirely fair.
>
> Margaret Elder's was the one that upset me the most. Because I'm very fond of Margaret. And I just . . . It kind of seemed to me like someone else looking at this might not understand. Yet, what else would you evaluate anyone on but your own feelings and your own policies on certain things.

Real and Ritual Aspects of the Evaluation Procedure   Not every teacher at Taft expressed concern about the evaluation procedure, but it was clearly on the minds of many of them and for some, including several whose accounts have been presented in this chapter, the procedure aroused feelings of anxiety and resentment. Dissatisfaction was focussed particularly on the brevity of Ed's classroom visits and on the subjective nature of his assessment of teaching effectiveness. The evaluation conferences between teacher and principal based on such observations tended to follow a ritualistic format in which teachers formally expressed their gratitude for Ed's suggestions (just as he had done during his evaluation at the central office) while he drew upon the authority of his position and experience to make generalizations about each teacher's overall effectiveness based on data clearly more impressionistic than empirical. Teachers who did not feel overly anxious about the procedure or who had received favorable review were not inclined to express misgivings about whether Ed had an adequate basis for his judgment. As one primary teacher explained: "I think he knows a lot more than his few minutes of classroom observation might tell him. And I think he's very perceptive in the few minutes he's in."

Ed's behavior in regard to classroom visits suggested that he did not like making them for purposes of formal teacher evaluations. He seemed to prefer being an unobtrusive observer, dropping in to a class for a brief moment on some errand, casting an eye about the class, and departing. What to some teachers was a year without any "real" visit at all was to Ed a year in which he felt he had remarkably close touch. At the end of the first three weeks of school he reported having been in all 18 classrooms, none less than two times, with an estimated total of 64 visits.

> I've been in rooms more often this fall than I have been in recent years in administration. Partly because I felt I had to, with some of the problems. But I've enjoyed it. I've really felt I've had more contact with students and teachers by this point in the year than I have ever had.

The total evaluation procedure, with its required observations and conferences culminating in the preparation of the final evaluation report, served both real and ritual functions at Taft School.[11] Somewhat paradoxically, the ceremony seemed to assume its more ritualistic function in terms of teachers who technically were being most critically judged (i.e., a teacher being evaluated for tenure), and to have its real effect on teachers whose "judgment day" was still a year or two away. Among the three teachers at Taft for whom evaluation time spelled trouble, Mrs. Skirmish still had one year of probationary status to serve before she would be judged for tenure, Mrs. Elder had two years, and Mr. New, whose position as an intern teacher was officially regarded as temporary status, still faced a full three-year probationary period. Only one teacher at Taft was actually "up" for tenure, and she went "sailing through."

The evaluation ceremony appeared to serve the needs of the organization better than it served the needs of the individuals in it. That is, at the personal level the preparation of the evaluations produced anxiety on the part of many principals because of the magnitude and touchiness of the task, and anxiety on the part of many teachers because of the meaning of the task. On the other hand, at the cost of these individual anxieties, the ceremony provided a midyear reaffirmation of the status hierarchy by which schools are organized and administered. The evaluation ceremony reaffirmed organizational rules and policies imposed within the hierarchy, with the effect of keeping the locus of power in the central office and meting out detailed elements of responsibility rather than delegating authority and responsibility on a broad basis.

The evaluation ceremony had both public and private dimensions. The principal's classroom observations, and the fact of private one-to-one conferences held in Ed's office behind doors that were otherwise usually open, were highly visible aspects of the procedure. The policy of requiring each teacher to read and sign his own evaluation form added another public dimension from the administrator's point of view, and I suspect that it was the fact that principals were required to lay their entire formal evaluation statement before their teachers that had resulted in keeping the formal evaluative machinery so apparently simple. Much of the crucial information about evaluation had to be channeled through informal, officially off-the-record statements such as the comments exchanged about Taft teachers during Ed's own evaluation conference with central office personnel, or through correspondence to which teachers were not witness. Yet the content of each individual's evaluation, particularly the negative aspects of it, was a matter of private concern among the teachers. Perhaps in a few instances teachers who had close professional confidants (for example, a teacher located in the same part of the building and at the same or an adjacent grade) discussed critical aspects of Ed's verbal and

---

[11] The term "ritual" is not intended to suggest either that the evaluation ceremony was unimportant or was treated lightly by any of the participants in it. Anthropologist Estelle Fuchs has pointed out the importance of ritual ceremony in the teacher evaluation process, particularly in the first administrative observation of a beginning teacher, and how a supervisor who fails to carry out the ritual satisfactorily may leave the teacher unsure about whether he has passed the ordeal (Fuchs 1969:159). It is possible that by attempting to minimize the formal nature of his visits Ed actually created more rather than less uncertainty and apprehension among his teachers, the very opposite of his intention. It should also be noted that the apprehension associated with evaluation procedures was not limited to beginning teachers, but extended to experienced teachers in probationary status who were not new to teaching but who were new to the school.

written recommendations of their evaluations, but if so it was done in the privacy of small groups rather than among the faculty-at-large. The teachers who felt they had received what Mrs. Skirmish described as "black" evaluations kept such matters to themselves. They had assumed, rightly, that most of the faculty being evaluated had received, in some variation or another, the principal's stamp of approval. And each had also assumed, at least tentatively, that only individually had he or she been denied the necessary endorsement to continued teaching at Taft.

Socialization in Other Contexts   The emphasis in the present chapter has been on the socializing influence of the evaluation procedure as Ed Bell used it for purposes of incorporating new teachers into or systematically getting them out of Taft School. The process of integrating teachers into the school extended much beyond the drama of the evaluation ceremony. There were many facets of the socialization process too mundane, too petty, and too remote from the teaching function in the school to be made explicit in an evaluation conference or to be made explicit at all. Teachers had to learn, for example, what types of telephone calls were appropriate to make and receive during various parts of the day, what variations in dress style were acceptable, the extent to which outsiders were welcome in the school or classroom (husbands of some of the younger teachers were frequently on hand after school; boy friends of the two unmarried teachers were not), and how late in the afternoon they were expected to stay at school. The latter issue was a particularly sensitive one among the new teachers. This discussion of socialization in other contexts draws upon that one specific problem for illustration.

The consensus of staff opinion was that Ed expected everyone to remain at school each afternoon until at least four o'clock. No written rule or formally announced policy existed. There was some ambivalence in school board policy regarding how late teachers were to stay, and the exact interpretation of that directive, as with many like it, seemed to be left to the discretion of individual administrators. On matters which principals felt that they had discretionary power in interpreting policy, they could enforce a statement to the letter, interpret it liberally, or, in matters of little consequence, perhaps even ignore it. Regarding the hour for leaving the building, the important aspect for the teachers at Taft was to know what Ed expected. Ed told one teacher:

> It's district policy to remain in the building one-half hour after the kids leave, and I interpret that to mean half an hour after the last kids leave [i.e., the 3:30 dismissal of the upper-grade youngsters]. Primary kids need less time in school, but primary teachers need more time to prepare. Otherwise everyone would want to teach primary just for the shorter hours.

It is important to recognize that schools place great emphasis on the value of time. They regiment the day into blocks of time that make it possible to account for every instructional minute. Punctuality is preached and practiced as a virtue. Taft School had 24 clocks coordinated with a master clock in the office and an automated buzzer system audible throughout the building and grounds. In the office Ed kept two kitchen timers which were used as reminders for imminent events and to monitor the time allotted for brief errands, particularly if children requested to make a quick trip home for some acceptable reason during the school day. The concern about time was not limited only to the behavior of pupils. Central office personnel endeavored to insure that the district got all the "time" it had contracted with its administrators and even worried about the length of time some of their colleagues took at coffee breaks. Collectively the district's administrators were asked to direct their attention to problems of time accountability, such as whether a substitute teacher should be required to remain after school as long as a regular teacher. In conversation principals discussed the problem of teachers too anxious to leave school each day. One principal had coined the term "heel skinners" to describe teachers who, if unchecked, would leave the school building so soon after dismissal that departing children might suffer having their heels bruised as the teacher raced them to the door. Tom Nice related, "I gently remind teachers to check by the office if they are leaving before 4:30. Otherwise, what can I tell parents if they should call?"

Within the school district hierarchy, the concern which individuals expressed regarding their own "hours" seemed to be related to satisfying their respective and immediate superordinates; worry regarding the hours on the job spent by others was directed toward immediate subordinates. Ed was annoyed with the lack of recognition on the part of the central office staff of the long hours he spent each week, and he was piqued at "owing" the district a few hours at the end of the year. At the same time, he conveyed the importance of putting in a full day to his teachers, especially in terms of their departure in the afternoon. He left problems of *pupil* accountability and punctuality to his teachers. If Ed spoke to a child about getting to school on time, he acted only at the request of a teacher; such problems were not among his own pressing concerns.

From an administrative view, the length of the day one spent visibly engaged in schoolwork seemed to be taken as a critical index of commitment. Teachers who wished to leave early on specific days typically presented Ed with high priority reasons (family emergencies, medical appointments) or reaffirmed their commitment through wanting to leave early because of sheer exhaustion. One new teacher who requested to leave "early" every Friday for part of the year was refused Ed's permission to do so, although she was recognized for being one of the teachers to arrived earliest each morning. Ed's refusal to allow her to leave early was frequently discussed during the ensuing weeks, and the story served to reinforce staff suspicion that their principal paid undue attention to the hour when each person left the building after school. Among staff who felt somewhat at odds with Ed for any other reason, the story also provided a whipping boy for more general feelings of disenchantment.

Even for the final teacher day at school, the moment of departure became a subject of discussion among the new teachers several days before the end of the term. They anticipated that many of them would finish their record-making and classroom clean-up by early afternoon. Four days before school was to let out one new teacher remarked to me: "Some of us were talking about when we would leave on the last day. We thought maybe two o'clock."

"Is that official?" I asked.

"Oh, no, that's just the earliest we could get away. I guess it's too early. Maybe at 3:00 or 3:30 people will start leaving. But I don't think people will stay until 4:00 o'clock."

On the afternoon of that last day, a Saturday, there were indications of uncertainty and uneasy joking about departing "early" even among old-timers. The following midafternoon dialogue ensued between two of the senior teachers in the faculty room.

FIRST TEACHER: (entering the room) That's it! I'm finished!
SECOND TEACHER: Are we free to go? It isn't even three o'clock yet.

FIRST TEACHER: Well, I'm going!
SECOND TEACHER: I guess we do have tenure, don't we. I'll go tell Mary Lou. I'm riding with her.

Ed made his feelings quite explicit about the relationship between the hours one spent at school and a commitment to teaching during a conversation with Mrs. Skirmish following one of his visits to her classroom.

ED: I've had some question about the length of the day and your commitment to it.
ALMA: I don't go home before four o'clock hardly ever, Ed, except for those few times I asked you. With the extra time on this new reading program, I'm actually teaching a longer day now. I just can't get here before eight o'clock.
ED: I don't mean that you should. I don't get here earlier than that myself. But I did want you to have this warning early enough about the length of the school day.

Through a comment of explanation Ed made afterward regarding the latter conversation, he revealed something of his strategy for getting a certain level of performance out of his teachers—you asked more of yourself than you asked of them. He was speaking of one of his fellow principals, one whose style of administration was far more casual than Ed's own:

He's not exactly one for getting to school on time or for being there all the time. He could *never* have talked to Alma the way I did. He doesn't have that kind of commitment. Of course, he may show his commitment in other ways.

Regardless of the relationship between hours spent at school and teaching effectiveness, long hours did appear to be regarded as indicative of one's dedication. Ed had another new teacher who tended to scurry in late and leave early. He was somewhat resigned to her schedule, since family obligations were inevitably the complicating factor, but he had begun to give some warning signals to her. "Your class 'has your number,'" he commented one morning as she arrived just before the last morning bell. On another occasion he said of her, "She does a good job . . . when she's here."

The endorsement written by a senior principal for a teacher who was being considered for promotion to a principalship revealed the kind of behavior which principals apparently like to see, "I thought he was a real worker. He was one of the first to arrive, one of the last to leave."

Partial Immunity to the Socialization Process The evaluation process subtly reaffirmed that teachers, like principals and school buildings, belonged to the school district rather than to individual schools. At Taft School this fact was illustrated by the differential way in which two teachers, Mrs. Skirmish and another of the primary teachers, Mrs. Robin, were dealt with in the annual evaluation ceremony. Both teachers transferred to Taft at the same time and from the same school. Both were spending their first year at Taft School. Mrs. Robin, the younger of the two teachers by two decades, was completing her fourth year of teaching in the district. The previous year she had been awarded tenure. District policy did not require that she be evaluated again for two more years. At the end of the year she stated that Ed had never "really" seen her teach and had prepared no evaluation report on her for the central office. An evaluation report *was* required concerning Mrs. Skirmish, although she was completing her tenth year of teaching. Yet the two teachers were equally new to Taft School, and Ed actually knew far less about the younger woman either personally or professionally than he did about Alma. The system dictated that he direct his efforts to only one of these teachers, and that is what he did. Mrs. Robin's immunity to the evaluation procedure was a consequence of formal procedures established within the district.

For certain other teachers, immunity to the evaluation procedure, and actually to a great deal of the total socialization process, was a function of their personalities and/or their superb willingness or ability to adapt to the demands of the situation. In teaching, as with other complex sets of interrelated skills by which certain people more easily accomplish goals or win games, some people are identified early as "naturals" or are recognized for being proficient enough to "make the team." The one "third year" teacher who received tenure was at least in the latter category, and Kay Johnson, though only a first year teacher, had already begun to look to Ed like she might be a born teacher. Such people were immune to the negative implications of teacher socialization, and thus procedures like evaluation tended to provide positive reaffirmation of the mutual respect and dedication to high purposes shared between teacher and principal.

Because of circumstances external to the school district, two other young teachers at Taft were relatively immune to the evaluation procedures and to the full impact of the socialization process, even though both of them were probationary teachers, and one of them, Mrs. Brightside, was new to the staff during the year. Their immunity stemmed from the fact that their careers as teachers were secondary to the careers of their husbands. Both teachers learned early in the school year that they would be leaving the community the following June to accompany their husbands to new assignments.[12] Technically they had to be evaluated, and Ed followed the same evaluation procedure with each of them

---

[12] A third teacher, Mrs. Manning, resigned early in the year. Discovering that she was pregnant within the first few weeks of the school year, she was virtually immune to the pressures of professional socialization. She had been outspoken on several occasions, provoking Ed and several of the senior teachers. She "skipped" PTA meetings, and on one occasion boldly made a personal appointment on an afternoon scheduled for a faculty meeting. Initially Ed had encouraged her to "do the professional thing" and teach at least until Christmas. As the weeks wore on, he found he had been able to find a satisfactory replacement for her much earlier than he originally planned.

that he did with every other teacher whom he was required to evaluate. At the same time, the evaluation proceedings in those two cases had only a personal meaning, not an institutional one, since Ed would never formally have to commit the district to awarding tenure. Neither teacher expressed concern over the evaluation procedure itself. One said of Ed's classroom visits:

> He certainly doesn't get in the way. He really doesn't come in often enough to make me nervous. And when he does come in, he's so subtle about it, you don't make that big a deal about it.

The other teacher felt that Ed was "positive" about her teaching even though he had observed her class on a "noisy" day:

> Ed's not real critical. If you're really working with the kids and like them, this is what he feels is important. If you're getting things done in your way and it's kind of noisy in your room, OK. Because when I had my—oh, what do they call that, when he has to come and observe . . . that "evaluation"—he was very complimentary. He said that maybe the noise level was a little high at times, but if I could live with it and I could get them quiet when I needed it, that was OK, too. Makes you feel very good. I know my noise level is too high at times, and it doesn't panic me that he knows it. But then, maybe he's made me feel so good that my own self-concept is good.[13]

Neither of these two latter teachers expressed anxiety about the evaluation procedure or seemed affected by the shadow it cast over the interactions between the principal and some other probationary teachers. On the last day of school, there were tears in their eyes as they bid farewell to their colleagues. One of the departing teachers had wrapped two little gifts for Ed. The first was a booklet, *The Wisdom of Charlie Brown,* inscribed, "I hope you find Charlie Brown's philosophy as helpful as I have found yours." The other gift was a miniature trophy for the "World's Greatest Boss." The second teacher sobbed her way through her final parting in the front office: "Goodbye, Mr. Bell. I'll sure miss this place. As soon as I have a baby old enough to show off, I'll be back."

Comment

Events pertaining to evaluation, the most important formal aspect of teacher socialization, transpired in a fraction of time during the year. They have been spelled out in detail here because of their critical nature for faculty and administrator alike, but not because they consumed a great number of hours at school. The evaluation task set Ed most clearly apart from his teachers and challenged him with difficult decisions which he faced with an indecisiveness of his own that only added more stress for all concerned—including Ed. Taft School, like any human group, was not without its conflict, but this chapter should not create an

---

[13] Although this teacher did not appear threatened by the formal evaluation procedure, she nonetheless acted in such a way as to present a good image of herself as a teacher to her principal. In relating an incident of a classroom problem, she told me: "I never did talk to Ed about that. I felt he was so busy. And I was disappointed I wasn't handling the situation better. So I talked to the intern supervisor. *I really didn't want Ed to know I was having a problem.* I don't know why I didn't. I think that I didn't want him to know I couldn't handle it and that I was feeling all shook-up."

impression of the school as unusually conflict-ridden. One must keep in mind that I have drawn extensively from the accounts of the only three teachers who felt themselves to be recipients of less-than-satisfactory evaluations and that my presence as an observer provided them with an unusual opportunity to unburden their problems to an interested but uninvolved outsider. Recall also that Ed did not actually file a negative report on any of these teachers.

If the evaluation of teachers is, as it appeared to be in Ed's case, one of the most critical of the professional tasks of a career principal, then the special skills he brings to that task and the special resources on which he can draw in performing it warrant careful attention. I watched for behavior in this regard and listened for clues in every setting in which I found principals talking about their work and their worries. The little I gleaned in the way of specific comment is included in this and prior chapters.

I could never escape a personal feeling that Ed made his assessments about new staff quickly (probably on first impression), independent of performance observed in the classroom, and then subsequently accumulated whatever evidence he felt he needed to support those impressions. Although he tended to be cautious when screening candidates for his school or the district, once he decided to accept a candidate for the Taft faculty, the extent of his enthusiasm and optimism took a predictable upward swing. From that moment on, he accumulated negative information only slowly and reluctantly. If the balance of his assessment did shift to a negative impression, however, he found it exceedingly difficult to reassess or even to review his judgment, even though he continued to experience ambivalence and nagging doubts once he felt compelled to render an unfavorable evaluation. I do not know whether his doubts arose primarily because of the tenuous professional basis he had for making judgments about teachers or from the touchy personal business of having ultimately to reveal them.

10/Behind many masks

Oh, wad some power the giftie gie us
To see oursels as others see us!

Robert Burns

"Look out for our new principal, Dad. She goes right into the crowd and disguises herself as a person." A speaker at the annual meeting of the State Association of Elementary School Principals reported receiving this advice from his third-grade son just prior to Open House for the new school year. Principals and other educators in the audience responded with expected laughter at the story. Yet the implication that principals are divested of human qualities and must, therefore, "disguise themselves as people" was not completely a laughing matter among the administrators I encountered. Like Ed, school principals everywhere appear to share a self-conscious concern with their professional image.

The present chapter draws attention to the varying perceptions which people who frequently came into contact with Ed Bell in his professional role had of him as *a* principal and as *the* principal of Taft School, thus providing a view "in" from the outside. The chapter which follows views the principalship in complementary fashion from the inside out, exploring the hopes and dreams which principals share about someday reaching a more positive, more professional, and more precise role definition than that suggested by the wide-ranging and often conflicting opinions and perceptions presented here.

The chapter title, "Behind Many Masks," has been borrowed from an article written by anthropologist Gerald Berreman (1962) in which he discusses the function of impression management in carrying out an intended role. This chapter draws upon volunteered and solicited comments collected throughout the study to illustrate a variety of "masks" which Ed wore, including those which he donned in conscious efforts at impression management as well as masks which others perceived independently from or in spite of Ed's efforts to monitor the image he presented. The comments range from those representative of widely-shared opinions to others unique to the speaker or to the occasion. Collectively, they lend support to the wisdom of an adage often repeated among administrators: "No matter what you do, you can't please everyone."

Other than the selection of comments and, in the case of the teacher statements that comprise a large portion of the chapter, the identification of categories for sorting recurring themes, little is offered here in the way of analysis or synthesis. The comments form a mosaic. To understand fully the psychological processes underlying Ed's perception and rationalization of this mosaic extends beyond the limits of the inquiry. At the same time, all of the attitudes described here are part of, and thus provide clues about, those very processes. The impressions presented include those of the school secretary, the superintendent of schools, pupils, parents, and teachers.

THE SCHOOL SECRETARY'S
IMPRESSION OF THE PRINCIPAL

Ed is a real nice guy to work for. Personality-wise, he is a very fine person. I don't think I've ever had any personality clashes with him.

Every once in a while I'll get the feeling that Ed just talked all day about what a wonderful school this is—not only Ed, but the teachers—what a wonderful school, what a great set-up it is, how much it's doing for the children, how much progress they're making, and that this is the only way, that everybody else is wrong.

The other day I said to my husband that I've almost gotten the feeling that maybe Ed isn't so sure of himself. Because he'll say, "I know there's an easier way, but I think we're right." Or, "Maybe I'm not right, but I think I'm doing right." There's always somebody right there to jump in and say, "Oh yes, you're right. We're doing it the right way." Sometimes I get the feeling that maybe subconsciously he isn't so sure. He's looking for someone to back him up and say, "Oh, yes, you are right." And they always do.

Ed gets pretty wrapped up in other things he's doing and forgets things. Then some sort of report or something is past due. All of a sudden, here it is. I am a little overwhelmed by it all because I didn't know about it to begin with. And he tends to be a little bit forgetful sometimes. But for the most part he's a pretty fine person to work for. I think he's pretty fair. Sometimes he's maybe a little bit too democratic. It's a lot easier if he would just make a decision rather than asking everybody about it.

As far as I'm concerned, there is somewhat of a gap here between the classified and the certified. The teacher aide and I have talked about this. We aren't the only classified people in the building, but the janitors stick to themselves and the cooks are over in the other end, so we are the only ones in the building that are classified that get together [with the certified staff]. And there has been times when we both felt that maybe we weren't quite as good.[1]

I think the children like him very much. They don't hesitate to come in and tell him about anything—whether it's somebody picking flowers or any little thing. Sometimes I'm not sure if I should censor these or not. When he's real

---

[1] The teacher aide did not share this view. She explained in an interview:

I haven't felt at all that I have been left out because I am not a teacher. I haven't felt that they respect me any less because I don't happen to be as well educated or be a teacher. The secretary was terribly upset one day at this clear distinction that was made between the classified and the certificated people. It arose out of answering a phone call.

Ed told her that he felt it was better that one of the professional persons handle it. This annoyed her greatly. She was quite sure she could handle the situation as well as any professional person. She said, "I just get tired of this distinction that's made all the time between the classified and certificated people." Well, I have never felt this distinction at all, not in any way, shape, or form.

busy, I definitely do. But I'm not sure whether he always wants the children to come in any time and tell him about any little thing, when they definitely could and should be handled by someone else.

I know, and I'm sure he does too, that there are a lot of disgruntled parents in the neighborhood. I think maybe I've gotten some complaints over the phone that he hasn't even heard. People tend to spout off to the first person they talk to. And living in the neighborhood, I've gotten a lot of this. I ran into one woman who didn't even live in the area who was upset with Ed for something. I didn't bother to find out what. She was lambasting him pretty good. I think that there are a lot of parents that back Ed up. But there are an awful lot of parents that are not real happy with the way things are going.

One thing—and this is probably completely irrelevant, but others have mentioned it to me, and I've noticed it too—Ed tends to be a little cheap. This kind of grates on me sometimes. I'm probably one of the most Scotch persons you've ever met. I'm quite frugal. But sometimes his cheapness kind of gets to me. It's almost funny, really. The first day I was here, before the teachers came, just Ed and I were here, and we'd worked at various things during the day. During the morning we took time out for coffee, and we went home for lunch. And in the afternoon he said, "Would you like to have a coke? We've got some cokes and stuff in the refrigerator." I said, "Well, all right." He went in there and he got out a coke and opened it up and handed it to me and he said, "Do you have any change?" And it kind of threw me, because the way he—I mean, I don't mind buying my own coke, certainly, but it just kind of threw me for a minute. I almost laughed. But this has been typical.

I guess he borrowed the secretary's car a great deal last year. And she was kind of put out because he never offered to buy her any gas. Her car isn't an economy model like mine—it was quite a gas hog.

Oh, the fact that he hasn't paid his faculty dues or the candy cane money, or any of that. In fact, he's the only one that hasn't paid *anything*. At one point, he told me that he was sure he had paid on it, and that he thought I was mistaken. I went back and checked all my receipts from the very first of the year, and he hadn't.

Someone was trying to figure out how many goodies—how many cookies or whatever they were going to bring. And someone else said, "Well, plan on thirty, and then maybe an extra half a dozen for Ed." I don't think anybody really resents it, but it was just kind of a joke. I mean, everybody realizes that this is the way he is.

One day he was there in the faculty room and he was going around looking through the sacks and he said, "Well, this orange has been here for about three days, I guess nobody wants it." Or he'll look through the refrigerator and say, "I guess nobody wants this or that." You know, it just seems kind of funny.

I guess I consider myself somewhat of a frustrated teacher and I sometimes think to myself, "Well, I think I can do a little bit better than that or deal with this situation a little bit differently, with better results." And probably I couldn't, but I have felt this at times.

THE SUPERINTENDENT'S IMPRESSION OF THE PRINCIPAL

When the superintendent of schools expressed interest in discussing the progress I was making with the study, I made a formal appointment to meet with him at his office. I did not make notes during our conversation, but I later recorded excerpts from his remarks that pertained most immediately to Ed Bell:

Ed Bell is an enigma to me. Sometimes in a meeting he will give his idea or his version of a problem and then he'll refuse to listen to any other viewpoint—he'll just sit there and shrug his shoulders. He's very protective of his teachers, though, and he wants them to be comfortable.

You know, he went through all that trouble with Mrs. Skirmish without complaining. Here she was having a little prayer for her children every morning in class. And then telling them there was no Santa! Why, Carolyn Goddard almost blew her lid when she heard about that. We don't try to get information about things like that, you understand. It just comes to us, in all sorts of ways.

I'm glad you have found him easy to work with in your study. You once commented about his "openness." I'm glad to hear it. I think that Carolyn Goddard is worried about his inflexibility. As a matter of fact, I think our teachers generally are more open to suggestion and more willing to act [than the principals]. Sometimes I wonder whether these administrators around here really think in depth or just keep scratching the surface.

I guess you know Ed is an active member of his church and a real believer. I was out to lunch just yesterday with one of the members of Ed's congregation. Ed spends a lot of time going to church, and I guess he gets along real well with all those Christian people. Maybe that's why he's so open as a principal—maybe he figures he's in God's hands.

PUPIL IMPRESSIONS OF THE PRINCIPAL

During the study I asked all fifth- and sixth-grade pupils at Taft School to write about their principal.[2] Here is the statement that one sixth-grade girl wrote. Hers was one of the most detailed accounts prepared by any pupil.

Mr. Bell is a good principal, in a way, I like him and everything, but he doesn't give a person a chance to say their side of the story, if something has happened. A pretty long time ago, about 6 girls and I were playing foursquare. Some boys ran in the middle of the square and swiped our ball. Naturally, we tried to get it back, but they threw it in a huge puddle. Then they pick it up and were going to throw it at us. Well, we started running and we darted into the nearest shelter, which was a bathroom.[3] Mr. Bell saw us go in so he came in and said for us all to go to the office, and wait. He was gone for a pretty long time, so we picked out someone to be the talker. Pretty soon our teacher came around the corner and we told her what happened. She was on our side all the way and thought the boys were in the wrong. Finally, Mr. Bell came in, looked straight at us and said if he ever saw us in there again, he would call our parents and then expel us from school. Well, we aren't hoods, or whatever people like that are called. We were all good with work, and good with other kids and teachers. Well, he didn't give us a chance to say a thing, and I think that's a pretty bad quality for a principal. That answers "What kind of a Principal," and "One time I won't forget."

---

[2] One hundred and forty-two pupils in the three fifth-grade and three sixth-grade classrooms responded anonymously to three questions, "What kind of a principal is he?" "Pleasant memories are . . ." and "One time I won't forget." Responses to the question, "What kind of a principal is he?" generally evoked a favorable response (74 percent of the boys, 84 percent of the girls). At the same time almost half of the boys (46 percent, in contrast to 27 percent of the girls) cited a negative experience in responding to the question, "One time I won't forget. . . ."

[3] Probably no category of portals presents any greater supervisory or administrative challenge than the doors to the girls' lavatories in American elementary schools.

I'll tell you about a pleasant memory, I am in Student Council. Everybody thought it would be nice to have a candy machine for after school. Mr. Mason took Mr. Bell's place one day, because Mr. Bell was busy. Mr. Mason thought it was a pretty good idea because that could get money for our school treasurey, but Mr. Bell said a plain and flat NO! But it was fun while it lasted!

Some sample responses written by other pupils to each of the three questions are presented below:

What Kind of a Principal Is Mr. Bell?

To me he is the cutest and nicest principal I've ever met. To others he may be an ordinarily man.

Mr. Bell is the kind of a principal who helps you figure it out.

Mr. Bell is a very nice principal he never gets Mad at you and he helps you about all Kinds of things.

He is a babesh cause when you get in troble he babes you.

A Dam stopit one.

I like Mr. Bell real well for a principal but I sure wouldn't want him for a relitive.

Mr. Bell is a fine principal. Many times I don't agree with him, but of course that's normal. I get mad when he interrupts us for announcements in the middle of class.

He is okay but when you get in trouble he gets to talking about his family and how good it is.

Pleasant Memories Are . . .

When Mr. Bell understood us when we got in trouble.

Mr. Bell came and had dinner with the sixth-grade Camp Fire Girls.

One day when he was going to xeplle me. Then didn't.

When I leave this school I won't have any pleasant memories.

I will probably remember Mr. Bell but I won't remember much about him. I think he is a good principal but sometimes he's sorta strick. I don't have any good memories about him or any bad ones.

One Time I Won't Forget

One time I had a note from my mom that said I didn't have to take "hot lunch" if I didn't want it. I didn't want it so I didn't buy it. Bell called me to the office about 10 times over that one *stupid* lunch.

The time I went into his office for the first time. To get in troble.

I won't fore get the time when my freind and I were blamed fore bilding a fire in the bath room.

I will remember two things about him. He always is blinking like he has something in his eyes. And then on the intercom he always starts out with music. I know that he plans what he is going to say but it doesn't always come out that way.

When about 20 of us six grade boys got in trouble for breaking a school rule I felt a little responsible. So I was really trying to solve the problem and really talking it up. Everybody except for me was keeping their mouth shut, but they liked it because I got them off the hook from being suspended.

I won't forget the time my 5 grade teacher was sick and Mr. Bell came in and took over. He told us about the hurricanes and tornedoes when he was little. And when his robe came off in a tornedo. And he found it someplace on a hill.

At the last part of the 5th grade he finally (after 5 years) remembered my name. I'll never forget that!

I won't forget when Mr. Bell was in his office after school was out for the day and the gym was closed and my friends and me wanted to play basketball in the gym and he play with us instead of working.

I'll never forget the time I fell and split my chin and he took me home and looked worried. But I think he was worried because the school would have to pay for the accident.

PARENTS' IMPRESSIONS OF THE PRINCIPAL

Incidental Comments Made by Parents[4]

I don't like that principal, because he won't talk to you. And if he does, he just gives you a bunch of double-talk.

I like the way he tries to explain things to you.

I don't like the way he runs that school: sex education; no discipline; kids are not taught what they are supposed to be taught.

I think that the principal is overly concerned with parents.

I think that he is a good Christian.

He's doing an excellent job.

Parent Impressions Related by the Counsellor

The parents who are unsatisfied with some of the things that are going on really don't have too much to stand on as far as valid reasons for being non-cooperative. There have been some unfortunate things happen and Mr. Bell just happened to be the one who was dealing with them at that time.

He received a card over Christmas time from some parents that had moved to another city and had written back. They were parents who came into school quite often and were quite familiar with the routine here. They were very happy in the manner that their own children were dealt with at school. They wrote back that they didn't think they appreciated Taft School as much until they had moved away.

I would say that most parents have a real positive attitude toward the school. There is that small percentage that wouldn't be satisfied. If they had the moon, they'd still need something else.

[4] These comments were volunteered by parents living in the Taft School attendance area during interviews conducted as part of a related but independent field study carried out by John A. Olson during 1968 (see Olson 1970).

Parent Impressions of the Principal Reported in Written Statements Made by Pupils

Sixth-grade girl: My parents don't know Mr. Bell because my mother and father don't have time to. My mother comes to conferences but that's about all. The reason my father doesn't come is because he thinks that it is a mother doty to take care of our problems.

Sixth-grade girl: My parents both know Mr. Bell very well. We belong to the same church.

Fifth-grade girl: I think my mother and father both know Mr. Bell pretty well but my mother knows him better I think because she is P.T.A. president.

Sixth-grade boy: My mother thinks he is a nice man. But my father never met him.

Sixth-grade girl: My parents don't like him very well because he delays things all the time.

Parent Impressions Related by Teachers

Ed has gotten notes from parents asking him what the role of the principal is! They want him to discipline their children and to spank them and do these things. You know—the *old* role of principal. And he refuses to do it. He's gotten notes from George Parson's folks. They're probably very displeased with the principal. George is in the sixth grade now. His mother came to school once this year. She didn't see why we didn't just spank George and make him behave. They were real disgusted with us.

All the parents I talked to during parent conferences—and I think only two or three of my parents did not show up—were very pleased with this school and the standards that were used. Some of them said to me, "You can use any method you want to control my child."
The parents seem pleased with the school and the way it's run. I don't think any of them have ever said anything to me about Mr. Bell. I think Mrs. Skirmish has had some trouble with parents and their ideas with the way a school should be run and the way this one's being run.

I've never heard a parent say a bad thing about Ed or a good thing. I've never heard any parent reactions. From my observations, they seem to feel pretty free at PTA to visit with him and talk with him.

One family whose oldest boy I had here three years ago was so violently opposed to Ed that they showed up at the superintendent's office a couple of times to make complaints. I'm very happy that over a period of three years—I have their daughter in my class at the moment—they have changed their attitude considerably. They felt that Ed was sort of wishy-washy. It has taken this long to suggest to them that far from being weak, his position has actually been one of real strength.

My particular room is very poor in attending PTA meetings. Many of the parents have never been to PTA. I am still meeting parents for the first time [in March]. And in first grade, that shouldn't be so. There are some parents that I've never met. There are some that I should have met much sooner than I did.

Maybe they're so extremely confident in the school they have no worries. Or else they're just not interested and have other things to do. Quite a number of my parents didn't even come when we had Open House. And there were two times when school was open in the evening for parents to come to the rooms and they were either unable to come or didn't come.

TEACHER IMPRESSIONS OF THE PRINCIPAL

> I contradict myself?
> Very well, then, I contradict myself;
> (I am large—I contain multitudes.)
>
> Walt Whitman, *Song of Myself*

The teacher comments which comprise the remainder of this chapter are taken from two sources—taped interviews and staff questionnaires. The topics which have been used to sort out these comments represent recurring themes whenever Taft teachers discussed their school and their principal. It is interesting to note how frequently teacher comments include comparisons: they compare Taft with other schools, Ed with other principals, and school years past with the school year present. Instances of such comparisons can also be found among teacher comments quoted in previous chapters. The tactic of comparing appears to provide another means by which teachers attempt to socialize or counter-socialize a principal.

The Principal's Job as Taft Teachers Described It

I think a principal should be fair, he should be professional in his actions and use good discretion at all times. He should be an intelligent person. He should be liberal-minded, personable, able to get along with all kinds of people—teachers, parents, children. He should have a stable kind of home relationship and hopefully not too many other pressures.

I think Ed is doing an excellent job as an administrator. I think it's a job a lot of people couldn't do and wouldn't want to do. As some of our "profs" [professors] have told us, that's the last thing they'd ever be—an elementary school principal.

I think the position of principal is a lousy one. I think it can be vicious. One of the better things education might do would be to work toward making the principal a rotating position in which various members of a faculty were to assume this position for a time.

The fiction is that a principal becomes the educational leader in his school. The fact is that if the principal does become the educational leader, his school and teachers are apt to develop an independence which is threatening to superintendents. So the principal who does assume this job to any extent is apt to find himself threatened in one way or another from above. The principal who acts in tune with district policy becomes more or less an organizational figurehead in the school. So one can take one's choice in the principalship of playing ball or playing the game half way. It isn't a great position to be in.

I'm one to believe that a principal is still a principal and that his role is different than that of just another person. You might say that he's the boss. I don't feel that I'm his equal. I don't know if that's because I'm a woman or because I'm a teacher. But I still feel that he should be the one that has the . . . I don't want to say "ruling," because that isn't true, and that's not at all true of Ed . . . but I do feel that there should be a different role between the principal and teacher.

I heard one teacher say to my student teacher last year, "Just remember that *you don't work for him, you work with him."* I think this is true. But you can work with someone and he can still have a different role. I believe that he should be the leader of the school.

Working "for" and Working "with" Ed Bell

Ed's Leadership Style

He seems to have a way of getting things accomplished without being really too directive, or should I say "bossy," about it, but still gets the job done.

He doesn't want to be treated too formally as "the boss." He wants to be treated as one of the staff, be called by his first name, to be kidded with and spoken to in the same tone of voice and in the same way in which you speak to any of the rest of the teachers. I like this. Someone that wants a real strong leader, that doesn't want to make a lot of decisions on their own, wants some one else to carry the burden for him, wouldn't like this at all.

In a few cases I think perhaps he needs to take a little stronger leadership role. But if he did this, he would not be as understanding a person where we are concerned when he looked in on our weaknesses and our difficulties within the classroom. So we have to make up our mind one way or the other, because I don't think he can be both.

He's made a climate where we can do things when we're ready. It used to be, though he didn't say *"You have to do it,"* that he talked about it so constantly that we knew that this was the thing that was expected of us. We almost felt obligated to do some of these things before we were even ready for them.

Ed doesn't pressure us at all. We had a science program coming over the TV and we had this new math, and we were still trying to do as much as we did in language arts. And Spanish came in that year. All the teachers were trying to get *everything* in. Ed told us to slow down, that we were driving ourselves, and that if we didn't get something taught this year, they would get it next year. Then he laughed and said, "That sounds funny for an administrator to say."

I have had an impression that he sometimes expects a program that he has outlined to be followed. For example, we have been having quite a hassle here in the third and fourth grade about lunchroom. The teachers have been mulling it over to see what they could do to create some kind of order in the lunchroom. And in the middle of these discussions Ed will step in and say, "Well, now, do this and this and this and this." And this settles the matter—there you are.

He does try to be direct. I think this is not because of who he is personally but who he is professionally and what he feels is expected of him. And I think he fails at it miserably when he does. It confuses me sometimes. In education, *even as a principal* you can't just be who you are. You still have to put on some kind of different mask. I think that's unfortunate, that's the thing. The one thing that I feel is a shortcoming is: *when he tries to play the role of principal, he doesn't do a very good job of it.*

Like he was trying to tell us all at the first of the year that we should attend the school board meeting. It didn't seem right. The words seemed to be coming out of the wrong mouth or something. There was a directive from downtown that everybody was supposed to attend one meeting. He was very concerned that we go. He wanted us to go because he didn't want us all to show up at the meeting when the board was going to talk about salaries and not any of the others. He said something like, "Everybody ought to go, it's very interesting and you'll

all be glad you went." Sandra Manning challenged him,[5] "Well, if it is so interesting, why do you have to tell us to go? You know we would all just go anyway."
He said, "Sandra, I would rather that you just talk to me about that after the
meeting, and let's don't take the time now to discuss it." The fact that he had
told us to do it was different, and the way he kind of cut her off was a different
Ed than I had been used to seeing.

In some ways he seems to be unsure of what kind of administrator he wants
to be. Sometimes there's a little vacillation, a little change from one role over to
another. I think personally he's a fine, warm person. When he's an administrator
of that type he does a good job. But when he tries to be an "administrator," as
sometimes I think he thinks he's supposed to be, he doesn't do a very good job.

Two types of persons seem uncomfortable here with Mr. Bell—the dependent
person, adult or child, and the person who needs to win. The former seeks
more direction than he receives. The latter finds no game set up to win.

Uncertainty and indecision are among Ed's weakest points. You never know
for sure what to expect from him.

One of his strong points is that he can change his mind without feeling
threatened.

"Backing" Teachers

This particular boy that I have in my class that I am concerned about, I know
that Ed is really backing me up. I know that Ed has backed me up to the
mother when the mother has more or less wondered if I were doing the kind of
job I should be doing. And I really appreciate that, because it concerns me to
think I have something out for her boy or whatever it might be.

Now this idea, and I've heard it from other people, that Ed does not support
his teachers is partly true and partly false. If it came to a showdown between
the teacher and a student it would really depend upon the circumstances. I
feel that I have to be very, very careful about everything I say to the children.
They might go home and say something, you know, and the parents will call up.
He's very public-minded.
I wonder if it did come down to something between me and a student that
didn't look very good on my part, just what he would do. I might get chewed out.
I might have it coming. But I think a lot of teachers feel that it would be nice to
have a principal just take their side no matter what.

The principal I had before would tell the parents one thing and you another.
You would think he was on your side, but you could never depend on it. And
that is something with Ed. I know that if he tells you something, he'll tell the
same thing to the parents.

I know that Ed has made it quite clear that he will not stand for any hitting of
a child or ever defend a teacher in that case.

I have been in a couple of schools in which the principals gave me the opinion
that as long as I was doing what I thought was right, they not only backed me
up but were interested in having me work this way. I feel that the same condition exists here.

---

[5] Mrs. Manning was the teacher who resigned early in the school year. The episode described here provides an example of the "immunity to socialization" discussed in the
previous chapter.

Getting Around the Building

A principal should get around the building a little bit more and be more aware of things. I see Ed in the front office quite often, but I don't see him around too often.

I like the way he stays in the school as much as he can. The kids don't have a picture of him as somebody that sits in an office that they get sent to. He's out in the hall working with the kids. He's in and out of your classroom and very relaxed and easy and it doesn't bother me at all. He's a good politician for Taft School, besides being a good principal. Every time a group of teachers comes in and he gets a cup of coffee he comes and sits down and talks with his faculty.

Perhaps he doesn't get in to the classrooms. You know the tremendous responsibility and the number of activities and phone calls and parents and contacts and all of this comes up unexpectedly. It's pretty hard with this many in the staff to get into the classrooms and be down there often enough to really get a clear picture of what is going on. But he's a pretty keen person at sizing up individuals. I feel perhaps he learns most of what he needs right there in the staff room in listening and participating and general conversations among the teachers there.

Children see him mostly before school or after school or in the lunchroom—he does come into the lunchroom every so often to visit—or the playground. He doesn't come out to the playground too often, but he does come up occasionally.

In the classroom he is really just in-and-out at various times. I haven't been aware of him staying for more than five minutes at any one time in the two years that I've been here.

[The same teacher also said:]

Ed is busy all day with his main interest, children. He's in and out at different times. Not often, but I never see him sitting at his desk just thumbing through papers. I've had one principal in this district who was a "coffee-room sitter."

When they see him, little first-graders will always talk to him on a very informal basis. And pleasantly. Happy about their conversations with him. For one thing, I think they like to see a man image every so often. And he interacts with them very freely and often.

I'm not in contact with him too much because he doesn't really come around to the classroom too often and I've not found it necessary to go in and just talk things over.

I would like to see him be around a little bit more. He compliments me on things that I do when I don't feel that he knows that I really do these things, because he's not coming to the classroom. He was in maybe five minutes one day just fixing the clock, but he's never just come in to see my room. He's never been in here for one lesson or anything.

I would like a principal to come around and see what's going on. I think that they need to, especially in first grade, because most men haven't worked in a primary grade before. I think he should probably be around the children more in different situations rather than just over the loudspeaker. I think it would be nice for him to come in more often.

I got along with my first principal fine. He never stepped into my classroom the whole two years I was there. He was simply biding out his time until his retirement was up.

Public Relations

I think he takes a lot of time working with parents, trying to convince them that our school's way is a good way.

I think he took the defeat of the tax election real personally at first. I know he took a lot of time beforehand to try to talk to parents and get them to know Taft School and what we as a faculty and he himself is trying to do for their kids.

He is overly concerned with parental acceptance. He tries too hard to impress parents, other educators, and the community.

I like his attitude about the importance of community relations, that we've got a job to do with our school having it as an image in the community. I agree with this.

I think he's grown every year in his ability to work with parents, to make them feel that the school is theirs as well as ours (those of us who work here). I think he's had very good public relations with parents that I've worked with.

In the fall, when we had parents here for the Room Desserts, he attended all of them at every grade level. We always have a big turnout for those at the beginning of the year, and he came in to each. He either made a formal statement or just visited with every parent that he had time to talk to.

Sometimes I don't understand why he wants to attend so many public functions. He believes a lot in public relations with people involved in the school. I feel public relations are important, but I don't feel that we have to go out of the way to hold meetings and things just for the fact of involving parents. I don't believe in especially going out of my way to impress people with what's going on. If they want to know what is going on, I think they'll be interested enough to come ask and to look for themselves.

Ed likes to involve parents. In any little problem that comes up, he wants to get a committee to come and do it. If a committee of parents wants to come, then teachers have to come, too. My whole life isn't involved around the school. I give my full time to it in preparing and when I'm at school, but when I go home from school I've done everything I need to at school. I don't need to carry it home with me. I have another life at home. I'm not involved in school 24 hours a day. Just 16!

Treating the Staff as Equals

Taft School is a good place to work. I think it is mainly because Ed is such a "personably-type-person" and is willing to work with us as equals, not just as a superior above us.

Ed is real open with all of us. I am more on a working relationship with him than I was with the woman principal I worked for. I felt I was really an underdog with her. It was more on a formal basis. I called her by her last name. She'd call us by our first names when we were by ourselves. But when we were in front of children or in other groups she'd call us by our last names. We weren't part of the team like Ed sets up in this kind of atmosphere.

I feel he's liberal with children, but I don't believe he is with teachers. I work on weekends, and I asked if I could leave before four o'clock on Fridays. He said no, because it was school district policy. And I mentioned that I'm here at school every morning between seven and seven-thirty, and many nights I'm here until five or five-thirty. I saw no point of him saying, "No," that I couldn't leave. I didn't really feel like I should have to ask him to leave, but I did. I don't know why it is, but I didn't feel that this was consistent with his philosophy toward children.

One of the things I have noticed that I have objected to around here is the difference between classified and professional people. The daytime custodian came in one day and said that he had taken some boys apart that were fighting. The principal, instead of talking to the boys, tells *him* that *he's* not supposed to say anything to the kids. Right in front of the kids. And tells him, "When you see things, you remember that you're the custodian and you're not to say anything to anybody." And then he puts an arm around each of the boys and talks as if, "You boys are fine, but that guy . . . [laugh] is the bad guy." I believe Ed definitely has a class consciousness as far as custodians are concerned. They are "lower" people. This is not consistent with his philosophy of "school's the place where everybody lives together and everybody's equal."

I have used the teacher aide in various ways with the children in the classroom. I expect every child to respect her the same as a teacher. I try to instill that within them. But Ed's idea is, "Well, all the kids know, of course, that they don't have to do what the teacher aide or any of these other people tell them." I think the aide is well aware of this, too. She probably hasn't said it in so many words, but I can sense that she feels like she has to be more apologetic.

About Meetings

Ed expects a religious-type commitment to be present at PTA, staff meetings, and guidance.

My main gripe is PTA. We all feel like we are required to come every time. If we don't, we know that it is something that is displeasing to Ed. So we do come. But sometimes I wonder if maybe we shouldn't have the choice of whether to come or not.

It was really ridiculous at a lot of meetings, because there were twice as many teachers as there were parents. Of course, if the teachers are required to come, and the parents aren't, that's natural.

PTA isn't a real fascinating business. But Ed has never once said to me, "We expect our teachers to go to PTA meetings." This was what was told to me at my other school. But I'd get home and I'm tired and everything and I'd think, "Oh, gee, Ed would be so disappointed if his teachers didn't show up." And he makes you feel that you don't want to disappoint him, because he thinks you're pretty great and don't disappoint him in that.

I appreciate Ed's tremendous interest in guidance. This has helped me tremendously in the classroom—the people he has brought in to help us with this, the guidance meetings they hold.

As far as the staff goes, we seem to get hung up on things like at guidance meetings. I don't think we get a great deal accomplished.

We never make appointments on faculty-meeting day. Hair appointments are the worst. Ed once chewed out someone right in front of everyone, after she left, because she had a hair appointment.

I feel there is a value in many of the meetings, but some meetings are called that are of no value. I feel there should be a definite purpose other than just meeting to have a meeting. I've felt that sometimes our faculty meetings were just simply because he felt there needed to be one. There was nothing in particular that was talked over. He has an agenda that may be half an hour, forty-five minutes, or an hour. Everything's covered, and then he'll say, "Is there anything else?" And then he'll start up on something else.

Somebody said that they thought some of the Wednesday meetings that Ed called were unnecessary. Gee, I haven't felt like I've been very "meeting'd" this year. But this person thought they were kind of useless because we never communicated at them. And perhaps they are, because even without meetings the faculty communicates so much on individual children and things. So maybe he does call unnecessary meetings. It's never bothered me.

This year we've had fewer faculty meetings than ever. On the other hand, his contact on a personal level seems to be stronger. In other words, rather than gather us together and promote ideas, he makes suggestions as he sees one in the hall and as things come up. Perhaps at the moment he feels that the faculty is getting enough group activity through the [in-service] course that is being offered here. But I hope this isn't so. I hope that after the course folds, we will continue to be the same flexible group that I feel we are at the moment.

Another gripe that we have is that our staff meetings are too long and too one-sided and have been in the past. I spoke to Mr. Bell about that just a week or so ago. We were talking about the help the teachers would need in the Social Living program next year. He said that he thought perhaps we needed an in-service class of some kind such as we'd had in this past year. He said, "Of course, we haven't had the staff meetings." I said, "And our communication has been as good, hasn't it, Mr. Bell?" He said, "It's been better, because we had a common problem that we were working on."

So I think he's a little dense here in not realizing that when he sits in the staff meeting and doesn't get any feedback from the teachers that he should know that either this is not a problem to the teachers or he's going about it in the wrong way. In the classroom, he would expect us to realize it, if we got no feedback from the youngsters.

Handling Details

He's a very fair and honest man. But he forgets things, puts them off too long, forgets to tell us. Like when they are going to order books, if we knew about it ahead of time we could spend our money more wisely. He'll tell Bob Mason there's only three more days to do this, there's some of this money that has to be spent, so we all rush about madly. That's his weakness. It's that way in everything. He forgets to tell us, or he just forgets. It kind of "bugs" teachers. It's just part of his personality. He's such a nice, relaxed person, and so easy to work with and everything. I think he just overlooks it.

There are some principals that go "clip, clip, clip." They are hard to work for, and they get on everybody's nerves, but they get everything done with top-notch efficiency. Then there are others that are relaxed and easy going, and it's easy on the teachers. I think you accomplish more in a school with that atmosphere. But then you have to put up with this "forgetting" aspect.

In a building like this, there is sometimes a breakdown in communication. I think you find this in any group of real busy people. Something will be going to happen or something will be needed and there's the old standing joke with Ed: "Here it is. No hurry; it was due ten minutes ago."

Sometimes I wish he'd make a decision when he says. Right now it's our duty schedule. He'll say, "I'll do anything you tell me to, to make it better." But I'm a teacher. I have other problems. Why doesn't he just *do it*?

Ed's Positive and Reassuring Manner

One of the most important things about Ed is the fact that he seems to have confidence in his teachers.

I've enjoyed working here tremendously and really appreciated all the help that Ed has given me. He's always a morale booster. He always tries to find positive things to say that will reassure us, and this is a big help. Sometimes we all feel depressed about what we're doing and wonder if we are doing as effective a job as we might.

I have had a beautiful experience with Taft School. I have nothing but good things to say about Ed, mostly because he makes me feel so good. I think he has this attribute, whether you're really doing a great job or not, of making you feel like you are, and so then you try all the harder.

I give Ed credit for the faculty getting along the way they do. I give him lots of credit for the kids feeling about the school the way they do, because he gives this feeling to the teachers who, in turn, give it to their kids. I don't think the kids have a feeling about, "Gads, here's the principal." If they do, it's just kind of a carry over from their parents.

I'd like to give him credit for the hot lunch program, but [laugh] I can't do that. Although I think he probably makes the cooks feel just as good as he does the teachers, when he has an opportunity to.

I felt really bad when I had to tell Ed that I couldn't come back next year. But he was "really a doll about it," as Kay and I say all the time. He made me feel good about leaving. *He makes me feel good about everything!*

He's very supportive in things that you do in the room with the children or whatever you are studying at the time. All for it, you know. He gives you the idea that you're really doing a good job. Never critical. I've just never been afraid of him or afraid that he might have some doubts about me.

He gives you a good feeling about yourself and makes you feel like you're wanted in the school and part of his staff. He wants us all to work together, which I think we do quite well, and help each other out—this cooperative feeling.

Ed was constantly reassuring me that he was sure I was doing the best that I could. He knew that I was having some problems but, in his attitude, he gave me confidence that I was a professional person, and that I could handle them. And I think his confidence in me gave me confidence in myself to be able to handle these problems.

Accepting New Ideas

I think Ed really gets in and works with us and tries to help us figure out the problems and difficulties we are having and tries to help us come to some conclusions. We are always evaluating the kinds of things we've done and how we could improve situations for ourselves and for the children both. If things aren't working well, he's always willing to help us try and do something a little bit different. At the other school I was at, once something was set up, nothing would be changed. It was static.

He is progressive in the sense that he likes to experiment with new ideas. And he's willing to take a gamble on something. As long as you know your purposes and what you are doing and keep pretty close to the ground, he'll go along with it.

When I heard there was an opening here I came over and visited with Mr. Bell for an hour and a half. I felt that he was quite liberal in letting teachers try anything they wanted to that they had a good reason for doing, that he would like to try new things and not stay in a rut. One of his strong points is that he keeps up on new educational methods.

Ed's Philosophy of Education[6]

Ed's biggest emphasis in teaching is developing the most in any child—developing their own self-concept first and subjects second.[7] I like that.

This school isn't typical of those I've worked in before. I think that, compared with other principals, Ed is a rather unusual person. I think he has an extreme dedication to what he's doing. He believes very strongly in the things he believes in—to the extent that sometimes he might get carried away with his belief and not get down to the actual situation.

I think he's very dedicated and believes in everything he says. He doesn't just quote philosophy and not practice it. I think he is wise enough to see that maybe Taft School is too far to the progressive side of education, but he feels this is better than being too far the other way.

I think he changes a little bit every year. He's always questioning himself and his motives and his philosophy. He's always wondering, "Am I really doing the right thing or thinking the right thing?"

I feel that he is pretty lenient and open-minded. And yet I feel that I don't know in which direction he really would like progress to be made.

Almost always when we get into a discussion, Ed pulls us back to the fact, "Well, what's best for the youngster?" Not what's best for the teacher, what's best for the principal, or what's best for the parents. What's best for the youngster! I think we need constantly to be reminded of that in education.

[The same teacher also said:]

As I've told Ed several times, "Let's cut out the philosophizing and get to the things we really need to get at." Because he really does like to philosophize. You need some dreamers and people who philosophize, but as I've often said, "There's a time and a place, and right now we've got to get this job taken care of and planned for, because this is going to come up tomorrow or the next day whether we are ready for it or not." I think he's cut down tremendously on this.

The "Loose Structure" at Taft School

If I read Ed correctly, he has a theory that schools are children-oriented and that children should take a great part and a great responsibility in their own education. He likes a fair amount of freedom and pretty loose standards.

I believe that Ed is seeing that children should have some boundaries put around them that they aren't just allowed to run free. I taught here in the summer school and I didn't agree with the way the children behaved in the classroom. This probably was the philosophy at the time. I have felt that things were tightening up a little bit more, *which I agree with*.

Ed does not spell things out clearly enough as to his expectations, particularly along the line of structure. How much structure should we have in our classrooms, and how much freedom? We got into sort of a hassle about it last year.

---

[6] Because of the preoccupation which teachers exhibited toward "structure" at Taft School, comments on that particular aspect of Ed's philosophy are considered separately. The superintendent of schools once made a comment to a group of principals that provides a rather different perspective from those presented here: "Individuals in a school district only have attitudes. There is only *one* basic philosophy in a district."

[7] See Jules Henry's observation, "In the United States there is a sharp division between those who think that the primary function of a teacher is to facilitate a child's emotional adjustment, and those who think that the teacher's main function is to teach subject matter" (1960:297).

It kind of boiled down to the point where it was just an individual thing. If you liked an unstructured classroom, you could have one. If you liked it structured . . . well, everyone felt that he liked the unstructured better.

The new teachers didn't know what to make of it. When I talked with Sally Jensen—she was new that year—she said, "Well, what is this? What does he want? Does he want us to structure the classroom, or give them a lot of freedom, or what?"

And I said, "To tell you the truth, I've been here a year and a half and I still don't know myself!"

I think all of the teachers this year have sort of drawn in a little bit more, because the two examples that we saw of an unstructured situation were such disasters in the sixth grade. Sandra Manning's class, for one. Of course, she's gone. And Wally Adam's room. ["Is it an unstructured room?" I asked.] Don't you know! Oh, gee, you haven't lived. That's "The Jungle." They do as they please. He just gives them a lot of freedom to express themselves. I think that a lot of us look at that as an example of an unstructured situation and we don't want to have our rooms look like that.

I think the Intern Supervisor is the one who brought the word "structure" in and used it very frequently. She wanted to know how she could structure the program better. And then it became a dirty word as some of us wanted to know just what she was trying to do and to whom she was trying to do it and who was being structured. I think that some of us convinced her that she wasn't really trying to structure the program for the kids but by the same token was trying to structure the whole faculty into a program.

I think Ed's back to realizing, where children are concerned, that in the fall we have to start out slowly and not just turn the children loose. Kids will be kids, no matter how long you work at it. He's worked with the children and with the staff in trying to give the children every bit of freedom and responsibility that they're able to handle. Not every bit they want, which was the situation last year. This year he realizes that there's some limitations that have to be set.

One of Ed's weakest points is his seeming distrust of structure in classroom and school organization.

I taught my first year in another city under a woman principal, which of course is sort of a different atmosphere than it would be under a man. In that school things were much more structured then they are here. The children would be expected to march down the hall, be quiet, and more or less toe the line. And children that didn't do these things were immediately sent to the principal. This was her major responsibility, to handle the discipline.

I probably operate better in a structured atmosphere than a nonstructured one, but I like to think I'm somewhere in between. I'm structured in that I know what my plans are for the day. I'm unstructured in the fact that if we don't get to them, who cares? And that I try to give children a lot of time to do things on their own. I mean, I'm not over them all the time, but yet I know where I'm going from day to day.

One teacher was quite dissatisfied with her evaluation. That was Margaret Elder. She is more or less of the old school. She said that Ed seemed to follow a pattern throughout her whole evaluation of terming her as being a "structured" teacher. She felt that it wasn't exactly fair and that she wasn't as entirely structured as all of this.

Structured means having lines in the halls, having a very clean school, having very low noise level classrooms, having pretty structured things for the kids to do, not much working in groups, not too many messy projects. I take my kids out to read a story underneath the trees—I'm not sure that would really be approved of in lots of schools. Now I'm talking about the extreme structured situation. I wonder if, in a situation like that, the faculty room would be as fun. I think you'd feel structured in the faculty room if your classroom was that way.

I can only think of one teacher on this faculty that has felt a little uncomfortable in this situation at first. That was Margaret Elder, but I think that even she has come to feel more comfortable in it. I'm sure she was used to a more structured way in the building, and she had her class more structured. I imagine she felt a little bit of pressure from the rest of the faculty, and perhaps Ed, to relax somewhat.

[Margaret Elder said:]

Taft is quite a loosely structured sort of system and there are some people who can't work here too well. I haven't quite decided whether I can work here well or not, because evidently I'm a rather structured person and I like a little more formalized structure to sort of wield my way around. I do think it would be wise to stay at least another year and give myself a chance. There must be something to this informal situation that I'm not aware of.

Accepting "Individual Differences" among the Teachers

I think that Ed is a very liberal-minded person. I can tell from things he's talked to me about. In hiring me, one thing that was interesting is that when my name came up there must have been some question about my being Jewish and that he thought this would add to the school.

He allows teachers to be individuals in the way they handle their classroom.

He's too lenient toward parents' and children's personal needs and not understanding toward teachers' individual personal needs.
[The same teacher also said:]
One of his strong points is that he is aware of individual needs.

I think Ed gives a lot of leeway as far as how we teach. I think he realizes that each teacher teaches in a different way. He doesn't expect us to fit into any set pattern.

I think Ed kind of chooses teachers who he knows can fit in with his philosophy.
[The same teacher said:]
An ideal principal is somebody like Ed who can get three-fourths of our teachers working together and that can work with somebody as liberal as Wally Adam and as structured as Margaret Elder and handle them both, even though maybe he disagrees with some things Wally does and some things Margaret does.

Wally Adam is an example of Ed's acceptance of (should I say tolerance of?) differences in teacher behavior. There have been other "Wallys."

I know that Ed admires Wally's philosophy of education but I've also heard Ed laying him out for something he did, too.

Organization and communication are Ed's weakest points. Sometimes teachers are uncomfortable because guidelines are not clear and may appear to be different with different teachers. Even the autonomy to use unique teaching techniques or differ in classroom management may not be clear or completely consistent.

[The same teacher also said:]

One of Ed's strongest points is his consistency in allowing teachers to be autonomous.

A "Comfortable" School

I have been real comfortable at this school in that I've been allowed to do as I wanted. And I feel quite comfortable around Mr. Bell, as I have the other principal I worked for. I feel that this should be something that every teacher should feel. It would be rather difficult to work for someone that you didn't feel relaxed around.

I really think Ed's a wonderful principal. There's very few schools where the children like the principal as well as they do here and feel like the school belongs to them and are as comfortable as they are.

I've substituted and been in a lot of different schools. Each school has a different atmosphere. It depends on the principal, really. In this school I think you have the least pressure put on you of any school I know.

Another thing that is very good about this building is the way our staff room is used, to discuss children and problems, exchange ideas, give suggestions, have fun among the staff, pull jokes on each other.

One of Ed's real strong points is making almost anyone who comes in here feel comfortable and feel relaxed and feel wanted and feel needed.

I had a real comfortable feeling here last year, even though it was my beginning year. The cooperation was extremely high. I think it's probably even more so this year.

I think one of Ed's strongest points is his ability to create a happy—sometimes slap-happy—school environment for children and teachers.

A Special Regard for Ed

Maybe it's just because I work with them and know more about how they feel, but I'd say the third- and fourth-grade teachers have a real intense feeling of loyalty to Ed and what a great guy he is and what a great principal. I think first and second grade has this same sort of feelings, although maybe it's not as intense. Now, in fifth and sixth grade, I think maybe Martha Duchess knows him better than anybody here. She can tease him better. I think Wally Adam has lots of respect for him, but I don't feel Wally needs a principal to make him feel good.

[Wally Adam said:]

Rather than think of Ed as a leader, I think of him as being a very strong colleague. The word "leader" is a very poorly defined word in our society. For instance, I suspect that many of our leaders are drivers. Or many of our leaders are people who are merely sitting where they are on the crest of a wave and they're better balancers, and what appears to be leadership is merely a juggling of situations or an adjustment of positions so that the person on top can remain there. It appears to be very strong leadership, but actually it's being in the right place and anticipating where to be on a particular issue. I really think it is very fortunate for me that I have a person like Ed in his position. He and I have "clicked" on a personal level.

[Martha Duchess said:]

I'm a person that speaks her mind pretty frankly, and so Mr. Bell and I are on a pretty friendly, pretty *frank* basis where our work is concerned. Perhaps this is because I've known him as long as I have and worked with him as long as I have. I suppose you would say to some extent we're personal friends outside the school, although family-wise we're not close this way. It's more just to run in for the weekend or an evening or something of this kind. We don't make any particular point of making engagements or going back and forth for dinner or this type of thing.

I know most all of the principals personally, except the newer ones that have come in the last few years. I think if I had to pick someone to work with, from what I know and what other teachers have talked about in their buildings and so on, that I probably couldn't pick anyone that I would enjoy working with as much. Perhaps this is just personality. We happened to hit it off.

[The counsellor said:]

I'm probably quite spoiled. If I had to be moved to another school and under a different administrator, I just probably wouldn't be too happy about that right away. You get used to somebody and know how they think and how they operate, and you can just about read what they are thinking and what they are expecting you to do or wanting you to do. Then you operate in that manner. I think that probably I have this insight into a lot of people, and Mr. Bell is one of them.

Comment

The common element among these disparate sets of opinions is that they all pertain to Ed Bell or to Taft School perceived as a function of Ed's management of it. The comments are in context in terms of Ed's life, because they represent the varied and often contradictory sets of expectations which he confronts in the course of his everyday work. At the same time, they are out of context in terms of each speaker's unique personality and experience vis-à-vis Ed and the school. It is difficult to know how individuals wished their principal would act when their own expectations were self-contradictory, to know how deeply certain of these stated convictions were held, or to assess what actual impact they had. For example, whether or not pupils like and respect their principal—or even know who he is— may have little to do with accomplishing the institutional purposes of the school or satisfying the personal motives of those who are present at it. I suspect that those who were "comfortable" at Taft School exhibited more ambiguity in their perceptions and expectations of Ed and thus were able to make greater accommodation for his behavior, while those who were less satisfied set expectations calculated to show him always at a disadvantage.

There were at least two techniques which Ed employed to buffer himself from the conflicting and sometimes antagonistic views held by those about him. One was through his ability to bare his soul of problems that bothered him, often, it seemed, to the first person who happened along. Ed appeared remarkably able to shrug off many of the kinds of threats and comments that can drive principals "up the walls," not only the rumors of conspiracies to "get" administrators that occasionally circulate within the ranks of public school employees and the communities they serve but also the lesser innuendos and audible asides forever cast in a principal's direction. For comments that penetrated too deeply to be easily dismissed, Ed's reaction was frequently to discredit the authority or competence of the source to his select audience.

Ed's second means for reducing the impact of the variation to which he was continually exposed was to surround himself with coteries of like-minded confidants whose opinions and judgments he sought because they were customarily sympathetic and inevitably supportive of him personally. At school this coterie consisted of a psychologically nurturing group of older female teachers with whom, usually in individual conversations, he shared many of his problems. Among his administrative colleagues Ed had a comparable and almost-as-nurturing group consisting of several of the male principals senior to him. By surrounding himself professionally with such persons, Ed was able to filter out much of the dissonance to which he was subjected and to dissipate among confidants that which he could not otherwise ignore. There are obvious advantages to such behavior from the point of view of individual mental health, but the procedure was not foolproof. Relatively unimportant differences of opinion did occasionally "get to" Ed in spite of his armour of personnel, and important differences of opinion and indications of stress sometimes escaped him as he attempted in typical style to acknowledge them but to pass over them too lightly.

11 / Patience and prudence

Patience: The Eternal Search for Role

If principals dream of a time when they no longer will have to face such disparate expectations as those which seem to pervade their professional lives, they do so because the dream itself affords some comfort rather than because they believe such a day could ever be a reality. What they do think about and talk about—the one possible hope in which most of them are willing to invest energy as well as concern—is in their eternal search for an "improved" role. Like many of their other collective behaviors, their search for role entails elements of group ritual and elements of individual patience and hope. The group activity brings a certain degree of satisfaction through the recognition of mutual awareness and expressed determination; but the basic problem, frequently defined as lack of an adequate role definition, remains unresolved and essentially unchanged despite the energy expended and the accompanying good intentions. The literature directed to elementary school principals, particularly in their major professional journal, shows a constant parade of articles addressed to the continuing and self-conscious examination of their present role and a preoccupation with what the role might or should become.[1]

The search for role is in-group talk. Administrators do not publicly declare their anxiety concerning role definition among patron statuses like parents or teachers, and the extent of their dissatisfaction with the principalship is not usually made explicit to their central office superiors. But in the privacy of their own formal and informal conversations, discussions of role consume a substantial part of their time.

There are two heavily intertwined but separable components to the preoccupa-

[1] Titles of articles appearing in the *National Elementary Principal* during 1966–67 included, "Beyond Survival for the Elementary Principal" (September); "A New Image of the Elementary School Principal" (September); "Reflections of a Fledgling Administrator" (November); "Training Administrators for Inner-City Schools: A Proposal" (January); "A District Superintendent Looks at the Principal" (February); "A Look Ahead at School Administration" (April). In addition to similar titles the following year, two of the six annual issues (April and May) were devoted to the special theme, "The Changing World of the Elementary School Principal."

tion with a changing role. One component emphasizes change in the historical sense—that the duties and responsibilities of the principal have changed dramatically in the recent past, well within the memory of present old-timers; and forces acting to change society or the schools inevitably will produce continuing change in the duties and responsibilities of the principalship of the future. During the period of this study, the effects of a new and unprecedented "teacher militancy,"[2] though far away geographically and probably a long way off in time from comfortable suburban elementary schools like Taft, gave principals everywhere some cause for alarm. If some principals remained unperturbed, their national organization, their journals, and their invited speakers did their best to alarm them. Such efforts to arouse concern were not wasted on Ed. Toward the end of the field study he was alerting other colleagues to the importance of becoming knowledgeable about "collective bargaining and negotiations," and warning that the district and state should be planning a course of action rather than just waiting for things to happen. Because of his interest, the local principal's association asked him to be its official representative at a one-day conference sponsored by the State Education Association on this topic. Ed's concern was for the role that principals would play should teacher groups become sufficiently powerful to negotiate directly with school boards. The opinions he had heard convinced him that principals were wise to maintain their identification with "management":

> We're already on the management side. I wish we weren't, because it can get in the way of educating kids, but the gap is there, and I just have to admit it. We're too small a group to make much difference anyway—it's the teachers who are powerful. A couple of years ago, I would have joined the teachers in any such action [for example, a strike], but now I think I can do more good by keeping out of it. Where principals have gone on strike, they have often not been rehired because they did not have tenure as administrators. Where they have stayed around, they can act as arbitrators between teachers and school boards.

As a result of the arguments he heard at the conference, Ed tempered his position:

> I think I came away from that meeting with a new idea, that teachers and administrators *can* stay in the same camp for a long while, maybe indefinitely. We have more in common with teachers than with the superintendent. He's *really* management.

The other related aspect of concern toward their role reflected a concern for up-grading the principalship so that as the role evolved it would improve in quality and become more professional. This quest was echoed constantly in the recurring rhetorical question that principals ask: "What *should* we be doing as principals?" The topic was a pervading reason for principals to convene and hear an outside speaker reflect on the subject, or to share personal points of view with their colleagues, as illustrated by the following episodes.

---

[2] Wags pointed out that in some metropolitan school districts where teachers went on strike in the late 1960's any student who missed as many days as the teachers did would have been expelled summarily from school.

What Is Our Role? A Guest
Speaker Gives His View

Comments made during an after-dinner talk at a principals' meeting illustrate the intertwining between the facts of the changing role and the dream of an improved one. The occasion was one of the monthly meetings of the County Association of Elementary School Principals. The meeting was attended by Ed and about 50 of his fellow principals. The evening consisted of dinner in the cafeteria of the host school, a brief business meeting, an invited talk, and the inevitable building tour. The speaker was the president of the state organization of elementary principals. He was a principal in the state's largest school district; his own school had 35 teachers and 800 pupils ranging from kindergarten through grade eight. The speaker was introduced toward the close of the meal after the customary silver-ware-against-water-glass signal for attention. The introduction was made by program chairman Louis Baker, a principal from Ed's district: "Harold Mullen, our speaker, is a person who has travelled around the state a lot and who can tell us something and give us a perspective on what it means to be a principal."

The speaker began by explaining he was going to be informal in presenting some of his thoughts, for he had not prepared a formal address. Until that afternoon, he reported, he had not been sure whether he was going to be able to make the long drive to attend the meeting, for he had not been feeling well for the last few days ("Out in the eastern part of the state they call what I have 'crowbar diarrhea'—the doctor told me to take a laxative and to stay in bed, but that didn't seem like very good advice"). Before beginning his comments on the principalship, he followed the custom observed by many speakers at these voluntary professional meetings of "warming up" the audience:

> Back when I was just getting started in administration I remember going in to see the superintendent and asking about a raise. The superintendent agreed that I deserved one, but he told me, "The budget is pretty tight this year. Come around next year, Harold . . . if you're still with us."
>
> While I was eating dinner, I asked your program chairman, Louis Baker, how long he had been working in the district. He told me he'd been working ever since the superintendent told him he was considering letting him go.

He began his "serious" discussion of the elementary principalship by describing some current problems facing principals, including the urgent need for a state-wide kindergarten program (his district was one of the few which offered kindergarten), the extensive use made of school buildings (his own building was in use 18 hours a day), and new problems in professional negotiations. Yet in spite of the significance of the pressing problems that confront the elementary principal, he said that in his opinion the position had continued to be an inferior one in the educational hierarchy. He made a frequently-heard analogy contrasting educators—specifically principals—with the medical profession: "We should read professional papers in groups like this. I wonder why I don't share any of the things I do or have seen in schools. How do we keep our ideas out in front?"

Excerpts from his comments reflect the same concerns voiced almost universally by old-timers who have experienced changes in the principalship through the years:

We aren't doing what we *should* be doing. We never seem to have enough time.

When I first started in administration, three years was all the preparation required. Today you have to have a master's degree plus 33 units to hold a state credential for elementary administration. Of course in those days teachers weren't prepared to teach, and the principal spent all his time helping new teachers. Today the colleges prepare them to teach, and we do other things.

I'm struggling to hold on to the role of the school principal as I have known it, but I'm watching it change. It may be that in a few years there won't be any role of elementary school principal as we know it. In Switzerland, they don't even have elementary principals—they just pass the job around among the staff.

I think elementary principals are a kind of people who have an extra-ordinary concern for youngsters.

At that last state meeting of the elementary principals, I heard the State Superintendent of Schools say—I'm not sure whether it was in the whole session or in a private meeting afterward—that the way the federal government is moving today, if it isn't checked, education may be taken over by people outside the group of professional educators.

As we sit in the principal's office, what chance do we have to learn what our roles can be? Just keeping the school functioning is almost more than one person can handle. Take my own school, for instance. I have 35 teachers, over 800 kids from kindergarten through grade eight including the seventh and eighth grades run as a junior high school program. I have over 50 certified people working in the building, and I have two full-time secretaries.

When I started as a principal, the assistant superintendent advised me, "Harold, 75 percent of your time should be spent in evaluation, instruction, and curriculum." I couldn't even do it then. Today, it's reversed. I don't spend 25 percent of my time with the people who are handling the instructional program.

At the conclusion of the talk, the principals rose in applause. The program chairman concluded the presentation in folksy style intended as a compliment: "Thank you very much, Harold, for a general, real, nonacademic speech." His emphasis on the word "real" indicated that the speaker had addressed himself to the problems of the principalship as only an insider can understand them.

At another meeting of the same organization later in the year, the principals heard substantially the same message about the problem of role definition in their work, this time from a professor of educational administration. The professor referred to problems of "role conflict" and "role dilemma" confronting principals. He indicated that the increased attention being given to professional negotiations in education finally was going to force an answer to an age-old question that principals had never resolved, namely, whether they are basically teachers or not, and thus, in negotiation, whether they represent labor or management.[3] "I am convinced the position is pretty ambiguous, the waters are pretty muddy," the

---

[3] Like Ed, most principals seem loath to ally themselves in either camp. As a West Coast high school principal whose opinion was subsequently printed in a national newsletter explained, principals should neither align themselves with the superintendent as part of the management side nor with teachers as part of the labor side, for theirs is the "unique position" of "being always on the side of the kids." (Quoted in "PDK News Notes and Quotes" 9(1) September 1969.

professor warned. Unless elementary principals do something about it, they're going to get pushed here and there."

What Is Our Role? A Committee
Talks over the Problem

Ed shared the misgivings of his colleagues about the problems of role. He also felt some personal responsibility to do something about them. During the period in which this study was made, Ed was, to borrow a phrase from Margaret Mead, "coming of age" in the principalship. He was firmly and permanently established as a principal; he had accepted the principalship as his professional career goal; and, at the urging of more senior colleagues, he had begun playing an active part in implementing the internal, organizational activities of the principal associations. If the role of the principal was in trouble, Ed wondered whether the organization of which he was president, the Regional Association of Elementary School Principals, had a part to play: "We have to decide whether this group wants to wait to see what will come about or to do something about it."

To review how the regional association might better serve its membership, Ed arranged a special meeting to explore ideas for action. Calling the meeting was his first major administrative act of the new school year as president of the association (October of the second year of the field study). Ed's intent was to provide a forum where a representative group of principals could identify their own problems. As stated in the letter Ed mailed to the invited participants, "The committee assignment will be to determine action that principals in our region would like to see or recommend to our organization. Such action might have state-wide or local implications. . . . Come with ideas, your own or those borrowed from others."

The group that met consisted of nine principals. Ed had invited one principal from his own district, Lou Baker, to accompany him and to serve on the committee. Two of the principals who attended were first-year administrators. There was one female administrator in the group; by acclaim she was chosen to act as secretary.

How the meeting evolved, and the concerns that emerged during the discussions, are revealed through excerpts presented from the dialogue. The dialogue suggests the degree of self-consciousness about role that I felt to be implicit but pervasive among the principals throughout the study. In the public contexts in which principals usually found themselves, such self-consciousness typically was indicated by no more than a brief comment, an exchange of "knowing glances," or heads nodded silently in agreement. On this occasion the principals sought to make their problems sufficiently explicit to provide a basis for action, and their remarks were made within the sanctuary of their peers.

As the dialogue shows, the topic of "salaries" emerged rather quickly; eventually it was singled out as the immediate problem toward which the group should address its attention.[4] Although salary was a frequent topic of discussion among

---

[4] Educators at virtually any level show a remarkable proclivity to discuss the problem (but not necessarily the amount) of their salaries, either covertly or blatantly, any time they gather. Principals appear particularly susceptible to this behavior. Their remarks suggest that salary and status are perceived as synonymous, or that salary is the "test" of status.

the principals, there was an extenuating circumstance for the introduction of the topic at this meeting. The report of a salary study committee appointed by the president of the state organization of elementary principals had only recently been completed, submitted, and accepted at the annual meeting of that organization. Subsequently the report had been circulated to every elementary principal in the state. Principals had not yet had an opportunity to discuss the report with colleagues outside their own districts.

If the interpretation is correct that the eternal quest for a better role is a ritual activity, then even if the report of the new salary study had not been available, or if salary problems in some form had not ultimately become the center of the committee's attention, it seems unlikely that the discussion of "role" would have gone much further than it did. The usual complaints were aired, the usual solution was proposed: somebody (else) ought to do a role study. Ed's part in the process was "to get things started" and then to let others carry on without him.

The Discussion

Ed raised his voice to be heard above the voices of several informal conversations and suggested that everyone refill his (styrofoam) coffee cup and take a place around a large table in the library of the host school.

ED: It seems to me we sort of meet together, swap stories, have some coffee, get some inspiration, and so forth, whenever our professional organizations get together, and then we return home to do pretty much as we always do. Maybe we ought to do some other kinds of things. For example, we could put together ideas we might want action on, even immediately, like recommendations to our legislators or to our state organization. Or we might make resolutions to feed to our Resolutions Committee, because they aren't really set up to formulate new ideas. I'd like to call on Pete Simpson for his ideas on this.

PRINCIPAL SIMPSON: (an active member of the organization and an officer in the state principal's association) The elementary school principal should provide more leadership. We go to meetings and workshops, but are there things we could do to help our status and also help the education of boys and girls?

PRINCIPAL: (from a small town) You're right! I went to one meeting and all I heard was a talk on "How to Collect Lunch Money." I thought that was pretty procedural. I was hoping for something on a little higher level.

ED: Yes, we all share these problems. Jerry [principal of the host school], why don't you take it from here [i.e., act as chairman]. I'll be glad to sit in today, but if you meet again, I may not meet with you.

PRINCIPAL JERRY: O.K.

ED: There are a couple of other principals who are interested but who couldn't make it today. Martin Albert couldn't come—he has a school carnival which they are getting ready to put on real soon, maybe today. And another principal already had a meeting called for today, getting ready for our next conference. We should have checked meeting schedules first.[5]

It was not by conscious design, but neither is it completely coincidental, that the activities described in the monograph begin (see Chapter 2, "A Day in the Life") and end (the present chapter) with salary as a focus of discussion in professional meetings.

[5] Ed had expected to attend the other meeting himself. Once he learned of the conflict, he asked Bill St. Claire to attend in his place. The practice of "sitting-in" for others on committees seemed to be common among these educators and raises interesting questions as to the perceived function of individual participation and presence at such meetings.

By the way, Martin was interested in knowing how many of you here are from districts where the administrative salary schedule is tied in with the teacher's schedule and how many are on separate administrative salaries? I guess by now you are all familiar with that report of the study committee headed by Professor Gray that worked last summer on administrative salaries. They recommended a "minimum ratio" of 1.33 [i.e., that the maximum scheduled salary for principals be at least 33 percent more than the maximum salary for teachers].

PRINCIPAL BAKER: I think we could do a better job if we looked into the role of the elementary school administrator. Right now it's a bastard job. Just what are we supposed to do? Is it instructional? I think a better thing for us to look at [than salaries] is the job.

How about the new principals—is it a good training they're getting? What do they know? We all came through the old program, but what are these younger fellows getting? I believe now that any school in the state with eight teachers has to have an administrator with a credential.

PRINCIPAL SIMPSON: May I add that when Professor Gray worked on this committee he came up with the fact that in some cases the job of the principal is pretty limiting.

ED: Maybe some of you here aren't aware of this report. Should we have someone read it aloud? [Heads nodded agreement. One of the first-year principals read the summary from a copy of the report.]

In addition to the "minimum ratio" of the administrative salary schedule to the teachers salary schedule noted above, the report recommended 1) provision for a series of increments leading to the maximum salary, 2) that every school district establish a separate salary schedule for its principals based upon the teachers' salary schedule and the teachers' work year, and 3) that each principal's salary be increased by a series of carefully elaborated ratios. These special ratios, to be negotiated in establishing the salary schedule of each district, were designed to account for certain factors common to the principalship but subject to variation from one school and district to the next, including:

a. leadership responsibilities

b. specialized preparation (advanced graduate study)

c. days required beyond the teaching year

d. size of school

e. years of previous administrative experience

f. additional responsibilities beyond those normally associated with the administration of an elementary school (for example, driving the school bus).

To illustrate how the recommendation could be implemented, the report provided an example of an administrator's salary based on an index figure comprised of four specific facets, with the facets serving as multipliers beyond the basic teacher salary schedule:

Facet 1:   The first responsibility of an administrator is to be an educator, thus his base salary is derived from the teacher salary schedule.

Facet 2:   The administrator works a longer year than teachers. His salary is increased at the rate of 2½ percent a week for the length of his extended contract.

Facet 3:   A responsibility factor allows an additional ½ percent of salary for each full-time teacher up to a maximum of 24 teachers (12 percent).

Facet 4:   Since the principal becomes more effective and valuable with additional years of administrative experience, he is allowed an experience factor of one percent a year to the maximum allowed to teachers.

After the reading aloud of sections of the report, the discussion resumed.

RURAL PRINCIPAL: Those "Facets" don't take into account things like supervising the district's transportation system or looking after the community use of the building. Shouldn't the principal be paid for that?

ED: If duties like that are included in what we do now, then they will just come to be expected. Maybe this is a good time to get out of such duties.

NEW PRINCIPAL: I was taking a class from Professor Gray when this report was being developed. He explained to us why these particular factors were included. As a matter of fact, he gave us some first drafts before the report was ready for circulation.

ED: All this may be pretty academic. Maybe we ought to discuss what *we* can do, what *we* can deal with and reasonably take action on.

NEW PRINCIPAL: I like that Facet Number One, that administrators are teachers first and foremost, and that it is better to tie in and work on a ratio than to try to get a uniform salary schedule. We were talking about this during the drive here in the car this morning. Myron Lieberman was our guest speaker at the last state meeting and he told us that administrators ought not to tie their salaries to the coat-tails of the teachers [see Lieberman 1966]. But I think we should tie them in.

PRINCIPAL BAKER: You know, another thing we should be working on is to get sabbatical leaves for administrators. It's so difficult to keep up with new developments when we never get any time.

PRINCIPAL JERRY: You're right. You hire one or two new teachers and listen to them and you don't even know what they're talking about.

ED: How does the school board see the administrator? Don't you think they see us as the guys who get the dogs off the field? I think they need to be informed that there is a need for leadership in the elementary schools.

PRINCIPAL BAKER: I never have worked with a superintendent who really understands the role of the elementary school administrator!

NEW PRINCIPAL: Why don't we foot the bill for a couple of guys to go to the Regional Educational Lab [one of the series of regional laboratories established in 1965 by the Office of Education] and do a role study of the administrator for a year or so. I think the teachers are moving ahead in doing things like that in spite of the administrators these days.

ED: As far as studies go, that's what CASEA[6] is doing, isn't it, Harry?

PRINCIPAL SIMPSON: To do an effective job as principal requires a longer length of time than we have. We need to work all year through if we are going to get to know the community.

NEW PRINCIPAL: Here's another thing. I got assigned to a 16-teacher school in our district, and 15 is our cut-off point. So I'm getting $800 a year more than some of my friends who have been in it [administration] for several years. They're not happy about it.

PRINCIPAL JERRY: I'm not sure about whether being the principal of a big school

---

[6] CASEA refers to the Center for the Advanced Study of Educational Administration, one of a series of research and development centers established by the Office of Education beginning in 1964. The researcher was associated with CASEA while conducting the present study. It became necessary to explain for the benefit of the new principals that the study I was conducting was not a role study, at least not in terms of what these principals were interested in. Excerpts from that dialogue are included in the protocol.

is any more work. I don't know whether a principal in a small school works less or just does his job better.

ED: How far are you going to carry this business of "size?" Last year I had a total of 17 *student teachers*—shouldn't that enter into it?

ANOTHER PRINCIPAL: What about adjusting the salaries for things like setting up the bus schedule, or coming down to open up the building in the evening?

NEW PRINCIPAL: If all these extra duties were put on a percent basis maybe we would price the principalship right out of existence because school districts would have to pay principals too much for their noninstructional problems.

ED: Well, we've been at this for an hour and ten minutes and I'm not sure that we are getting anywhere except to criticize a report made by Professor Gray.

ANOTHER PRINCIPAL: We have to decide if we are going to accept a report like Harry's [the present monograph] or if we are going to go ahead to ask our regional principal's association, or some other group like the state or national elementary principal association, to do it.

PRINCIPAL JERRY: Maybe this is a good time for you all to go through our cafeteria line and get your lunches. We'll have to go to a different room to eat lunch. Then you can continue your discussion.

The school hot lunch that day included chicken, mashed potatoes and gravy, salad, freshly baked corn bread, ice cream cups, milk, and coffee for adults. Conversation among the principals during the meal turned first to the problem of having state support for schools rather than making school districts dependent on local property taxes for such a large part of their support. One principal offered, optimistically, "When the Vietnam War stops, the money which is supporting it will go into buildings for education." Someone more pessimistic replied, "When Vietnam ends, there will probably be someone else to fight. I hate to see us tie in our budget for education to a war budget."

During a lull in the conversation, I asked the principals to elaborate on the kind of investigation into the principalship they would like to see. "If you had the opportunity to get CASEA to do any kind of study that would help you, what would you ask for? My study will only be about what you *do,* but you already know that." Their responses set them in motion for continuing the deliberations begun that morning.

PRINCIPAL: We need to make better use of our time.

NEW PRINCIPAL: I need to know, what should I be doing?

OBSERVER: Research can't answer that. At least, not my kind.[7]

ANOTHER PRINCIPAL: We need to know how we can exercise better leadership, and to find rapid ways of getting things moving, like the machinery for a meeting like this.

ANOTHER: We need to know about how to manipulate a staff. Like this sensitivity stuff that some fellow from the Regional Education Laboratory was talking about.

ANOTHER: We need to find out more about the curriculum. And about evaluation.

[7] The ethnographic approach was only one of a variety of ways in which researchers at CASEA were approaching the study of educational administration. Educators particularly interested in the problem of role definition in the principalship and the specific kinds of in-school problems enumerated at the meeting described here are referred particularly to Becker *et al.* 1971, Schmuck and Nelson 1970, and Schmuck, Runkel, *et al.* 1972.

ANOTHER: I think one thing we need to know more about these days is the impact of teacher's unions and what their place is going to be. Especially in our larger communities.

ED: I think we'd be way out in left field if the union came along and managed to split us off from the teachers.

NEW PRINCIPAL: Principals should be more involved with policy making at the district level. I've just been handed two chapters of a new policy statement from the central office. It deals with teachers and principals. I'm supposed to be one of the principals who is preparing it, but I think the stuff is actually being written by the superintendent and the school board.

ED: I promised our host we'd be out of here by 1:30 and it's almost that time now. So where do we go from here? Let's hear a list of the major points we have developed so far.

PRINCIPAL JERRY: Here's a list I've been keeping: principals' salaries, the union problem, sabbatical, the role of the principal, and policy making.

ED: Which one of these do we want to pursue? We can't do them all.

PRINCIPAL: Maybe *salaries* is a good one to start on.

ANOTHER PRINCIPAL: I think that's a good one.

ED: Does someone want to make a formal motion?

ANOTHER PRINCIPAL: I move we take this salary proposal of Professor Gray and work with it.

ED: How many are in favor? [The motion passed unanimously, but Ed expressed dissatisfaction with it.] Personally, I don't think that goes far enough.

NEW PRINCIPAL: Then I move that the salary proposal be studied, passed on, and sent to the state organization with our recommendations. [The new motion was passed unanimously.]

PRINCIPAL JERRY: I think the next thing to do is to read and study this salary proposal, to tear it apart, and to put it together again.

PRINCIPAL SIMPSON: Couldn't we also be thinking about such things as future building needs in education? Some long-range problems, as well as short-range things like salaries?

NEW PRINCIPAL: Could we also get some information on federal grants? I'm probably the worst person there is for being informed. I've never written my congressman or anybody. But I need to know about legislation and grants, like this "Title III."

ED: We had speakers who told us about those new programs at our regional meeting last spring. But you weren't there, of course. Could we also make better headway for principals as a group if we had a full-time representative in the state teachers' association office?

ANOTHER PRINCIPAL: Could we also look at the in-service offerings as viewed by elementary principals? It's pretty expensive to send teachers off to in-service meetings, and maybe some meetings are more worthwhile than others.

ANOTHER PRINCIPAL: It's expensive for principals to get around to meetings, too. I'd like to know what some other districts do about things like paying mileage, registration fees, and paying for meals and lodging.

ED: Well, let's try and decide on a time and place for the next meeting of this group. I probably won't go to the next meeting. I think you can carry on just as well without me.

ONE PRINCIPAL: You'd be welcome to meet at my school. We have room for you, and we are pretty centrally located for the different counties.

ANOTHER PRINCIPAL: By the way, what's the name of this committee?

ANOTHER: Let's call ourselves the "Salary Study Committee."

ANOTHER: That might be a little too specific. Why don't we just call ourselves the "Study Committee."

Ed did not attend the subsequent meeting of the study committee. Since the committee had charged itself to analyze a resolution that already had been passed earlier that month at a general assembly of the state organization, it charged itself with a somewhat redundant task except for helping to further publicize the original report. And because it came at a time when school boards throughout the state were preoccupied with reviewing the machinery by which salary schedules for teachers were negotiated, the "demands" of the principals virtually were ignored while all eyes, including those of the principals, focused on the increasing power being assumed by representatives of teacher groups in large urban school districts.

The meeting Ed had called provided an opportunity for a small group of principals to express concern for their role and to share a sense of "action-orientedness" within the ranks of their own professional association. The problem toward which the committee decided to direct its attention was handled through a familiar pattern: relegating consideration to further study and further meetings. Beyond the initial identification of the "role problem," in reaffirmation of their constant awareness of it, their collective and pervasive self-consciousness about the ideal role of the principal demanded no further action and suggested no possibilities for resolution. No one argued that the problem did not exist, but no one (except an administrator of two months' experience) seriously considered doing anything about it. Old-timers knew, and the newcomers who were going to remain as principals would soon learn, there is a distinction between the patience required in the eternal search for an ideal role and the prudence necessary to survive in the real one.

Prudence: How to Survive in the Principalship

To dwell excessively on what the principalship might become is to flirt with disenchantment. Not everyone assigned to the principal's office can sustain himself there; those who wish to abide successfully *in* the principalship must be able to abide *with* it. Survival does not seem to entail doing the job outstandingly well—no one can persistently satisfy so many individuals representing so many divergent interests—but rather doing it well enough to remain in the position at all. The process of surviving at times precludes principals from exhibiting those very aspects of their work that they hope someday to see enhanced. For example, consider two kinds of behavior often heralded as the quintessence of the principals' role: *instructional leadership* and *agent of change*.

The opportunities for Ed Bell to exert "leadership" at Taft School were hardly awesome. Indeed, the constraints on his behavior tended to preclude leadership in many of the actual roles he had to play. Even in his conscious attempts to be an exemplary model of a gentleman and adult for the pupils in the school, or to be an exemplary model of a tireless and selflessly dedicated educator among his staff, Ed played the role of a person superbly sensitive to being what he felt others expected him to be. For the most part, the exercise of the authority of his office was parcelled out to him policy by policy and directive by directive. His freedom was to make no serious mistakes. A brief exchange between Ed and Norman

Olds revealed that Ed was well aware of constraints on his professional freedom:

NORMAN OLDS: I think we're one of the most progressive districts in the area—
    the state—maybe in the nation. Look at the variety of programs here, and the
    freedom the administrator has at each school.
ED: Yeah. *As long as no one says anything*, you're OK.

Principals today are bombarded with the notion that they are, and ought to be, agents of change in the public schools.[8] In recent years they have been introduced to a vocabulary of change that draws heavily on cultural anthropology: change agent, acculturation, innovation, diffusion, cultural dynamics. Again, the facts speak otherwise—the principal may well be the point of last and least change. Most changes adopted by individual school districts are initiated from the "top down," resulting from administrative fiat at the central office (see Miles 1964); to a lesser degree, classroom changes come about through grass-roots efforts by teachers, particularly through techniques that become vogue in teacher training and graduate programs in education. Principals do indeed work among constant changes in personnel and programs; an examination of the complex and varied activities that comprise the professional life of a principal like Ed Bell suggests that forces of change swirled constantly about him. Principals also talk a great deal about change. But I did not see any evidence that Ed actually contributed to this foment. The school principal is successful in his work to the extent that he is able to contain and constrain the forces of change with which he must contend as a matter of daily routine; whatever force he exerts on the dynamics of the school contributes to its stability, even when he wants to act, or believes he is acting, in a way that will encourage an aura of change.

On several occasions when new programs were discussed, Ed's comments revealed his ambivalence about formally introducing change at Taft School. As far as maintaining an *image* of Taft as a school receptive to new ideas, he was all for it: "I always like to think that this school, the staff, and myself are thought of as being cooperative for new kinds of things."

When his general pose of receptivity for change was tested with specific application, Ed became more prudent. The following exchange was recorded during a guidance committee meeting regarding a new program (Behavior Modification) being tried in some local schools:

ED: I'm not so excited about starting something new that appears to be "the
    answer." And especially to letting someone come in to upset all the good
    things we have going now.
TEACHER: Yes, but if we wait until something is accepted, it takes 12 years.
ANOTHER TEACHER: Yes, that's the way it is in education.
ED: Well, that's why I don't want to be against every idea, either.

When it came to specific instances of change, Ed's receptivity reflected his sensitivity to the possible complications and implications for the school's many

---

[8] For example, "A principal of an elementary school stands at the apex of all educational progress—from kindergarten through college" (Hencley *et al.* 1970:v).

audiences. His judgments were often, but not invariably, a compromise. In the case of the early-late reading program inaugurated during the year, Ed firmly supported the program change as a marked improvement for teaching reading. He staunchly (almost stubbornly) defended the program against one teacher's strong opposition and some subsequent parental complaining about it. He lauded the collective efforts of "the teachers" for having introduced the change, although three of the six teachers concerned were new to the school that fall:

> My teachers saw this in other classes in other schools. We just can't get to the kids, otherwise. So they were the ones who started it.

On a more sensitive issue dealing with sex education in the curriculum at Taft, Ed discouraged a proposed innovation because it looked to him to be a change that might arouse more displeasure among parents (and other teachers) than could be offset by any benefits that might be derived. The central office had announced that new sex education films designed for the upper-elementary grades were available for classroom use. Ed arranged a film preview session with the upper-grade teachers, the nurse, and the counsellor. In a discussion following the preview, the question arose whether to show sex education films to mixed classes of sixth-graders or to provide separate showings for boys and for girls. Mr. Adam stated that he wished to show the films to his entire class. Ed and the other teachers preferred having the boys view the films at one showing, the girls at another. Adam remained firm in his stated preference but agreed to "go along" with the wishes of the others. Ed consoled him with his often-repeated cliché: "We must move as rapidly as we can, as slowly as we must." Then he added:

> This school is doing a lot of pioneering already. I'd hate to see anything happen to spoil that—including getting our ears lopped off.

Taft School was "pioneering" several programs and services considered innovative among schoolmen: a full-time guidance counsellor; a resource teacher; special help available through the school social worker and the school district's teacher for blind pupils; use of educational television; an emphasis on individualized reading; and, eventually, conducting pilot programs in behavior modification.[9] These programs, however, neither originated at nor were unique to Taft School. Substantially similar programs existed at each of Columbia's other schools and, as financial resources permitted, at most schools throughout the state and nation. Even the adoption of the early-late reading schedule at Taft, for all the commotion it caused, was hardly a startling breakthrough. Several of the district's schools followed a similar program, and such an alternative is one of a limited number of scheduling possibilities that have gone in-and-out of fashion in elementary schools

---

[9] Serving as a speaker on a panel presented for local educators regarding this latter "innovation," Ed summarized the program in a way that inadvertently revealed a tendency to reduce the impact of the new element by emphasizing its traditional rather than its unique features: "But there's really nothing new under the sun. Good teachers have been doing these things in classrooms all along." This is another example of what I have discussed elsewhere (Wolcott 1974) as the tendency to reduce and constrain variation and thus to keep things "manageable."

for decades. In the Columbia School District the decision about adopting the early-late program appeared to rest with each principal, although Ed was careful to secure the endorsement of the Director of Elementary Education before putting it into effect.

The only time Ed used the word innovation during the year was in referring to his idea of having the primary pupils scrape their luncheon trays and then return to their tables rather than exit immediately onto the playground. One of the most creative changes he made went unheralded, unrecorded, and perhaps unrecognized by himself as innovative, at least in the extent to which it departed from traditional ways of thinking about classrooms. Two children from homes near Taft School attended special classes elsewhere in the district for pupils deemed to be mentally retarded. The two returned from their special classes via the first afternoon school bus each day and walked to their homes. Ed noticed one of these children waving to upper-grade Taft pupils still in their classrooms one afternoon and he wondered if the "Special Ed" children might enjoy spending an extra hour in a regular classroom at Taft School. Their parents were receptive, the teachers were willing, and the plan was carried out.

I have suggested that principals customarily are expected to express an interest in change and to feel a sense of freedom that they *could* effect change if they so elected, even though their role tends to restrict and even to preclude them from actually fostering changes that are not inevitable. At one point, maintaining even the *appearance* of acting in the dynamic role of agents of change was denied the principals of the Columbia School District. In a rather unusual action, the superintendent issued a directive that, for one year only, no new programs were to be initiated. The policy was intended to be pragmatic rather than simply reactionary. A proliferation of new programs in past years, a rapid expansion in the size of the school district, and recent voter resistance in approving school budget increases seemed to warrant a period of assessment and evaluation. The directive was referred to cryptically as "The Moratorium," a label the superintendent vigorously tried to suppress. "This isn't a 'moratorium,' as one reporter described it," he explained to Ed and a group of principals, "but they [the press] want their fun." On another occasion he explained, "Moratorium means *not doing anything,* and we never said that." The superintendent emphasized that rather than "starting new things up all the time," the year was to be devoted to an evaluation of existing programs. Nevertheless, the embargo was impossible to ignore. In discussions among their colleagues, some principals supported the superintendent's rationale (Tom Nice agreed, "I think we *should* level off for awhile"), but Ed found it the basis for a note of dejection: "There's no use of us looking at new programs, because we aren't going to start any new programs this year."

Yet for all the complexities of their multi-client operation, for all the stress and anxiety of dealing with problems and personalities in endless numbers and variations, for all the inequities they explicitly identified (such as long hours, endless meetings, inadequate salaries, lack of appreciation for their role) or the strains resulting from unresolved and perhaps unidentified differences between the reality of their actual role and the hope of identifying a more significant ideal one, Ed and his colleagues liked their positions and wished to keep them. They had learned to live with the shortcomings of the role. As Ed noted during an infrequent moment of resignation,

> Sometimes I ask myself, "I wonder just how important is all of this work I do?" It's not like bales of hay that you can count, or sacks of oats. But I guess I've gotten used to it.

Ed and his fellow career principals had not only gotten used to the drawbacks of the position, but were also aware of special attractions in their work. They enjoyed what one principal-turned-professor described as the "power, thrill, and consequences of administration." They found what Ed referred to as "a lot of satisfaction" in the authority of a position associated with and dedicated to the altruistic purposes of public education yet unencumbered with the minute-to-minute demands of classroom teaching. Any references to resuming fulltime teaching responsibilities included the telltale adverb: going "back" into the classroom was obviously a regression in one's career. As principals are keenly aware, American society does not heap accolades on middle-aged men who have reached their zenith instructing ten-year-olds—especially if they are recognized as administrative has-beens. Ed confirmed his preference for administration in an exchange with Mr. Adam:

ADAM: It's so nice, Ed, to have you doing this administering and me sitting back and having the fun of teaching.
ED: Well, this can be fun, too. I understand some of the boys in secondary want to get out of administration because of ulcers. But there aren't any ulcers here.[10]

In spite of the female-dominated institutions they administered, the principals in the district also constituted an almost exclusively male group of peers. Their positions provided them with as much and perhaps more opportunity for interaction with those peers than any other role in public schools.

Another facet of being a principal that Ed and at least some of his colleagues enjoyed, and one that entailed a host of cues for survival, was what they perceived as their professional and personal visibility and the need for them to behave as *exemplary* citizens, to be admired even if not necessarily to be envied by members of the community-at-large. Perceiving themselves to be held in such esteem was a mixed blessing. As with other professional and paraprofessional groups, the feeling created a certain amount of anxiety and antagonism, a sense of always being on-stage. As one principal expressed it, "If you want to find out about this town, go out and buy a big Cadillac. Then see how long before you are called in for a conference."

At the same time, maintaining an exemplary image did provide a full-time assignment and a continuing opportunity to show the extent of one's superdedica-

---

[10] Technically, Ed overstated the point. At least one elementary school principal in the district had recently undergone treatment for ulcers and continued to follow a strict diet. He regularly munched Gelusil tablets to keep his stomach soothed through the school day. Except for their complaints about never having enough *time*, however, neither Ed nor his colleagues referred to the principalship as a pressure job.

tion. What seemed remarkable among elementary principals collectively was the extent to which they not only accepted the responsibility for maintaining the image but seemed personally to have internalized the image of the professional role in which they served. At least one observer has characterized them collectively as "too good to be true":

> A recent study of the biographical characteristics of a nationwide sample of elementary school principals shows that the portrait they present is that of the "good child." Indeed, the portrait is that they are "too good to be true"—or, shall we say, to be authentic (Halpin 1966:212).

If one combs through the comments other people made about Ed during the course of the study for the positive traits that were identified, the list of his virtues could literally be drawn to read like the Scout Law: trustworthy, loyal, helpful, friendly, courteous, kind, obedient, cheerful, thrifty, brave, clean, and reverent. If at times Ed's efforts to exemplify such behaviors were too apparent or strained, the self-consciousness of the effort did not negate that this was the kind of person, principal, and model he sought to be. To the extent that Waller's description of schools as "museums of virtue" (Waller 1932) remains apt today, then the principals serve as the head curators, those on whom the responsibility of preserving that virtue rests most securely. Ed sought constantly and consciously to make Taft School a place where children and teachers did right things because they themselves recognized them as right.

Initially I was inclined to interpret Ed's "goodness" as idiosyncratic. It was apparent that his fundamentalist upbringing in a Midwest farm family continued to exert its influence on his behavior as a nondrinking, nonsmoking, churchgoing, devoted Christian man. I recorded many individuals' comments, some admiring but others hinting at excess, concerning Ed's religious commitment, capped by a nickname assigned to him by a former teacher and of which he was probably unaware, "Evangelical Ed." In many ways, Ed's behavior seemed so conspicuously virtuous that it obscured the fact that his behavior, compared with that of his fellow principals, was a matter of degree, not of kind. As the fieldwork continued, I found the goodness theme manifested in the behavior of all the principals encountered in the study, both through their self-conscious efforts to be admirable citizens and through the comments they directed to or about others who deviated from the straight and narrow path. Their adherence to the Puritan ethic[11] provided them with a set of personal standards above the reproach of even their severest critics. It gave them a constant set of values that could be applied to virtually any problem on which a schoolman might be called for a pronouncement, ranging from pornography smuggled into school (Norm Olds recounted, "I sent word home that if the father wanted those 'dirty' playing cards the kid had brought he could come get them—they'd be in my office. But no one ever did.") to the private and personal drinking behavior of a colleague ("I could have built up quite a little nest egg just with the money he spent drinking during that conference").

---

[11] For a brief explanation of the Puritan ethic as it relates to the public schools, see Goldhammer et al. (1967:142n). The identification of and contrast between traditional and emergent values affecting the schools has also been analyzed by Spindler (1959, 1963c), Lee (1963), and others.

My observations have led me to the thesis that elementary school principals, in the course of their double socialization into teaching and into the principalship, internalize the lower middle-class ethos epitomized in the public schools to such an extent that it becomes their personal ethos as well. They act in such a way that they make the school's commitment and effort toward improving the human condition a believable one; they become, each to the extent of his individual commitment and capability, exemplars of the virtues espoused at school as living testimony that human beings are perfectable and that the schools play a crucial role in this regard.[12] Their long exposure to and reinforcement within their special niche in the educational institution provides continuing recognition, reaffirmation, and reward for their goodness. Virtue is its own reward, but it is also a marketable quality for survival in the principalship. Ultimately the professional demeanor of goodness, reinforced initially during the process of induction into teaching and subsequently intensified through a promotion into administration, comes increasingly to characterize not only the "status personality" associated with the position of principal but a pervasive part of each principal's total personality structure. In terms of "character formation" as an educational objective of the public elementary school, the school principal seems himself to be the most successful product.

As a prescription for behavior, this ethos draws attention to the qualities a principal should demonstrate as a good person; it provides prescriptions for a life style but not for an administrative style. How then does an administrator proceed to carry out his responsibilities? Many principals, certainly including Ed among them, seek to humanize the institutions they serve by showing more understanding toward their subordinates than they feel is sometimes exhibited to them by those at the top of the organization or external to it. At times, however, the requirements of the institution are perceived to overshadow or preclude the opportunity for acting as a "good guy." Ed faced such moments when he confronted the possibility of not submitting endorsing recommendations for certain of his teachers, or when he felt that teachers needed to be reminded of institutional obligations (for example, hours for departing from the building) or professional ones (such as attending PTA meetings). Under such circumstances one may see principals dealing with those beneath them in the hierarchy in ways remarkably similar to the manner in which they are dealt with by those above, thus paradoxically perpetuating and reinforcing a system even though they feel themselves to be sometimes at odds with it. Ed tended to act formally in accomplishing the business of the organization, particularly in performing expected rituals like holding meetings, evaluating personnel, interviewing prospective candidates, or "cooling out" irate

---

[12] My general impression of characteristic principal behavior is remarkably similar to a description Herbert Gans provided for a whole social class in America, the lower middle class:

If left to themselves, lower middle class people do what they have always done: put their energies into home and family, seeking to make life as comfortable as possible and supporting, broadening, and varying it with friends, neighbors, church, and a voluntary association. Because this way of life is much like that of the small-town society or the urban neighborhood in which they grew up, they are able to maintain their optimistic belief that Judeo-Christian morality is a reliable guide to behavior (Gans 1967:203).

Gan's description "fits" Ed's life style and provides an appropriate portrayal of the life style of many of his fellow principals. Ed himself was an eidolon of the work-morality ethic.

parents (see Goffman 1952). His occasional reversion to formal administrative behavior prompted one teacher (Mr. New) to make the observation reported earlier:

> I think personally he's a fine, warm person. When he's an administrator of that type, he does a good job. But when he tries to be an "administrator," as sometimes I think he thinks he's supposed to be, he doesn't do a very good job.

When Ed and his cohorts "tried to be administrators," their behavior precipitated the same criticisms from their subordinates that the principals expressed as subordinates of others. These pages provide many instances to illustrate how Ed tended to administer as he was administered. The annoyances most noted by those below Ed and attributed by them to his influence had counterparts in the annoyances he experienced at the hands of his own higher-ups. Consider the following examples for illustration:

Talking. Ed felt that most meetings with the superintendent were a waste of time—the superintendent did all the talking and yet was very roundabout if one tried to put him on the spot for an answer. Ed had a similar reputation among many teachers, parents, and even pupils.

Penny-pinching. Ed was frustrated by the penny-pinching practices of the school district. His staff expressed similar annoyance with Ed's personal habits in this regard.

Lack of recognition. Ed sometimes wondered whether central-office personnel fully appreciated the extent of his dedication to education and to the school district. In turn, some of the teachers at his school expressed a hesitancy about whether Ed fully appreciated *their* efforts and dedication in classroom instruction.

Putting in time. Ed expressed annoyance in feeling that the hours he spent in the building were considered more important than the overall quality of the program of his school. Some teachers expressed precisely the same views toward Ed's expectations that they not leave the building before a certain hour each afternoon.

Lack of authority invested in one's role. For all the committees and conferences designed to democratize the organization, power was exercised from above. A great deal of the power was exercised as veto power; Ed could usually say "no" but he could not always say "yes" without appealing to a higher authority.[13] But there were also ultimate decisions which could be made about what a subordinate could do and where he could do it. The principals had power over their teachers but were, in turn, subjected to comparable authority over their own actions. The practice of reassigning principals to different schools on the basis of administrative whim was a dramatic way of emphasizing ultimate authority. As one principal said of the transfers, "If anybody didn't want to transfer . . . well . . . you just *were* transferred." It is clear from their comments that some Taft teachers shared similar feelings regarding ultimate decisions concerning their careers.

Principals were aware of such problems as these, but they saw little recourse for alleviating them. During their summer workshop session, removed from the immediate press of daily school routine, they discussed how their own behavior and their failure to "put themselves in the place of the teachers" perpetuated the administrative hierarchy:

[13] See Abbott (1965:48): "Hierarchical relationships tend to over-emphasize the right to veto and to under-emphasize the right to affirm."

"We do silly little things to teachers that don't do much for their image."

"I think there are things that go on in a district that filter down and we just pass them on down."

"I know I forget, sitting in the office, how much pressure there is on teachers."

I have suggested that one answer to the problem of being a principal is to put one's efforts into personalizing the role and to behave, or think of oneself as behaving, as an exemplary individual. Prudence does indeed dictate, however, that administrators must don many masks to accomplish institutional goals. They cannot always be "nice guys" and get their work done. When they *have to* and do act, they are accused of acting "just like administrators." That accolade might be deemed a compliment in some institutional settings, but such behavior is not universally heralded in the elementary school setting among status-conscious adults toward whom a principal is expected to act more like a colleague and peer than a boss.

Neither being a good person nor administering as he is administered provides guidelines for a principal that give him a practical answer to nagging questions like "What should I be doing *now?*" "What problem should I tackle next?" The answer for the principals I met and observed to the question of what to do next seemed to be to let the position run them. Perhaps it is this absence of a self-generating sense of direction that provides the most telling and frequently heard criticism of elementary school principals both within professional education and by outsiders. After conducting interviews with principals in 67 elementary schools, the authors of one study were moved to include the following "subjective observation" into their report:

> Most of the principals seemed unable to identify what the school needed most, plans under way to improve it, or problems viewed as first order of business in producing a better school. The principals, for the most part, were eager—hungry—to query our staff about what they saw as promising in various parts of the country but were inarticulate regarding the implications of these or any other ideas for their own schools (Goodlad and Klein 1970:67).

Ed administered Taft School by attending to literally any problem brought to his attention unless he was already engaged with a problem of higher priority.[14] As we have seen, he coped sympathetically with an infinite variety of immediate problems from the moment he arrived at school (sometimes problems were so "stacked up" on his arrival it was ten minutes before he had time to remove his hat and overcoat) until the moment he left it. He often returned for another meeting in the evening and in the interim he confronted impatient problems on the telephone at home. But when the last of the day's problems was "finished," so was he. Like an on-duty fireman, he responded to one emergency after another. He had remarkable resources he could mobilize whenever a problem looked like it might get out of hand, whether a new and needy family in the community was unable to send money for the children's lunches, the salt-water aquarium needed more sea

---

[14] Management professor Peter F. Drucker has suggested that the only comprehensive definition of an administrator is "a man whose time is being wasted by everybody else" (Drucker 1967:30).

water, or he felt he had to "see what's wrong with the university" when a supervisor's evaluation left a classroom teacher infuriated and a student teacher in tears.

In fireman-like fashion, once the urgent problems were contained, the principal returned to his "station" to relax, to anticipate the next emergency, and, perhaps, at times of low anticipated danger, to engage in a bit of emergency-prevention. For Ed, the alternatives after taking care of the emergencies or routines (including showing the building to "visiting firemen") were to have another cup of coffee in the faculty room, to return telephone calls or to initiate new ones (most frequently to his wife or to a nearby colleague like Tom Nice or Bill St. Claire), or to "take a walk down the hall" to sample the instructional and deportmental climate of the school.

The matter of initiating telephone calls to colleagues during a lull in the day's work or after some episode requiring an administrative decision was not as casual as it may appear. Most principals in the district (there was at least one "loner") seemed inclined to want and need to keep track of each other, to share their problems, and to assess their procedures for handling specific and unique situations against the opinions of their colleagues. Even the *absence* of any pressing problem was enough to lead someone as gregarious as Ed to call a close cohort like Bill St. Claire to assure himself, "Are things quiet over there, too?" Any serious problem was bound to be discussed somewhere with colleagues—either by telephone or in the informal conversations facilitated by the frequency of their numerous formal meetings. The major informal functions of their frequent gatherings included not only a continuing exchange of information about what was going on in other schools or districts but also a forum for comparing notes or assessing the climate of opinion among their colleagues.[15]

In the course of the typical school day Ed was called on so often for little emergencies and for such a number and variety of formal and informal encounters that he had developed patterns of behavior by which he actually avoided the few opportunities he did have for giving his sustained and uninterrupted attention to a single thought or activity. Even programs that he formally endorsed, like PTA, or activities such as the in-service training program or the weekly guidance committee meetings that he helped to initiate, found his own attendance, participation, and attention sporadic. Except for the occasional meetings behind his closed office door with faculty or parents, Ed did literally nothing at school without the constant threat of interruption.

Depending on his own interpersonal needs, a principal in a large school district may exercise some choice whether to let the people or the paperwork preempt the major portion of his time, for he confronts a multitude of both. Ed opted for personal interaction. He delegated the task of filling out forms and handling details to his secretary.[16] He conducted most school business verbally rather than

---

[15] In discussing this phenomenon with me, a former principal observed, "I hadn't consciously pondered the fuzzy role identification too many of us labor under, and how often we need to reassure each other and ask for help on problems not even particularly 'tough,' but I guess it's universal, at least among elementary principals" (Anna Kohner, personal communication).

[16] For example, one morning Ed needed to refer to school board policy in preparing a form requested by the central office. He started thumbing through the loose-leaf binder

by issuing a barrage of memos and directives to his subordinates. As one of his teachers had observed, he was not an "office-sitter." During the rare moments when neither a pressing matter of paperwork nor the opportunity for conversation presented itself for his attention, he sat at his desk only briefly for any uninterrupted period of time; if no interruptions occurred spontaneously, he himself would initiate some new action or interaction. During the time and motion study, as reported in Chapter 5, the average (median) length of time I observed him working without interruption at his desk was one minute. Frequently I recorded instances when he was engaged in multiple activities such as conferring with pupils or a teacher in the office, signaling to someone else in the outer office, and signing forms prepared by the secretary, while still another party waited "on hold" on the telephone. The door to his office usually was open, serving constantly to beckon staff, visitors, and even the more outgoing pupils, to "stick their heads in and say hello."

The consequence of Ed's problem-centered orientation brought his actual behavior somewhat into harmony with the expectations of those about him. It also provided him with a practical goal against which he could personally measure his administrative success. This goal was the immediate containment of any and every actual and anticipated problem that might possibly disrupt the "smooth" operation of the school. More than this, he also attempted to give at least token recognition to virtually every event, comment, or complaint that came to his attention.[17] Unable to draw on any special body of knowledge or set of unique skills to a position in which he had to perform adequately but wished to perform exceedingly well, Ed brought instead a conscious, almost tangible quality of superdedication to try to do anything for everybody. He remained ever on-call and available for action, as evidenced by long hours spent at school each day, numerous responsibilities and assignments accepted, new programs tacitly encouraged, and an endless procession of new staff, pupils, parents, and outsiders inducted patiently into the operation of the school. Remote as these functions may be from a ritual quest for a more professional role, they nonetheless present a job description of infinite duration that render service to the institution and provide a man some personal sense of having done a day's work. For whether Ed was engaged in a twelve-second encounter with a hurt thumb, a twelve-minute search for a record player for a substitute teacher, or a twelve-day administrators' workshop with his colleagues attempting to define an ideal elementary school, his behavior seemed to be guided by an unwritten rule that is at once the *raison d'être* for the role of the elementary school principal and the perfect obstacle to ever achieving a radical change in that role: *every problem is important.*

---

housing the ever-increasing and changing regulations of the school district which he referred to as "The Bible." Then he suddenly handed the book to the secretary. "You cost the district less than I do," he joked with her. "You look it up."

[17] It is important to realize that what Ed did was influenced not only by the problems brought to him but also by the people who had the easiest "access" to him. At Taft School these people were mostly noninstructional personnel: the secretary, the nurse, the counsellor, the intern supervisor, and, via telephone, other principals and central office personnel. The teachers were usually in class. The resource teacher's office was at the other end of the building.

Epilogue / Reactions and reflections

Some readers might be interested in knowing Ed's reaction to the completed ethnography. I have kept his reactions separate from the main body of the text but include them here as an editorial postscript, accompanied by some reflections of my own about the principalship as an office and as a human activity. The descriptive chapters constitute the essence of the study. In the comments that follow I have exhibited less of the restraint characteristic of the ethnographer as observer. There are, however, a few more things which I can say about the principalship, and I do not want to evade responsibility to educator colleagues by failing to indicate some lessons one might draw from this study or to social science colleagues by failing to suggest some avenues for analysis and further inquiry.

Ed's Reaction to the Study

I completed my major editing of the manuscript in Africa during a period of sabbatical leave. I arranged for Ed to have his first opportunity to read the manuscript by receiving a copy as soon as the retyping was finished. I waited several months to hear from him, and I must confess that his pause gave me pause as well. Finally a letter came.

His reaction was mixed. Overall, his response brought to mind Huck Finn's succinct review of Mark Twain's efforts with *The Adventures of Tom Sawyer*: "There was things which he stretched, but mainly he told the truth." Ed thought the study fair and honest, although he felt that I had put undue emphasis on certain events and problems which made them appear out of proportion to the school year. His observation provides a good opportunity for reviewing the difference between being a principal and studying the principalship. The cultural anthropologist is interested in how people resolve problems, particularly those problems which are recognized collectively and which are resolved through adaptive patterns of behavior that are learned and shared. I had sought diligently to identify how Ed and other principals go about solving them. I now realize that Ed and I were at cross-purposes in that regard. His commitment was to resolve and thus to eliminate problems and, when possible, to prevent them from ever happening; mine was to search them out and to keep them constantly in mind in an effort to describe and to understand how principals behave.

Happily, Ed's faith in the project survived the ordeal of his first reading of the manuscript, and although he doubted that his wife would ever completely forgive my including a mother-in-law's appraisal of her housekeeping, he reaffirmed his hope and confidence that others would find the completed monograph useful. On the negative side, he admitted distress because he felt that at times he personally and the principalship in general appeared rather inept. He particularly pointed out that many of the things which principals do—like chasing dogs off the school-grounds or tracing a missing sandwich—are done not because principals want to do them but because other people expect it. I think he is absolutely right in linking the limitations of the principal's role with the restraints imposed by constantly having to meet the expectations of a multitude of others. The demands of a position in which "every problem is important" mitigate the opportunity for constructive accomplishment. The principalship is thusly burdened and hampered by the traditions that have grown up around it.

Ed was also concerned that the portrayal might serve to discourage people from considering a career in the principalship. I would argue that more information like this, rather than less of it, will help principals and would-be principals assess the limitations of the position in terms of individual personalities, capabilities, and aspirations. There are principals for whom the job is "just right" and who seem "just right" for it. I think Ed is one of them. Personally and professionally I have known some individuals tragically trapped and others ecstatically elated in full-time assignments to the principal's office. With predictable regularity Ed eagerly anticipated each coming school year; a friend of mine returning to a similar post in southern California wrote of facing "another year of hell"; a nun who had just completed her first year as principal of a parochial school in the midwest reflected,

If something is going wrong, you hear about it right away. But is anything going right? I'm not looking for any "thank you," but there's just nothing rewarding about the job.

Beyond the luxury of personal satisfaction there are also individuals holding a principalship for whom the assignment is inappropriate in terms of their talents and personalities, and there are those who are blatantly incompetent, as boldly suggested by the title of a nation-wide study contemporary with this one: *Elementary School Principals and Their Schools: Beacons of Brilliance and Potholes of Pestilence* (Becker *et al.* 1971). However, the realization that one does not belong in the principalship may bring little solace to someone who recognizes that his only options for the foreseeable future are to *hold on* to the position anyway or *go back* to classroom teaching, the latter with its implication of returning to a "lower" status or being unable to cope with the demands of an administrative post.

Lingering Thoughts on the Principalship as an Office

Teachers are sometimes noted for at least giving the *appearance* of being an "authority-resisting lot." Perhaps this is because their role is ultimately so vulnerable to the influences of power and status within both the educational system and the broader community which they serve. I must admit to a strain of that authority-resisting nature in my own personality, and I sometimes wondered if, as a former teacher, I harbored a subconscious (or at least carefully suppressed) wish to unveil the administrative superstructure in public schools as mindless, senseless, and superfluous to the processes of schooling. However, in spite of the limitations and "shortcomings" of the principal's role, of which these pages may appear to be a veritable catalogue, it seems pointless to lament that schools are bureaucracies (with the implication that they could be something else) or that they could be run better (or at all) without some form of administrative structure. This study was not designed to provide an evaluation of the role of principal but to provide a description of what a principal does, and I hope that defenders of the role find as much here in support of its strengths as detractors will surely find to argue its limitations. Presumably there are other possible administrative arrangements for organizing schools, although Americans may need to be reminded that just as their schools reflect their society, so does the organization of those schools reflect customary arrangements for managing it. In whatever form the administrative structure takes, however, the extent of specialization and differentiation that characterize the occupation of teaching and the organization of schools necessitate hierarchical ordering. Someone is going to be in charge.

Anthropologist Anthony Wallace has pointed out that "the most primitive cultures employ administrative processes—even though there may be no full-time administrative role as such—by providing for *ad hoc* leaders in kin group activities, in group hunting, in combat, in the management of complex tasks" (1970:117). The elaboration of administrative systems has increased with advances in man's technological complexity and with population density. In order to meet the requirements of the vast numbers of people in industrial societies, modern man finds himself confronted increasingly by the complex, relatively stable, and permanent forms of administrative structure which we refer to as *bureaucracies*. Maintaining an adequate level of supply and service for modern urban populations in which no member alone can provide the necessities of life, Wallace writes, "requires a level of coordination in plans of extremely high complexity that only those organizations called bureaucracies can supply" (p. 118). Thus, he continues, the most important social, and cultural, problem of the modern world is not to look for ways to avoid or to eliminate bureaucracies but to *design more effective ones.*

I find it genuinely useful to think about the utility and need for bureaucracies as an administrative form of social organization in complex societies, in contrast to the constant but ritual din made by those who channel their energies toward pointless plotting about how to overthrow or eliminate them. Such administrative structures are prerequisite to organizing human activities in complex urban settings where the absence of interpersonal commitments precludes other modes of social organization—kinship structures or local groups—from serving as viable alternatives. Our efforts should be directed at keeping our bureaucracies effective rather than merely lamenting our dependence on them or arguing that they are incapable of being improved. Furthermore, as psychologist Seymour Sarason has pointed out in his insightful discussion of the principalship (Sarason 1971:110–150), if we are going to blame "the system" for whatever one considers to be its defects, then we need also to blame it for its virtues. Educational bureaucracies are as remarkable as they are awful. They are capable of mobilizing resources and accommodating their varied clients far beyond the imagination of a single individual. Whatever pride and proprietary interest Ed Bell felt toward "his" school, he could not have created it by himself.

Wallace argues that the problem of the interface between bureaucracy and its clients increases constantly with increasing technology, urbanism, and population. He identifies two eroding forces to which bureaucracies are especially susceptible. One is their susceptibility to seizure by those who would exploit them for their own purposes, a charge which schoolmen face constantly but to which elementary school principals are typically guilty only to the extent of regarding their institutions individually as "my school." Taft School was hardly a den of corruption. The second eroding force is the low level of responsiveness of many bureaucracies to the claims of their clientele:

> Bureaucracy is apt to fail to serve those dependent upon it for services, not through any intention of harm, but from a host of difficulties that can perhaps be lumped together under the rubric of insensitivity (Wallace 1970:119).

It is interesting to think about the principalship as a position peculiarly suited as a link between the educational bureaucracy and the individual human lives of a large number of children and adults. Consider how Ed Bell occasionally epitomized the insensitivity of the bureaucracy, at times ameliorated it, and at times overcame its (usually unintentional) insensitivity and replaced it with a human sensitivity of his own. On the dimension of maintaining the quality of institutional responsiveness those in the principals' office face a constant challenge. But it is their *vigilance* that is being evoked here, not a rash of guilt feelings to be assuaged by enrolling in a three-unit course in sensitivity training, for a lack of bureaucratic responsiveness may be a function of out-moded elements in the system, lack of knowledge or training, or a host of other possible institutional or personal contributors.

I rather doubt that the challenge to underwrite the quality of responsiveness in their institutions will strike principals as the kind of changed role they seek in their eternal search, and it seems necessary to speak to the problems of change as principals envision it. I imagine that the role of the school principal is changing. Principals themselves insist that it is, and senior colleagues among them can point to changes they have seen from one generation of administrators to the next within the span of their own careers. Further, any role must change as the society in which the role is enacted changes, and certainly there are changes occurring in American society generally and within the ranks of the tens of thousands of teachers and the millions of pupils who are part of that society. Principals seem, in fact, to be scrambling about looking for how they fit in a changing picture of school organization in which they are increasingly bypassed or ignored in negotiation proceedings and in which alternative staffing arrangements increase administrative responsibilities for personnel at other levels within the hierarchy.

On another dimension, the minor but continual shifts within the administrative organization of the school district, the literal as well as figurative drawing and redrawing of boundaries around individual domains, the reshuffling of administrative personnel (of the individuals mentioned in these pages who had not retired or left the school district at the time of publication, almost everyone had been reassigned either to new positions or, as in Ed's case, to different schools), and the constant changes of pupil and teacher personnel served constantly to alter virtually every school-related interpersonal network. Such "repetitive minor reorganization," as Wallace notes elsewhere, is characteristic of all administrative structures, from the most simple to the most complex, and he observes:

> As they are perceived from the inside—at least in my experience—such reorganizations almost always are achieved to the accompaniment of considerable complaint, apprehension, and bickering. The changes do not always seem to make much difference in productivity, but usually when the matter has been settled "the air seems a bit clearer" and morale is apt to be a bit higher. The process evokes memory of the old adage, "The more things change, the more they stay the same." And, indeed, one may suspect that the function of these reorganizations is fundamentally conservative in the literal sense; they work to purify and preserve the essential structure (Wallace 1971:7).

This "capacity for internal reorganization," serving both to combat the effects of institutional aging which tend to erode them internally as well as to renew their ability to respond to the external forces of their clients, gives administrative structures their survival advantage over both kinship and consensual community structures and accounts for the fact that they can outlive those alternate forms of social organization. Thus administrative structures exhibit the necessary and complementary capacities for stability and change—usually with just enough capacity for change to insure their permanence.

It is ironic and even paradoxical that school administrators have been so touted in recent years as "agents of change." I believe that their contribution in education is quite the opposite of change, and although that contribution is equally essential to the institution, it happens to be an unheralded function both within the institution itself and in a society that reveres novelty and change. *School principals serve their institutions and their society as monitors for continuity.* Unlike the preliterate setting, where schools are introduced from outside to act as agents of directed social change, schools in complex, bureaucratically organized societies serve to maintain tradition and continuity. School administrators make a major contribution in maintaining this continuity. The real change agents of schools in modern societies are the young teachers, the young parents, and the pupils themselves.

Viable social systems need the stabilizing effect of a heavy load of "cultural ballast" if they are to maintain continuity with the past. Principals, though relatively few in number, have the considerable weight of authority and tradition on their side and an obvious personal commitment to keeping the system—including their own places in it—substantially intact. Insulated as they are within the layers of the educational hierarchy, with educators "above" them in the central office and educators "below" them in the classroom, they occupy an ideal position for acting as formal bearers of organizational and societal tradition. They are never acknowledged for this contribution to the stability of the institution they serve. More often they are indicted for their seeming resistance to change, for their predictable conservatism, for being constantly "behind the times" or "out of it." Their reaction to this perennial indictment has also been predictable. They have become ritually preoccupied with *talk* about change and expert at initiating continual minor reorganization within their own domains; one even hears them alluding to the danger of moving too quickly, leaving "others" behind. Since their positions require them simultaneously to present the appearance of change and to provide the stabilizing effects of continuity, their response has been to become agents of the rhetoric of change rather than agents of change itself (see Halpin 1969:5).

Examining the role of the principal as a "stability-maintaining" one lends an interesting perspective for analyzing and predicting patterns of administrative behavior. For example, consider the critical process of incorporating new teachers into the school. Taking only individual cases, Ed's experience with his "new" teachers—and their experiences with him—suggest a variety of forms that teacher socialization may take. Individuals were socialized *out of* as well as *into* teaching roles at Taft School, and the course and process of socialization differed from one individual to the next even in the same wing of the school building. Neither Ed's effectiveness as a socializer nor his relative importance compared with the peer group of teachers emerges clearly from the data. At least one teacher arrived "presocialized," a natural complement to the Taft faculty. Other teachers—in this case young wives anticipating careers at home rather than at school—seemed relatively free from the full effects of Ed's socialization efforts because their lives were little dependent upon teaching success. The recognition of this latter type of teacher, exhibiting an apparent "immunity to socialization," may be useful to researchers interested in dimensions of teacher socialization. Attention seems too often to have been focused on the overt processes and skills called into play by the socializers, too little on the varied circumstances of each individual who aspires to enter or remain in teaching. At the same time, if one looks for a common denominator in Ed's treatment of all teachers being incorporated into the "fold," we see him acting consistently on behalf of the institution to organize the diversity that he confronted, both real and imagined, in terms of its tolerances for that diversity as he assessed it.

It is tempting to posit a relationship between the heavy reliance on individual socialization which accompanies incorporation into a school faculty and the slow rate of change of the institution itself, comparable to the relationship that has been hypothesized in comparing socialization processes in traditional and changing societies (see Cohen 1971). At present, however, our understanding of socialization as process lags substantially behind our inclination to affix that term to virtually any learning of socially prescribed behavior, whether referring to the acquisition of an entire cultural heritage (enculturation) or to a beginning teacher's realization of the importance of keeping pupils quiet in the school's library and corridors. An inquiry into the principalship may have been a poor vantage point for learning much about the complexities of teacher socialization, yet it is interesting to note that Ed perceived positive changes in all new teachers who remained on the faculty, and he saw no evidence of change on the part of at least one teacher who did not stay. Perhaps there is a distinction to be made between socialization by and into the formal role of educator, essentially a matter of compliance and submission, and socialization into the informal education subculture, a process involving more complex options and consequences.

A Note on the Training of Administrators

I hope that persons charged with the preparation of elementary school principals will find it useful to assess those programs in light of the realities of the position as reported in these chapters. In my opinion such programs miss their mark. They tend to train for the superintendency or for central office jobs, doting on specialized aspects of school district administration which, at least in urban school districts, are handled by specialists who relegate only the simplest tasks to administrators at individual schools.

Opportunities for examining relevant and critical aspects of the principalship—especially relating to the delicate task of evaluating teaching performance—are explored lightly if touched upon at all. The regret is not so much that the art of evaluation is poorly developed but that administrators feel compelled (and in fact are compelled) to present a facade of having pursued a totally rational course in their evaluation procedures when their true rationality haunts them with the knowledge that human judgments about other humans are never made on purely analytical bases. The processes, problems, and consequences of evaluation procedures deserve better attention than they receive in the preparation of school administrators.

I think principals might also find utility in their training programs in grappling with the processes involved in studying American society and American subcultures, including an exploration of how their own formal role reflects ideal statements about American "culture" but often puts them squarely at odds with the realities of it. They would benefit from a better understanding of the anthropologist's distinction between education, viewed as cultural process, and "schooling," the latter comprising only one aspect of the former. Perhaps they could turn their attention to an analysis of how they themselves have been successfully inculcated with an idealized set of norms which bring "school and society" into a unity for them that is by no means perceived as such by all of their clients. As administrators, they need skill in recognizing when conflicts between the community-at-large and their own norms and values lie at the root of sometimes seemingly minor problems at school, especially those concerned with manners and morals. Indeed, conflict itself would play a more valuable factor in school administration if principals could learn to recognize its integrative functions rather than assume it to be only and always a disruptive social force.

In similar vein to becoming serious students of American society, principals-in-training might also learn how to analyze the immediate bureaucratic system of which they are part. As Sarason has observed after years of working with schoolmen, "the principal's actual knowledge of the characteristics of the system is frequently incomplete and faulty to the degree that his conception or picture of what the system will permit or tolerate leads him to a passive rather than an active role" (1971:142). Principals are inclined to anticipate and to interpret trouble in relation *to the system* (especially in such familiar domains as emphasizing the school's custodial and legal responsibilities or the unstated but invariably undesirable "implications" of veering from established policies) without reviewing the factual basis for their judgments or contemplating when and how the limits of the system need to be probed, reviewed, or reconsidered. Yet even among principals within the same school district, Sarason notes, the range in practices

> . . . is sufficiently great so as to suggest that the system permits and tolerates passivity and activity, conformity and boldness, dullness and excitement, incompetency and competency. One of the most distinguishing characteristics of the modal urban school system is the diversity in quality and practice it contains (Sarason 1971:142).

Can training programs help administrators achieve a more analytical perspective in discerning between actual and assumed limitations of bureaucratic systems, or must this be left to vagaries of individual personality?

Early in the fieldwork I was struck with how often a principal is called upon to settle questions concerning personal property or personal rights, and how seldom his pronouncements take into account the total context of the problem or the typically antithetical roles the principal plays as detective, prosecutor, witness, judge, warden, and parole officer. I think it might be valuable for a principal to be able to analyze his "cases" from a judicial point of view—not in terms of courses explicating school law or state educational codes but from the perspective of a philosophy of justice. Expediency apparently forces principals to pass judgments which would be unthinkable in the adult world and should perhaps be unthinkable in school as well. Pupils summoned to the principal's office for matters of deportment learn some strange lessons about human rights and human dignity. Organized minorities have been lashing out at school-derived injustices, but a careful analysis of school life might reveal that the administration of school justice is typically mishandled for everyone. Maybe it is well to learn early in contacts with public officials that might makes right. But there is the possibility that principals could teach a better sense of the nexus between individual rights and collective responsibility if they themselves were more consciously aware of the complex business of administering justice.

These areas suggested for attention in training programs share a common purpose: helping school administrators to better understand the social processes in which they are engaged. Yet even a greater understanding of social processes seems unlikely to resolve the problem of the lack of technical expertise that characterizes the principalship. I doubt that the role ever will be characterized by the kind of esoteric knowledge and special jargon that marks better-defined (and more highly regarded) professions. Principals need problems more than they need answers. The fact that their role has become firmly entrenched in spite of corresponding development in its technical evolution can be taken to suggest that its technical dimensions are not its critical ones.

Lingering Thoughts on the Principalship as a Human Activity

Loyal coteries surrounding any of the successful principals I have known have never been able to identify precisely what it was about these administrators that made them effective where others were not. I have gone to some lengths in Chapter 10 to show how varied and sometimes self-contradictory were the feelings of the teachers at Taft School toward Ed Bell. Yet while fumbling to find words to describe what they *do* like about an effective principal, many a teacher will observe firmly, "But I can tell you the kinds of things he does *not* do" and will launch into examples of a seemingly endless list of arbitrary, overbearing, rude, thoughtless, or demeaning actions which haunt all administrations and plague many.

Some principals seem able to enlist a personal and voluntary followership far exceeding the loyalty they can command through their superior position in the administrative structure. They are blessed with a special talent for leadership, able, as Wallace suggests, to obtain their ends more constructively through sugges-tion and willing cooperation in an atmosphere of mutual concern with common problems. Wallace makes a useful distinction between *managers* and *leaders,* and his observations are cogent in distinguishing customary performance expected of *all* principals (and of comparable roles in other bureaucracies) from a special quality exhibited by some of them:

> A manager, as his title suggests, is a person who manages other human beings (i.e., he tells them what to do) and makes his living at it. The professional man-aging of men is an ancient and respectable form of human activity, with a history that reaches back to the Mesopotamian Neolithic. A manager is distinct from a leader: the manager's word is backed by force; the leader's by the willing-ness of persons to follow (Wallace 1952:112).

A manager may also be a leader—but it is not necessary that he be one. The principalship is a manager's task. In addition to the prerequisites for selection, the constraints on the position are too many, the opportunities too few, to make it sufficiently attractive to recruit and retain many truly dynamic leaders. Yet there is no question that some principals exhibit more capacity for leadership in the job than others. They create a sense of purpose among a majority of those with whom they interact. They seem able to capitalize on the potential of the institu-tion while others are rendered helpless by its limitations. I am not ready to go so far as one principal who insisted that the principal "makes all the difference" in a school, but neither would I ever argue that he makes no difference at all.

One of the curious dimensions of being an elementary school principal is that, like many institutional roles, it makes great demands in personal commitment, in time and in energy, and yet seems to limit the options one has for displaying that commitment once made. A "super-dedicated" principal like Ed has difficulty finding ways to throw himself more fully into the role he has accepted for a life-time career. In spite of the long hours he puts in already, I think Ed would be willing to give even more time and effort than he does to his school duties, but as he perceives the role it neither allows nor asks more of him. No one really cares whether he goes back to the building in the evenings and on weekends. He can be at school until after midnight on a school budget election day in May, yet be required to "pay back" two and a half hours a day in June because of a contract overlap. No one insists that he take the concerns of the day home with him and continue to worry about them. Greater attention to the school's instructional pro-gram on his part would probably be perceived by his staff as a sign of his dissatis-faction with their present efforts, and overt efforts at involvement in that direction would be perceived as interference. Fostering teacher creativity is infinitely more complex than stifling it.

As a result, Ed's own need for involvement has found other outlets. His increased professional activity is organizational but not necessarily educational; he is becoming more active in education without becoming a better educator. In fact, his professional activity diminishes the time he has available for interacting with teachers and pupils at Taft. The position enables him to work *on behalf* of children but precludes opportunity for sustained interaction *with* them. Even among pupils sent to the office on matters of deportment, Ed's responsibility is only to attend to the problem; someone else will actually look after the child.

Ed devotes a great deal of time and energy to participation in church activities. Similarly, his colleagues made frequent references to other non-school activities in which they found opportunity for satisfaction and involvement on their own terms: family, home, and garden; travel; camping, hunting and fishing; and personal hobbies. What seems to distinguish school principal involvement in these avocations from comparable involvement among other occupational categories is the degree to which principals emphasize the intrinsic satisfaction of outside pursuits rather than a deserved respite from their occupational tasks. In spite of their personal commitment to a work-ethic morality, I was not sure that they felt themselves to have a convincing claim toward needing or deserving time off. They seemed especially sensitive toward the popular public notion that school people do not really hold full-time jobs, and too exasperated with the accusation to find a systematic way to dispel it. They were reticent about describing holiday plans outside professional circles and almost indignant if chided about going "on vacation" during any period when they would in fact be on duty. A career in the principalship provides no surcease from ambivalence, although ambivalence is not a prerequisite to the office.

Of course, hope is not a prerequisite for the office, either. But that does not stop Ed from looking forward to his next year, and his next. Hope is a very human quality. And human qualities are what the principal's office needs.

Principals who find personal satisfaction in their work seem to lean toward one or the other of two different (but not necessarily antithetical) styles: those who create a mini-technology of their own, or those like Ed Bell who are attracted by the potential for human development and human interaction in an elementary school. The former develop skills at facets of management, such as efficiency in reporting and scheduling, craft in maintaining or developing the physical plant, adroitness in anticipating new curricular fads. Rather than complement the bureaucracy, they become part of it. The task they set for themselves is to maximize its (technical) efficiency so that the system can work for others as well as it has already worked for them. They serve the bureaucracy with special sensitivity to the expectations of those superior to them in its hierarchy.

The latter group work within the same institutional framework but find their purpose in a commitment to the promise of education and to the human aspects of the enterprise. Their inclination is to make the bureaucracy serve its clients rather than have clients serve the bureaucracy, and, as their patience and energy allow, they attend thoughtfully to ways in which the system can better serve everyone, especially those over whom they exert formal authority. They strive for quality in their interaction although usually they must content themselves with the quantity of it. They enjoy the responsibility of playing even a small part in so many lives and feel rewarded when either the position or their own unique personalities enables them to make a genuine and positive difference in the life of a child or another adult.

References

Abbott, Max G., 1965, "Hierarchical Impediments to Innovation in Educational Organizations." In Max G. Abbott and John T. Lovell, eds., *Change Perspectives in Educational Administration*. Auburn University, School of Education, Auburn, Ala.

Adams, Richard N., and Jack J. Preiss, eds., 1960, *Human Organization Research: Field Relations and Techniques*. Homewood, Ill.: Dorsey Press.

American Association of School Administrators, 1960, *Professional Administrators for America's Schools*. Thirty-eighth yearbook, American Association of School Administrators, National Education Association, Washington, D.C.

Atwood, Mark S., 1964, "Small Scale Administrative Change: Resistance to the Introduction of a High School Guidance Program." In Matthew B. Miles, ed., *Innovation in Education*. Bureau of Publications, Teachers College, Columbia University, New York.

Babchuk, Nicholas, 1962, "The Role of the Researcher as Participant-Observer and Participant-as-Observer in the Field Situation." *Human Organization* 21:225–228.

Barr, Donald, 1971, *Who Pushed Humpty Dumpty? Dilemmas in American Education*. New York: Antheneum.

Becker, Gerald, Richard Withycombe, Frank Doyel, Edgar Miller, Claude Morgan, Lou Deloretto, and Bill Aldridge, under the direction of Keith Goldhammer, 1971, *Elementary School Principals and Their Schools—Beacons of Brilliance and Potholes of Pestilence*. University of Oregon, Center for the Advanced Study of Educational Administration, Eugene.

Becker, Howard S., 1952a, "The Career of the Chicago Public School Teacher." *American Journal of Sociology* 57:470–477.

———, 1952b, "Social Class Variations in the Teacher-Pupil Relationship." *Journal of Educational Sociology* 25:451–465.

———, 1953, "The Teacher in the Authority System of the Public School." *Journal of Educational Sociology* 27:128–141.

———, 1958, "Problems of Inference and Proof in Participant Observation." *American Sociological Review* 23:652–660, (No. 6, December).

———, 1963, *Outsiders: Studies in the Sociology of Deviance*. New York: Free Press.

———, and Blanche Geer, 1957, "Participant Observation and Interviewing, a Comparison." *Human Organization* 16:28–35.

Benedict, Ruth, 1938, "Continuities and Discontinuities in Cultural Conditioning," *Psychiatry* 1:161–167.

Berreman, Gerald D., 1962, *Behind Many Masks: Ethnography and Impression Management in a Himalayan Village*. Monograph No. 4, Society for Applied Anthropology, University of Kentucky, Lexington.

Biddle, Bruce, 1967, "Methods and Concepts in Classroom Research." *Review of Educational Research* 37:337–357.

Birdwhistell, Ray L., 1970, *Kinesics and Context: Essays on Body Motion Communication*. Philadelphia: University of Pennsylvania Press.

Blood, Ronald E., 1966, "The Function of Experience in Professional Preparation, Teaching and the Principalship." Unpublished Ph.D. dissertation, Claremont Graduate School, Claremont, Calif.

Boyan, Norman J., 1951, "A Study of the Formal and Informal Organization of a School Faculty." Unpublished doctoral dissertation, Harvard University, Cambridge, Mass.

Burnett, Jacquetta Hill, 1969, "Ceremony, Rites, and Economy in the Student System of an American High School." *Human Organization* 28:1–10.

————, n.d., "Event Analysis in the Microethnography of Urban Classrooms (Urban Puerto Rican 7th Graders at Home and at School)." Bureau of Educational Research, University of Illinois, Urbana. Mimeographed.

Carlson, Richard O., 1962, *Executive Succession and Organizational Change—Place-bound and Career-bound Superintendents of Schools*. University of Chicago, Midwest Administration Center, Chicago, Ill.

————, 1972, *School Superintendents: Careers and Performance*. Columbus, Oh.: Merrill.

Carlton, Patrick W., 1968, "Teacher Salary Negotiations: A Case Study and Analysis." Portland: Oregon Education Association Press. Lithographed.

Christiansen, Winfield S., 1954, "The Influence of the Behavior of the Elementary School Principal upon the School He Administers." Unpublished doctoral dissertation, School of Education, Stanford University, Stanford, Calif.

Cohen, Yehudi A., 1971, "The Shaping of Men's Minds: Adaptations to Imperatives of Culture." In Murray Wax et al., *Anthropological Perspectives on Education*. New York: Basic Books.

Cruickshank, William M., James L. Paul, and John B. Junkala, 1969, *Misfits in the Public Schools*. Syracuse, N.Y.: Syracuse University Press.

Department of Elementary School Principals (DESP), 1958, "The Elementary School Principalship—A Research Study." *The National Elementary Principal*, 37th Yearbook of the Department of Elementary School Principals, National Education Association, Washington, D.C.

————, 1968, *The Elementary School Principalship in 1968*. Department of Elementary School Principals, National Education Association, Washington, D.C.

Dodd, Peter C., 1965, "Role Conflicts of School Principals." Harvard University, Graduate School of Education (Office of Education, Cooperative Research Project No. 853, Final Report No. 4) Cambridge, Mass.

Dreeben, Robert, and Neal Gross, 1965, "The Role Behavior of School Principals." Harvard University, Graduate School of Education (Office of Education, Cooperative Research Project No. 853, Final Report No. 3) Cambridge, Mass.

Drucker, Peter F., 1967, "The Effective Administrator." In Report on the First Annual Conference of the School of Community Service and Public Affairs. University of Oregon, Eugene.

Eddy, Elizabeth M., 1967, *Walk the White Line*. New York: Doubleday.

————, 1969, *Becoming a Teacher*. Columbia University, New York: Teachers College Press.

Elkins, Benjamin, 1950, "Status, Problems, and Practices of Beginning Elementary School Principals." Unpublished Ph.D. dissertation, School of Education, Northwestern University, Evanston, Ill.

Fishburn, Clarence E., 1955, "Teacher Role Perceptions in the Secondary Schools of One Community." Unpublished Ed.D. dissertation, School of Education, Stanford University, Stanford, Calif.

Fleming, Emett Eugene, 1967, "Innovation Related to the Tenure, Succession and

Orientation of the Elementary Principal." Unpublished doctoral dissertation, Northwestern University, Evanston, Ill.

Foskett, John M., 1967, *The Normative World of the Elementary School Principal.* University of Oregon, Center for the Advanced Study of Educational Administration, Eugene.

Friedrich, Paul, 1967, "Review of L. L. Langness, The Life History in Anthropological Science." *American Anthropologist* 69:235–236.

Fuchs, Estelle, 1966, *Pickets at the Gates.* New York: Free Press.

———, 1969, *Teachers Talk: Views from Inside City Schools.* New York: Doubleday.

Gallaher, Art, Jr., 1965, "Directed Change in Formal Organizations: The School System." In *Change Processes in the Public Schools.* University of Oregon, Center for the Advanced Study of Educational Administration, Eugene.

Gans, Herbert J., 1962, *The Urban Villagers.* New York: Free Press.

———, 1967, *The Levittowners.* New York: Pantheon.

Goffman, Erving, 1952, "On Cooling the Mark Out." *Psychiatry* 15:451–463.

———, 1961, *Encounters.* Indianapolis: Bobbs-Merrill.

———, 1963, *Behavior in Public Places.* New York: Free Press.

Gold, Raymond L., 1958, "Roles in Sociological Field Observations." *Social Forces* 36:217–223.

Goldhammer, Keith, John Suttle, William D. Aldridge, and Gerald L. Becker, 1967, *Issues and Problems in Contemporary Educational Administration.* University of Oregon, Center for the Advanced Study of Educational Administration, Eugene.

Goldman, Samuel, 1966, *The School Principal.* New York: Center for Applied Research in Education, Inc.

Goldschmidt, Walter, 1972, "An Ethnography of Encounters: A Methodology for the Enquiry into the Relation between the Individual and Society." *Current Anthropology* 13 (No. 1):59–78.

Goodenough, Ward H., 1957, "Cultural Anthropology and Linguistics." In Paul L. Garvin, ed., *Report of the Seventh Annual Round Table Meeting on Linguistics and Language Study.* Monograph series on languages and linguistics, No. 9, Washington, D.C.: Georgetown University Press, pp. 167–173.

Goodlad, John I., M. Frances Klein, *et al.*, 1970, *Behind the Classroom Door.* Worthington, Oh.: Charles A. Jones Publishing Co.

Gouldner, Alvin W., 1959, "Organizational Analysis." In Robert K. Merton, Leonard Broom, and Leonard S. Cottrell, Jr., eds., *Sociology Today.* New York: Basic Books.

Griffiths, Daniel E., John S. Benben, Samuel Goldman, Laurence Iannaccone, and Wayne J. McFarland, 1963, "Teacher Mobility in New York City: A Study of the Recruitment, Selection, Appointment, and Promotion of Teachers in the New York City Public Schools." New York University, School of Education, Center for School Services, New York. Lithographed.

———, David Clark, Richard Wynn, and Laurence Iannaccone, 1962, *Organizing Schools for Effective Education.* Danville, Ill.: Interstate Printers and Publishers.

———, Samuel Goldman, and Wayne McFarland, 1965, "Teacher Mobility in New York City." *Educational Administration Quarterly* 1:15–31 (Winter).

Gross, Neal and Robert E. Herriott, 1964, "The Professional Leadership of Elementary School Principals." Harvard University, Graduate School of Education (Office of Education, Cooperative Research Report No. 853, Final Report No. 1) Cambridge, Mass.

———, and Anne E. Trask, 1964, "Men and Women as Elementary School Principals." Harvard University, Graduate School of Education (Office of Education, Cooperative Research Report No. 853, Final Report No. 2) Cambridge, Mass.

Gussow, Zachary, 1964, "The Observer-Observed Relationship as Information about Structure in Small-group Research." *Psychiatry* 27:230–247.

Hall, Edward, 1966, *The Hidden Dimension*. New York: Doubleday.

Halpin, Andrew W., 1966, *Theory and Research in Administration*. New York: Macmillan.

———, ed., 1967, *Administrative Theory in Education*. New York: Macmillan. Originally published in 1958.

———, 1969, "A Foggy View from Olympus." *Journal of Educational Administration* 7:3–18.

———, 1970, "Administrative Theory: The Fumbled Torch." In Arthur M. Kroll, ed., *Issues in American Education*. New York: Oxford.

———, and Don B. Croft, 1960, "The Biographical Characteristics of Elementary-school Principals." Unpublished report to the Cooperative Research Branch, USOE, Contract #214 (#6905), Bureau of Educational Research, University of Utah, Salt Lake City.

Hencley, Stephen P., Lloyd E. McCleary, and J. H. McGrath, 1970, *The Elementary School Principalship*. New York: Dodd, Mead.

Hemphill, John K., Daniel E. Griffiths, and Norman Frederiksen, 1962, *Administrative Performance and Personality*. Bureau of Publications, Teachers College, Columbia University, New York.

Hentoff, Nat, 1966, *Our Children Are Dying*. New York: Viking.

Henry, Jules, 1960, "A Cross-cultural Outline of Education." *Current Anthropology* 1:267–305.

———, 1963, *Culture against Man*. New York: Random House.

Iannaccone, Laurence, 1958, "The Social System of an Elementary School Staff." Unpublished doctoral dissertation, Teachers College, Columbia University, New York.

———, 1962, "The Whitman Study, the Application of Sociological Field Study Methods to the Informal Organization of an Elementary School Staff." Faculty Research Seminar, School of Education, New York University. Mimeographed.

Jackson, Philip W., n.d., "Keeping an Eye on the Teacher: Comments on Classroom Observing." In Sidney C. Eboch, ed., *Novel Strategies and Tactics for Field Studies of New Educational Media Demonstrations*. Ohio State University, Research Foundation, Columbus. Papers presented at a conference held May 10–12, 1965.

———, 1968, *Life in Classrooms*. New York: Holt, Rinehart and Winston.

Kaufman, Bel, 1964, *Up the Down Staircase*. Englewood Cliffs, N.J.: Prentice-Hall.

Khleif, Bud B., 1969, "Issues in Anthropological Fieldwork in Schools." Department of Sociology, University of New Hampshire, Durham. Mimeographed.

Kimball, Solon T., 1955, "The Method of Natural History and Educational Research." In G. D. Spindler, ed., *Education and Anthropology*. Stanford, Calif.: Stanford University Press.

———, 1961, "An Anthropological View of Learning." *The National Elementary School Principal* 40:23–27.

———, 1965, "The Transmission of Culture." *Educational Horizons* 43:161–186.

King, A. Richard, 1967, *The School at Mopass*. New York: Holt, Rinehart and Winston.

Kinsey, Alfred C., Wardell B. Pomeroy, and Clyde E. Martin, 1948, *Sexual Behavior in the Human Male*. Philadelphia: Saunders.

Kluckhohn, Clyde, 1941, "The Use of Personal Documents in Anthropology." In Louis Gottschalk, Clyde Kluckhohn, and Robert Angell, *The Use of Personal Documents in History, Anthropology, and Sociology, Part II*. New York: Social Science Research Council.

Kluckhohn, Florence, 1940, "The Participant-observer Technique in Small Communities." *American Journal of Sociology* 46:331–342.

Kozol, Jonathan, 1967, *Death at an Early Age*. Boston: Houghton Mifflin.

Landes, Ruth, 1965, *Culture in American Education: Anthropological Approaches to Minority and Dominant Groups in the Schools.* New York: Wiley.

Langness, L. L., 1965, *The Life History in Anthropological Science.* New York: Holt, Rinehart and Winston.

Leacock, Eleanor Burke, 1969, *Teaching and Learning in City Schools.* New York: Basic Books.

Lee, Dorothy, 1963, "Discrepancies in the Teaching of American Culture." In George D. Spindler, ed., *Education and Culture: Anthropological Approaches.* New York: Holt, Rinehart and Winston.

Leis, Philip E., 1972, *Enculturation and Socialization in an Ijaw Village.* New York: Holt, Rinehart and Winston.

Lieberman, Myron, and Michael Moskow, 1966, *Collective Negotiations for Teachers: An Approach to School Administration.* Chicago: Rand McNally.

Lindquist, Harry M., 1971, "A World Bibliography of Anthropology and Education, with Annotations." In Murray Wax *et al.*, eds., *Anthropological Perspectives on Education.* New York: Basic Books.

Lohman, Joseph D., 1937, "The Participant-observer in Community Studies." *American Sociological Review* 2:890–897.

Lutz, Frank W., and Laurence Iannaccone, 1969, *Understanding Educational Organizations: A Field Study Approach.* Columbus, Oh.: Merrill.

Mann, Floyd C., 1951, "Human Relations Skills in Social Research." *Human Relations* 4:341–354.

McDowell, Harold D., 1954, "The Principal's Role in a Metropolitan School System: Its Functions and Variations." Unpublished doctoral dissertation, University of Chicago, Department of Sociology, Chicago, Ill.

Miles, Matthew B., ed., 1964, *Innovation in Education.* Bureau of Publications, Teachers College, Columbia University, New York.

Miller, S. H., 1952, "The Participant-observer and 'Over Rapport.'" *American Sociological Review* 17:97–99.

National Education Association Research Report, 1967, "Estimates of School Statistics 1967–68." Research report 1967 R–19. National Education Association, Washington, D.C.

Olesen, Virginia, and Elvi Waik Whittaker, 1967, "Role-making in Participant Observation: Processes in the Researcher-actor Relationship." *Human Organization* 26:273–281.

Olson, John A., 1969, "Mapping: A Method for Organizing Data about Your School Attendance Area." Oregon School Study Council Bulletin, Vol. 12, No. 7. College of Education, University of Oregon, Eugene.

———, 1970, "Ecological-demographic Considerations for Educational Planning: A Micro-study of a Suburban Elementary School Attendance Area." Unpublished doctoral dissertation, College of Education, University of Oregon, Eugene.

Parkinson, C. Northcote, 1957, *Parkinson's Law and Other Studies in Administration.* Cambridge, Mass.: Riverside Press.

Powdermaker, Hortense, 1966, *Stranger and Friend: The Way of an Anthropologist.* New York: Norton.

Ranniger, Bill Jay, 1962, "A Summary of the Job Responsibilities of the Elementary School Principal." Unpublished doctoral dissertation, School of Education, University of Oregon, Eugene.

Redfield, Robert, 1957, *The Primitive World and Its Transformations.* Ithaca, N.Y.: Cornell University Press.

Rohner, Ronald P., 1969, *The Ethnography of Franz Boas.* Chicago: University of Chicago Press.

———, and Evelyn C. Rohner, 1970, *The Kwakiutl Indians of British Columbia.* New York: Holt, Rinehart and Winston.

Rose, Robert Louis, 1969, "Career Sponsorship in the School Superintendency."

Unpublished doctoral dissertation, College of Education, University of Oregon, Eugene.

Rosenfeld, Gerry, 1971, *"Shut Those Thick Lips!": A Study of Slum School Failure*. New York: Holt, Rinehart and Winston.

Rothman, Esther, 1971, *The Angel Inside Went Sour*. New York: David McKay Company.

Ryan, Kevin, ed., 1970, *Don't Smile Until Christmas: Accounts of the First Year of Teaching*. Chicago: University of Chicago Press.

Sarason, Seymour B., 1971, *The Culture of the School and the Problem of Change*. Boston: Allyn and Bacon.

Schmuck, Richard, and Jack Nelson, 1970, "The Principal as Convener of Organizational Problem Solving." Bureau of Educational Research Report, Vol. 2, No. 2, University of Colorado, Boulder.

————, P. J. Runkel, S. Saturen, R. Martell, and C. B. Derr, 1972, *Handbook of Organization Development in Schools*. Palo Alto, Calif.: National Press Books.

Schwartz, Morris, and Charlotte Schwartz, 1960, "Problems in Participant Observation." *American Journal of Sociology* 60:343–353.

Sexton, Patricia Cayo, 1969, *The Feminized Male—Classrooms, White Collars, and the Decline of Manliness*. New York: Random House.

Sharpe, Russell T., 1956, "Differences between Perceived Administrative Behavior and Role Norms as Factors in Leadership." Unpublished doctoral dissertation, School of Education, Stanford University, Stanford, Calif.

Shipnuck, Murray E., 1954, "Perceived Hostility in Administrator-teacher Relationships." Unpublished Ed.D. dissertation, School of Education, Stanford University, Stanford, Calif.

Sieber, Sam D., 1968, "The Case of the Misconstrued Technique." *Phi Delta Kappan* 49:273–276.

Sindell, Peter S., 1969, "Anthropological Approaches to the Study of Education." *Review of Educational Research* 39:593–605.

Smith, Alfred G., 1968, "Communication and Inter-cultural Conflict." In Carl E. Larson and Francis E. X. Dance, eds., *Perspectives on Communication*. Milwaukee: University of Wisconsin Press.

Smith, Louis M., 1967, "The Micro-ethnography of the Classroom." *Psychology in the Schools* 4:216–221.

————, and J. A. M. Brock, 1970, "Go, Bug, Go!: Methodological Issues in Classroom Observational Research." Occasional Paper Series, No. 5, Central Midwestern Regional Educational Laboratory, Inc., St. Ann, Mo.

————, and William Geoffrey, 1965, "Teacher Decision-making in an Urban Classroom." U. S. Office of Education Cooperative Research Report No. S–048, Washington, D.C.

————, and William Geoffrey, 1968, *The Complexities of an Urban Classroom: An Analysis toward a General Theory of Teaching*. New York: Holt, Rinehart and Winston.

————, and Pat M. Keith, 1967, "Social Psychological Aspects of School Building Design." Final Report, Project S–223, Bureau of Research, U. S. Office of Education, Washington, D.C.

————, 1971, *Anatomy of Educational Innovation: An Organizational Analysis of an Elementary School*. New York: Wiley.

Spindler, George D., ed., 1955, *Education and Anthropology*. Stanford, Calif.: Stanford University Press.

————, 1959, *The Transmission of American Culture*. Cambridge Mass.: Harvard University Press.

————, 1963a, "Anthropology and Education: An Overview." In George Spindler, ed., *Education and Culture: Anthropological Approaches*. New York: Holt, Rinehart and Winston.

————, 1963b, "Personality, Sociocultural System, and Education among the

Menomini." In George Spindler, ed., *Education and Culture: Anthropological Approaches.* New York: Holt, Rinehart and Winston.

——, 1963c, "The Role of the School Administrator." In George Spindler, ed., *Education and Culture: Anthropological Approaches.* New York: Holt, Rinehart and Winston.

Tilden, Charles H., 1953, "Administrative Adaptation to Social Forces." Unpublished Ed.D. dissertation, School of Education, Stanford University, Stanford, Calif.

Tolbert, Rodney N., 1968, "Should You Employ That Male Elementary Teacher?" *The National Elementary Principal* 47:40–43.

Turner, Ralph H., 1960, "Sponsored and Contest Mobility and the School System." *American Sociological Review* 25:855–867.

University Council for Educational Administration, 1967, "The Madison Simulation Materials. Edison Elementary Principalship." University Council for Educational Administration, Columbus, Oh.

Vidich, Arthur J., 1960, "Participant Observation and the Collection and Interpretation of Data." *American Journal of Sociology* 60:354–360.

——, and Charles McReynolds, 1971, "Rhetoric Versus Reality: A Study of New York City High School Principals." In Murray Wax *et al.*, eds., *Anthropological Perspectives on Education.* New York: Basic Books.

Wallace, Anthony F. C., 1952, "Housing and Social Structure: A Preliminary Survey, with Particular Reference to Multi-storey, Low-rent, Public Housing Projects." Philadelphia Housing Authority. Xerox microfilm copy produced in 1969.

——, 1970, *Culture and Personality.* New York: Random House.

——, 1971, *Administrative Forms of Social Organization.* Reading, Mass.: Addison-Wesley Modular Publications, No. 9.

Waller, Willard, 1932, *The Sociology of Teaching.* New York: Wiley. Science Edition Printing, 1965.

Warren, Richard L., 1968, "Teacher Encounters: A Typology for Ethnographic Research on the Teaching Experience." Stanford Center for Research and Development in Teaching, Stanford, Calif. Mimeographed.

——, 1969, "Parents and Teachers: Uneasy Negotiations between Socialization Agents." Stanford Center for Research and Development in Teaching, Stanford, Calif. Mimeographed.

——, n.d., "The Classroom as a Sanctuary for Teachers: Discontinuities in Social Control." *American Anthropologist*, forthcoming.

Wolcott, Harry F., 1967a, "Anthropology and Education." *Review of Educational Research* 37:82–95.

——, 1967b, *A Kwakiutl Village and School.* New York: Holt, Rinehart and Winston.

——, 1969, "Concomitant Learning: An Anthropological Perspective on the Utilization of Media." In Raymond V. Wiman and Wesley C. Meierhenry, eds., *Educational Media: Theory into Practice.* Columbus, Oh.: Merrill.

——, 1970, "An Ethnographic Approach to the Study of School Administrators." *Human Organization* 29:115–122.

——, 1971, "Handle with Care: Necessary Precautions in the Anthropology of Schools." In Murray L. Wax *et al.*, eds., *Anthropological Perspectives on Education.* New York: Basic Books.

——, 1974, *The Elementary School Principal: Notes from a Field Study.* In George D. Spindler, ed., *Education and Cultural Process: Toward an Anthropology of Education.* New York: Holt, Rinehart and Winston.

Zelditch, Morris, Jr., 1962, "Some Methodological Problems of Field Studies." *American Journal of Sociology* 67:566–576.

About the Author

Harry F. Wolcott was born in Oakland, California, in 1929. He made his home in the greater Bay Area during his early years, with studies at the University of California at Berkeley, San Francisco State College, and Stanford University, cumulating in a Ph.D. from Stanford in 1964. During that period he also served in the army and taught school in two California communities. His dissertation topic was a study of a Kwakiutl Indian village and the one-room school where he taught at Village Island in the Alert Bay region of British Columbia, published as *A Kwakiutl Village and School* (Holt, Rinehart & Winston, 1967).

His graduation from Stanford corresponded with President Lyndon Johnson's funding of the Great Society. The University of Oregon was authorized to establish a federally funded research center called the Center for the Advanced Study of Educational Administration. That may explain why Wolcott's first independent study, *The Man in the Principal's Office* (Holt, Rinehart & Winston, 1973), conducted under the auspices of the center, dealt with a study in educational administration rather than in some other, more broadly conceived aspect of education.

Wolcott remained at the University of Oregon throughout his career, serving on the faculties of education and anthropology. Another field-based research project resulted in the monograph *Teachers versus Technocrats: An Educational Innovation in Anthropological Perspective*. All three of these monographs have recently been reissued by AltaMira Press.

As interest grew in ethnographic research, Wolcott turned attention to that topic with a series of books dealing with various aspects of method, including *Transforming Qualitative Data* (Sage, 1994); *The Art of Fieldwork* (AltaMira, 1995); *Ethnography: A Way of Seeing* (AltaMira, 1999); and two editions of *Writing Up Qualitative Research* (Sage, 1990 and 2001). On the substantive side, his most recent book is *Sneaky Kid and Its Aftermath: Ethics and Intimacy in Fieldwork* (AltaMira Press, 2002).